TRAVEL GUIDES

SOUTHWEST USA
& LAS VEGAS

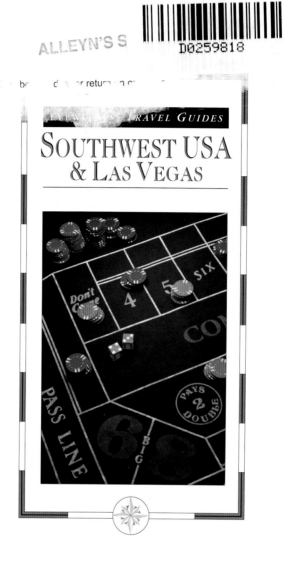

DK EYEWITNESS *TRAVEL GUIDES*

SOUTHWEST USA
& LAS VEGAS

DORLING KINDERSLEY
LONDON • NEW YORK • SYDNEY • DELHI
PARIS • MUNICH • JOHANNESBURG
www.dk.com

A DORLING KINDERSLEY BOOK

www.dk.com

Produced by Duncan Baird Publishers
London, England

MANAGING EDITORS Michelle de Larrabeiti, Rebecca Miles
MANAGING ART EDITOR Vanessa Sayers
EDITORS Liz Atherton, Georgina Harris, Judith Ledger
DESIGNER Dawn Davies-Cook
DESIGN AND EDITORIAL ASSISTANCE Kelly Cody, Jessica Hughes
VISUALIZER Gary Cross
PICTURE RESEARCH Ellen Root
DTP DESIGNER Sarah Williams

CONTRIBUTORS
Donna Dailey, Paul Franklin, Michelle de Larrabeiti, Philip Lee

PHOTOGRAPHERS
Demetrio Carrasco, Alan Keohane, Francesca Yorke

ILLUSTRATORS
Gary Cross, Eugene Fleurey, Claire Littlejohn,
Chris Orr & Associates, Mel Pickering, Robbie Polley,
John Woodcock

Reproduced by Colourscan (Singapore)
Printed and bound by South China Printing Co. Ltd., China

First published in Great Britain in 2001
by Dorling Kindersley Limited
80 Strand, London WC2R 0RL

Copyright 2001 © Dorling Kindersley Limited, London

A CIP CATALOGUE RECORD IS AVAILABLE FROM THE BRITISH LIBRARY.

ISBN 0 7513 2743 3

**The information in this
Dorling Kindersley Travel Guide is checked annually**.
Every effort has been made to ensure that this book is as up-
to-date as possible at the time of going to press. Some details,
however, such as telephone numbers, opening hours, prices,
gallery hanging arrangements, and travel information are liable
to change. The publishers cannot accept responsibility for any
consequences arising from the use of this book.
We value the views and suggestions of our readers very highly.
Please write to: Senior Publishing Manager, Dorling Kindersley Travel
Guides, Dorling Kindersley, 80 Strand, London WC2R 0RL.

◁ **Tall saguaro cacti in the Sonoran Desert, southern Arizona**

CONTENTS

**View over Grand Canyon's
North Rim in northern Arizona**

ARIZONA

**Flute players petroglyph from
Walnut Canyon, Arizona**

Mesa Arch overlooking Canyonlands National Park in southern Utah

Visitors enjoying a trail ride at a dude ranch in southern Arizona

Hispanic pottery

Half-size replica of the Eiffel Tower at Paris Hotel, Las Vegas

San Xavier del Bac Mission in Tucson, southern Arizona
(see pp88–9)

HOW TO USE THIS GUIDE

THIS TRAVEL GUIDE helps you to get the most from your visit to the Southwest US. *Introducing the Southwest* maps the region, and sets it in its historical and cultural context. The region includes the two states of New Mexico and Arizona, the city of Las Vegas, and sizeable chunks of Colorado and Utah. Each chapter describes important sights, using maps, photographs, and illustrations. Recommended restaurants and hotels are listed in *Travelers' Needs*, as is advice on accommodations and food. The *Survival Guide* has tips on such issues as transportation and tipping.

THE SOUTHWEST REGION BY REGION

The Southwest has been divided into five regions, each of which has its own chapter. Two of these regions are further divided into areas. All major towns and attractions have been numbered on an Area Map at the start of each chapter.

A locator map shows where you are in relation to the rest of the region.

Sights at a Glance lists the chapter's sights by category: Historic Towns and Cities, Areas of Natural Beauty, etc.

2 Area Map
An overview of the landscape and history is followed by a map that numbers and locates all sights.

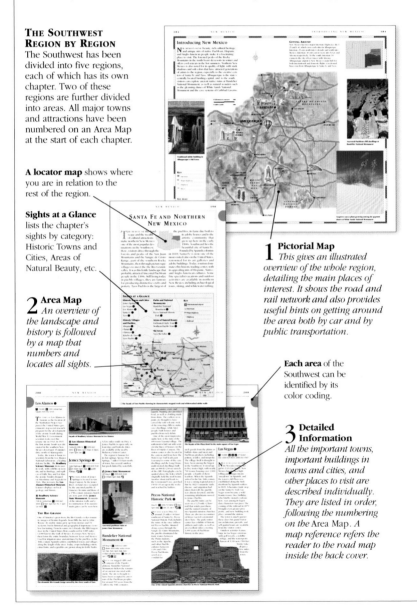

1 Pictorial Map
This gives an illustrated overview of the whole region, detailing the main places of interest. It shows the road and rail network and also provides useful hints on getting around the area both by car and by public transportation.

Each area of the Southwest can be identified by its color coding.

3 Detailed Information
All the important towns, important buildings in towns and cities, and other places to visit are described individually. They are listed in order, following the numbering on the Area Map. A map reference refers the reader to the road map inside the back cover.

LAS VEGAS

This unique city has its own chapter, which is introduced by a historical feature. The main sights are numbered and plotted on the *City Map*, as are points of interest in the Greater Las Vegas area. The information for all the sights is easy to locate within the chapter as it follows the numerical order on the map. The city has its own *Practical Information* section, which offers useful advice on shopping, entertainment, and gambling.

1 Introduction
The landscape, history, and character of Las Vegas are described here, showing how the city was developed and what it offers the visitor today.

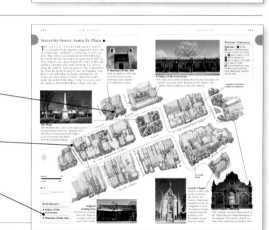

2 City Map
For easy reference, sights are numbered and located on a map.

3 Street-by-Street Map
This provides a bird's-eye view of the heart of a sightseeing area.

A suggested route for a walk is shown in red.

Stars indicate the sights that no visitor should miss.

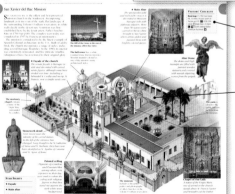

For all top sights, a Visitors' Checklist provides all the practical information you need to plan your visit.

4 Top Sights in the Southwest
These are given two or more full pages. Historic buildings are dissected to reveal their interiors; interesting districts are given street-by-street maps; national parks and forests have maps showing facilities and trails.

Introducing
The Southwest

Putting the Southwest on the map

For the purposes of this guide the Southwest has been taken to include Arizona, New Mexico, the Four Corners area, which takes in southwestern Colorado and southern Utah, and the city of Las Vegas. The region is contained by borders with Mexico in the south, California in the west, and Texas in the east, and covers around 326,000 sq miles (835,000 sq km). The region is sparsely populated since 60 percent of its population of around 10 million live in the cities.

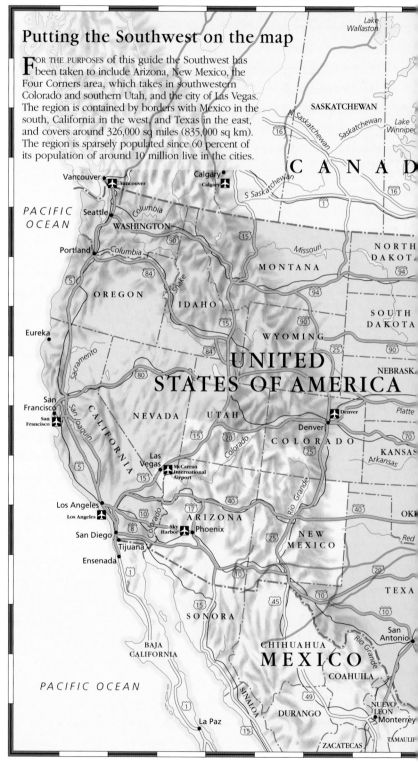

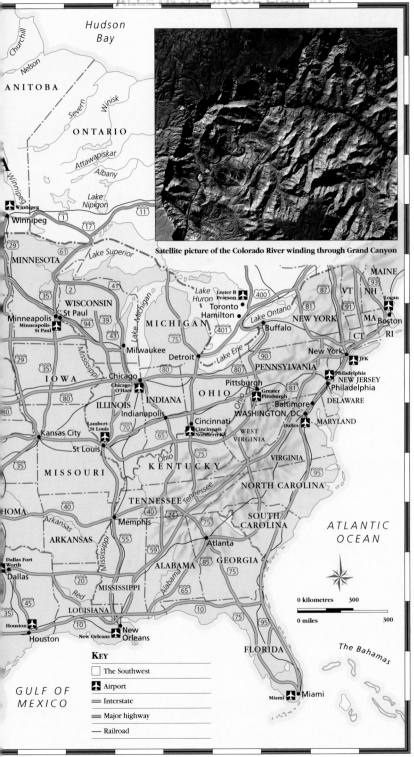

Satellite picture of the Colorado River winding through Grand Canyon

KEY

- [ ] The Southwest
- ✈ Airport
- ━ Interstate
- ━ Major highway
- — Railroad

0 kilometres 300

0 miles 300

A PORTRAIT OF
THE SOUTHWEST

DISTINGUISHED BY ITS DRAMATIC LANDSCAPE, *the Southwest is a land of twisting canyons, cactus-studded desert, and rugged mountains. For more than 15,000 years, the region was inhabited by Native Americans, but by the 20th century Anglo-American traditions had mingled with those of the Hispanic and Native populations to create the Southwest's multicultural heritage.*

America's Southwest includes the states of Arizona and New Mexico, southwestern Colorado and southern Utah, and the city of Las Vegas, Nevada. Perceptions of this region are influenced by the landscape: the red sandstone mesas of Monument Valley, the tall saguaro cacti in Arizona's Sonoran Desert, the staggering scale of Grand Canyon, and the adobe architecture of New Mexico. At the heart of the region is its defining geological feature – the Colorado Plateau – a rock tableland rising more than 12,000 ft (3,660 m) above sea level and covering a vast area of around 130,000 sq miles (336,700 sq km). The plateau was created by the same geological upheavals that formed the Rocky Mountains. Subsequent erosion by wind, water, and sand molded both hard and soft rock to form the plateau's canyons, mesas, and mountains.

Skull of a buffalo

Many of these natural wonders are now protected by national parks. Grand Canyon is the second most-visited national park in the US, and among southern Utah's national parks, Zion also ranks high in popularity. The region's underground attractions are no less beautiful,

Cacti and dried chiles adorn this flower shop in Tucson's historic El Presidio district

◁ Spring flowers, sand verbena, and dune primrose cover the desert landscape with the exquisite cave formations of Carlsbad Caverns in New Mexico and the recently opened Kartchner Caverns in southern Arizona.

FLORA AND FAUNA

The hot, dry climate of the Southwest's desert areas has spawned a host of specially adapted plants and animals. The ubiquitous cactus comes in many forms, from the giant saguaro to the stubby cholla. There are more than a hundred species, all with far-reaching root systems and fleshy pads for storing water. During spring and early summer the region's deserts are famous for their explosion of colorful desert flowers, while ponderosa pine, yucca, agave, sagebrush, and chaparral, such as scrub oak and manzanita, dominate the region's higher elevations. The mountains in the north of the region support dense forests of Douglas fir, aspen, and other conifers.

Across the Southwest coyotes, roadrunner birds, lizards, rattlesnakes and hawks are numerous, with the higher elevations home to bear, mountain lion, deer, and elk.

Sonoran black-tailed prairie dog

Southeastern Arizona is also known for its hummingbirds. The lower reaches of the Colorado River and the Gila and Rio Grande rivers in New Mexico attract shorebirds and cranes. The spadefoot toad is designed to survive the harsh desert environment – it can lie under the sand for up to two years, only emerging to reproduce when the rains come.

Most parts of the region enjoy more than 300 days of sunshine a year, yet around 90 percent will receive as little as 2 in (5 cm) and no more than 20 in (50 cm) of annual rainfall. Sudden summer rainstorms on the Colorado Plateau cause flash floods. Summer temperatures in the desert, often reach more than 100°F (38°C) but can drop by up to 30°F (10°C) after sunset. Temperatures fall 3–5°F (1–2°C) for every 1,000 ft (300 m) in elevation, giving the peaks of northern Arizona flora similar to that in parts of Canada.

SOCIETY

The Southwest is a crossroads of the three great cultures that shaped America: Native American, Hispanic, and Anglo-American. The Spanish language is prominent, not only in bi-lingual New Mexico but also in Arizona and Colorado. Everyday English is peppered with a range of Spanish phrases, reflecting a regional heritage stretching back to the 16th century. While US history usually focuses on developments in the East-Coast British colonies, Spanish explorers were in the Southwest in 1540, 80 years before the Pilgrims landed at Plymouth Rock.

Flowering cacti in Arizona's Sonoran Desert

Looking out from Mummy Cave Overlook in Canyon de Chelly's Canyon de Muerto

A host of Native American languages are also spoken across the Southwest, reflecting the far longer history of the region's native inhabitants. The Hopi and other Pueblo peoples trace their ancestry back to the ancient peoples who built the elaborate cliff dwellings at Mesa Verde, Canyon de Chelly, and Chaco Canyon. The Navajo, famous for their rugs and jewelry, occupy the largest reservation in the US, stretching across the northern ends of both Arizona and New Mexico. The Apache and several other tribes also occupy land here. Today's native populations have a hand in the government of their own lands and have employed a variety of ways to regenerate their economies – through casinos, tourism, the production of coal, and crafts such as pottery, baskets, and Hopi *kachina* dolls. Some native festivals and dances are open to visitors, although, for spiritual reasons, some are private affairs. These traditions

Navajo rug

have held through time, and today's architecture, design, and distinctive cuisine, reflect the influence of Spanish and Native cultures.

A trinity of religions is dominant in the Southwest. Native American spiritual beliefs are complex, as each tribe has different practices often tied to ancestors and the land. Because these beliefs are considered to be private, it is difficult for visitors to get beyond a surface understanding. The Roman Catholicism brought here by the conquering Spanish has a more visible presence. It is the main religion in much of the region, although a number of Protestant denominations are also prominent. Utah's residents, however, are predominantly Mormon.

Hopi *kachina* doll

POLITICS

When Arizona and New Mexico gained statehood in 1912, they became part of the democratic republic of the United States of America. The Constitution of the US

Mountains rise behind the towering walls of Hoover Dam across the Colorado River bordering Nevada and Arizona

In the 1930s, dam building projects were initiated in the western states, starting with the Hoover Dam. By the 1960s, however, it was clear that in order to generate electricity, irrigate farms, and supply cities, more dams were needed. The controversial Glen Canyon Dam, opened in 1963, flooded a vast area of natural beauty, as well as Native ruins and sacred sites. Today, many local tribes have asserted ownership of the water on their lands. Water has also been channeled increasingly toward urban use as farmers in need of cash sell or lease their water rights.

was influenced by the ideals of both the French and American revolutions of the late 18th century. The federal government is divided into the executive branch of the President and his cabinet, and a legislative branch, with the House of Representatives and the Senate, each composed of members elected by each state. The judicial branch of government is headed by the Supreme Court, which is the final arbiter of legal disputes and any changes to the written Constitution. Each state also passes its own laws and has its own elected government. Visitors should be aware that laws on speed limits, alcohol consumption, and taxes may vary across the Southwest.

Today, the states of Arizona and New Mexico are the US's fifth and sixth largest states. Despite the fact that the region's population is increasing, it remains one of the least populated in the US. The cities of Phoenix, Tucson, Santa Fe, Albuquerque, and Las Cruces account for around 60 percent of the Southwest's population. Such intense urbanization has put pressure on the region's resources, particularly water, which has become one of the most pressing issues facing the Southwest.

Chile wreath, Santa Fe

THE ECONOMY

Manufacturing, high technology, and tourism have taken over from mining and ranching as the region's principal employers. However, mining and agriculture, remain important elements of the region's economy. There are huge reserves of oil and natural gas in parts of New Mexico and Utah. Agricultural products include livestock, cotton, and citrus fruit. New Mexico is the country's main chile producer, and ranks fifth in the nation for dairy production.

Both state and federal governments are major employers in the region. Since World War II, when the Manhattan Project developed the first atomic bomb at Los Alamos, New Mexico has been an important center for defense research and the development of nuclear weapons technology. Today, other research projects including biotechnology, especially the Genome Project (which maps all human genes) and computer technology, attract scientists to the Southwest.

Hikers at the start of the Bright Angel Trail in Grand Canyon

CULTURE AND THE ARTS

Vast wilderness and a warm climate make outdoor leisure popular in the Southwest. There are miles of hiking trails, rivers for whitewater rafting, lakes for water sports, ski resorts, and some of the nation's finest golf courses. One of the best ways to experience the landscape is on a trail ride, while armchair cowboys can attend that great Southwestern event – the rodeo.

Phoenix, Tucson, Santa Fe, and Albuquerque are home to symphony orchestras, theater, opera, and dance companies. A flourishing Hispanic music scene and Native American traditional dances meet in the fusion sound of Carlos R. Nakai, a Navajo flautist who has performed classical music and jazz. International star performers visit such cities as Phoenix and Las Vegas, which is most famous for its dazzling casinos.

**Las Vegas star Wayne Newton
entertaining the audience**

One of the region's most famous attributes is the quality of light found in the hills of northern New Mexico. Georgia O'Keeffe's paintings of the local landscape in the 1940s helped to make the area around Santa Fe a mecca for all kinds of artists. Today, the city has the second largest art trade in the US. Native artisans also produce fine artifacts: the pottery of Maria Martínez of San Idelfonso Pueblo is highly regarded, as are the paintings of Navajo R. C. Gorman, and the work of Pueblo potter Nancy Youngblood Lugo.

The Southwest is as much a state of mind as it is a geographical region. The attractions of the landscape and a romantic sense of the past combine to conjure up the idealized legends of the "Wild West." For many visitors, the Southwest offers the chance to indulge that bit of cowboy in their souls.

Landscapes of the Southwest

T HE COLORFUL, beautiful, and varied landscape of the Southwest has been shaped by volcanic eruption, uplift, and wind and water erosion. For much of the Paleozoic Era (between about 570 to 225 million years ago) the region was mostly covered by a vast inland sea that deposited over 10,000 ft (3,048 m) of sediment, which eventually hardened into rock. Following the formation of the Rocky Mountains, some 80 million years ago, rivers and rainfall eroded the rock layers and formed the deep canyons and arches that distinguish the landscape of the Southwest.

The central geological feature of the region is the Colorado Plateau, which covers some 13,000 sq miles (34,000 sq km). The plateau is cut through by many canyons, including Grand Canyon *(see pp58–63)*.

Coral Pink Sand Dunes State Park's *shimmering pink sand dunes cover more than 50 percent of this 3,700-acre (1,497-ha) park* (see p149).

The butte formations of Monument Valley *(see pp164–5)* are the result of erosion and their tops mark the level of an ancient plain.

The mountains *of the Southwest are part of the Rockies and were formed during volcanic activity and continental plate movement some 65 million years ago. Snow-covered peaks, forests of pine and juniper, spruce and fir, streams and small lakes fed by snow melt, as well as alpine meadows are all found in this area.*

GEOGRAPHICAL REGIONS

Despite the great variations in the landscape, more than 70 percent of the land is classified as desert, with four distinct areas: the Great Basin, Chihuahuan, Sonoran, and Mojave deserts *(see pp20–21)*. Each area supports flora and fauna uniquely adapted to their harsh environment.

KEY

☐ Great Basin Desert

☐ Chihuahuan Desert

☐ Sonoran Desert

☐ Mojave Desert

Colorado Plateau

Foothills of the Rocky Mountains

Grasslands

Large areas of grassland once covered the broad river basins of New Mexico and Arizona. However, little of this landscape remains as it was largely turned to desert through overgrazing by Anglo-American ranchers in the 1880s.

Canyons such as this one at Zion National Park (see pp154–55) *started life when a stream began to cut a relentless path into the rock. As the cut grew deeper, erosion by wind, rain, and ice began widening it, and the stream carried away the debris.*

The orange sand of Monument Valley's desert floor is dotted with sagebrush and ponderosa pines.

MESAS, BUTTES, AND SPIRES

Like canyons, mesas come in many sizes. Some very large ones measure over 100 miles (161 km) across and are often the result of land being forced up by geological forces. Other mesas, buttes, and spires are hard-rock remains left behind as a large plain cracked, and then eroded away.

The Colorado Plateau is crossed by river-forged canyons. Elevations here range from 2,000 ft (6,000 m) above sea level to around 13,000 ft (3,900 m). Dramatic variations in the landscape include desert, verdant river valleys, thickly forested peaks, and eroded bizarre sandstone formations.

Desert Flora and Fauna

DESPITE THE fact that around 70 percent of the Southwest region is occupied by desert, it is not an arid, lifeless wasteland. There are four distinct deserts: the Sonoran, the Chihuahuan, the Great Basin, and the Mojave. The Sonoran Desert has one of the richest arrays of flora and fauna in the country. The Chihuahuan Desert supports hardy yuccas and agaves, and its hills and plains are covered with a dry, wheat-colored grass. The Great Basin is a cooler desert and home to a variety of grasses and desert animals. Spring rains and run-off from the mountains can transform even the driest deserts. At such times some 250 species of flower bloom in the Mojave.

Bighorn sheep are shy, elusive creatures and are not easily spotted. Now a protected species, they are being gradually reintroduced throughout the desert areas.

All living things in these southwestern desert regions adapt remarkably well to their harsh environment; the plants in particular are capable of storing water when it is available and using it sparingly during dry periods.

THE SONORAN

Found in southern Arizona, the Sonoran's summer "monsoons" and winter storms make it the greenest of the deserts. It is famous for the tall saguaro cactus *(see p86)*, some of which attain heights of 50 ft (15 m) and provide a home for such desert animals as the Gila woodpecker and the elf owl.

THE CHIHUAHUAN

Mainly found in Mexico, the Chihuahuan also reaches north to Albuquerque, New Mexico, and into parts of southeastern Arizona. Cacti, agaves, and yuccas, and lizards, rattlesnakes, and coyotes survive in conditions that include snowfall in winter and high temperatures and thunderstorms in summer.

The desert tortoise can live for more than 50 years. It is now a protected species and is increasingly difficult to spot.

The javelina is a strange piglike mammal that wanders the Chihuahuan and Sonoran deserts in small packs.

Prickly pear cacti flower in spring and are among the largest of the many types of cacti that flourish in the Sonoran Desert.

Yucca plants have been gathered for centuries and have many uses: their fruit can be eaten, and the roots make shampoo.

DANGERS IN THE DESERT

The danger of poisonous desert creatures has often been exaggerated. Although some desert creatures do, on rare occasions, bite or sting people, the bites are seldom fatal unless the victims are small children or have serious health problems. To avoid being hurt, never reach into dark spaces or up onto overhead ledges where you can't see. Watch where you place your feet, and shake out clothes and shoes before putting them on. Never harass or handle a poisonous creature. If you are bitten, stay calm and seek medical help immediately.

The desert scorpion *is golden in color. Its bite is venomous so anyone who has been bitten should go to a hospital for an antidote.*

The Gila monster *is the only venomous lizard in the US. It is a slow-moving rarely seen inhabitant of the desert regions, and will only bite if it feels threatened.*

THE GREAT BASIN

With its canyons, cliffs, mesas, and buttes, the landscape of the Great Basin Desert appears most characteristic of the region. It extends from the far northwest corner of Arizona into eastern Utah and Oregon, and its scattering of cacti, sage, and mesquite is home to the bighorn sheep and various types of rattlesnake.

THE MOJAVE

This vast desert extends into central and northern Arizona. The Mojave is dry for most of the year, but a small amount of winter rain results in a display of wildflowers in spring. Other flora and fauna found here include creosote bush, cacti, yucca, jackrabbits, desert tortoises, and bighorn sheep.

Sagebrush *is a pervasive subshrub that covers vast areas of the cooler Great Basin Desert. It smells of sage.*

The blacktailed jackrabbit *is born with a full coat of muted fur to camouflage it from predators such as the coyote.*

Golden eagles *can be seen high in the sky in daytime as they hunt for prey across the Great Basin Desert.*

The Joshua tree *was named by Mormons who pictured the upraised arms of Joshua in its branches.*

Architecture of the Southwest

THE HISTORY OF ARCHITECTURE in the Southwest reaches back to the Ancestral Puebloan or Anasazi builders of such cities as Mesa Verde *(see pp180–81)*, demonstrating skilled craftsmanship. Across the region, historic architecture can be seen in many towns and cities, with the adobes of their old-town districts arranged around a central plaza. But there are also other architectural styles, from the Spanish Colonial of the 18th century to those of the 19th and early 20th century. Wooden storefronts, Victorian mansions, and miners' cottages all lend a rustic charm to many mountain towns, and one of the 20th century's most famous architects, Frank Lloyd Wright, set up an architectural school in Scottsdale *(see p81)*.

San Felipe de Neri Church, Albuquerque Old Town

TRADITIONAL ADOBE

Adobe ovens *(hornos)* at El Rancho de las Golondrinas

The traditional building material of the southwestern desert is adobe, a mixture of mud or clay and sand, with straw or grass as a binder. This is formed into bricks, which harden in the sun, then built into walls, cemented with a similar material, and plastered over with more mud. Adobe deteriorates quickly and must be replastered every few years. Modern adobe-style buildings are often made of cement and covered with lime cement stucco painted to look like adobe. Original dwellings had dirt floors and wooden beams *(vigas)* as ceiling supports. Roofs were flat, with pipes *(canales)* for water run-off.

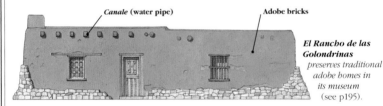

Canale (water pipe)   Adobe bricks

El Rancho de las Golondrinas *preserves traditional adobe homes in its museum* (see p195).

SPANISH COLONIAL

In the 17th and 18th centuries, Spanish Colonial missions combined the Baroque style of Mexican and European religious architecture with native design, using local materials and craftsmen. This style underwent a resurgence in the 20th century as Spanish Colonial Revival, from 1915 to the 1930s, being incorporated into private homes and public buildings. Red-tiled roofs, ornamental terracotta, and stone or iron grille work were combined with white stucco walls. A fine example is Tucson's Pima County Courthouse *(see p84)*, with its dome adorned with colored tiles.

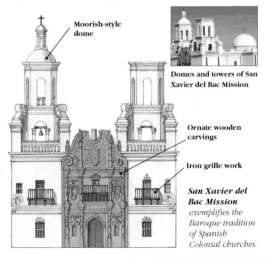

Moorish-style dome

Domes and towers of San Xavier del Bac Mission

Ornate wooden carvings

Iron grille work

San Xavier del Bac Mission *exemplifies the Baroque tradition of Spanish Colonial churches.*

MISSION REVIVAL

Similar in spirit to Spanish Colonial trends, the early 20th-century Mission Revival style is characterized by stucco walls made of white lime cement, often with graceful arches, flat roofs, and courtyards, but with less ornamentation. A fine example of a Mission Revival-style bungalow is the J. Knox Corbett House in Tucson's Historic District *(see p84)*. Built of brick but plastered over in white to simulate adobe, it has a red-tile roof and a big screen porch at the back.

Façade of the J. Knox Corbett House

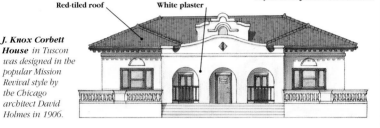

Red-tiled roof   White plaster

J. Knox Corbett House in Tucson was designed in the popular Mission Revival style by the Chicago architect David Holmes in 1906.

PUEBLO REVIVAL

Santa Fe Museum of Fine Arts

Pueblo Revival was another southwestern style that became particularly fashionable in the first three decades of the 20th century. It featured adobe or simulated adobe walls, with projecting *vigas,* and flat roofs with *canales.* The second and third stories were usually set back to resemble multistory pueblo dwellings, such as Taos Pueblo *(see p206),* hence the name. Features include rounded parapets, framed portal windows, and wood columns. This style has been used frequently in public buildings; the Museum of Fine Arts in Santa Fe *(see p194)* is an outstanding example.

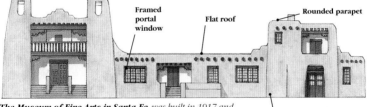

Framed portal window   Flat roof   Rounded parapet

The Museum of Fine Arts in Santa Fe was built in 1917 and was the first building in Pueblo Revival style in the city. A central courtyard providing shade from the sun is one of its features.

Adobe wall

CONTEMPORARY ARCHITECTURE

Two of America's most prominent architects, Frank Lloyd Wright (1867–1959) and Paolo Soleri (*b.* 1919), practiced in the Southwest. Wright's "organic architecture" advocated the use of local materials and the importance of the setting. His architectural complex at Taliesin West *(see p81)* included a school, offices, and his home. It was built from desert stones and sand, and the expansive proportions reflect the Arizona desert. In the 1940s, Italian Soleri studied at Taliesin. In 1956 he established the Cosanti Foundation *(see p81)* devoted to "arcology," a synthesis of architecture and ecology that minimizes the waste of energy endemic in modern towns.

Interior of Taliesin West, designed by Frank Lloyd Wright

Colonizers of the Southwest

THE REMOTE WILDERNESS areas of the Southwest were among the last regions of the US to be colonized by Anglo-Americans, in the mid- to late 19th century. The Spanish were the first Europeans to reach this area in the 1500s, led by soldier and explorer Francisco Vasquez de Coronado (1510–54), and Santa Fe was established in 1610. In 1752, the Spanish established the first European settlement in Arizona at Tubac. Kit Carson and fellow fur trappers explored east–west routes in the mid-19th century, while the Mormons founded Salt Lake City in the 1840s. In the later 19th century, explorers and prospectors, most notably US national hero John Wesley Powell, traveled across the region.

Inscription Rock *rises over a natural spring in New Mexico (see p163), and was a restng place for travelers over centuries. The rock features Zuni petroglyphs and graf-fiti, including Oñate's carved name.*

The Butterfield Stage route *was established in 1858. Sanctioned by Congress to provide a twice-weekly service for isolated Westerners, it aided the establishing of settlements in remote areas.*

ROUTES OF THE COLONIZERS
The promise of gold brought the first Spanish travelers to the Southwest in the 1500s. Various groups of colonizers and traders soon followed, forging many new routes across this rugged region.

KEY

— Coronado Trail

— Oñate Trail

— Santa Fe Trail

— Butterfield Stage route

— Old Spanish Trail

— Powell Expedition

— Anza Trail

— Camino Real

-- State boundaries

UTAH

NEVADA

CALIFORNIA

ARIZONA

Los Angeles

Colorado River

Fort McDowell

San Diego

Fort Yuma

Tucson

MEXICO

Juan Bautista de Anza*, Spanish commander of the Tubac settlement* (see p84)*, explored the Anza Trail from 1774 to 1776. Reaching the Pacific Coast, Anza went on to found San Francisco.*

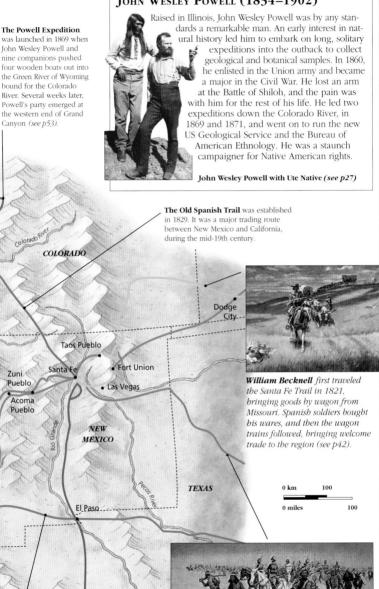

JOHN WESLEY POWELL (1834–1902)

Raised in Illinois, John Wesley Powell was by any standards a remarkable man. An early interest in natural history led him to embark on long, solitary expeditions into the outback to collect geological and botanical samples. In 1860, he enlisted in the Union army and became a major in the Civil War. He lost an arm at the Battle of Shiloh, and the pain was with him for the rest of his life. He led two expeditions down the Colorado River, in 1869 and 1871, and went on to run the new US Geological Service and the Bureau of American Ethnology. He was a staunch campaigner for Native American rights.

John Wesley Powell with Ute Native *(see p27)*

The Powell Expedition was launched in 1869 when John Wesley Powell and nine companions pushed four wooden boats out into the Green River of Wyoming bound for the Colorado River. Several weeks later, Powell's party emerged at the western end of Grand Canyon *(see p53)*.

The Old Spanish Trail was established in 1829. It was a major trading route between New Mexico and California, during the mid-19th century.

Colorado River

COLORADO

Dodge City

Taos Pueblo

Zuni Pueblo

Santa Fe   Fort Union

Acoma Pueblo   Las Vegas

Rio Grande

NEW MEXICO

Pecos River

TEXAS

El Paso

| 0 km | 100 |
| 0 miles | 100 |

Chihuahua

William Becknell *first traveled the Santa Fe Trail in 1821, bringing goods by wagon from Missouri. Spanish soldiers bought his wares, and then the wagon trains followed, bringing welcome trade to the region (see p42).*

Juan de Oñate, a Spanish fortune-seeker, first traveled the Camino Real in 1598. He named part of this harsh, desert path "Journey of the Dead" but safely reached the Rio Grande *(see p39)*.

Francisco Vasquez de Coronado (1510–1554) *headed north from Mexico in 1540 with 336 soldiers and 1,000 Native Americans to spend two years exploring the region. His route became the Coronado Trail.*

Native Cultures of the Southwest

Hopi wicker plaque

THE NATIVE PEOPLES of the Southwest have maintained many of their distinct ways of life, in spite of more than 400 years of hardship since the arrival of the Spanish in 1539. Disease, armed conflict, and brutal attempts at cultural assimilation have forged the determination of Native groups to retain their cultural identity. Since the mid-20th century they have led political campaigns for the restoration of homelands and compensation for past losses.

Today, there are more than 50 Native reservations in the Southwest, the Navajo Reservation being the largest. Native peoples are found across the region, working in cities and running modern farms. In most tribes, a growing economy based on tourism and gambling has brought much-needed revenue, but battles over land rights and environmental issues are ongoing.

Rodeo at a Mescalero Apache reservation near Ruidoso, New Mexico

THE APACHE

DESPITE THEIR reputation as fierce warriors, reinforced by their legendary leaders Cochise and Geronimo *(see p42)*, the Apache were mainly hunter-gatherers thought to have roamed south from their Athabaskan-speaking homelands in northern Canada during the 15th century. Just as, historically, the Apache lived in bands, so today they are divided into three main groups: the Jicarilla, Mescalero-Chiricahua, and Western Apaches.

Successful management of their natural resources has ensured a degree of economic stability. The Jicarilla Reservation in northern New Mexico is noted for its excellent hunting and fishing programs, and the Mescalero Reservation in southern New Mexico, near the city of Ruidoso *(see p224)* boasts a ski area and a casino.

Visitors are welcome at the Apache reservations, to watch rituals such as the Nah'ih'es or Sunrise Ceremony which marks a girl's transition to womanhood. Dances, festivals, and rodeos are also held on reservations *(see pp32–5)*.

THE NAVAJO

WITH A POPULATION of more than 200,000, the Navajo Nation is the largest reservation in the Southwest, covering more than 25,000 square miles (64,750 sq km) in Arizona, New Mexico, and southern Utah. The spiritual center of the Navajo Nation is Canyon de Chelly *(see pp168–71)* where Navajo

farmers still live, tending the sheep that were introduced by the Spanish and using their wool to make rugs.

The Navajo are generally welcoming to visitors and act as guides in Monument Valley and other sites on their land *(see pp164–5)*. They have resisted building casinos to raise money, basing their economy on tourism and the sale of natural resources such as oil, coal, and uranium. However, many Navajo are opposed to the pollution that strip-mining and other industrial enterprises have brought.

While many Navajo now live off the reservation in cities and towns, the traditional dwelling, the hogan, remains an important focus of their cultural life. Today's hogan is an octagonal wood cabin, often fitted with electricity and other modern amenities, where family gatherings take place.

Navajo religious beliefs are still bound up with daily life, with farmers singing corn-growing songs and weavers incorporating a spirit thread into their rugs. Colorful and intricate sand paintings still play a part in healing ceremonies, which aim to restore *hozho*, or harmony, to ill or troubled individuals.

Navajo Indian woman shearing the wool from a sheep

THE PUEBLO PEOPLE

COMPRISING 20 tribes in New Mexico, including the Zuni, and the Hopi in Arizona, the Pueblo people share religious and cultural beliefs. However, there are

HOPI SPIRITUALITY

Religion is a fundamental element of the Hopi lifestyle. Their religious ceremonies focus on *kachina* (or *katsina*), spirit figures which symbolize nature in all its forms. Familiar to visitors as the painted, carved wooden dolls available in many gift stores, the *kachina* lie at the heart of Hopi spirituality. During the growing season (December to July), these spirit figures are represented by *kachina* dancers who visit Hopi villages. During the rest of the year, the spirits are believed to reside in a shrine in the high San Francisco Peaks, north of Flagstaff. Hopi religious ceremonies are often held in the *kiva*, a round underground chamber, usually closed to visitors *(see p161)*. Other Pueblo tribes also use kivas for ceremonial events, a practice thought to date from the days of the Ancestral Puebloans.

Young Hopi Rainbow Dancer

linguistic differences, with five languages spoken in different pueblos. Most Pueblo tribes trace their ancestry to the Ancestral Puebloan people *(see pp160–61)*, who spread across the area from around 300–200 BC. Acoma Pueblo, also known as "Sky City" because of its high position on a sandstone mesa, is thought to be among the oldest inhabited pueblos in the country. Nineteen of the pueblos are strung out along the fertile valley of the Rio Grande River Valley. Their history and varied culture is traced at Albuquerque's impressive Indian Pueblo Cultural Center *(see pp214–5)*.

Today, most pueblos produce distinctive arts and crafts, such as the artistic pottery of the Hopi or the fine jewelry of Zuni. The colorful ceremonies of the Rio Grande Pueblos vary from village to village, with the Corn Dance being the most common. Held on various dates from late spring to summer *(see p33)*, the dance is meant to insure a successful harvest. Visitors should behave respectfully, remembering that despite the festive atmosphere, these dances are religious rituals. Much Pueblo ceremony is carried out in private, away from the eyes of tourists.

Tohono O'odham painters restore frescoes at San Xavier del Bac

THE TOHONO O'ODHAM

ALONG WITH their close relatives, the Pima people, the Tohono O'odham live in southern Arizona's Sonoran Desert. Due to the harsh nature of the environment here, neither tribe has ever been moved off its ancestral lands. However, both tribes are among the most anglicized in the region. The Pima were guides to the US Army during the Indian Wars of the 1860s. Today's Tohono O'odam are mainly Christian, the mission church of San Xavier del Bac is on Tohono O'odham land south of Tucson *(see pp88–9)*, but still hold some of their traditional ceremonies, such as the Nawait or Saguaro Wine Festival and the Tcirkwena Dance. They are also known for their fine basketwork.

THE UTE

THIS TRIBE ONCE reigned over a vast territory. As late as the 1850s their lands covered 85 percent of Colorado. Steady encroachment by settlers and mining interests eventually forced them to resettle. Today, the Ute welcome visitors to their two reservations along the southern Colorado border. The Ute Mountain Reservation is home to the little known but spectacular Ancestral Puebloan ruins of Ute Mountain Tribal Park *(see p172–3)*, and the southern Ute Reservation attracts thousands of visitors each year to the popular Sky Ute Casino, Lodge, and Museum. The southern Utes also hold a colorful Bear Dance on Memorial Day weekend that is open to the public.

Ute woman sewing moccasins with Mount Ute in the background

Native Art of the Southwest

Hopi-made coiled basket

THE NATIVE PEOPLES of the American Southwest have a proud artistic heritage. They produced painted pottery, basketwork, and jewelry of distinction for centuries, often using stylized images of animals and plants to express their spiritual relationship with nature. As the region's tourist trade developed, in the 19th century, such products became sought after by visitors. In the 20th century a Native fine art movement began with watercolors, which initially depicted Native ceremonies. Such works proved popular with collectors and marked the beginning of an interest in and market for southwestwern Native art. Today, artists work in all media, including sculpture, video, and installations, and in all styles such as abstract expressionism or realism.

Basketwork *is a tradition associated with all Native peoples of the Southwest. Braided, twined, or coiled from willow or yucca leaves, the baskets are decorated differently according to the tribe.*

Rugmaking *traditions in the Southwest belong to the Navajo and Pueblo, with Puebloan examples dating from prehistoric times. Navajo weaving is best known; these rugs were sought after by tourists as early as the mid-1800s, and by the late 19th century colorful regional distinctions emerged.*

NATIVE AMERICAN PAINTING

The Apache developed the art of animal-skin painting in which warriors celebrated their deeds in pictographs. Designs, often scenes of men and horses in battle or hunting, were scratched on the surface and color added with bone or brush. After 1900 a fine art movement developed, including fine impressionistic and abstract works such as *Red Tailed Hawk* (1986) by Hopi/Tewa artist Dan Namingha.

Pottery *originated around 200 BC with the coiled pots of the Mimbres people. These mid-20th-century pots are a polished blackware vase from Taos Pueblo* (left) *and a patterned jar from Acoma* (above).

Contemporary sculpture by Native American artists can be seen in galleries across the Southwest. They include this piece called Dineh *(1981) by famous American sculptor Allan Houser.* Dineh *is the word the Navajo use to describe themselves. This is a modernist work, cast in bronze, whose smooth planes and clean lines appear to represent the dignity and strength of this couple.*

EARLY NATIVE AMERICAN ART

Outstanding examples of early Southwestern pottery, basketwork, and hide paintings have been marvelously preserved because of the area's dry climate, in spite of the fact that they are made from perishable organic materials such as clay, yucca fiber, and painted animal skins. As a result, more is known about early indigenous art here than in any other part of North America. The earliest pieces date back to around 200 BC, with textiles a later development. By AD 600, the styles of the three main groups: the Hohokam, Mogollon, and Ancestral Puebloan peoples had begun to merge and to absorb outside influences, seen in the Mexican designs on some ancient pots.

Ancient pottery bowl

Silverwork *has been produced by the Navajo, Zuni, and Hopi peoples for centuries. Since the mid-19th century, Navajo jewelers have incorporated Spanish styles. Zuni and Hopi silver is made in a different way. They adopted an intricate overlay process in the 1930s, distinguished by raised silver patterns against a dark background.*

Carving *focuses mainly on wooden dolls, or* kachinas, *whittled mostly from pine or cottonwood. The Pueblo peoples, especially the Hopi, are noted for their masked figurines, which depict* kachina *spirits.*

The Southwest: backdrop for the Movies

THE PANORAMIC DESERT LANDSCAPE of the Southwest is familiar the world over thanks to the countless movies that have been filmed here. As legendary actor John Wayne once said: "TV you can do on the back lot; for the real outdoor dramas, you have to do them where God put the West." Monument Valley *(see pp164–5)* is famous for its association with John Ford's Westerns, while the stark beauty of southern Utah, particularly around the Moab and Kanab areas, has appeared in several films. The popular idea of the "Wild West" *(see pp54–5)* has been formed more through film than by any other medium, and visitors to the Southwest may find much of its scenery strangely familiar. Many TV series and commercials have also been shot here.

Old Tucson Studio *was built for the 1940 motion picture* Arizona. *The studio is still a popular movie location and is now also home to a family-oriented, Wild West theme park (see pp86–7).*

Johnson Canyon, *near Kanab* (see p148), *was the location of the 1962 film* How the West was Won. *It is a western town set that was built for the 1952 movie* Westward the Women. *Today, the set is open to visitors.*

JOHN FORD AND MONUMENT VALLEY

John Ford was not the first director to shoot a movie using Monument Valley's spectacular buttes as a backdrop. That honor goes to George B. Seitz, who filmed *The Vanishing American* there in 1924. But it was John Ford's genius that captured the spectacle of the West as people had never seen it before. His first movie there, *Stagecoach* (1939), so enthralled audiences that it brought the Western back into vogue and made the young John Wayne into a star. Ford set a new standard for movies, bringing the grandeur of the West to the big screen, and setting off a "studio stampede" of directors wanting to utilize the beauty of the region. In all, over 60 movies and countless TV shows, commercials, and videos have used Monument Valley as a spectacular panoramic backdrop.

Moab's *snow-capped mountains, red rock formations, and deep river canyons* (see p141) *have been the backdrop for over 100 major motion pictures, including* Thelma and Louise *in 1991.*

Director John Ford on the set of Stagecoach

Robert Zemeckis *used Monument Valley in 1990 as the backdrop for the third installment of his* Back to the Future *series of films, starring Michael J. Fox and Christopher Lloyd.*

THE SUNDANCE FILM FESTIVAL

Actor and director Robert Redford owns the Sundance Resort, which combines an environmentally responsible mountain vacation development with an institute for the promotion of the cinematic arts. Founded by Redford in 1981, the Sundance Film Festival takes place annually in the second half of January. The majority of screenings, which showcase independent film- and documentary-makers, are not held at the Sundance Resort (about 75 miles (121 km) northwest of Moab), but in Park City and at the Tower Theater in Salt Lake City. The festival has become America's foremost venue for innovative cinema and attracts the big Hollywood names. Tickets sell out quickly, so make ticket and lodging reservations ahead.

Robert Redford at the Sundance Film Festival in 1998

Monument Valley was favored by John Ford, who directed nine movies using the area dubbed "Ford Country" and other southern Utah sites as backdrops. Many, like the 1956 epic The Searchers, *are considered classics.*

Dead Horse Point State Park (see p143) has long been used by directors who want a spectacular setting. It was seen in the 1991 film Thelma and Louise *and, more recently, actor Tom Cruise free-climbed up the sheer cliff-face in the thrilling opening sequence of* Mission Impossible: 2.

Tombstone was the setting for the 1993 film of the same name (see p92). *Starring Val Kilmer, Sam Elliott, Bill Paxton, and Kurt Russell, it is a modern interpretation of the Western genre.*

Lake Powell is the most spectacular artificial lake in the US (see pp150–51). Its stark and otherworldly beauty has been used as a set for such diverse movies as the 1967 Dean Martin Western Rough Night in Jericho, *the 1965 biblical epic* The Greatest Story Ever Told *(pictured here), with Charlton Heston, and the 1968 science fiction classic* Planet of the Apes.

THE SOUTHWEST THROUGH THE YEAR

THE WEATHER in the Southwest is well known for its extremes, ranging from the heat of the desert to the ice and snow of the mountains – temperatures vary according to altitude, so the higher the elevation of the land, the cooler the area will be. Because the climate can be unbearably hot during the summer, particularly in Arizona, southern Utah, and New Mexico, many people prefer to travel to the Southwest during spring and fall. This part of the world is particularly beautiful in fall, with its astounding array of golds, reds, and yellows in the forests and national parks. The area's diverse mix of Native, Hispanic, and European (Anglo) cultures gives visitors the opportunity to experience many different kinds of festivals and celebrations.

Stringing ristras at the Hatch Chile Festival

SPRING

ALTHOUGH THE weather can be unpredictable in the spring, many festivals and celebrations are held at this time throughout the Southwest. Around Easter, prayers for a good harvest inspire several of the festivals and rituals held in the pueblos.

MARCH

Guild Indian Fair and Market *(first weekend)*
Phoenix. Held at the Heard Museum, the fair features Indian dancing, arts, crafts, and Native American food.
Rio Grande Arts and Crafts Festival *(mid-Mar)*
Albuquerque. This popular festival features handcrafted items from more than 200 artists and craftsmen.

Native dancer at the Guild Indian Fair and Market, Phoenix

Hispanic musicians or *mariachis* play at a Cinco de Mayo celebration

APRIL

Taos Film Festival *(mid-Apr)*
Taos. Film screenings at locations throughout Taos.
American Indian Week *(mid-Apr)* Albuquerque. Arts and dancing at the Indian Pueblo Cultural Center.
Gathering of Nations Pow Wow *(late Apr)* Albuquerque. A festival of more than 5,000 Native American performers and traders from 300 tribes.
Square Dance Festival *(late Apr)* Red Rock State Park. A three-day festival including performances and workshops.

SUMMER

THE WARM summer weather is the time for many open-air events, from such sports activities as boat racing and rodeos to cultural events as diverse as country music and opera. The weather in July and August, however, can be extreme, especially in southern Arizona, which sees very high temperatures and violent summer storms.

MAY

El Cinco de Mayo *(5 May)*
Many southwestern towns. Festivities to mark the 1862 Mexican victory over the French include parades, dancing, and Mexican food.
Tularosa Rose Festival *(first weekend)* Tularosa. This annual festival includes music, arts and crafts, and food as well as roses.
T & C Fiesta *(first weekend)* Truth or Consequences. Annual festival featuring a rodeo, a parade, street entertainment, and an old-time fiddlers competition.

Santa Cruz Feast Day *(early May)* Taos and Cochiti pueblos. Celebrations include blessing the fields and a colorful corn dance.

Tucson Folk Music Festival *(late May)* Tucson. A wide selection of folk music at various venues in Tucson.

La Vuelta de Bisbee *(mid-May)* Bisbee. A professional, 80-mile (129-km) bicycle race in the Bisbee area.

Great Rio Grande Raft Race *(mid-May)* Albuquerque. Kayaks, canoes, and homemade boats are used in this race to Rio Bravo bridge.

Helldorado Days and Rodeo *(late May)* Las Vegas. A week-long festival of rodeo events and art shows.

JUNE

San Antonio Fiesta *(13 June)* Sandia Pueblo. This festival welcomes visitors and features tribal dancing.

The Annual Bluegrass and Country Music Festival *(mid-Jun)* Telluride. One of the West's biggest music events is held outdoors here.

Utah Summer Games *(late June)* Cedar City. The games include a marathon, cycling, tennis, and swimming.

New Mexico Arts and Crafts Fair *(late Jun)* Albuquerque. Traditional arts and crafts, plus food and entertainments.

Utah Shakespeare Festival *(Jun–Aug)* Cedar City. Plays are produced in three theaters across the town.

Taos Summer Chamber Music Festival *(Jun–Aug)* Taos and Angel Fire. This festival takes the form of a series of outdoor concerts.

JULY

UFO Encounter *(early Jul)* Roswell. A series of lectures on UFOs, also featuring concerts and entertainment.

An exhibit at Roswell's UFO Encounter event

Nambe Falls Celebration *(early Jul)* Nambe Pueblo. Traditional dancing, food, and arts and crafts in a beautiful hillside setting.

Fourth of July *(4 July)* Most Southwestern towns. Celebrations include parades, fireworks, rodeos, sports, music festivals, and ceremonial Indian dances.

Flagstaff Festival of the Arts *(early Jul–mid-Aug)* Flagstaff. A celebration of the arts, featuring films, concerts, plays, and operas.

Frontier Days *(first week)* Prescott. The oldest professional rodeo in the world, featuring calf roping and wild horse racing.

Taos Pueblo Pow Wow *(second week)* Taos Pueblo. Traditional ceremonies and dances at the Taos Pueblo.

Rainbow Dancers at Nambe Falls Celebration

Native American Arts and Crafts Show *(mid-July)* Indian Pueblo Cultural Center, Albuquerque. Features handmade arts and crafts both on exhibit and for sale.

Spanish Market *(last weekend)* Santa Fe. Features arts and crafts by contemporary Hispanic artists.

Ruidoso Art Festival *(last weekend)* Ruidoso. This juried event is an annual showcase for top-quality arts and crafts. Many of the pieces are on sale to visitors.

Santa Fe Opera *(Jul–Aug)* Santa Fe. The company performs a variety of operas in an open-air arena .

Chamber Music Festival *(Jul–Aug)* Santa Fe. One of the finest chamber music festivals in America is held at venues throughout the city.

AUGUST

Old Lincoln Days *(first weekend)* Lincoln. A festival featuring a re-enactment of the death of Billy the Kid, including the *Last Escape of Billy the Kid* pageant.

Inter-Tribal Indian Ceremonial *(mid-Aug)* Red Rock State Park, near Gallup. Fifty tribes take part in dances, pow wows, parades, rodeos, and races. Includes arts and crafts.

Bat-Flight Breakfast *(mid-Aug)* Carlsbad Caverns. Participants can enjoy an outdoor breakfast, while watching thousands of bats as they return to the caves.

Indian Market *(third weekend)* Santa Fe. Held since 1922, the market is an opportunity to buy a wide selection of high quality Native arts and crafts.

Great American Duck Race *(fourth weekend)* Deming. Includes live duck racing, a tortilla toss, a best dressed duck contest, concerts, food, and Deming's biggest parade.

Annual Bluegrass and Country Music Festival in Telluride

FALL

THE AUTUMNAL forests and mountains of the Southwest are striking, ablaze with brilliant yellows, reds, and golds. Fall is one of the best seasons for touring and sightseeing because the temperatures become cooler and more comfortable.

SEPTEMBER

San Esteban Feast Day
(early Sep) Acoma Pueblo. The annual feast day of this pueblo brings together hundreds of Acomans and includes the Harvest Dance.
Navajo Nation Fair and Rodeo *(early Sep)* Window Rock. The largest Indian fair in the US features a parade, a rodeo, traditional song and dance, and arts and crafts.
Hatch Chile Festival *(early Sep/Labor Day weekend)* Hatch. Cooking, music, and arts and crafts in the center of the chile-growing industry.

The All-American Futurity *(early Sep/Labor Day)* Ruidoso Downs Racetrack. Quarter horse race with prize money in excess of $2 million.
New Mexico State Fair *(mid-Sep)* New Mexico. One of the largest state fairs in the nation, with rodeos, carnivals, exhibits, and music.
Fiesta de Santa Fe *(weekend after Labor Day)* Santa Fe. Festivities to commemorate Don Diego de Vargas' reconquering of the city in 1692 *(see p40)*.
Rendezvous of the Gunfighters *(Labor Day weekend)* Tombstone. Includes a parade, stagecoach rides, chili cook-offs, and mock shootouts.

OCTOBER

Kodak™ Albuquerque International Balloon Fiesta *(early Oct)* Albuquerque. More than 850 balloons take part in this event, which is the largest of its kind in the world.

The Whole Enchilada Festival *(first weekend)* Las Cruces. Featuring the world's largest enchilada *(see p249)*, as well as arts and crafts.
Geronimo Days *(second week)* Truth or Consequences. Celebrations with Native American, Hispanic, and cowboy entertainers.
Lincoln County Cowboy Symposium *(second weekend)* Ruidoso. A celebration of life in the Old West, with cowboy poets, storytellers, and musicians.

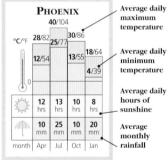

Calf roping at Lincoln County Cowboy Symposium

LAS VEGAS

°C/°F	Apr	Jul	Oct	Jan
	27/81	29/81		
	20/68		16/61	
	7/45	8/46		
				-2/28
☀ hrs	11	12	10	8
☂ mm	8	13	8	18
month	Apr	Jul	Oct	Jan

39/102

PHOENIX

°C/°F	Apr	Jul	Oct	Jan
	28/82	30/86		
		25/77	18/64	
	12/54	13/55		
			4/39	
☀ hrs	12	13	10	8
☂ mm	10	25	10	20
month	Apr	Jul	Oct	Jan

40/104

Average daily maximum temperature

Average daily minimum temperature

Average daily hours of sunshine

Average monthly rainfall

Climate
The climate varies across the region. Phoenix and the southern areas have hot and dry summers and mild, sunny winters, whereas such northern areas as Southern Utah, Arizona, and New Mexico have snowy winters that are colder due to their higher elevation.

GRAND CANYON (SOUTH RIM)

°C/°F	Apr	Jul	Oct	Jan
		29/84		
	16/61		18/64	
		12/54		
			3/37	5/41
	-1/30			-7/19
☀ hrs	11	11	9	8
☂ mm	26	45	27	33
month	Apr	Jul	Oct	Jan

SANTA FE

°C/°F	Apr	Jul	Oct	Jan
		27/81		
	15/59	14	17/63	
	2		3	4/39
				-8/18
☀ hrs	10	10	9	7
☂ mm	27	61	31	18
month	Apr	Jul	Oct	Jan

MOAB (UTAH)

°C/°F	Apr	Jul	Oct	Jan
		37/99		
	22/72		23/73	
		18/64		
	5/41		5/41	4/39
				-8
☀ hrs	10	10	9	6
☂ mm	19	20	30	17
month	Apr	Jul	Oct	Jan

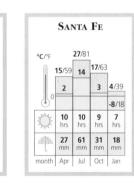

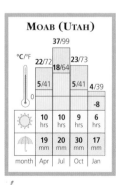

Helldorado Days *(third weekend)* Tombstone. The festival features re-enactments, parades, a carnival, music, and street entertainment.
Fat Tire Festival *(last week)* Moab. The festivities include mountain bike guided tours, workshops, and a hill climb.

WINTER

CHRISTMAS in the Southwest is celebrated in traditional American style, with lights decorating almost every building and tree. The ski season stretches from mid-November to early April in the region's many resorts. Skiing, snow-boarding, and ice-skating are all popular.

NOVEMBER

Festival of the Cranes *(mid-Nov)* Socorro. Festival held during the November migration of whooping cranes to the Bosque del Apache Wildlife Refuge *(see p218)*.
Southwest Arts and Crafts Festival *(mid-Nov)* Albuquerque. Featuring artists from across America, this is New Mexico's only juried national arts event.

DECEMBER

La Fiesta de Tumacacori *(first weekend)* Tumacacori. Festival held on mission grounds to celebrate the Native American heritage of the upper Santa Cruz Valley.

A skier descending the Ridge in Taos Ski Valley

Guided Night Walk *(Christmas Eve)* Santa Fe. A tour of the town's sights illuminated by Christmas lights.
Las Posadas Procession *(for nine days leading up to Christmas)* Albuquerque. Candlelit processions circle the Old Town Plaza as a reminder of Mary and Joseph's search for shelter.

JANUARY

Fiesta Bowl Festival and Parade *(New Year's Day)* Phoenix. College football at the ASU Sun Devil Stadium.
PGA Phoenix Open *(Jan)* Phoenix. PGA's annual golf championship in Phoenix.
San Ildefonso Pueblo Feast Day *(late Jan)* San Ildefonso Pueblo. Ceremonial dances commemorate this feast day.
Southern Arizona Square and Round Dance & Clogging Festival *(late-Jan)* Tucson. The festival attracts thousands of dancers.

Saguaro Cactus illuminated by Christmas lights

FEBRUARY

Tubac Festival of the Arts *(early Feb)* Tubac. A highlight of the town's calendar, and one of the most important arts and crafts festivals in southern Arizona.
Silver Spur Rodeo *(first weekend)* Yuma. Along with the rodeo, this festival features arts and crafts and Yuma's biggest parade.
Tucson Gem and Mineral Show *(first two weeks)* Tucson. Open to visitors, this is one of the biggest gem and mineral shows in the US.
La Fiesta de los Vaqueros *(late Feb)* Tucson. A rodeo and other cowboy events, plus the world's largest non-motorized parade.

Player at PGA Open golf championship in Phoenix

THE HISTORY OF
THE SOUTHWEST

THE SOUTHWEST IS KNOWN *for its landscape, dominated by desert, deep canyons, and high mesas. Despite the arid conditions native civilizations have lived here for thousands of years, adjusting to the arrival of other cultures – the Hispanic colonizers of the 17th and 18th centuries and the Anglo-Americans of the 19th and 20th. Its rich history has created a fascinating multicultural heritage.*

Long before the appearance of the first Spanish explorers in the 1500s, the Southwest was in-habited by a variety of native populations. Groups of hunters walked here across the Bering Straits over a land bridge that once joined Asia with North America around 25,000–35,000 years ago. Descendants of these primitive hunter-gatherers, sometimes called Paleo-Indians, gradually fanned out across the American continent as far south as present-day Argentina. The early inhabitants of the Southwest endured centuries of hardship and adaptation to develop the technology and skills required to survive the rigors of life in this arid landscape.

Kachina doll

THE FIRST INHABITANTS

The first Native American peoples in the Southwest region have been called the Clovis, named for the site in New Mexico where stone spearheads were found embedded in mammoth bones. This hunter society roamed the area in small groups between 10,000 and 8,000 BC. Gradually, however, their prey of large Pleistocene mammals died out, and tribal people turned to roots and berries to supplement their diets. Anthropologists believe settled farming societies appeared gradually as the popu-lation grew, and that new crops and farming techniques were introduced by migrants and traders from Mexico in around 800 BC, when corn first began to be cultivated in the region.

Among the early farmers of the Southwest were the Basketmakers, named for their finely wrought baskets. Part of the Early Ancestral Puebloan, or Anasazi, culture, these people are thought to have lived in extended family groups, in pithouse dwellings. These were holes dug out of the earth up to 6 ft (2 m) deep, with roofs above ground. The Basketmakers were efficient hunters, using spears and domesticated dogs. They kept turkeys, whose feathers were highly valued as decoration.

By around AD 500, agrarian society was well established in the Southwest and large villages, or pueblos, began to develop. These usually centered around a large

TIMELINE

	30,000 BC	20,000 BC	10,000 BC
Stone spear point		**10,000–8,000 BC** Nomadic Clovis culture hunted in New Mexico. They made tools out of mammoth ivory and stone	**800 BC** Corn brought to the Southwest from Mexico. Start of agriculture, although the semi-nomadic quest for food still predominates
	30,000–25,000 BC First nomadic people cross Bering Strait land bridge from Asia to North America	**10,000 BC** Man reaches the tip of South America	**5,000–500 BC** Cochise people arrive in southeastern Arizona. Also known as people of the "Desert Culture"

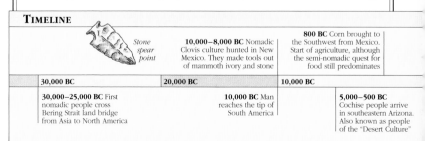

◁ **Papago Indian woman from Pima County, Arizona, 1903**

pithouse that was used for communal or religious use – the forerunner of the ceremonial kiva, which is still very much in use today (see p161).

ANCIENT CULTURES

By AD 700 there were three main cultures in the Southwest: the Hohokam, the Mogollon, and the Ancestral Puebloan. They had slowly developed, from around 200 and 300 BC, into societies based on settled communities and cultivated crops.

Hohokam pot

Ancestral Puebloan people began to build more elaborate dwellings that grew into cities such as Chaco Canyon (see pp174–5) in AD 800 and Mesa Verde (see pp180–81) in AD 1000. These settlements were mysteriously abandoned in the 12th and 13th centuries (see p161). It is thought the people migrated to the Pueblo Indian settlements along the Rio Grande valley and northwest New Mexico, and to Hopi mesa and Acoma, where their descendants live today.

The Hohokam farmed the deserts of central and southern Arizona between 300 BC and AD 1350. Their irrigation systems enabled them to grow two crops a year. It is thought that today's Tohono O'odham (Papago) and the Pima Indians of southern Arizona are descendants of the Hohokam (see pp26–7).

The Mogollon were known for their pottery and adjusted to an agrarian lifestyle when agricultural crops arrived from Mexico. They are thought to have become assimilated into Ancestral Puebloan groups and their descendants living in the north of the region.

THE NAVAJO AND THE APACHE

The Navajo and Apache peoples originated in the Athabascan culture of the north of the American continent, in Canada and Alaska. The Navajo moved south between 1200 and 1400, while the Apache are thought to have arrived in the Southwest some time in the late 15th century.

The Navajo were hunters who took to herding sheep brought by the Spanish. There were four Apache groups: the Jicarilla, the Mescalero, the Chiricahua, and the Western Apache, who continued their nomadic lifestyle. The Apache were known as skillful warriors, especially the Chiricahua Apache of southern Arizona, whose leaders Cochise and Geronimo fought Hispanic and Anglo settlers in an attempt to deter them from colonizing the area in the late 19th century.

Navajo cornfield near Holbrook, Arizona, in 1889

THE ARRIVAL OF THE SPANISH

In 1539, the Franciscan priest, Fray Marcos de Niza, led the first Spanish expedition into the Southwest region. He was inspired by hopes of finding wealthy Indian cities, such as those the Spanish had conquered in South America, and the desire to convert native populations to Christianity. His

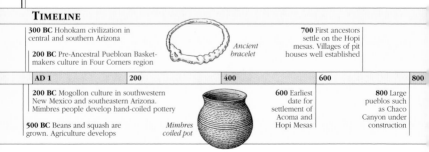

TIMELINE

300 BC Hohokam civilization in central and southern Arizona

200 BC Pre-Ancestral Puebloan Basket-makers culture in Four Corners region

Ancient bracelet

700 First ancestors settle on the Hopi mesas. Villages of pit houses well established

AD 1	200	400	600	800

200 BC Mogollon culture in southwestern New Mexico and southeastern Arizona. Mimbres people develop hand-coiled pottery

500 BC Beans and squash are grown. Agriculture develops

Mimbres coiled pot

600 Earliest date for settlement of Acoma and Hopi Mesas

800 Large pueblos such as Chaco Canyon under construction

HOPI MESA AND ACOMA PUEBLO

The Hopi villages of Old Oraibi and Walpi, and the Acoma Pueblo perch on high mesas in north-eastern Arizona and northern New Mexico. Dated to AD 1150, they are believed to be America's oldest continually occupied settlements. The Ancestral Puebloan forebears of the Hopi and Acoma peoples arrived between AD 1100 and 1300, a period known as the "Gathering of the Clans." The first to arrive was the Bear Clan, from Mesa Verde. Others came from Canyon de Chelly, Chaco Canyon, the cliff dwellings of Keet Seel, and Betatakin in the Navajo National Monument.

Acoma pueblo, New Mexico *(see p217)*

expedition sent an advance party into Zuni tribal lands. Messages came back describing villages that Marcos identified as the fabled kingdom of gold, or Cibola. The priest never got there, but the myth of riches persisted.

A year later, Francisco Vasquez de Coronado *(see p216)* returned with 330 soldiers, 1,000 Indian allies, and more than 1,000 head of livestock. He conquered the trading center of Zuni Pueblo and spent two years traversing Arizona, New Mexico, Texas, and Kansas in search of Cibola. Coronado's brutal treatment of the Pueblo people, sacking homes and burning villages, sowed the seeds for the Pueblo Revolt 140 years later.

THE COLONY OF NEW MEXICO

Without gold, the Spanish lost interest until Juan de Oñate's 1598 expedition. He set up a permanent colony called New Mexico, which included all of the present-day states of New Mexico and Arizona, as well as parts of Colorado, Utah, Nevada, and California.

Spanish attempts to conquer the Indian pueblos led to bloody battles. Oñate's cruelty, coupled with harsh conditions and bad harvests, caused many settlers to flee the colony. A new governor, Don Pedro de Peralta, was instated in 1610, and Santa Fe became the capital.

Engraving by Norman Price of Coronado setting out to discover a legendary kingdom of gold in 1540

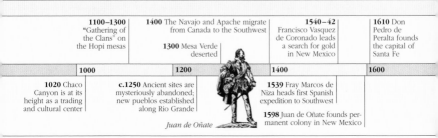

1100–1300 "Gathering of the Clans" on the Hopi mesas	1400 The Navajo and Apache migrate from Canada to the Southwest	1540–42 Francisco Vasquez de Coronado leads a search for gold in New Mexico	1610 Don Pedro de Peralta founds the capital of Santa Fe
	1300 Mesa Verde deserted		

1000	1200	1400	1600
1020 Chaco Canyon is at its height as a trading and cultural center	c.1250 Ancient sites are mysteriously abandoned; new pueblos established along Rio Grande	1539 Fray Marcos de Niza heads first Spanish expedition to Southwest	
		1598 Juan de Oñate founds permanent colony in New Mexico	

Juan de Oñate

Despite the harsh conditions, more settlers, priests, and soldiers began to return to the area, determined to subdue the native people and to suppress their religious practices.

Illustration of the 1680 Pueblo Indian Revolt

THE PUEBLO REVOLT

As the colonists spread out, they seized Pueblo farmlands and created huge ranches for themselves. The Pueblo people refused to work for them and continued to resist the new religion. When, in 1675, three native religious leaders were hanged in Santa Fe and more than 40 others publicly whipped, Popé, a Pueblo leader, started a resistance movement. The uprising on August 9, 1680, resulted in the deaths of 375 colonists and 21 priests, with the remaining 2,000 settlers driven south across the Rio Grande.

The Pueblo people did not manage to rid the region of the Spanish. In 1692, Don Diego de Vargas reclaimed Santa Fe. There were signs, however, of a relatively more tolerant relationship between Indian and colonizer.

THE END OF THE SPANISH ERA

By the late 18th century, the Spanish wanted to extend their power to California and secure the Pacific coast against the English and the Russians. Their first Arizona settlement was at Tubac, near Tucson in 1752. In 1775, Juan Bautista de Anza reached the Pacific Coast and founded San Francisco in Alta California *(see p24)*.

As the Southwest opened up, Anglo-Americans were presented with new trading opportunities. In the Louisiana Purchase of 1803, Napoleon sold Louisiana, an enormous area of about 828,000 sq miles (2.2 million sq km) of land, to the recently formed United States. The US and New Mexico now shared a border, but the Anglos proved the stronger power.

The fight for Mexico's independence from Spain began on September 16, 1810, but it was not until 1821 that independence was finally declared.

THE MISSIONS

In the late 17th century, Jesuit missionary Father Eusebio Kino lived alongside and established a rapport with the Pima people of southern Arizona. He initiated the Jesuit practice of bringing gifts of livestock and seeds for new crops, including wheat. Those natives involved in the missionary program escaped forced labor. Kino inspired the natives living south of Tucson, at a place called Bac, to begin work on what was to become the Southwest's most beautiful mission church, San Xavier del Bac (*see pp88–9*). When Kino died in 1711, there were around 20 missions across the area.

Father Eusebio Kino

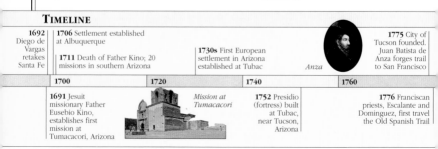

TIMELINE

1692 Diego de Vargas retakes Santa Fe	**1706** Settlement established at Albuquerque		**1775** City of Tucson founded. Juan Batista de Anza forges trail to San Francisco
	1711 Death of Father Kino; 20 missions in southern Arizona	**1730s** First European settlement in Arizona established at Tubac *Anza*	

1700   **1720**   **1740**   **1760**

1691 Jesuit missionary Father Eusebio Kino, establishes first mission at Tumacacori, Arizona	*Mission at Tumacacori*	**1752** Presidio (fortress) built at Tubac, near Tucson, Arizona	**1776** Franciscan priests, Escalante and Dominguez, first travel the Old Spanish Trail

The Republic of Mexico was founded in 1824. Newly independent Mexicans were glad to do business with their Anglo-American neighbors, who brought much-needed trade after the Spanish block on goods going west.

ANGLO-AMERICAN SETTLEMENT

Conflicts over land rights marked the period following the 1803 Louisiana Purchase. While the Hispanic and Native inhabitants of the region were happy to trade with the Anglos, they were angered by the new settlers who built ranches and even towns on lands to which they had no

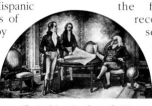
The Louisiana Purchase of 1803

legal right. By the 1840s the United States had embarked on a vigorous expansion westward, with settlers accompanied by United States' soldiers. In 1845 the US acquired Texas and, when Mexico resisted further moves, the president sent an army to take control of New Mexico, starting the Mexican War. The Treaty of Guadalupe-Hidalgo ended the conflict in 1848, and gave the US the Mexican Cession (comprising California, Utah, including Nevada and parts of Wyoming and Colorado, and New Mexico, which included northern Arizona) for $18.25 million. In 1854 the United States bought southern Arizona through the Gadsden Purchase for $10 million. While each region had its own territorial capital for administering law, they were not able to elect national representatives to Congress.

THE IMPACT OF THE AMERICAN CIVIL WAR

When the Civil War broke out in 1861, many Southwesterners had Confederate sympathies, siding with the southern states against the north, or Union. They tried to declare Arizona a Confederate territory but in 1862, Union forces repelled Confederates at Glorieta Pass, near Santa Fe. In 1863, the federal government recognized Arizona as a separate territory, and drew the state line that exists between it and New Mexico today. After the Civil War, reports of land and mineral wealth in the West filtered back east, and Anglo settlement of the West rapidly increased. Rich lodes of gold, silver, and copper were discovered in Arizona, and mining camps such as Tombstone, Jerome, and Bisbee in Arizona *(see pp92–93)*, and Silver City in New Mexico became boomtowns. In Colorado, Silverton, Ouray, and Telluride *(see pp178–9)* also grew up around the mining industry in the late 19th century.

Engraving depicting an Apache attack on Anglo settlers (c.1886)

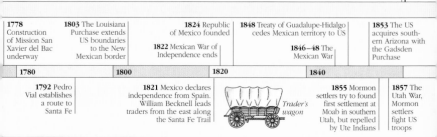

| 1778 Construction of Mission San Xavier del Bac underway | 1803 The Louisiana Purchase extends US boundaries to the New Mexican border | 1824 Republic of Mexico founded | 1848 Treaty of Guadalupe-Hidalgo cedes Mexican territory to US | 1853 The US acquires southern Arizona with the Gadsden Purchase |
| | | 1822 Mexican War of Independence ends | 1846–48 The Mexican War | |

1780	1800	1820	1840

| 1792 Pedro Vial establishes a route to Santa Fe | 1821 Mexico declares independence from Spain. William Becknell leads traders from the east along the Santa Fe Trail | *Trader's wagon* | 1855 Mormon settlers try to found first settlement at Moab in southern Utah, but repelled by Ute Indians | 1857 The Utah War, Mormon settlers fight US troops |

The Arrival of the Anglo-Americans

THE FIRST NON-SPANISH PEOPLE of European descent, or Anglo-Americans, to arrive in the Southwest were "mountain men" or fur trappers in the early 1800s. They learned survival skills from Native tribes, married Native women, and usually spoke more than one Native language, and Spanish.

The opening of the Old Spanish Trail in 1776, and the forerunner to the Santa Fe Trail from St. Louis in the East in 1792, made the region accessible to traders and settlers *(see pp24–5)*. Yet it was only after Mexican independence was declared in 1821 that the territory opened up to Anglo traders who brought luxury goods such as oranges, silk handkerchiefs, and whisky. American soldiers arrived in 1846, and by the 1850s the US Government had taken the region from the Mexicans. The Anglos, determined to subdue both Native and Hispanic populations, wrested away their lands to make way for vast ranches and towns such as Tombstone, which grew around the discovery of silver in 1877.

Mountain Man
Jim Bridger was one of many rugged individuals to open up trade routes to the west in the 1820s.

The Mexican War
This lithograph shows a battle in the 1846–8 war between the US and Mexico. After capturing Mexico City, the Americans agreed to pay $18.25 million in exchange for possession of New Mexico and California.

APACHE WARRIORS

The nomadic Apache lived in small communities in southeastern Arizona, and southern and northwestern New Mexico. Seen as a threat to the settlement of these territories, the US military was determined to wipe them out. The hanging of one of Chief Cochise's relatives in 1861 instigated a war which lasted more than a decade until Apache reservations were established in 1872. In 1877, a new leader, Victorio, launched a three-year guerrilla war against settlers that ended only with his death. The most famous Apache leader, Geronimo, led a campaign against the Mexicans and Anglos from 1851 until he surrendered in 1886 and was sent to a reservation in Florida.

Apache leader Geronimo, in a fierce pose in this picture from 1886

Mining Boom Prospector
In the second half of the 1800s, the region was a magnet for miners seeking their fortune. In reality, few individuals profited as large companies swiftly gained control of the mining areas.

The Coming of the Railroad
In 1869, the transcontinental railroad brought an influx of miners, adventurers, and tourists to the Southwest, and saw new industries emerge.

The Long Walk
Portrait of Navajo leader, Manuelito (1818–1894) taken after the Long Walk. More than 8,000 Navajo were sent to New Mexico in 1864. Many died on the way.

WAGON TRAINS ON THE SANTA FE TRAIL
Charles Ferdinand's *The Attack on the Emigrant Train* (1856) depicts the conflicts between the Apache and traders and settlers who poured into the Southwest after the establishment of the Santa Fe Trail *(see pp24–5).*

Apache were often depicted attacking wagon trains. The Apache, who had a fierce reputation, felt justifiably threatened by Anglo settlers.

Anglo-American Influence
John Gast's American Progress *(1872) shows Indians pursued by a woman in a white robe – a symbol of American culture. The schoolbook represents education; trains, ships, and settlers are all signs of "civilization."*

A group of cowboys roping a steer, painted by C. M. Russell (1897)

LAND DISPUTES

After the Civil War, the US Government set about clearing more land for settlers. In 1864, more than 8,000 Navajo people were forced from their lands and made to march "The Long Walk" of 400 miles (644 km) east to a reservation at Bosque Redondo in New Mexico. Some died en route as a result of the harsh weather and many more from disease at the reservation. In 1868, the Navajo were given 20,000 square miles (51,800 sq km) of land across Arizona, New Mexico, and southern Utah. The Chiricahua Apache continued to fight against forced settlement for most of the 19th century until their defeat and the surrender of their leader, Geronimo, in 1886.

In the 1870s, vast areas of the Southwest became huge cattle and sheep ranches. Battles between farmers, smallholders, and ranchers were common. Frequent "Range Wars"

Engraving showing Billy the Kid shooting a man in a bar

included the Lincoln County War, known for its famous protagonist, Billy the Kid (*see p54*). As Anglo ranchers seized land, the New Mexicans' tradition of communal land use was overturned and many indigenous farmers lost their livelihoods.

By the 1880s four major railroads crossed the region bringing new Anglo settlers in search of prosperity. They came fully believing in their right to exploit the resources of this new land, and the railroad became a catalyst for new industries in the region, such as lumberjacking, cattle farming, and mineral mining. Luxury goods brought from the East by rail also made life a little easier.

New Mexico and Arizona were granted statehood in 1912. In the years leading up to and following World War I, Arizona, in particular, experienced an economic boom because of its rich mineral resources.

TIMELINE

1877 Copper found at Bisbee, Arizona. Silver discovered at Tombstone, Arizona.

Geronimo (1829–1909)

1886 Indian Wars end with the surrender of Geronimo

1912 New Mexico and Arizona become 47th and 48th states of the Union

1917 The US enters World War I

1860	1880	1900	1920

1868 Navajo Reservation established in the Four Corners region

1878 The Lincoln County War begins in Lincoln, New Mexico

1881 Gunfight at OK Corral. Billy the Kid shot in New Mexico

1889 Phoenix becomes the territorial capital of Arizona

Grand Canyon steam train

1901 Grand Canyon railroad opens, bringing tourists to the region

THE DEMAND FOR WATER

As the region's population expanded, water supply became a pressing issue, and a series of enormous, federally funded dams were built to channel precious water for the burgeoning population of such cities as Phoenix. Dam- and road-building projects aided the region's economy and attracted even more settlers.

The Hoover Dam was constructed between 1931 and 1936, but by the 1960s even that proved inadequate. Glen Canyon Dam was completed in 1963, flooding forever an area of great beauty. The dam created the huge reservoir of Lake Powell, destroying a number of ancient Native ruins.

The issue of water continues to be a serious problem in the Southwest as the population keeps on rising. Projects to harness water from any available source are under debate.

WORLD WAR II

The legacy of the war years changed the economic course of the Southwest. New Mexico's sparsely populated and remote desert areas provided secret research, development, and testing sites for the first atomic bomb, starting with Los Alamos and the Manhattan Project in 1945 *(see p186)*. Military installations such as the Titan Missile Base in southern Arizona and New Mexico's White Sands Missile Range were of national importance during the Cold War period of the 1950s.

Military research, computer technology, and other industrial off-shoots led to urbanization and a post-war population boom. Today, Phoenix and Albuquerque are among the fastest-growing cities in the US.

Patriot missile test at White Sands, New Mexico

The Southwest continues to be a major center for national defense research and development, as well as for research into space travel.

THE SOUTHWEST TODAY

The Southwest's economy continues to prosper, and its population is still growing, augmented by numbers of winter residents or "snowbirds." Ever-increasing numbers of tourists visit the region's scenic and historic wonders, preserved in the area's national parks. Established in the early 20th century, the parks have encouraged a heightened awareness of both conservation issues and Native cultures and their legacies, all of which will help guard the Southwest's precious heritage for generations to come.

Return of an early 19th-century Ancestral Puebloan artifact

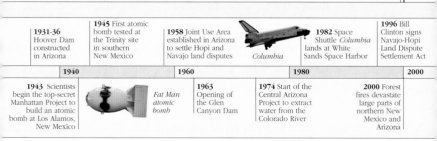

1931-36 Hoover Dam constructed in Arizona	1945 First atomic bomb tested at the Trinity site in southern New Mexico	1958 Joint Use Area established in Arizona to settle Hopi and Navajo land disputes	1982 Space Shuttle *Columbia* lands at White Sands Space Harbor	1996 Bill Clinton signs Navajo-Hopi Land Dispute Settlement Act
			Columbia	

1940	**1960**	**1980**	**2000**

1943 Scientists begin the top-secret Manhattan Project to build an atomic bomb at Los Alamos, New Mexico	*Fat Man atomic bomb*	1963 Opening of the Glen Canyon Dam	1974 Start of the Central Arizona Project to extract water from the Colorado River	2000 Forest fires devastate large parts of northern New Mexico and Arizona

ARIZONA

Introducing Arizona

THIS LARGE EXPANSE of land is a region of stunning natural beauty. In Arizona's southwest corner lies the hostile, but eerily beautiful, Sonoran desert. Its boundaries are occupied by the cities of Tucson and Phoenix, the state's biggest city and its economic center. To the north, the landscape changes, rising through high desert plateaus toward forests, canyons, and mountains. Here, the city of Flagstaff and the picturesque mountain towns of Sedona and Jerome attract thousands of visitors. The state's most famous sight is Grand Canyon *(see pp58–63)*, which draws millions of tourists to Arizona every year.

The distinctive buttes of Cathedral Rock overlooking a fishing lake at Red Rock crossing near Sedona

GRAND CANYON NATIONAL PARK
93
66
40
KINGMAN
BULLHEAD CITY
40
93
LAKE HAVASU CITY
72
60
10
QUARTZSITE
10
95
Gila River
YUMA
8
ORGAN PIPE CACTUS NAT. MON

GETTING AROUND

Phoenix is a major hub for international and domestic flights. Driving, however, is the preferred option and Arizona has a good network of well-maintained highways. Northern Arizona is bisected by I-40 and I-10 cuts across the south; I-17 is the main north-south artery. Amtrak operates two train services that cross Arizona, and Greyhound buses run regular services to Arizona from major cities across the US.

KEY

- Interstate
- Major highway
- Highway
- River

SEE ALSO

- ***Where to stay*** pp230–45
- ***Where to eat*** pp246–63

Skyscrapers dominate the skyline of Downtown Phoenix

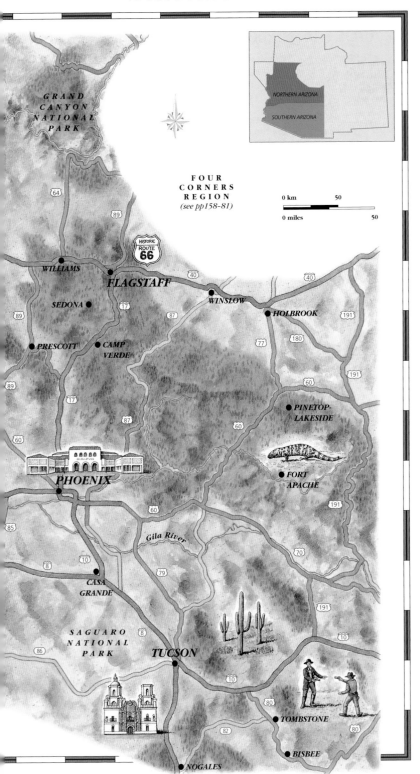

NORTHERN ARIZONA

SOUTHERN ARIZONA

**FOUR
CORNERS
REGION**
(see pp158–81)

0 km   50

0 miles   50

GRAND
CANYON
NATIONAL
PARK

HISTORIC
ROUTE
66

64

89

WILLIAMS

FLAGSTAFF

40

WINSLOW

40

SEDONA

17

87

HOLBROOK

191

89

77

180

PRESCOTT

CAMP
VERDE

89

17

87

60

191

PINETOP-
LAKESIDE

60

PHOENIX

FORT
APACHE

191

60

85

Gila River

70

8

10

CASA
GRANDE

79

SAGUARO
NATIONAL
PARK

8

191

86

TUCSON

10

10

10

80

TOMBSTONE

80

82

BISBEE

NOGALES

Route 66 in Arizona

Route 66 Flagstaff sign

Route 66 is America's most famous road. Stretching for 2,448 miles (3,941 km), from Chicago to Los Angeles, it is part of the country's folklore, symbolizing the freedom of the open road and inextricably linked to the growth of automobile travel.

Known also as "The Mother Road" and "America's Main Street," Route 66 was officially opened in 1926 after a 12-year construction process linked the main streets of hundreds of small towns that had been previously isolated. In the 1930s, a prolonged drought in Oklahoma deprived more than 200,000 farmers of their livelihoods and prompted their trek to California along Route 66. This was movingly depicted in John Steinbeck's novel *The Grapes of Wrath* (1939).

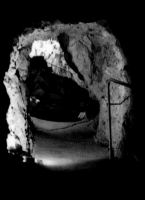

Seligman *features several Route 66 stores and diners. Set among Arizona's Upland mountains, the road here passes through scenery that evokes the days of the westward pioneers.*

Route 66 *in Arizona passes through long stretches of wilderness bearing none of the trappings of the modern world. The state has the longest remaining stretch of the original road.*

KEY

▬ Route 66
= Other roads
-- State lines

0 kilometers 40
0 miles 40

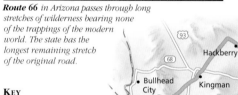

Oatman *is a former gold-mining boomtown. Today, its historic main street is lined with 19th-century buildings and boardwalks. Gunfights are regularly staged here.*

***The Grand Canyon Caverns**, discovered in 1927, are around 0.75 miles (1.2 km) below ground level. On a 45-minute guided tour visitors are led through football field-sized caverns adorned with stalagmites and seams of sparkling crystals.*

Route 66 in Popular Culture

In the 1940s and 1950s, as America's love affair with the car grew and more people moved west than ever before, hundreds of motels, restaurants, and tourist attractions appeared along Route 66, sporting a vibrant new style of architecture. The road's end as a major thoroughfare came in the 1970s with the building of a national network of multilane highways. Today, the road is a popular tourist destination in itself, and along the Arizona section, enthusiasts and conservationists have helped to ensure the preservation of many of its most evocative buildings and signs.

Locator Map

— *Route 66*

☐ *Map area*

Bobby Troup, composer of the popular song, *Route 66*, in a 1948 Buick convertible

Holbrook was founded in 1882 and is another Route 66 land-mark. It is famous for Wigwam Village, a restored 1950s motel, where visitors can stay in rooms that are de-signed to resemble Indian teepees.

(map with towns: Parks, Winona, Winslow, Joseph City, Chambers, Navajo, Flagstaff area)

Flagstaff is home to the famous Museum Club roadhouse, a large log cabin, built in 1931. It became a nightclub nicknamed "The Zoo," which was favored by country musicians traveling the road, including such stars as Willie Nelson.

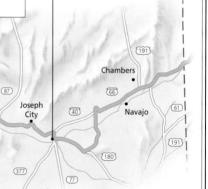

Williams *is known for its many nostalgic diners and motels. Twisters café (see p251), also known as the Route 66 Place, is crammed with road memorabilia, including the original 1950s soda fountain and bar stools.*

The Geology of Grand Canyon

GRAND CANYON'S multicolored layers of rock provide the best record of the Earth's formation of anywhere in the world. Each stratum of rock reveals a different period in the Earth's geological history beginning with the earliest, the Precambrian Era, which covers geological time up to 570 million years ago. More than two billion years of history have been recorded in the canyon, although the most dramatic changes took place relatively recently, four million years ago, when the Colorado River began to carve its path through the canyon walls. The sloping nature of the Kaibab Plateau has lead to increased erosion in some parts of the canyon.

A view of Grand Canyon's plateau and South Rim

View of the North Rim
The canyon's size and beauty are what make it one of the most-visited sights in the US (see pp58–63).

Canyon rim

KAIBAB LIMESTONE
TOROWEAP FORMATION
COCONINO SANDSTONE
HERMIT SHALE

SUPAI GROUP

REDWALL LIMESTONE

TEMPLE BUTTE LIMESTONE

MUAV LIMESTONE

BRIGHT ANGEL SHALE

TAPEATS SANDSTONE

SHINUMO QUARTZITE

HAKATAI SHALE

DIABASE SILL

BASS FORMATION

RECORD OF LIFE

The fossils found in each layer tell the story of the development of life on Earth. The oldest layer, the Vishnu Schist, was formed in the Proterozoic era, when the first bacteria and algae were just emerging. Later layers were created by billions of small marine creatures whose hard shells eventually built up into thick layers of limestone.

The Asymmetrical Canyon
The North Rim of Grand Canyon is more eroded than the South Rim. The entire Kaibab Plateau slopes to the south, so rain falling at the North Rim flows toward the canyon and over the rim, creating deep side canyons and a wide space between the rim and the river.

The Surprise Canyon Formation
Classified by geologists in 1985, this new strata can be seen only in remote parts of the canyon. It was formed 335 million years ago.

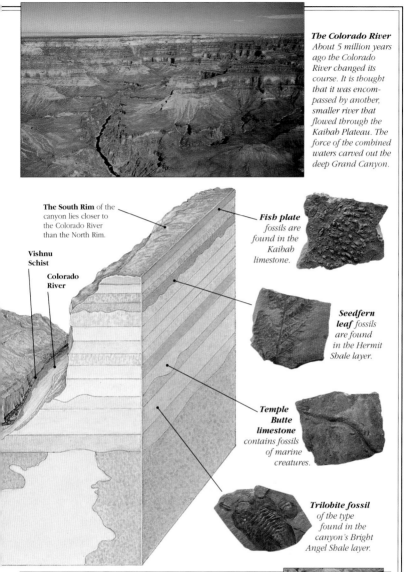

The Colorado River
About 5 million years ago the Colorado River changed its course. It is thought that it was encompassed by another, smaller river that flowed through the Kaibab Plateau. The force of the combined waters carved out the deep Grand Canyon.

The South Rim of the canyon lies closer to the Colorado River than the North Rim.

Vishnu Schist

Colorado River

Fish plate *fossils are found in the Kaibab limestone.*

Seedfern leaf *fossils are found in the Hermit Shale layer.*

Temple Butte limestone *contains fossils of marine creatures.*

Trilobite fossil *of the type found in the canyon's Bright Angel Shale layer.*

HOW THE CANYON WAS FORMED

While the Colorado River accounts for the canyon's depth, its width and formations are the work of even greater forces. Wind rushing through the canyon erodes the limestone and sandstone a few grains at a time. Rain pouring over the canyon rim cuts deep side canyons through the softer rock. Perhaps the greatest canyon-building force is ice. Water from rain and snowmelt works into cracks in the rock. When frozen, it expands, forcing the rock away from the canyon walls. The layers vary in hardness. Soft layers erode quickly into sloped faces. Harder rock resists erosion, leaving sheer vertical faces.

Crack formed by ice and water erosion

The Wild West

ROMANTICIZED IN A thousand cowboy movies, the "Wild West" conjures up images of tough men herding cattle across the country before living it up in a saloon. But frontier life was far from romantic. Settlers arriving in this wilderness were caught up in a first-come-first-serve battle for land and wealth, fighting Native Americans and each other for land.

The rugged life of the mining prospectors and ranch cowboys helped to create the idea of the American West. Today, visitors can still see mining ghost towns such as Chloride *(see p70)* or enjoy re-enacted gunfights on the streets of Tombstone. In the late 19th century, however, such survival skills as good shooting often co-existed with a kill-or-be-killed ethos.

Old mining cottages, such as this one, may be seen in the Southwest's many former mining towns. The region's mining past can be traced in towns such as Oatman (see p70) and Bisbee (see p92).

A reward poster for William Bonney (better known as Billy the Kid), who was one of the Wild West's most notorious outlaws. He was eventually tracked and killed by Sheriff Pat Garrett at Fort Sumner on July 14, 1881 (see p225).

Deadwood Dick *was the nickname of cowboy Nat Love – earned because of his cattle-roping skills. Although there were around 5,000 black cowboys, there are no sights or museums commemorating them in the Southwest today.*

Cowboys were famous for their horsemanship and sense of camaraderie. The painting shows two friends attempting to save another.

The Questionable Companionship (1902) *by Frederic Remington highlights the tensions between Native Americans and the US army, who had played a central role in removing tribes from their ancestral lands.*

all over the west they wear

LEVI STRAUSS & CO.S
COPPER RIVETED
Overalls.

Cowboy fashion began to appear in advertisements in around 1900. The ever popular Levi Strauss denim clothing can be bought across the region (see p265).

Guided trail rides are a great way to explore the Wild West and are part of the package of activities available at dude ranches (see p271). These ranches offer visitors the opportunity to experience the contemporary cowboy lifestyle.

Horses were vividly depicted in Remington's dramatic action scenes. They were painted with astonishing realism, revealing a profound knowledge of their behaviour and physique.

SOUTHWESTERN COWBOYS

New York-born artist Frederic Sackrider Remington (1861–1909) became well known for his epic portraits of cowboys, horses, soldiers, and Native Americans in the late 19th century. One such example of his work is the oil painting *Aiding a Comrade* (1890), which celebrates the bravery and loyalty of the cowboy, at a time when they and small-scale ranchers were being super-ceded by powerful mining companies and ranching corporations. Remington lamented the passing of these heroes: "Cowboys! There are no cowboys anymore!"

THE GUNFIGHT AT THE OK CORRAL

One of the most famous tales of the Wild West is the Gunfight at the OK Corral, in Tombstone, Arizona (*see p92*). This struggle pitted two clans against each other, the Clantons and the Earps. The usual, often disputed, version features the Clantons as no-good outlaws and the Earps as the forces of law and order. In 1881 Virgil Earp was the town marshal, and his brothers Morgan and Wyatt were temporary deputies. The showdown on October 26 had the Earps and their ally Doc Holliday on one side and Billy Clanton and the McLaury brothers, Tom and Frank, on the other. Of the seven combatants, only Wyatt Earp emerged untouched by a bullet. Billy, Tom and Frank were all killed. Wyatt Earp moved to Los Angeles, where he died in 1929.

Scene from the 1957 film, *Gunfight at the OK Corral*, with Burt Lancaster and Kirk Douglas

GRAND CANYON AND NORTHERN ARIZONA

FOR MOST PEOPLE, northern Arizona is famous as the location of Grand Canyon, a gorge of breathtaking proportions carved out of rock by the Colorado River as it crosses the state on its way west to California. Northern Arizona's other attractions include the high desert landscape of the Colorado Plateau, with its sagebrush and yucca, punctuated by the forested foothills of the San Francisco Peaks. The Kaibab, Prescott, and Coconino National Forests cover large areas, and provide the setting for the lively city of Flagstaff as

well as for the charming towns of Sedona and Jerome. This region is also dotted with fascinating mining ghost towns such as Chloride and Oatman, a reminder that Arizona won its nickname, the Copper State, from the mineral mining boom that took place in the first half of the 20th century.

More than 25 percent of Arizona is Native American reservation land. The state is also home to several centuries-old Puebloan ruins, most notably the hilltop village of Tuzigoot and the hillside remains of Montezuma Castle.

SIGHTS AT A GLANCE

Historic Towns and Cities
Camp Verde **12**
Flagstaff **2**
Jerome **14**
Kingman **8**
Lake Havasu City **10**
Oatman **9**
Sedona **16**
Williams **7**

National Parks and Monuments
Grand Canyon **1**
Montezuma Castle National Monument **13**
Petrified Forest National Park **17**
Sunset Crater National Monument **4**
Tuzigoot National

Monument **15**
Walnut Canyon National Monument **5**
Wupatki National Monument **3**

Areas of Natural Beauty
Oak Creek Canyon **6**
Heart of Arizona Tour **11**

KEY
✈ International airport
═ Interstate
═ Major highway
─ Highway
─ Railroad

0 km 75
0 miles 75

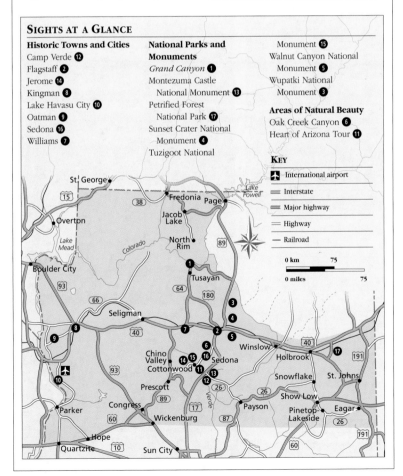

◁ Route 66 memorabilia decorating a shop on the Arizona section of the famous road *(see pp50–51)*

Grand Canyon ❶

GRAND CANYON is one of the world's great natural wonders and an instantly recognizable symbol of the Southwest. The canyon runs through Grand Canyon National Park *(see pp60–63)*, and is 277 miles (446 km) long, an average of 10 miles (16 km) wide, and around 5,000 ft (1,500 m) deep. It was formed over a period of six million years by the Colorado River, whose fast-flowing waters sliced their way through the Colorado Plateau *(see pp18–19)* which includes the gorge and most of northern Arizona and the Four Corners region. The plateau's geological vagaries have defined the river's twisted course and exposed vast cliffs and pinnacles that are ringed by rocks of different color, variegated hues of limestone, sandstone, and shale *(see pp52–3)*. By any standard, the canyon is spectacular, but its special beauty is in the ever-shifting patterns of light and shadow and the colors of the rock, bleached white at midday, but bathed in red and ocher at sunset.

Mule trip convoy
A mule ride is a popular method of exploring the canyon's narrow trails.

Havasu Canyon
Since 1300 Havasu Canyon has been home to the Havasupai Indians. Now a population of around 500 Indians lives on the Havasupai Reservation, making a living from the tourist trade.

Grandview Point
At 7,400 ft (2,250 m), Grandview Point is one of the highest places on the South Rim, the canyon's southern edge. It is one of the stops along Desert View Drive (see p61). *The point is thought to be the spot from where Spanish colonists had their first glimpse of the the canyon in 1540.*

North Rim
The North Rim receives roughly one tenth the number of visitors of the South Rim. While less accessible, it is a more peaceful destination offering a sense of unexplored wilderness. It has a range of hikes, such as the North Kaibab Trail, a steep descent down to Phantom Ranch on the canyon floor (see p60).

(see p60)

VISITORS' CHECKLIST

Road map B3. 🛈 *Canyon Visitor Center, Canyon View Information Plaza, south of Mather Point, Arizona (520) 638-7888.* ✈ *Grand Canyon Airport, Tusayan.* 🚃 *Grand Canyon Railway from Williams daily.* 🚌 *From Flagstaff and Williams.* 🕐 *South Rim: year round: daily. North Rim: summer only.* ● *North Rim: late Nov–mid-May: closed by snow.* 🌐 & *partial.* 🛍 🅿 🚻 🍴

View from Hopi Point
Projecting far into the canyon, the tip of Hopi Point offers one of the best sunset-watching spots along Hermit Road. As the sun sets, it highlights four of the canyon's beautiful sculpted peaks.

YAVAPAI POINT AT THE SOUTH RIM

Situated 5 miles (8 km) north of the canyon's South Entrance, along a gravelled stretch of the Rim Trail, is Yavapai Point. Its observation station offers spectacular views of the canyon, and a viewing panel identifies several of the central canyon's landmarks.

Bright Angel Trail
Used by both Native Americans and early settlers, the Bright Angel Trail follows a natural route along one of the canyon's enormous fault lines. It is an appealing option for day-hikers because unlike some other trails in the area, it offers plenty of shade and several seasonal water sources.

Grand Canyon National Park

GRAND CANYON NATIONAL PARK is a World Heritage Site
located entirely within the state of Arizona. The
park covers 1,904 sq miles (4,930 sq km), and is made up
of the canyon itself, which starts where the Paria river
empties into the Colorado, and stretches from Lees Ferry
to Lake Mead *(see p120)*, and adjoining lands. The area
won protective status as a National Monument in 1908
after Theodore Roosevelt visited in 1903, observing that
it should be kept intact for future generations as "... the
one great sight which every American ... should see."
The National Park was officially created in 1919.

The park has two main entrances, on the North and
South rims of the canyon, However, the southern section of the park receives the most visitors and can become
very conjested during the summer season *(see pp62–3)*.

North Kaibab Trail is a
challenging man-made route
following ridge lines and
offering panoramic views.

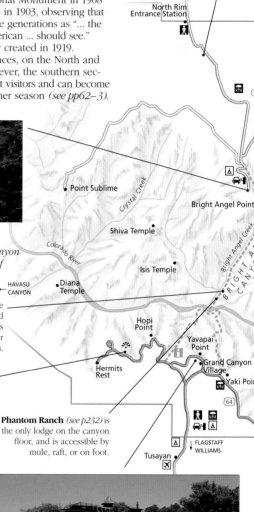

North Rim
Entrance Station

Point Sublime

Crystal Creek

Bright Angel Point

Shiva Temple

Colorado River

Isis Temple

BRIGHT ANGEL CANYON

Bright Angel Creek

HAVASU CANYON

Diana Temple

Hopi Point

Yavapai Point

Grand Canyon Village

Hermits Rest

Yaki Point

64

FLAGSTAFF
WILLIAMS

Tusayan

Grand Canyon Lodge
*Perched above the canyon at
Bright Angel Point, the Grand Canyon
Lodge has rooms and a number of
dining options* (see p63).

Bright Angel Trail starts from the
South Rim. It is a well-maintained
but demanding trail that descends
into the canyon and up the other
side to the North Rim.

Phantom Ranch *(see p232)* is
the only lodge on the canyon
floor, and is accessible by
mule, raft, or on foot.

Hermit Road
*This drive extends to the
Hermits Rest viewpoint.
A free shuttle bus ferries
visitors along the route
during summer.*

Grand Canyon Railway
*Restored steam trains make the 64-mile (103-km) trip from
the town of Williams to Grand Canyon Village.*

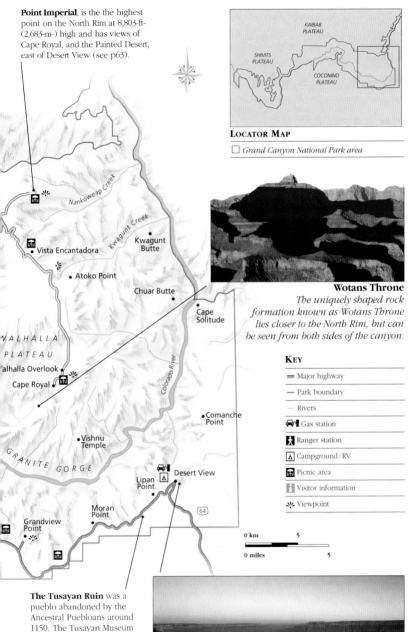

Point Imperial, is the the highest point on the North Rim at 8,803-ft-(2,683-m-) high and has views of Cape Royal, and the Painted Desert, east of Desert View (see p63).

LOCATOR MAP

☐ *Grand Canyon National Park area*

KAIBAB PLATEAU

SHIVITS PLATEAU

COCONINO PLATEAU

Nankoweap Creek

Vista Encantadora

Kwagunt Creek

Kwagunt Butte

Atoko Point

Chuar Butte

Cape Solitude

VALHALLA PLATEAU

Valhalla Overlook

Cape Royal

Colorado River

Comanche Point

Wotans Throne
The uniquely shaped rock formation known as Wotans Throne lies closer to the North Rim, but can be seen from both sides of the canyon.

KEY

▬	Major highway
—	Park boundary
—	Rivers
🚙	Gas station
🚶	Ranger station
Ⓐ	Campground/RV
⛱	Picnic area
ℹ	Visitor information
☀	Viewpoint

Vishnu Temple

GRANITE GORGE

Grandview Point

Desert View

Lipan Point

Moran Point

64

0 km   5

0 miles   5

The Tusayan Ruin was a pueblo abandoned by the Ancestral Puebloans around 1150. The Tusayan Museum now sits next to the site.

Desert View Drive
This route connects Grand Canyon Village with Desert View, and offers breathtaking views of both the central and eastern canyon.

Exploring Grand Canyon National Park

Bell near Hermits Rest

GRAND CANYON offers awe-inspiring beauty on a vast scale. The magnificent rock formations with towers, cliffs, steep walls, and buttes recede as far as the eye can see, their bands of colored rock varying in shade as light changes through the day. The park's main roads, Hermit Road and Desert View Drive, both accessible from the south entrance, overlook the canyon. Grand Canyon Village is located on the South Rim and offers a full range of facilities. Visitors can also enter the park from the north, although this route (Hwy 67) is closed during winter. Walking trails along the North and South rims offer staggering views but, to experience the canyon at its most fascinating, the trails that head down toward the canyon floor should be explored. The Bright Angel Trail on the South Rim, and the North Kaibab Trail on the North Rim, descend to the canyon floor, and are tough hikes involving an overnight stop.

Adobe, Pueblo-style architecture of Hopi House, Grand Canyon Village

🏨 Grand Canyon Village

Grand Canyon National Park.

📞 (520) 638-7888. ♿ partial.

Grand Canyon Village has its roots in the early 20th century, when the canyon was first recognized as a potential tourist attraction. The building of visitor accommodations started after the Santa Fe Railroad began operating a branch line here from Williams in 1901. The Fred Harvey Company constructed a clutch of well-designed, attractive buildings. The most prominent is the El Tovar Hotel (see p233). Opened in 1905, it is named after Spanish explorers who reached the gorge in 1540. The Hopi House also opened in 1905 – a rendition of a traditional Hopi dwelling, where locals could sell their craftwork as souvenirs. It was built by Hopi craftsmen and

designed by Mary E. J. Colter. An ex-schoolteacher and self-taught architect, Colter drew on Southwestern influences, mixing both Native American and Hispanic styles (see pp22–3). She is responsible for many of the historic structures that now grace the South Rim, including the 1914 Lookout Studio and Hermits Rest, and the rustic 1922 Phantom Ranch on the canyon floor.

Today, Grand Canyon Village has a wide range of hotels, restaurants, and stores. It can be surprisingly easy to get lost here since the buildings are spread out and discreetly placed among wooded areas. The Village

is not only the starting point for most of the mule trips through the canyon, but also the terminus for the Grand Canyon Railway.

The South Rim

Most of the Grand Canyon's 4.5 million annual visitors come to the South Rim, since, unlike the North Rim, it is open year-round and is easily accessible along Highway 180/64 from Flagstaff and Williams. The roads along this part of the canyon, **Hermit Road** and **Desert View Drive**, are closed to private vehicles from March to November each year. Both roads start at Grand Canyon Village and encompass a selection of the choicest views of the gorge. From Grand Canyon Village, Hermit Road extends 8 miles (13 km) to Hermits Rest and, in the opposite direction, Desert View Drive covers 23 miles (37 km) finishing at the stunning overlook of Desert View.

Beginning at Grand Canyon Village, Hermit Road meanders along the South Rim, its first viewpoint being **Trailview Overlook**, which provides an overview of the canyon and the winding course of the Bright Angel Trail. Moving on, **Maricopa Point** offers especially panoramic views of the canyon but not of the Colorado River, which is more apparent from nearby **Hopi Point**. At the end of Hermit Road lies **Hermits Rest**, where a gift shop, decorated in rustic style, is located in yet another Mary Colter-designed building. A short detour from this route leads to **Yavapai Point** from where it is possible to see Phantom Ranch. This is the

The interior of the Hermits Rest gift store with crafts for sale lining the walls

Desert View's stone watchtower on Desert View Drive

NEW PLANS FOR THE SOUTH RIM

The numbers of visitors touring Grand Canyon's South Rim has increased dramatically, and a summer visit to the canyon can be an extremely busy, traffic-congested experience. In 1995, the federal government announced plans to develop a transportation system here. To reduce the numbers of cars in the park, there is likely to be a light rail and bus service and extended off-site parking in place by 2003–2004.

South Rim entrance to the park

only lodging house available on the canyon floor, across the Colorado River *(see p232)*.

The longer Desert View Drive winds for 12 miles (20 km) before reaching **Grandview Point**, where the Spaniards are believed to have had their first glimpse of the canyon in 1540. Ten miles (16 km) farther on lie the pueblo remains of Tusayan Ruin where there is a small museum featuring exhibits on Ancestral Puebloan life. After a few miles, the road leads to **Desert View** where the watchtower was Colter's most fanciful creation, its upper floor decorated with early 20th-century Hopi murals.

The North Rim

Standing at about 8,000 ft (2,400 m), the North Rim is higher, cooler, and greener than the South Rim, with dense forests of ponderosa pine, birch, and Douglas fir. Visitors are most likely to spot wildlife on the North Rim. Mule deer, Kaibab squirrel, and wild turkey are among the most common sights. The North Rim is reached via Highway 67, off Highway 89A, ending at **Grand Canyon Lodge** *(see pp233 and 250)* there are visitor services, a campground, a gas station, restaurant, and a general store. Nearby, there is a national park information center, which offers maps of the area. The North Rim and all its facilities are closed between October and May, when it is often snowed in.

The North Rim is twice as far from the river as the South Rim, and the canyon really stretches out from the overlooks giving a sense of its 10-mile (16-km) width. There are about 30 miles (45 km) of scenic roads along the North Rim as well as hiking trails to high viewpoints or down to the canyon floor, (particularly the North Kaibab Trail that links to the South Rim's Bright Angel Trail.) The picturesque **Cape Royal Drive** starts north of Grand Canyon Lodge and travels 23 miles (37 km) to Cape Royal on the Walhalla Plateau. From here, several famous buttes and peaks can be seen, including Wotans Throne and Vishnu Temple. There are also several short, easy walking trails around Cape Royal, both along the top and below the rim. A 3-mile (5-km) detour leads to **Point Imperial**, the highest point in the canyon, while along the way the **Vista Encantadora** has delightful views and picnic tables overlooking the gorge.

Mule deer on the canyon's North Rim

The Bright Angel Trail

This is the most popular of all Grand Canyon hiking trails. The Bright Angel trailhead is at Canyon Village on the South Rim. The trail begins near the Kolb Studio at the western end of Grand Canyon Village and switches dramatically down the side of the canyon. It crosses the river over a suspension bridge, ending 9 hard miles (13 km) later at the Bright Angel Campsite, not far from the Phantom Ranch.

There are two resthouses and a fully equipped campground along the way. It is not advisable to attempt the whole trip in one day. Many walk from the South Rim to one of the rest stops and then return up to the rim. Temperatures at the bottom of the canyon can reach 110°F (29°C) or higher in summer. Day hikers should therefore carry a quart (just over a liter) of water per person per hour for summer hiking. Carrying a first-aid kit is also recommended.

Hikers taking a break on the South Rim's Bright Angel Trail

Breathtaking view of Grand Canyon at dusk ▷

Flagstaff ❷

Colorful Lowell Observatory sign

NESTLING AMONG the pine forests of Northern Arizona's San Francisco Peaks, Flagstaff is one of the region's most attractive towns. It is a lively, easy-going place with a good selection of bars and restaurants among the maze of old red-brick buildings that make up its compact downtown. Flagstaff's first Anglo settlers were sheep ranchers who arrived in 1876. The railroad came in 1882, and the town developed as a lumber center.

Flagstaff is the home of Northern Arizona University, which has two appealing art galleries, and is a good base for visiting Grand Canyon's South Rim, which is just under two hours' drive away. The surrounding mountains attract hikers in summer and skiers in winter.

The town of Flagstaff with the San Francisco Peaks as a backdrop

Exploring Flagstaff

Flagstaff's center is narrow and slender, channeling north toward the Museum of Northern Arizona and south to the University. At its heart is a pocket-sized historic district, an attractive ensemble of red-brick buildings, which houses the best restaurants and bars. Lowell Observatory is located on Mars Hill, a short distance from downown, and the popular Arizona Snowbowl ski resort is an enjoyable ten-minute drive to the north of the town.

🏛 Lowell Observatory
1400 West Mars Hill Road. ☎ (520) 774-3358. ◯ Apr–Oct: 9am–5pm daily; Nov–March: noon-5pm daily. ● public hols. ▨ 🚻 ✔

Tucked away on a hill about a mile northwest of the town center, the Lowell Observatory was founded in 1894 and named for its benefactor, Percival Lowell, a member of one of Boston's wealthiest families. He financed the observatory to look for life on Mars and chose the town because of its high altitude and clear mountain air. Although his theory was eventually proved wrong, the Lowell Observatory went on to establish an international reputation with its documented evidence of an expanding universe,

1930 Pluto dome at Flagstaff's Lowell Observatory

data that was disclosed to the public in 1912. One of the observatory's famous astronomers, Clyde Tombaugh, discovered the planet Pluto on February 18, 1930.

Visitors can inspect the main rotunda, with its assorted astronomical paraphernalia, and view the original photographic plates made by Tombaugh. A guided tour includes a video presentation on the observatory's history. Evening astronomy sessions can be arranged in advance.

🚻 Historic Downtown

Just ten minutes' walk from end to end, Flagstaff's historic downtown dates mainly from the 1890s. Many buildings sport decorative stone and stucco friezes and are now occupied by cafés, bars, and stores. Architecturally, several buildings stand out, particularly the restored Babbitt Building and the 1926 train station that today houses the visitor center. Perhaps the most attractive building is the Weatherford Hotel, which was opened on January 1, 1900. It was named after its owner, Texan entrepreneur John W. Weatherford, and was much admired for its grand two-story wraparound veranda and its sunroom.

🏛 Northern Arizona University
624 S. Knoles Dr. Flagstaff. ☎ (520) 523-9011. ◯ Times vary, so call in advance.

Flagstaff's lively café society owes much to the 16,000 students of Northern Arizona University (NAU). The main entrance point to the campus is located on Knoles Drive. Green lawns, stately trees, and several historic buildings make for a pleasant visit. Of particular note are two campus art galleries: the Beasley Gallery in the Fine Art Building, which features temporary exhibitions and student work, and the Old Main Art Museum and Gallery housed in Old Main Building – the university's oldest. This features the permanent Weiss collection, which includes works by the famous Mexican artist Diego Rivera.

Arts and Crafts swinging settee at Riordan Mansion

🏛 Riordan Mansion State Historic Park

1300 Riordan Ranch St. 【 (520) 779-4395. ○ May–late Sep: 8am–5pm daily; late Sep–Apr: 11am–5pm daily. ● public hols. 🖼 🚻

In the mid-1880s, Michael and Timothy Riordan established a lumber company that quickly made them a fortune. The brothers then built a house of grandiose proportions, a 40-room log mansion with two wings, one for each of them and their families. Completed in 1904 and now preserved as a State Historic Park, the house has a rustic, timber-clad exterior, and Arts and Crafts furniture inside.

🏛 Pioneer Museum

12340 Fort Valley Rd. 【 (520) 774-6272. ○ Mon–Sat 9am–5pm. ● Sun, public hols. 🚻

Flagstaff's Pioneer Museum occupies an elegant stone building that was originally built as a hospital in 1908. The museum opened in 1960 and incorporates the Ben Doney log cabin, which houses craft exhibitions. On display in the grounds are a steam locomotive of 1929 and a Santa Fe Railroad caboose. Inside, a particular highlight is a selection of Grand Canyon photographs taken in the early 1900s by photographers Ellsworth and Emery Kolb.

Arizona Snowbowl

Snowbowl Road, off Hwy 180. 【 (520) 779-1951. 🎿 Flagstaff Snow Report: (520) 779-4577. ○ Dec–mid-Apr.

Downhill skiing is available at the Arizona Snowbowl just 7 miles (11 km) north of town. The mountains here are the San Francisco Peaks, which receive an average of 260 in (660 cm) of snow every year, enough to supply the various ski runs that pattern the lower slopes of the 12,356-ft- (3,707-m-) high Agassiz Peak. Facilities include four chairlifts, and a ski school for beginners.

In summer, there is a hiking trail up to the peak, while for those less inclined to walk the Arizona Scenic Skyride is a cable car trip that offers spectacular views of the scenery.

🏛 Museum of Northern Arizona

(see pp68–9)

VISITORS' CHECKLIST

Road map: C3. 🏠 58,000. ✈ Pulliam Airport, 4 miles (6 km) south of town. 🚊 Amtrak Flagstaff Station, 1 East Route 66. 🚌 Flagstaff bus station, 399 South Malpais Lane. ℹ Flagstaff Visitor Center, at Amtrak depot, 1 East Route 66, Flagstaff (520) 774-9541. ○ 8am–5pm daily. ● public hols. 🖼 Flagstaff Festival of the Arts (early July to mid-August).

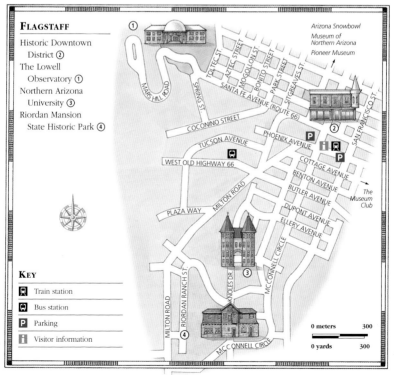

FLAGSTAFF

Historic Downtown District ②
The Lowell Observatory ①
Northern Arizona University ③
Riordan Mansion State Historic Park ④

Arizona Snowbowl
Museum of Northern Arizona
Pioneer Museum

The Museum Club

KEY

🚊 Train station
🚌 Bus station
🅿 Parking
ℹ Visitor information

0 meters 300
0 yards 300

Museum of Northern Arizona, Flagstaff

THE MUSEUM OF NORTHERN ARIZONA holds one of the Southwest's most comprehensive collections of Native American arts and crafts, as well as fine art and natural science exhibits. The collections are arranged in a series of galleries around a central courtyard. Beside the main entrance is the Archaeology Gallery, with the distinctive red and brown pottery of local Sinagua Indians. The award-winning anthropology exhibition in the Ethnology gallery documents 12,000 years of Hopi, Zuni, Navajo, and Pai tribal cultures on the Colorado Plateau. The gift shop sells contemporary Native American arts and crafts.

VISITORS' CHECKLIST

3101 North Fort Valley Rd.
☎ (520) 774-5213.
🕐 9am–5pm daily. ● public
hols. 🅰 🐾 🖵 🎁

★ Ethnology Gallery
This well-organized gallery houses important examples of Hopi silverwork, Zuni pottery, and kachina *dolls* (see p29) *dating from 1910.*

The inner courtyard has exhibits that focus on the variety of plants and animals found on the Colorado Plateau through the ages.

This part of the Ethnology Gallery replicates the inside of a kiva *(see p161).*

Babbitt gallery

Geology Gallery
A lifesize skeletal model of a Dilophosaurus is ringed by dioramas of ancient Arizona desert scenes.

KEY

☐ Archaeology Gallery
☐ Ethnology Gallery
☐ Babbitt Gallery
☐ Geology Gallery
☐ Historic courtyard
☐ Temporary exhibition space
☐ Non-exhibition space

Entrance

Archaeology Gallery

STAR SIGHTS

★ Ethnology Gallery

Museum Façade
Founded in 1928, the old building has a stone façade and is set in a pine forest.

Wupatki National Monument ❸

Road map C3. Forest Service Road 545, Sunset Crater/ Wupatki Loop Rd.
📞 (520) 679-2365. 🚉 Flagstaff. 🚌 Flagstaff. ⏰ 8am–5pm daily (longer in summer). ● Dec 25. 🎫 ♿ partial. ✔

COVERING MORE than 35,000 acres (14,000 ha) of sun-scorched wilderness to the north of Flagstaff, the Wupatki National Monument incorporates about 2,700 historic sites once inhabited by the ancestors of the Hopi people. The area was first settled after the eruption of Sunset Crater in 1064. The Sinagua people and their Ancestral Puebloan cousins realized that the volcanic ash had made the soil more fertile and consequently favourable for farming. The power of the volcanic eruption may also have have appealed to their spirituality. They left the region in the early 13th century, but no one really knows why (see pp160–61).

The largest site here is the Wupatki Pueblo, built in the 12th century and once a four-story pueblo complex of 100 rooms, housing more than 100 Sinagua. The structures rise impressively from their perch on a rocky outcrop overlooking the desert. A trail from the visitor center explores the remains, whose most unusual feature is its ballcourt. Here the Sinagua may have played at dropping a rubber ball through a stone ring without using their hands or feet.

Sunset Crater Volcano National Monument ❹

Road map C3. Hwy 45 off Hwy 89, Sunset Crater/ Wupatki Loop Rd.
📞 (520) 556-7042. 🚉 Flagstaff. 🚌 Flagstaff. ⏰ daily. ● Dec 25, Jan 1. 🎫 ♿

IN 1064, A MIGHTY volcanic eruption formed the 400-ft (120-m) deep Sunset Crater, leaving a cinder cone that rises 1,000 ft (300 m) above the surrounding lava field. Aptly named, the cone is black at the base and tinged with reds and oranges farther up. The one-mile (1.6-km) self-guided Lava Trail offers an easy stroll around the ashy landscape with its lava tubes, bubbles, and vents.

Walnut Canyon National Monument ❺

Road map C3. Walnut Canyon Road.
📞 (520) 526-3367. 🚉 Flagstaff. 🚌 Flagstaff. ⏰ 8am–4pm daily. ● Dec 25, Jan 1. 🎫 ♿ partial. ✔

LOCATED ABOUT ten miles (16 km) east of Flagstaff, off Interstate Hwy 40, Walnut Canyon houses an intriguing collection of cliff dwellings. These were inhabited by the Sinagua, ancestors of the Hopi, in the 12th and 13th

Petroglyph from Walnut Canyon

centuries. The Sinagua were attracted to the canyon by its fertile soil and plentiful water from nearby Walnut Creek.

Today, visitors can tour 25 cliff dwellings huddled underneath the natural overhangs, which are a feature of the canyon's eroded sandstone and limestone walls. The Sinagua left the canyon abruptly around the middle of the 13th century, possibly as a result of war, drought, or disease (see pp160–61). An interesting selection of Sinagua artifacts is on display in the Walnut Canyon Visitor Center.

Oak Creek Canyon ❻

Road map C3. ℹ️ (520) 774-9541.
🚉 Flagstaff. 🚌 Flagstaff. ⏰ 8am–5pm daily.

JUST SOUTH OF Flagstaff, Highway 89A weaves a charming route through Oak Creek Canyon on its way to Sedona (see p73). In the canyon, dense woods shadow the road, and the steep cliffs are colored in bands of red and yellow sandstone, pale limestone, and black basalt. This is a popular summer vacation area with many day-hiking trails, such as the East Pocket Trail, a steep wooded climb to the canyon rim. At nearby Slide Rock State Park, swimmers enjoy sliding over the rocks that form a natural water chute.

The Wupatki National Monument with ruins of a 12th-century pueblo building and San Francisco Peaks behind

Exterior view of Twisters, a retro-style diner off Route 66 in Williams *(see p251)*

Williams **7**

Road map B3. 🚶 *2,700.* 🚉 **i** *200 W. Railroad Ave. (520) 635-4061.*

THIS DISTINCTIVE little town, was named in 1851 for Bill Williams (1787–1849), a legendary mountain man and trapper who lived for a time with the Osage Indians in Missouri. The town grew up around the railroad that arrived in the 1880s, and when this was followed by a spur track to Grand Canyon's South Rim in 1901, Williams became established as a tourist center. By the late 1920s, the town was also a popular rest stop on Route 66 *(see pp50–51).*

Antique store in Chloride

Today, the town retains its frontier atmosphere, complete with Stetson-wearing locals and pick-up trucks. Most of its hotels and diners are arranged around a loop that follows Route 66 on one side and its replacement, Interstate Highway 40, on the other. Diners in town evoke the 1950s and are filled with nostalgic Route 66 memorabilia, including original soda fountains and posters.

Kingman **8**

Road map B3. 🚶 *35,000.* ✈ 🚉 🚌 **i** *120 West Andy Devine Ave. (520) 753-6106.*

LOCATED IN the middle of the Arizona desert, Kingman was founded by the Santa Fe Railroad as a construction camp in 1882. It developed into a small-time trading center, supplying the needs of nearby prospectors. In the 1920s, the town became an important rest stop on Route 66 and, during the 1930s Great Depression, it was crowded with dust bowl migrants fleeing the Midwest for California. Today, Kingman is a major crossroads at the junction of Interstate 40, Route 66, and Highway 93. Its location has spawned a number of roadside cafés and motels, but it retains some historic buildings.

Chloride, an ex-mining town, is an enjoyable day trip from Kingman. A boomtown during the late 19th century, this tiny village still has many of its original structures, including a raised wooden sidewalk and some fine shops and galleries.

Oatman **9**

Road map A3. 🚶 *100.* **i** *P.O. Box 423, Oatman (520) 768-6222.*

IN 1904, prospectors struck gold in the Black Mountains and Oatman became their main supply center. Today, Oatman is popular with visitors wanting a taste of its boomtown past.

Buildings from the town's heyday include the 1920s hotel, where movie stars Carole Lombard and Clark Gable honeymooned in 1939.

Lake Havasu City **10**

Road map A4. 🚶 *45,000.* ✈ 🚉 **i** *314 London Bridge Road (520) 453-3444.*

CALIFORNIA businessman Robert McCulloch founded Lake Havasu City in 1964. The resort city he built on the Colorado River was popular with the landlocked citizens of Arizona. His real brainwave, however, came four years later when he bought London Bridge and transported it from England to Lake Havasu. Some mocked McCulloch, suggesting that he had thought he was buying London's Gothic Tower Bridge, not this much more ordinary one. There was more hilarity when it appeared that there was nothing in Havasu City for the bridge to span. Undaunted, McCulloch simply created the waterway he needed. The bridge, and its adjoining mock-Tudor village complex, has since become one of Arizona's most popular tourist attractions.

London Bridge spans a man-made waterway in Lake Havasu City

Heart of Arizona Tour [11]

The Verde River passes through the wooded hills and fertile meadows of central Arizona, before opening into a wide, green valley between Flagstaff and Phoenix. The heart of Arizona is full of charming towns such as Sedona, hidden away among stunning scenery, and the former mining town of Jerome. Over the hills lies Prescott, once state capital and now a busy, likable little town with a center full of dignified Victorian buildings. The area's ancient history can be seen in its two beautiful pueblo ruins, Montezuma Castle and Tuzigoot.

Tips for Drivers

Recommended route: *From Sedona, take Hwy 89A to Tuzigoot, Jerome, and Prescott. Hwy 69 runs east from Prescott to the Interstate Highway 17, which connects to Camp Verde, Fort Verde, and Montezuma Castle.*
Tour length: *85 miles (137 km).*
When to go: *Spring and fall are delightful; summer is very hot.*

Sedona [1]
Set among dramatic red rock hills, Sedona is a popular resort, known for its New Age stores and galleries as well as for its friendly ambience.

Key

Tour route

Other roads

Tuzigoot National Monument [2]
Stunning views of the Verde River Valley are seen at this ruined hilltop pueblo, occupied until 1425.

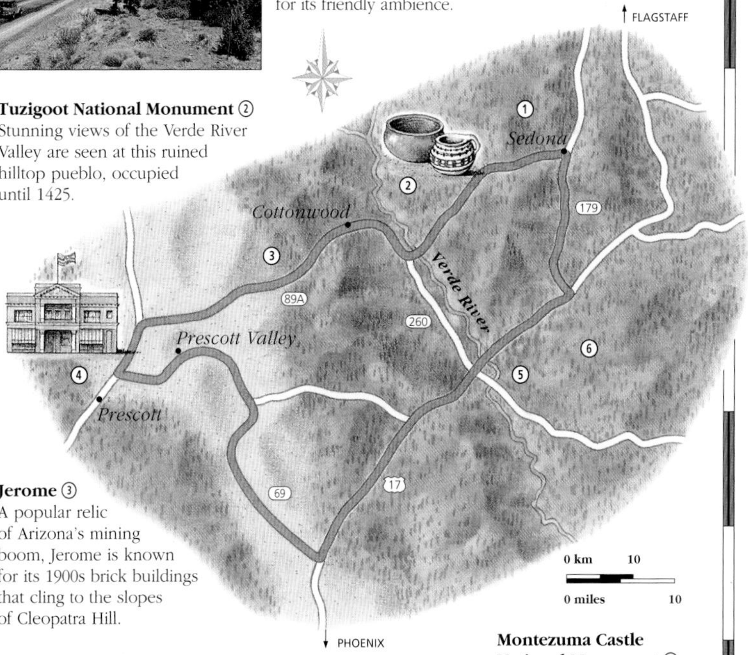
FLAGSTAFF
1
Sedona
2
Cottonwood
3
179
Verde River
89A
260
Prescott Valley
4
Prescott
5
6
69
17
0 km 10
0 miles 10
PHOENIX

Jerome [3]
A popular relic of Arizona's mining boom, Jerome is known for its 1900s brick buildings that cling to the slopes of Cleopatra Hill.

Montezuma Castle National Monument [6]
The Ancestral Puebloan ruins here date from the 1100s and occupy one of the loveliest sites in the Southwest.

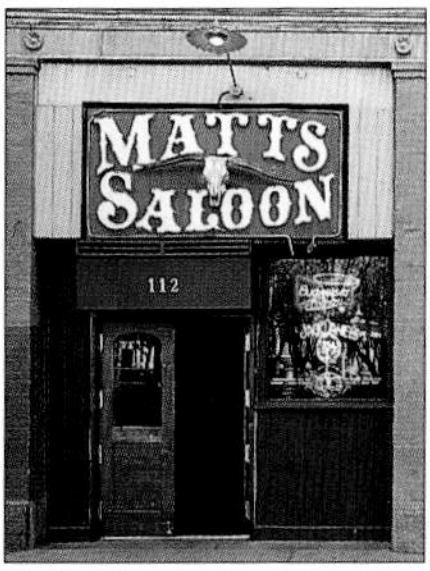
MATTS SALOON
112

Prescott [4]
This cool hilltop town is set among the rugged peaks and lush woods of Prescott National Forest, making it a popular center for many outdoor activities.

Camp Verde [5]
A highlight of this little town is Fort Verde. Built by the US Army in 1865, this stone fort is manned by costumed guides.

Pueblo remains of Montezuma Castle, built into limestone cliffs

Camp Verde ⓬

Road map B4. 🏃 *6,000*. ℹ️ *435 Main St. (520) 567-9294.* Ⓐ

F ARMERS FOUNDED the small settlement of Camp Verde in the heart of the Verde River Valley in the 1860s. It was a risky enterprise as the Apache lived nearby, but the US Army quickly moved in to protect the settlers, building **Fort Verde** in 1865. Today, Camp Verde remains at the center of a large and prosperous farming and ranching community. It was from Fort Verde that the army orchestrated a series of brutal campaigns against the Apache, which ended with the Battle of the Big Dry Wash in 1882. Once the Apache had been sent to reservations, Fort Verde was no longer needed and was decommissioned in 1891. Four of its original buildings have survived. The former army administration building contains a diverting collection of exhibits on army life. The interiors of the other three houses, on Officers' Row, have been returned to their original appearance. On weekends from spring to fall, volunteers in period costume act as guides and reenact scenes from the fort's daily life.

Costumed guides at Fort Verde State Historic Park

🏛 Fort Verde at Camp Verde State Historic Park
Off Hwy I-17 【 *(520) 567-3275.* ◐ *8am–4:30pm daily.* ● *Dec 25.*

Montezuma Castle National Monument ⓭

Road map C4. *Hwy I-17 exit 289.* 【 *(520) 567-3322.* ◐ *early Sep–end May: 8am–5pm daily; end May–early Sep: 8am–7pm daily.* 🅿️

D ATING FROM the 1100s, the pueblo remains that make up Montezuma Castle occupy an idyllic location, built into the limestone cliffs high above Beaver Creek, a couple of miles to the east of Interstate Highway 17. Once home to the Sinagua people, this cliff dwelling originally contained 20 rooms spread over five floors. Montezuma Castle was declared a National Monument in 1906 to preserve its excellent condition. The visitor center has a display on Sinaguan life and is situated at the start of an easy trail along Beaver Creek, which provides fine views of the ruins up above.

The National Monument also incorporates Montezuma Well, situated about 11 miles (18 km) away to the northeast. This natural sinkhole, 50 ft (15 m) deep and 470 ft (140 m) in diameter, had religious significance for Native Americans, with several tribes believing it was the site of the Creation. Over 1,000 gallons (3,790 liters) of water flow through the sinkhole every minute, an inexhaustible supply that has long been used to irrigate the surrounding land. A narrow trail leads around the rim before twisting its way down to the water's edge.

Jerome ⓮

Road map B4. 🏃 *500*. ℹ️ *Box K, Jerome (520) 634-2900.*

A PPROACHED FROM the east along Highway 89A, Jerome is easy to spot in the distance, its tangle of old brick buildings perched high above the valley, clinging to the steep slopes of Cleopatra Hill. Silver mining began here in the 1870s, but the town's big break came in 1912 when prospectors hit a vein of copper no less than 5 ft (1.5 m) thick. Just two years later, World War I sent the price of copper sky high and Jerome boomed. In the Wall Street Crash of 1929, however, copper prices tumbled and, although the mines survived until 1953, the boom times were over. To make matters worse, underground dynamiting had made Cleopatra Hill unstable, and the town began to slide downhill at a rate of 4 in (10 cm) a year. By the early 1960s, Jerome was virtually a ghost town, but its fortunes were revived by an influx of artists and artisans. Their galleries and stores soon attracted the tourists, and today Jerome is often busy with daytrippers wandering around the streets of the late 19th- and early 20th-century brick buildings that make up the town's historic center.

Façade of an early 20th-century store on Jerome's historic Main Street

The ford across picturesque Oak Creek at Red Rock Crossing, Sedona

Tuzigoot National Monument ⓯

Road map B4. *Follow signs from Hwy 89A.* ☏ *(520) 634-5564.* ⭘ *end May–early Sep: 8am–7pm daily; early Sep–end May: 8am–5pm daily.* ♿

PERCHED ON A solitary and slender limestone ridge, the ruins of Tuzigoot National Monument offer splendid views of the Verde River Valley. The pueblo was built by the Sinagua people between the 12th and 15th centuries and, at its peak, had a population of around 300. It was abandoned in the early 15th century, when it is believed the Sinagua migrated north to join the Ancestral Puebloans.

Tuzigoot was partly rebuilt by a local and federally funded program during the Depression in the 1930s. This emphasized one of the most unusual features of pueblo building, the lack of doorways. The normal pueblo room was entered by ladder through a hatchway in the roof, which was made of wood and mud. Sinaguan artifacts and art are on display at the visitor center.

Sedona ⓰

Road map C3. ⛰ 16,000. ✗ 🚌 ℹ *Forest Rd. (800) 288-7336.*

THE LITTLE TOWN of Sedona occupies a delightful location among the wooded hills and red-rock canyons south of Flagstaff. Fertile land and water attracted farmers to the area in the late 19th century. Today, the town has a reputation as a center for New Age living. This dates from the arrival of the psychic and writer Page Bryant. In 1981 she identified seven vortexes in the area, which she believed emanated electromagnetic energies that invigorated the soul. The subsequent influx of "New Agers" was followed by a burgeoning tourist industry that is reflected in the range of restaurants, hotels, stores, and fine art galleries here.

Sedona is a useful base for exploring the surrounding countryside. One pleasant excursion is along Red Rock

Cross section of petrified log

Loop Road. Just seven miles (11 km) long, the road gives access to Crescent Moon Ranch at Red Rock Crossing, a US Forest Service Recreation Area whose centerpiece is a picturesque ford across Oak Creek, used in many cowboy movies. Farther along Red Rock Loop Road is Red Rock State Park, where a gentle, wooded stretch of Oak Creek offers easy hikes and lovely picnic spots.

Petrified Forest National Park ⓱

Road map D3. *Off Hwy I-40.* ☏ *(520) 524-6228.* ⭘ *daily.* ● *Dec 25.* ♿

THE PETRIFIED Forest National Park is one of Arizona's most unusual attractions. Millions of years ago, ancient rivers swept thousands of trees downstream into a vast swamp that once covered this whole area. Here, groundwater transported silica dioxide into downed timber, eventually turning it into the quartz stone logs seen today, with colored crystals preserving the trees' shape and structure.

Running the entire length of the forest is the famous Painted Desert. This is an area of colored bands of sand and rock that change from blues to reds throughout the day as the shifting light catches the different mineral deposits.

The Painted Desert Visitor Center offers an orientation film. From here, a 28-mile (45-km) scenic road travels the length of the park. There are nine overlooks along the way, including Kachina Point, where the Painted Desert Wilderness trailhead is located. A free permit is required to backpack camp in the wilderness area. Near the south end of the road is the fine **Rainbow Forest Museum**, which has displays of different types of petrified wood, and explains the prehistory of the park.

🏛 **Rainbow Forest Museum**
Off Hwy 180 (south entrance).
☏ *(520) 524-3138.* ⭘ *daily.* ♿

Phoenix and Southern Arizona

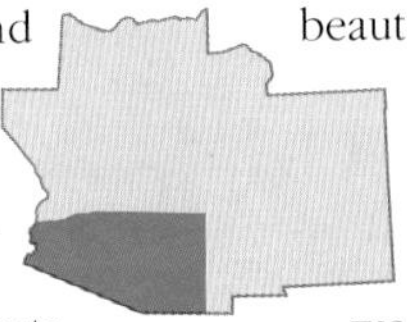

Mountain ranges and sun-bleached plateaus ripple the wide landscapes of southern Arizona, a staggeringly beautiful region dominated by pristine tracts of desert, parts of which are protected within the Saguaro National Park and the Organ Pipe Cactus National Monument. This land was first farmed around 400 BC by the Hohokam people *(see p38)* who carefully used the meager water supplies to irrigate their crops. When the Spanish arrived in the 16th century they built forts and established settlements across the region. This Hispanic heritage is recalled by the beautiful mission churches of San Xavier del Bac and Tumacacori and in the popular historic city of Tucson that grew up around the 1776 Spanish fort. When silver was discovered nearby in the 1870s, the scene was set for a decade of rowdy frontier life. Today, towns such as Tombstone, famous for the "Gunfight at the OK Corral", re-create this wild west era. The influx of miners also spurred the growth of Phoenix, a farming town established on the banks of the Salt River in the 1860s. Phoenix is now the largest city in the Southwest, known for its warm winter climate and recreational facilities.

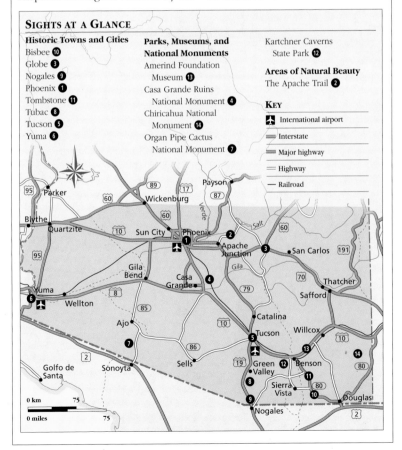

Sights at a Glance

Historic Towns and Cities

Bisbee 10
Globe 3
Nogales 9
Phoenix 1
Tombstone 11
Tubac 8
Tucson 5
Yuma 6

Parks, Museums, and National Monuments

Amerind Foundation Museum 13
Casa Grande Ruins National Monument 4
Chiricahua National Monument 14
Organ Pipe Cactus National Monument 7
Kartchner Caverns State Park 12

Areas of Natural Beauty

The Apache Trail 2

Key

International airport
Interstate
Major highway
Highway
Railroad

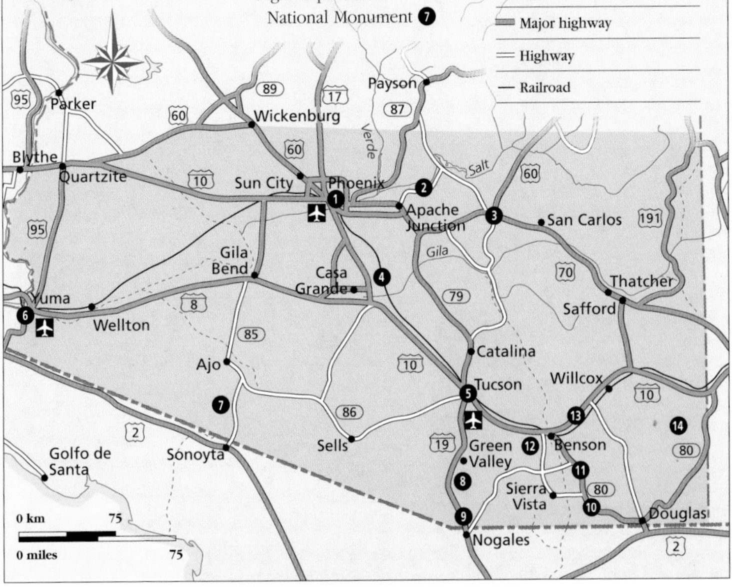

◁ **Visitors riding the range at the Lazy K Bar Guest Ranch near Tucson**

Phoenix ❶

Cash register at the Museum of History

PHOENIX IS A HUGE metropolis, stretching across the Salt River Valley. Farmers and ranchers settled here in the 1860s. By 1912, the city had developed into the political and economic focus of Arizona and was the state capital. As it grew, it absorbed surrounding towns, although each district still maintains its identity. Downtown Phoenix is now being reinvigorated. It is home to many historic attractions, including restored Victorian houses in Heritage Square, the Phoenix Art Museum, and the Heard Museum *(see pp78–9)* with its excellent collection of Native American artifacts.

The 1900 façade of the Arizona State Capitol Building

Exploring Downtown Phoenix

Downtown Phoenix, where the city began in the 19th century, is centered on Washington and Jefferson Streets, which run east to west between 7th Street and 19th Avenue. Central Avenue is the main north-south axis: to its east, parallel roads are labeled as "Streets," while roads to the west are "Avenues." City sights are mostly too far apart to see on foot, and driving is the best option. A DASH bus runs from Downtown to the State Capitol regularly on weekdays.

🏛 Arizona State Capitol Museum

1700 Washington St.
((602) 542-4675.
◯ 8am–5pm Mon–Fri.
● public hols. 🕙 10am & 2pm. ♿

Completed in 1900, the Arizona State Capitol housed the state legislature until they moved into nearby new premises in 1960. The building is a handsome structure,

topped by a copper dome. The interior is now a museum; guided tours include both original legislative chambers, which have been carefully restored, and a series of sepia photographs that document the history of Phoenix.

🏛 Arizona Mining and Mineral Museum

1502 West Washington St. ((602) 255-3791. ◯ 8am–5pm Mon–Fri; 1–5pm Sat. ● public hols. ♿

The search for precious stones and metals brought waves of prospectors to the Southwest in the years following the Civil War (1861–65). The riches they unearthed in Arizona's sun-seared hills were fabulous. A mountain of silver was discovered in the Dragoon Mountains near Tucson, while quantities of gold, silver, copper, and turquoise were found farther north in the Cerbat Mountains outside Kingman *(see p70)*. As word of the fortunes to be made in

Azurite and malachite rock

the area spread, thousands of prospectors converged on the Superstition Mountains to the east of Phoenix. However, many ended up destitute, never discovering the large deposits of gold rumored to be hidden in the hills.

This museum traces the colorful history of Arizona mining through photographs and displays of historic tools. There are also glittering examples of the various rocks the miners quarried, the most striking of which are the copper-bearing ores such as malachite and azurite, in vivid greens and blues.

🏛 Heritage Square

115 N. 6th St. ♿ partial.

Phoenix is a thoroughly modern city, which grew rapidly after World War II. Many of its older buildings did not survive this expansion. However, a few late 19th- and early 20th-century buildings remain, and the most interesting of these are found on Heritage Square. Rosson House is a handsome wooden mansion on Monroe Street dating from 1895. It has a wraparound veranda and distinctive hexagonal turret. Visitors may tour the house, which is furnished in period style (call 602 262-5029). Next door is the Burgess Carriage House, constructed in an expansive colonial style rare in the Southwest. The 1900 Silva House also features exhibits detailing Arizona's history. The tree-lined square with its cafés is pleasant for a stroll.

KEY

🛈	Visitor information
🅿	Parking

🏛 Arizona Science Center

600 E. Washington St. ((602) 716-2000. W www.azscience.org
🕐 10am–5pm daily. ● public hols.
♿ &

This ultra-modern facility has over 300 interactive science exhibits, covering everything from physics and energy to the human body, spread over three levels. The popular "All About You" gallery on Level One focuses on human biology. Here, visitors can take a virtual reality trip through the body. Level Three has "The World Around You," where visitors explore a 90-ft- (27-m-) long rock wall, as well as testing the surface temperature of different substances. The center also has a large-screen cinema on Level Two. It is popular with children, but there is something here for everyone.

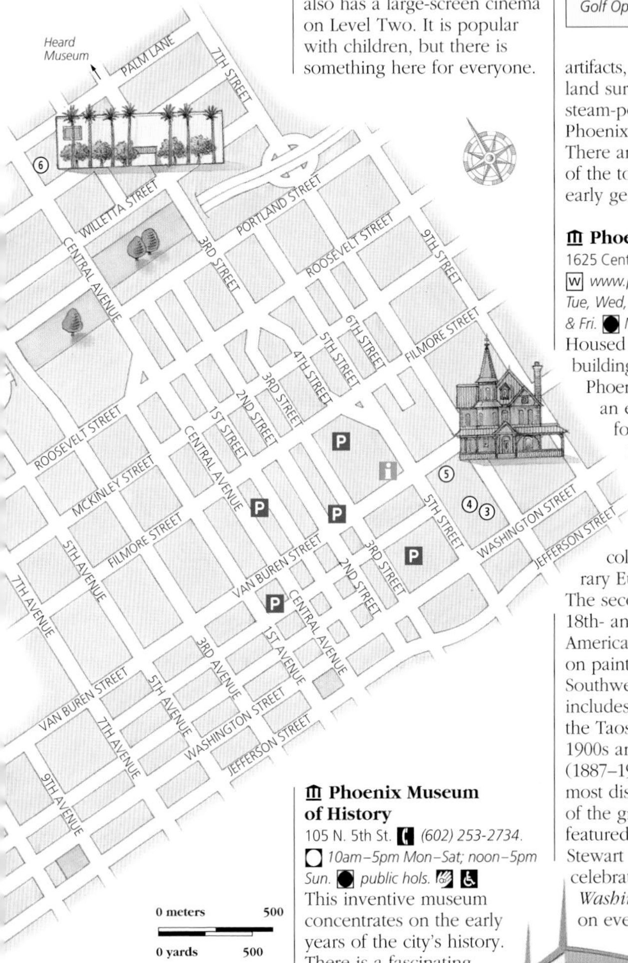

artifacts, including 19th-century land surveying equipment, a steam-powered bicycle, and Phoenix's first printing press. There are also reconstructions of the town's first jail and an early general store.

🏛 Phoenix Art Museum

1625 Central Ave. ((602) 257-1222.
W www.phxart.org 🕐 10am–5pm Tue, Wed, Sat & Sun; 10am–9pm Thu & Fri. ● Mon, public hols. ♿ &

Housed in an austere modern building, the highly aclaimed Phoenix Art Museum has an enviable reputation for the quality of its temporary exhibitions. These usually share the lower of the museum's two floors with a permanent collection of contemporary European and US art. The second floor features 18th- and 19th-century American artists, with a focus on painters connected to the Southwest. The exhibit here includes first-rate work from the Taos art colony of the 1900s and Georgia O'Keeffe (1887–1986) (see p203), the most distinguished member of the group. Among other featured artists are Gilbert Stewart (1755–1828), whose celebrated *Portrait of George Washington* (1796) is seen on every dollar bill.

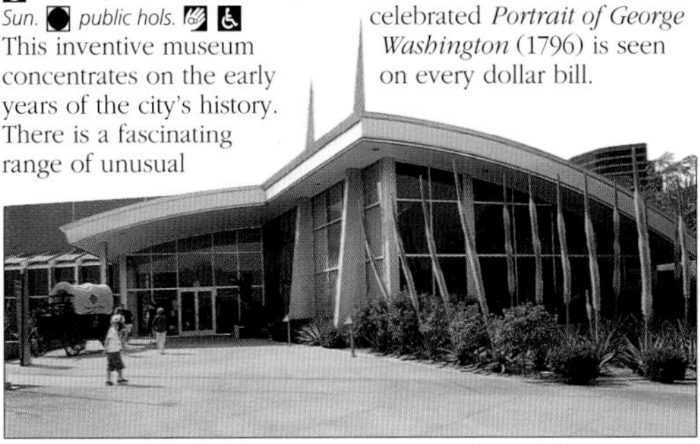

Heard Museum

🏛 Phoenix Museum of History

105 N. 5th St. ((602) 253-2734.
🕐 10am–5pm Mon–Sat; noon–5pm Sun. ● public hols. ♿ &

This inventive museum concentrates on the early years of the city's history. There is a fascinating range of unusual

Façade of the Phoenix Museum of History

SIGHTS AT A GLANCE

0 meters 500

0 yards 500

Heard Museum

THE HEARD MUSEUM was founded in 1929 by Dwight Heard, a wealthy rancher and newspaper tycoon who, with his wife, Maie, assembled an extraordinary collection of Native Southwestern American art in the 1920s. Several benefactors later added to the collection, including Senator Barry Goldwater of Arizona, who donated his *kachina* dolls.

The museum displays more than 30,000 works, but its star attraction is the "Native Peoples of the Southwest Gallery." This gallery details the three main cultural traditions of ancient Arizona: the Hohokam, Mogollon, and Ancestral Puebloan or Anasazi (*see pp26–7*). Baskets, pottery, and *kachina* dolls are the highlights, but there is also sumptuous silverwork by the Navajo, Zuni, Hopi, and Apache peoples.

Heard's original hacienda-style façade remains, despite the museum's recent enlargement

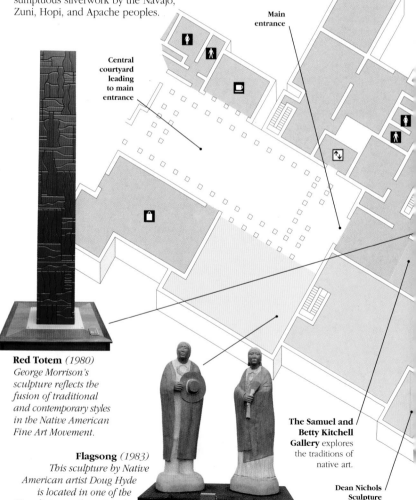

Central courtyard leading to main entrance

Main entrance

Red Totem *(1980)*
George Morrison's sculpture reflects the fusion of traditional and contemporary styles in the Native American Fine Art Movement.

Flagsong *(1983)*
This sculpture by Native American artist Doug Hyde is located in one of the Heard's tranquil courtyards.

The Samuel and Betty Kitchell Gallery explores the traditions of native art.

Dean Nichols Sculpture Courtyard

Red Tailed Hawk
Painted in 1986 by Dan Namingha, this is an impressionistic view of a Hopi Kachina in hawk form. It is displayed as part of the Heard's fine art collection.

VISITORS' CHECKLIST

2301 North Central Ave, Phoenix, AZ 85004. 📞 (602) 252-8840; 📠 (602) 252-8848. 🌐 www.heard.org. 🚌 Phoenix Greyhound Station. ⏰ 9:30am–5pm daily. ⛔ public hols. 📷 ♿ ✓ 🍴 📱

Navajo Child's Blanket
Woven in the 1870s, this richly colored, traditional blanket is one of the highlights of the Sandra Day O'Connor Gallery, which documents the history of the Museum, and showcases the Heard family's early collection of Native American artifacts.

KEY

☐ Samuel and Betty Kitchell Gallery
☐ Crossroads Gallery
☐ Sandra Day O'Connor Gallery
☐ Ullman Learning Center
☐ Freeman Gallery
☐ Native Peoples of the Southwest Gallery
☐ Dean Nichols Sculpture Courtyard
☐ Pritzlaff Courtyard
☐ Temporary exhibition space
☐ Non-exhibition space

Ullman Learning Center features interactive exhibits related to Native American life.

Interactive Display
This gallery examines various themes relevant to Native Americans, such as the connection between culture and environment and the symbolism in textile designs.

The South Courtyard offers additional space for the museum's fine sculptures.

★ Native Peoples of the Southwest Gallery
Kachina dolls are just one example of the Native American artifacts displayed in this award-winning collection. Others include pottery, jewelry, and textiles.

STAR COLLECTION

★ **Native Peoples of the Southwest Gallery**

Exploring Metropolitan Phoenix

PHOENIX IS ONE of North America's largest cities. In addition to its city population of more than one million, Phoenix has a burgeoning number of residents in its metropolitan area, totaling almost three million. The city fills the Salt River Valley, occupying more than 2,000 sq miles (5,200 sq km) of the Sonoran Desert. It is famous for its winter temperatures of 60–70°F (16–21°C) and around 300 days of sunshine a year. This makes Phoenix a popular destination with both tourists and "snow birds," visitors who spend their winters here.

Metropolitan Phoenix includes the former town of Scottsdale, 12 miles (19 km) northeast of Downtown. Replete with air-conditioned malls, designer stores, hotels and restaurants, it is also a good base for visiting Taliesin West and Papago Park and is famous for its world-class golf courses *(see p268)*. Tempe, 6 miles (10 km) east of Downtown, is home to Arizona State University and the Pueblo Grande Museum, while finally Mesa has the Arizona Temple, a large Mormon church built in 1927.

SIGHTS AT A GLANCE

Camelback Mountain [4]
Cosanti Foundation [3]
Mystery Castle [7]
Papago Park [6]
Pueblo Grande Museum and Archaeological Park [5]
Scottsdale [2]
Taliesin West [1]

KEY

- Downtown Phoenix
- Metropolitan Phoenix
- ✈ International airport
- Interstate
- Under construction
- Major highway
- Highway
- Railroad

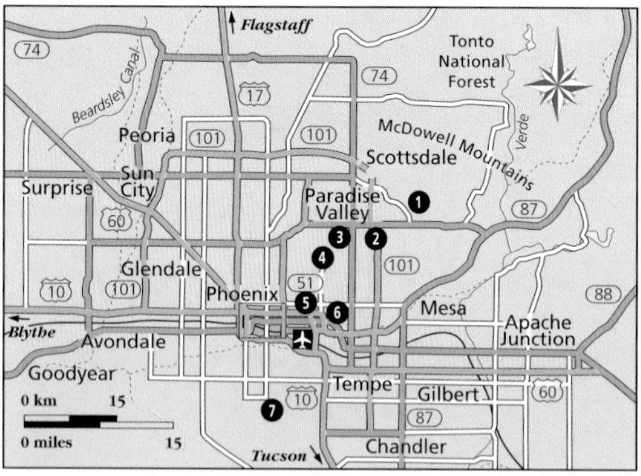

Scottsdale

Founded in the late 19th century, Scottsdale was named after its developer, army chaplain Winfield Scott (1837–1910), whose religious scruples helped keep the early settlement free from saloons and gambling. Scottsdale's quiet, tree-lined streets and desert setting attracted the famous architect Frank Lloyd Wright, who established Taliesin West here in 1937. The area still attracts artists and designers, but it is best known for its many golf courses – there are 175 in and around Scottsdale.

At the center of the district, to either side of Scottsdale Road between 2nd Street and Indian School Road, the streets are lined with low, brightly painted adobe buildings, which house many of the city's most fashionable restaurants as well as bars, antique stores, and art galleries. In addition to the Renaissance-style Borgata shopping mall, there is the El Pedregal Festival Marketplace, and Scottsdale Downtown with its arts shopping district around Main Street, Marshall Way, Old Town, and Fifth Avenue. Scottsdale is also the location for Phoenix's most popular shopping mall – Fashion Square – offering an array of designer stores and excellent restaurants *(see p264–5)*.

Scottsdale's elegant shopping mall, Fashion Square

Camelback Mountain

Scottsdale.

Named for its humped shape, Camelback Mountain rises high above its suburban surroundings just 7 miles (11 km) northeast of Downtown Phoenix. One of the city's most distinctive landmarks, the mountain is a granite and sandstone outcrop formed by prehistoric volcanic forces. Camelback Mountain is best approached from the north via the marked turn off McDonald Drive near the junction of Tatum Boulevard. From the parking lot, a well-marked path leads to the summit, a steep climb that covers 1,300 ft (390 m) in the space of a mile.

Camelback Mountain adjoins the Echo Canyon Recreation Area, a lovely wooded enclave with a choice of shady picnic sites.

Innovative design of the Cosanti Foundation gift shop

🏛 The Cosanti Foundation

6433 Doubletree Ranch Rd.,
Scottsdale. 📞 (480) 948-6145.
🕐 9am–5pm daily. ⬤ public hols.
💷 donation requested. ♿

In 1947, Italian architect Paolo
Soleri (b. 1919) came to study
at Taliesin West. Nine years
later, he set up the Cosanti
Foundation in Scottsdale to
further his investigations into
what he termed "arcology":
a combination of architecture
and ecology to create new
urban habitats (see p23).

Today, the Cosanti site consists of simple, low structures
housing studios, a gallery,
and craft workshops. This is
where Soleri and his workers
make and sell their trademark
windbells. The profits are
used to fund Soleri's main project, Arcosanti, a small town
that will be able to house
6,000 people in homes that
combine work and leisure

space. The project began
in 1970 and is still under
construction. Currently, 60
residents live there, using
energy generated by solar
greenhouses. Visitors can tour
the site, located 60 miles
(100 km) north of Phoenix
on Interstate Highway 17.

🏛 Taliesin West

Cactus Rd. at Frank Lloyd Wright
Blvd., Scottsdale. 📞 (480) 860-8810.
🕐 9am–4pm daily. 💷 ♿ 📷

Generally regarded as the
greatest American architect of
all time, Frank Lloyd Wright
(1869–1959) established the
600-acre (240-ha) Taliesin
West complex as a winter
school for his students in
1937. Wright had come to
prominence in Chicago
during the 1890s with a series
of strikingly original houses
that featured an elegant open-
plan style. Although noted for
his use of local materials such

as desert rocks and earth,
he also pioneered the use of
such contemporary elements
as pre-cast concrete (see p23).

Today, Taliesin West is home
to the Frank Lloyd Wright
School of Architecture, where
students live and work for up
to five years. The students also
work as guides to the complex.

Taliesin West is approached
along a winding desert road.
The muted tones of the low-
lying buildings reflect Wright's
enthusiasm for the desert setting. He was careful to en-
hance, rather than dominate,
the landscape, using local
stone covered with cement
to create the irregular walls,
colored red, yellow, and gray,
of the main building.

🏛 Pueblo Grande Museum and Archaeological Park

4619 E. Washington St. 📞 (602)
495-0901. 🕐 9am–5pm Mon–Sat;
1–5pm Sun. ⬤ public hols. 💷 ♿

Located 5 miles (8 km) east
of Downtown Phoenix, the
Pueblo Grande Museum
displays an ancient Hohokam
ruin, as well as many of their
artifacts, including cooking
utensils and pottery. Many
of these pieces come from
the adjacent Archaeological
Park, the site of a Hohokam
settlement from the 8th to
the 14th centuries. The site
was originally excavated in
1887, and today has an easy-
to-follow path which guides
visitors through the ruins.
Informative signs point out
the many irrigation canals
once used by the Hohokam
to water their crops.

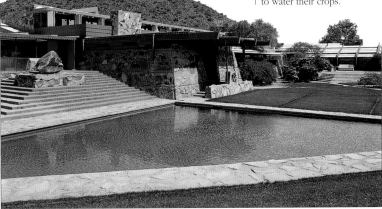

Taliesin West façade, designed to blend with the desert landscape

Cacti in the Desert Botanical Garden at Papago Park

♣ Papago Park

Galvin Parkway & Van Buren Street.
☎ *(602) 256-3220.*

Papago Park is located 6 miles (10 km) east of Phoenix's Downtown and is a popular place to unwind, with several hiking and cycling trails, picnic areas, and boating lakes.

Within the park, the **Desert Botanical Garden** is a 145-acre (59-ha) area devoted to more than 20,000 cacti and protected desert flora from around the world. The gardens are prettiest in spring, when many species flower. Guided tours are available, giving information on the extraordinary life cycles of the desert plants seen here.

The rolling hills and lakes of the **Phoenix Zoo** also occupy a large area of the Papago Park. The zoo reproduces a series of habitats including the Arizona-Sonora Desert and a tropical rainforest. Each

Trail's End sign at Phoenix Zoo

zone provides a home for more than 1,300 animals, their movement controlled by banks and canals rather than fences. A Safari Train provides a narrated tour of the zoo.

♣ Desert Botanical Garden

1201 N. Galvin Parkway. **☎** *(480) 941-1225.* ⏱ *May–Sep: 7am–8pm daily; Oct–April: 8am–8pm daily.* ● *major public holidays.* 🏷 🕭

🐾 Phoenix Zoo

455 North Galvin Parkway. **☎** *(602) 273-1341.* ⏱ *early Sep–Apr: 9am–5pm daily; May–early Sep: 7:30am–4pm daily.* ● *major public holidays.* 🏷 🕭 🌐 *www.phoenixzoo.org*

♠ Mystery Castle

800 East Mineral Road. **☎** *(602) 268-1581.* ⏱ *Oct–Jun: 11am–4pm Thu–Sun.* 🏷 🕭 *partial.*

Mystery Castle is possibly Phoenix's most eccentric attraction. In 1927, a certain Boyce Luther Gulley came to Phoenix hoping that the warm climate would improve his ailing health. His young daughter had loved building sandcastles on the beach, and since Phoenix was so far away from the ocean, Gulley set about creating a real-life fairy-tale sandcastle for her. He started work in 1930 and continued for 15 years, until his death in 1945. Discarded bricks and an assortment of scrapyard junk, including old car parts, have been used to build the structure. The 18-room interior can be seen on a guided tour, which explores the quirky building and its eclectic collection of antiques and furniture from around the world.

Façade of Phoenix's unusual Mystery Castle

The Apache Trail ❷

Road map C4. 🚌 **ℹ** *Globe Chamber of Commerce, 1360 N. Broad St., Globe (520) 425-4495 or Greater Phoenix Convention & Visitors Bureau, 50 N. 2nd St. (602) 254-6500* 🌐 *www.phoenixcvb.com*

HEADING EAST from Phoenix, Hwy 60 cuts straight across the desert to the suburb of Apache Junction at the start of Hwy 88. This road then begins its winding trail up into the Superstition Mountains. It is called the Apache Trail after the Native Americans who once lived here. The road is a wonderfully scenic mountain route that runs for 45 miles (72 km) up to Theodore Roosevelt Lake, which was created by the damming of the Salt River in 1911. Hwy 88 begins by climbing up into the hills and after 5 miles (8 km) reaches the Lost Dutchman State Park, named after the gold mine quarried here by Jacob Waltz and Jacob Weiser in the 1870s. These two miners cashed in a series of huge gold nuggets but kept the location of the mine to themselves. After their deaths, hundreds of prospectors worked these mountains in search of the famed gold mine but without success.

Beyond the state park, the highway passes by several campsites and through rugged terrain before reaching the tiny hamlet of Tortilla Flat, 17 miles (27 km) farther on, where there is an excellent café. This settlement is at the east end of slender Canyon Lake, the first of several Salt River reservoirs created to provide Phoenix with water. The lake has a marina, and 90-minute cruises are offered on *Dolly's Steamboat*. As the road climbs higher into the Superstition Mountains it becomes more difficult to negotiate, before it reaches the 280-ft- (84-m-) high Theodore Roosevelt Dam, where there is good fishing and a variety of watersports.

Three miles (5 km) east of the dam lies the **Tonto National Monument**, which comprises two large sets of

View of a section of the winding Apache Trail from Fish Creek Hill

ruined cliff dwellings. The Salado people, who created some of the superb pottery on display at the Heard Museum *(see pp78–9)* built these pueblos of rock and mud in the early 14th century. A steep, short trail leads up to the 19-room Lower Ruin, but the 40-room Upper Ruin can be visited only with a ranger. Guided tours are available between November and April.

Mining artifacts at the Gila County Historical Museum

⋂ Tonto National Monument
Hwy 88. 【 (520) 467-2241.
◯ 8am–5pm daily. ◪

Globe ❸

Road map C4. ▓ 6,000. ▦
🅷 Globe Chamber of Commerce, 1360 N. Broad St. (520) 425 4495. Ⓐ

THE MINING town of Globe lies about 100 miles (160 km) east of Phoenix in the wooded Dripping Spring and Pinal Mountains. In 1875, prospectors struck silver near here in what was then part of an Apache Reservation. The reservation was divested of its silver-bearing hills, and Globe was founded as a mining town and supply center. It was named for a massive nugget

of silver, shaped like a globe, which was unearthed in the hills nearby. The silver was quickly exhausted, but copper mining continued to thrive until 1931. Today, Globe has an attractive historic district with several notable late 19th- and early 20th-century buildings. The **Gila County Historical Museum** outlines Globe's history, with displays of a wide range of mining paraphernalia. On the south side of town are the Besh-Ba-Gowah Ruins, home of the Salado people in the 13th and 14th centuries.

⛏ Gila County Historical Museum
1330 N. Broad St. 【 (520) 425-7385. ◯ 10am–4pm Mon–Fri; Sat & Sun by appointment.

Casa Grande Ruins National Monument ❹

Road map C4. 【 (520) 723-3172.
◯ 8am–6pm daily. ⬤ public holidays. ◪ ♿

FROM AROUND 200 BC until the middle of the 15th century, the Hohokam people farmed the Gila River Valley to the southeast of Phoenix.

Among the few Hohokam sites that remain, the fortress-like structure that makes up the Casa Grande National Monument is one of the most distinctive. Built in the early decades of the 14th century and named the "Big House" by a passing Jesuit missionary in 1694, this sturdy four-story structure has walls up to 4-ft (1.2-m) thick and is made from locally quarried caliche, a hard-setting subsoil. Experts believe that the holes cut in three of the walls were used for astronomical observations, but this is conjecture. The interior is out of bounds, but visitors can stroll round the exterior. The visitor center has a small museum with some interesting exhibits on Hohokam history and culture.

Casa Grande is located 15 miles (24 km) east of Interstate Highway 10 (I-10) on the outskirts of the town of Coolidge. It should not be confused with the town of Casa Grande found to the west of I-10.

The fortresslike Casa Grande Ruins National Monument

Tucson ❺

DESPITE BEING ARIZONA's second largest city, Tucson has a friendly, welcoming atmosphere and a variety of interesting attractions to entertain the increasing number of visitors it receives each year. The city is located on the northern boundary of the Sonoran Desert in Southern Arizona, in a basin surrounded by five mountain ranges. When the Spanish colonizers arrived in the early 18th century they were determined to seize land from the local Tohono O'odham and Pima native tribes, who put up strong resistance *(see p40)*. This led the Spanish to move their regional fortress, or presidio, from Tubac to Tucson in the 1770s. The city was officially founded by Irish explorer Hugh O'Connor in 1775. Tucson's pride in its history is reflected in the careful preservation of 19th-century downtown buildings in the Barrio Historic District.

Exhibit at Arizona University

Contemporary glass skyscrapers in downtown Tuscon

Exploring Tucson

Tucson's major art galleries and museums are clustered around two central areas: the University of Arizona campus (lying between Speedway Blvd., E. Sixth Street, Park, and Campbell Avenues) and the downtown area, which includes the Barrio and El Presidio historic districts. The latter contains many of the city's oldest buildings and is best explored on foot, as is the Barrio Historic District, south of Cushing Street.

🏛 Tucson Museum of Art and Historic Block
140 N. Main Ave. 📞 *(520) 624-2333.*
🕐 *10am–4pm Mon–Sat, noon–4pm Sun.* ⬤ *Jun–Aug: Mon; public hols.*
🎫 *(free on Sun)* ♿ 🅿
The Tucson Museum of Art opened in 1975 and is located on the Historic Block, which also contains five of the Presidio's oldest dwellings –

most of which are at least a hundred years old. These historic buildings form part of the art museum and house different parts of its extensive collection. The Museum's sculpture gardens and courtyards also form part of the Historic Block complex.

The art museum itself displays contemporary and 20th-century European and American works. In the adobe Stevens House (1866), the museum shows its prized permanent collection of Pre-Columbian tribal artifacts, some of which are 2,000 years old. There is the Spanish Colonial collection with some stunning pieces of religious art. The 1850s Casa Cordova houses *El Nacimiento*, a lovely Nativity scene with

more than 300 earthenware figurines, on display from December to March every year. The J. Knox Corbett House, built in 1907, has Arts and Crafts Movement pieces such as an original Morris chair.

🏛 Pima County Courthouse
115 N. Church Ave.
The Courthouse's pretty tiled dome is a downtown landmark. It was built in 1927, replacing its predecessor, a one-story adobe building dating from 1869. The position of the original presidio wall is marked out in the courtyard, and a section of the wall, 3-ft- (1-m-) thick and 12-ft- (4-m-) high, can still be seen inside the building.

Both guided and self-guided walking tours of this interesting district are available from the Tucson Museum of Art.

⛩ El Presidio Historic District
The El Presidio Historic District occupies the area where the original Spanish fortress (presidio), San Agustin del Tucson, was built in 1775. More than 70 of the houses here were constructed during the Territorial period, before Arizona became a state in 1912. Today, these historic buildings are largely occupied by shops, restaurants, and offices, although archaeological excavations in the area have found artifacts from much earlier residents, the Hohokam Indians.

⛪ St. Augustine Cathedral
192 S. Stone Ave. 📞 *(520) 623-6351.*
🕐 *Services only; call for times.*

Stained-glass window in the cathedral

St. Augustine Cathedral was begun in 1896 and modeled after the Spanish Colonial style of the Cathedral of Querétaro in central Mexico. This gleaming white building features an imposing sandstone façade with intricate carvings of the yucca, the saguaro, and the horned toad – three symbols of the Sonoran Desert – while a bronze statue of St. Augustine, the city's patron saint, stands above the main door.

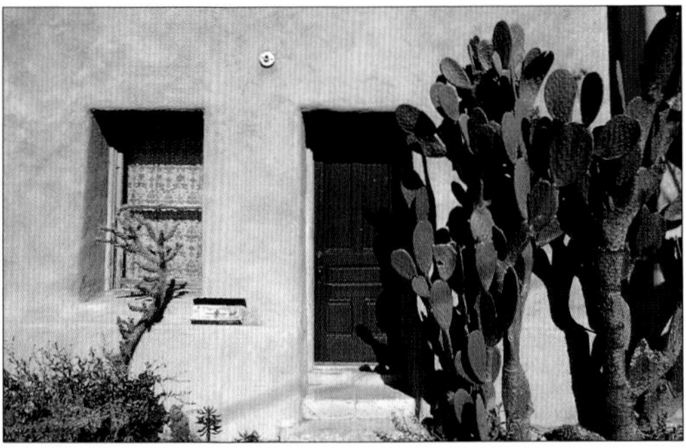
One of many 19th-century adobe houses in the Barrio Historic District

Visitors' Checklist

Road map C5. 👥 *750,000.* ✈ *Tucson International, 10 miles (16 km) south of downtown.* 🚆 *Amtrak Station, 400 E. Toole Ave.* 🚌 *Greyhound Lines, 2 S. 4th Ave.* ℹ *Metropolitan Tucson Convention & Visitors Bureau, 130 S. Scott Ave. (520) 624-1817; (800) 638-8350.* 🎉 *La Fiesta de los Vaqueros (late Feb); Tucson Folk Music Festival (May).*

🏛 Barrio Historic District

This area was Tucson's business district in the late 19th century. Today, its streets are quiet and lined with original adobe houses painted in bright colors. On nearby Main Street is the "wishing shrine" of **El Tiradito**, which marks the spot where a young man was killed as a result of a lovers' triangle. Local people lit candles here for his soul and still believe that if their candles burn for a whole night, their wishes will come true.

🏛 The University of Arizona

Speedway Blvd. ☎ *(520) 621-2211.*

Several fascinating museums are located on or near the UA campus, about a mile (1.6 km) east of downtown. Among these, the **Arizona Historical Society Museum** traces the history of the state from the arrival of the Spanish in 1540, to modern times. The **University of Arizona Museum of Art** focuses on European and American fine art from the Renaissance to the 20th century. Opposite the Museum of Art is the **Center for Creative Photography**, which contains the work of many of the 20th century's greatest American photographers. Visitors can view the extensive archives by advance reservations. The **Flandrau Science Center** features a range of child-friendly interactive exhibits.

One of the most renowned collections of artifacts, covering 2,000 years of native history, is displayed by the **Arizona State Museum**, which was founded in 1893.

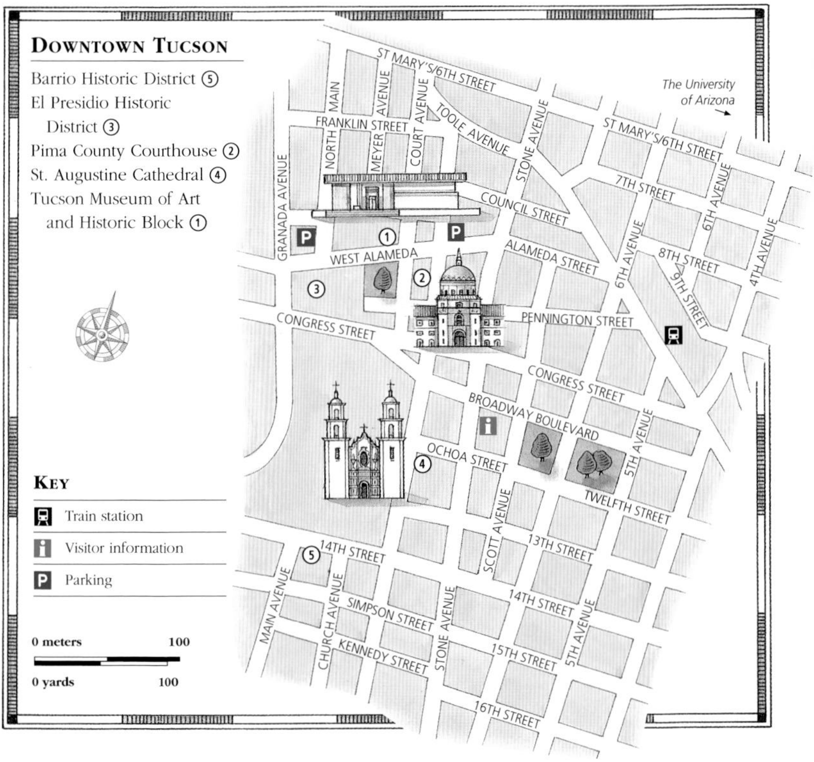
DOWNTOWN TUCSON
Barrio Historic District 5
El Presidio Historic District 3
Pima County Courthouse 2
St. Augustine Cathedral 4
Tucson Museum of Art and Historic Block 1
KEY
Train station
Visitor information
Parking
0 meters 100
0 yards 100
The University of Arizona
ST MARY'S/6TH STREET
FRANKLIN STREET
TOOLE AVENUE
NORTH MAIN
MEYER AVENUE
COURT AVENUE
STONE AVENUE
GRANADA AVENUE
COUNCIL STREET
7TH STREET
6TH AVENUE
4TH AVENUE
WEST ALAMEDA
ALAMEDA STREET
8TH STREET
9TH STREET
PENNINGTON STREET
CONGRESS STREET
BROADWAY BOULEVARD
5TH AVENUE
OCHOA STREET
TWELFTH STREET
SCOTT AVENUE
13TH STREET
14TH STREET
MAIN AVENUE
CHURCH AVENUE
SIMPSON STREET
KENNEDY STREET
15TH STREET
16TH STREET

San Xavier del Bac Mission

S AN XAVIER DEL BAC is the oldest and best-preserved
mission church in the Southwest. An imposing
landmark as it rises out of the stark, flat landscape
of the surrounding Tohono O'odham reservation, its
white walls dazzle in the desert sun. A mission was
first established here by the Jesuit priest Father Eusebio
Kino in 1700 (see p40). The complex seen today was
completed in 1797 by Franciscan missionaries.

Built of adobe brick, the mission is considered to be
the finest example of Spanish Colonial architecture in the
US (see p22). The church also incorporates other styles,
including several Baroque flourishes. In the 1990s its
interior was extensively renovated, and five *retablos*
(altarpieces) have been restored to their original glory.

**The Hill of the Cross, to the east
of the mission, offers fine views**

The bell tower's elegant,
white dome that reflects the
Moorish styles that are
incorporated into San Xavier's
Spanish Colonial architecture.

★ Façade of the church
*The ornate Baroque façade is
decorated with the carved figures
of saints (although some are much
eroded) including a headless St.
Cecilia and an unidentifiable
St. Francis, now a simple sand cone.*

**The mortuary
chapel** contains
a statue of the
Virgin Mary,
surrounded
by candles.

Stonework detail
*Over recent years the
identity of the carved statues
to the left of the entrance has
changed. Long thought to be St.Catherine
of Siena and St. Barbara, they have now
been identified as St. Agatha of Catania
and St. Agnes of Rome.*

Painted ceiling
*On entering the church,
visitors are struck by
the dome's ceiling with
its glorious paintings
of religious figures.
Vivid pigments of
vermilion and blue
were used to contrast
with the stark white
stone background.*

STAR SIGHTS

★ **Façade**

★ **Main altar**

★ Main Altar
The spectacular gold and red retablo mayor *is decorated in Mexican Baroque style with elaborate columns. More than 50 statues were carved in Mexico then brought to San Xavier where artists gilded and painted them with brightly colored glazes.*

VISITORS' CHECKLIST

Road map C5. 950 San Xavier Rd, 10 miles (16 km) south of Tucson on I-19. **(** (520) 294-2624. **◯** 8am–5pm daily. **♿ ◻** booths selling Native American fry bread. **◻**

Altar Dome
The dome and high transepts are filled with painted wooden statuary and covered with murals depicting scenes from the Gospels.

The patio is closed to the public but can be seen from the museum.

Chapel of Our Lady
This statue of the Virgin is one of the Church's three sculptures of Mary. Here she is shown as La Dolorosa *or Sorrowing Mother.*

The museum includes a sheepskin psalter and photographs of other historic missions on the Tohono O'odham reservation.

The shop entrance

Boats and watersports in the picturesque setting of Lake Yuma

Yuma

Road map *A4.* 🏛 *65,000.*
🚉 *Amtrak, 291 Gila St.* 🚌 *Grey-
hound, 170 E. 17th Place.* ℹ *Yuma
Convention and Visitors' Bureau, 377
Main St. (800) 293-0071.* 🅰

Yuma occupies a strategic
position at the confluence
of the Colorado and Gila
rivers in Arizona's far southwestern corner. Though noted
by Spanish explorers in the
16th century, it was not until
the 1850s that the town rose
to prominence, when the
river crossing became the
gateway to California for tens
of thousands of gold seekers.
Fort Yuma, built in 1849, also
boosted steamboat traffic
along the Colorado River.
  Today, Yuma's hot and
sunny winter climate makes it
a popular winter destination
for travelers or "snowbirds,"
escaping colder climes. Two
state historic parks highlight
its rich history: Yuma Crossing,
covering 20 acres (8 ha) along
the Colorado, looks at river
transportation and army life
in the later 1800s, while Yuma
Territorial Prison re-creates
conditions at the state's main
prison facility from 1876–1909.

Organ Pipe
Cactus National
Monument ❼

Road map *B5.* 📞 *(520) 387-6849.*
⭘ *Daily; visitor center 8am–5pm.*
📷 ♿ 🅿 🅰

The organ pipe is a
Sonoran desert species
of cactus, which is a cousin to
the saguaro *(see p86)* but with
multiple arms branching up

from the base, as its name
suggests. The organ pipe is
rare in the United States,
growing almost exclusively in
this large and remote area of
land along the Mexican
border in southwest Arizona.
Many other plant and animal
species flourish in this un-
spoiled desert wilderness,
although a lot of animals, such
as snakes, jackrabbits, and
kangaroo rats, emerge only in
the cool of the night. Other
cacti such as the saguaro, the
Engelmann prickly pear, and
the teddybear cholla are best
seen in the early summertime
when they give their glorious
displays of floral color.
  There are two scenic drives
through the park: the 21-mile
(34-km) Ajo Mountain Drive
and the longer 53-mile (85-
km) Puerto Blanco Drive. The
Ajo Mountain Drive takes two
hours and winds through
startling desert landscapes in
the foothills of the mountains.
The Puerto Blanco Drive
takes around four hours and

leads visitors through a range
of landscapes from desert to
the oasis at Quitobaquito
Spring. A variety of hiking
trails in the park range in
difficulty from paved, wheelchair-accessible paths to
wilderness walks. A visitor
center offers exhibits on the
park's flora and fauna, as
well as maps and camping
permits, and there are guided
walks available in winter.
  Be aware that the park is a
good two-and-a-half- to three-
hour drive from Tucson one
way. If you want to explore
this environment in any detail,
plan to camp overnight. Ajo,
34 miles (55 km) to the north,
has motels and services.

Tubac ❽

Road map *C5.* 🏛 *150.*
ℹ *Tubac Chamber of Commerce
(520) 398-2704.*

The royal Presidio (fortress)
of San Ignacio de Tubac
was built in 1752 to protect
the local Spanish-owned
ranches and mines, as well
as the nearby missions of
Tumacacori and San Xavier,
from attacks by local Pima
natives. Tubac was also the
first stopover on the famous
overland expedition to
colonize the San Francisco
Bay area in 1776. The trek
was led by the fort's captain,
Juan Bautista de Anza *(see
p40)*. Following his return,
the garrison moved north to

Rare cacti at the Organ Pipe Cactus National Monument

Mission church at Tumacacori National Historical Park

Tucson and for the next hundred years, Tubac declined. Today, the town is a small but thriving art colony, with attractive shops, galleries, and restaurants lining the streets around the plaza.

Tubac's historical remains are displayed at the **Tubac Presidio State Historic Park**, which encompasses the foundations of the original presidio in an underground display, as well as several historic buildings, including the delightful Old Tubac Schoolhouse. Also here, the Presidio Museum contains artifacts covering over one hundred years of Tubac's history, including painted altarpieces and colonial furniture.

ENVIRONS: Just 3 miles (5 km) south of town lies the beautiful ruined mission of **Tumacacori**. The present church was built in around 1800 upon the ruins of the original 1691 mission established by Jesuit priest, Father Eusebio Kino *(see p40)*. The Mission was abandoned in 1848, and today its weather-beaten ochre façade together with its brick columns, arched entry, and carved wooden door is an evocative reminder of former times. The cavernous interior is wonderfully atmospheric, with patches of exposed adobe brick and faded murals on the sanctuary walls. A small museum provides an excellent background on the mission builders and native Pima Indians. Week-end craft demonstrations, including tortilla making, basketry, and Mexican pottery, are held September through June. During the first weekend in December, La Fiesta de Tumacacori *(see p35)*, which

celebrates the cultural heritage of the upper Santa Cruz Valley, is held on the mission grounds.

♛ Tubac Presidio State Historic Park
Burruel St. & Presidio Drive.
(*(520) 398-2252.* ◯ *8am–5pm daily.* 🅿️ 🚻 🅿️
♛ Tumacacori National Historical Park
(*(520) 398-2341.* ◯ *8am–5pm daily.* ● *Dec 25, Thanksgiving.* 🅿️ 🚻 🅿️

Nogales ❾

Road map *C5.* 🔼 *19,500.* ✈️ 🚌
ℹ️ *123 W. Kino Park (520) 287-3685.*

Nogales is really two towns that straddle the US border with Mexico, at the end of Mexico's Pacific Highway. This is a busy port of entry, handling huge amounts of freight, including 75 percent of all winter fruit and vegetables sold in North America. The town attracts large numbers of visitors in search of bargains at shopping districts on both sides of the border. Decorative blankets, furniture, and crafts

Mexican pottery found in Nogales

are good value. There is a profound contrast between the US side and the ramshackle houses across the border, and visitors should be aware that the Mexican Nogales can be crowded with continuous hustle from street vendors eager for business. Still, it is a popular day-trip and there are several good restaurants here.

Visitors are advised to leave their cars on the US side, where attendants mind the parking lots, and to walk across the border. Those who drive across the border should check that their car insurance is valid in Mexico. Visas are required only for those traveling farther south than the town and for stays of more than 72 hours. US and Canadian citizens should carry a passport or birth certificate for identification as drivers' licenses are not sufficient proof of citizenship. Foreign nationals should make sure their visa status enables them to re-enter the US; those on the Visa Waiver Scheme *(see p276)* should have no problem. US dollars are accepted everywhere.

ASTRONOMY IN SOUTHERN ARIZONA

Southern Arizona's dry air and dark, clear nights have made it an international center for astronomy. Within a 75-mile (120-km) radius of Tucson, there is a cluster of prestigious observatories located in the mountains, including the Kitt Peak National Observatory, with its large telescopes, and the Fred Lawrence Whipple Observatory, both of which can be toured. Mount Graham International Observatory features some of the world's most advanced telescope technology. Opportunities for star-gazing are exceptional, but even without high-powered equipment, anyone can enjoy the countless constellations in the night skies.

Observatories in the mountains of southern Arizona

Bisbee ⑩

Road map C5. 🏛 *6,500.* 🚌
ℹ *Bisbee Chamber of Commerce, 31
Subway St. (520) 432-5421.*

THIS IS ONE of the most
atmospheric mining towns
in the Southwest. The discovery of copper here in the
1880s sparked a mining rush,
and by the turn of the century
Bisbee was the largest city
between St. Louis and San
Francisco. Victorian buildings
such as the landmark Copper
Queen Hotel still dominate
the historic town center, while
attractive clusters of houses
cling to the sides of the
surrounding mountains.

Today, visitors can tour the
mines that once flourished
here, such as the deep underground Queen Mine or, a
short drive south of town,
the Lavender Open Pit Mine.
Exhibits at the Bisbee Mining
and Historical Museum illustrate the realities of mining
and frontier life here.

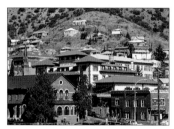
**The Victorian mining town of Bisbee clings
to the slopes of the surrounding mountains**

Tombstone ⑪

Road map C5. 🏛 *6,500.* ℹ
*Chamber of Commerce, PO Box 995.
(520) 457-9317.*

TOMBSTONE is a living legend,
forever known as the site
of the 1881 gunfight at the
OK Corral between the Earp
brothers and the Clanton
gang *(see p55).* The town's
historic streets and buildings
form one of the most popular
attractions in the Southwest.

Tombstone was founded
by Ed Schieffelin, who went
prospecting on Apache land
in 1877 despite a warning
that "all you'll find out there
is your tombstone." He found
a mountain of silver instead,

Re-enactment of the gunfight at the OK Corral, Tombstone

and his sardonically named
shanty town boomed with the
ensuing silver rush. One of
the wildest towns in the West,
Tombstone was soon full of
prospectors, gamblers, cowboys, and lawmen. In its heyday, the town was larger than
San Francisco. More than $37
million worth of silver was
extracted from the mines
between 1880 and 1887, when
miners struck an aquifer and
flooded the mine shafts.

In 1962 "the town
too tough to die"
became a National
Historic Landmark,
and, with much of
its historic down-
town immaculately
preserved, it attracts
many visitors, all
eager to sample the
unique atmosphere.
Allen Street, with its
wooden boardwalks,
shops, and restau-
rants, is the town's
main thoroughfare. The **OK
Corral** is preserved as a
museum, and re-enactments
of the infamous gunfight
between the Earp brothers,
Doc Holliday and the Clanton
gang are staged daily at 2pm.

Tombstone Courthouse on
Toughnut Street was the seat
of justice for the county from
1882 to 1929 and is now a
state historic site. It contains a
museum featuring the restored
courtroom and many historical
exhibits and artifacts, including
photographs of some of the
town's famous characters.
Toughnut Street used to be
known as "Rotten Row" as it
was once lined with miners'
tents, bordellos, and more
than one hundred bars.

Among other buildings worth
looking for in the downtown
area is the Rose Tree Inn
Museum, home of what is
reputedly the world's largest
rosebush. There is also the Bird
Cage Theater, once a bawdy
dance hall and bordello, and
so-named for the covered
"crib" compartments, or cages,
hanging from the ceiling, in
which ladies of the night plied
their trade. Nearby, the once
rowdy Crystal Palace Saloon,
still a bar, features some 42
bullet holes in its ceiling.

Just north of town, the
famous Boothill Cemetery is
full of the graves of those who
perished in Tombstone, peace-
fully or otherwise. This evocative place is not without the
occasional spot of humor.
Look for the marker lamenting
the death of George Johnson,
hanged by mistake in 1882,
which reads: "He was right,
we was wrong, but we strung
him up, and now he's gone."

🏛 **OK Corral**
Allen St. 📞 *(520) 457-3456.*
🕐 *9am–5pm daily.* 📷 ♿
🏛 **Tombstone Courthouse**
219 E. Toughnut St. 📞 *(520) 457-
3311.* 🕐 *8am–5pm daily.*
⬤ *Dec 25.* 📷 ♿

**Tombstone Courthouse in the
town center is now a museum**

Kartchner Caverns State Park ⓬

Road map C5. ☎ (520) 586-4100.
☐ 7:30am–6pm daily (cave tours
8:30am–4:30pm by reservation). ●
Dec 25. 🎥 ♿ 📷 obligatory. Ⓐ

T HE KARTCHNER Caverns are
one of Arizona's great
natural wonders. Located in
the Whetstone Mountains, the
caves were discovered in 1974
when two cavers crawled
through a sinkhole in a
hillside that led them into 7
acres (3 ha) of caverns filled
with colorful formations. Out
of concern to protect the
caves, they kept their discovery a secret for 14 years as
they explored this wonderland of speleotherms, or cave
formations, made of layers of
calcite deposited by dripping
or flowing water over millions
of years. In 1988 the land was
purchased by the state, but it
took 11 years to complete the
development that would allow
public access while conserv-
ing the special conditions that
enable these "wet" caves to
continue growing.

Before entering the caves,
visitors are introduced to the
geology of the formations at
the Discovery Center. Once
inside, visitors must not touch
the features, as skin oils stop
their growth. Along with huge
stalactites and stalagmites,
there is an abundance of
other types of formation such
as the aptly named 21-ft
(132-m) soda straw, the tur-
nip shields, and popcorn.

**Orange and white column
formations at Kartchner Caverns**

Amerind Foundation ⓭

Road map C5. ☎ (520) 586-3666.
☐ Sep–May: 10am–4pm daily.
● Jun–Aug: Mon & Tue; public
holidays. 🎥

T HE AMERIND Foundation is
one of the most important
private archaeological and
ethnological museums in the
country. The name Amerind
is a contraction of "American
Indian," and this collection
contains tens of thousands of
artifacts from different Native
American cultures. All aspects
of Native American life are
shown here, with displays covering Inuit masks, Cree tools,
and sculpted effigy figures
from Mexico's Casas Grandes.
The adjacent Amerind Art
Gallery has a fine collection
of western art by such prominent artists as William Leigh

(1866–1955) and Frederic
Remington (1861–1909).
The delightful pink buildings,
designed in the Spanish
Colonial Revival style (see
p22), are also of interest.

Chiricahua National Monument ⓮

Road map D5. ☎ (520) 824-3560.
☐ daily. ● 25 Dec. 🎥 ♿ 📷 Ⓐ

T HE CHIRICAHUA Mountains
were once the homeland
of a band of Apache people
and an impenetrable base
from which they launched
attacks on settlers in the late
1800s. This 12,000-acre (480-
ha) area now preserves
amazing rock formations,
which were created by a
series of volcanic eruptions
around 27 million years ago.
Massive rocks balanced on
small pedestals, soaring rock
spires, and enormous stone
columns make up the bizarre
landscape, which can be
viewed from the monument's
scenic drive and hiking trails.

The nearby town of Willcox
houses the intriguing **Rex
Allen Arizona Cowboy
Museum**, which is devoted to
a native son who became a
famous movie cowboy, starring
in 19 films in the 1950s.

🏛 **Rex Allen Arizona
Cowboy Museum**
155 N. Railroad Ave. ☎ (520) 384-
4583. ☐ 10am–4pm daily.
● public holidays. 🎥 ♿

Massive rock spires formed by million-year-old volcanic eruptions at Chiricahua National Monument

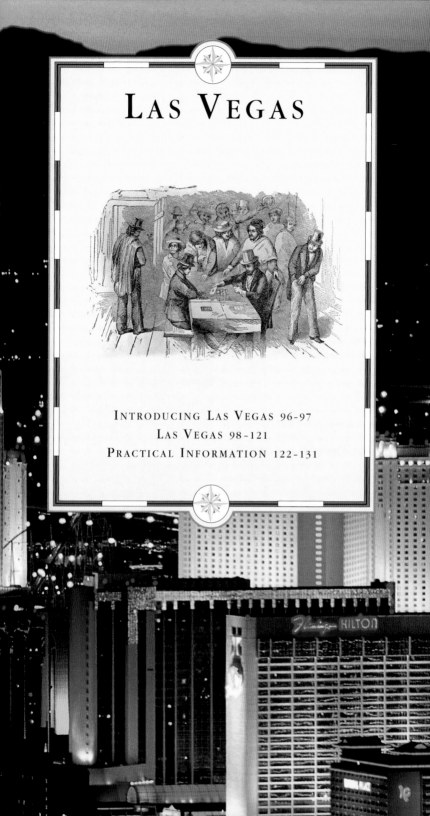

LAS VEGAS

The Changing Face of Las Vegas

NO OTHER CITY in the US has reinvented itself so often and with such profitable results as Las Vegas. Set in an unpromising landscape, bordering three deserts, artesian waters beneath the land first supported life here. Successive groups, from Native Americans to Mexican traders, Mormons, and railroad workers, all survived the environment. They added to a unique set of factors that gave birth to a Las Vegas they would barely recognize today.

No longer unique in offering casinos, the city still draws the crowds. Associated with some of the biggest names in show business, such as Frank Sinatra and Elvis Presley, with eccentric millionaires like Howard Hughes, with mobsters such as Bugsy Siegel, and above all with glamour, Vegas continues to fire the imagination as the fun city of stretch limos, showgirls, and an "anything goes" ethos for those who can pay for it.

Helen Stewart was a local ranch owner who sold her land to the railroad, which led to the founding of the city of Las Vegas in 1905.

DOWNTOWN LAS VEGAS
The city grew up around Fremont Street in Downtown Las Vegas in the early 1900s. By the 1960s *(see right)*, the area had began to suffer from competition from the Strip. Today, the area has been revived as the Fremont Street Experience *(see below right and p118)*.

Roulette was one of the games offered in Las Vegas once gambling was legalized in Nevada in 1931. The city was a hedonistic escape from the 1930s' Depression.

Construction of the Hoover Dam, 34 miles (55 km) from Las Vegas on the Colorado River, brought a rise in the city's fortunes (see p121). By the early 1920s Las Vegas had declined, and its population had fallen to 2,300. When construction began in 1931, money and people flowed into town, and by the early 1930s the population had swelled to around 7,500. Tens of thousands of visitors arrived to see the building of the dam and to enjoy the new gambling clubs springing up.

Benjamin Siegel, (left) called "Bugsy" behind his back, was a New York City gangster. He moved to Los Angeles in the 1930s and created the luxurious Flamingo hotel and casino in Vegas (see p111). He was killed by fellow investors only a year after the casino had opened in 1946, probably because other mobsters disliked his high profile. Although nothing remains of the original Flamingo building, there is still a tropical-themed luxury hotel on this spot.

HOWARD HUGHES

Billionaire Howard Hughes arrived in Las Vegas in November 1966, moving into a luxurious suite on the ninth floor of the Desert Inn hotel. When the hotel's management tried to move him out a few months later, Hughes bought the place for $13.2 million. Although he never left his room in four years, he spent some $300 million buying Vegas properties. These included the Silver Slipper hotel and casino across the Strip, whose blinking neon slipper disturbed him. As owner he had it switched off.

Hughes is credited with bringing legitimate business and a sanitized image to Vegas, sounding the death knell of mob investment in the city. In the 1960s, family oriented resorts such as Circus Circus opened, and such entertainment corporations as MGM, Hilton, and Holiday Inn began legitimate building programs. However, as recently as the 1970s and 80s mobsters were caught skimming profits from some Vegas hotels.

Billionaire entrepreneur Howard Hughes

THE STRIP

From a few low-rise buildings along a desert road in the 1960s to the glittering neon canyon of today, the transformation of the Strip has been remarkable (see pp102–105).

The Rat Pack, which included Peter Lawford, Sammy Davis Jr., Frank Sinatra, Joey Bishop, and Dean Martin, sealed Las Vegas' reputation as an entertainment mecca in the 1950s with shows at the now-demolished Sands hotel.

LAS VEGAS

R ISING LIKE A MIRAGE *out of Nevada's beautiful southern desert, Las Vegas is a glittering wonderland that promises fun to all its visitors. The city's unique attraction is its hotels with their fantastic architecture, re-creating such cities as New York and Venice. At the heart of these palaces lie the casinos where the lure of million-dollar jackpots draws almost 37 million visitors each year.*

Occupied by the Ancestral Puebloan peoples until around 1150 AD, the Las Vegas area was the home of several Native American tribes, including the Paiute, until Mexican traders arrived in the early 19th century. Mormon pioneers built a fort here in 1855, establishing the beginnings of a settlement in the area, which gradually developed. Officially founded in 1905, the city of Las Vegas expanded in the 1930s with the building of the Hoover Dam across the Colorado River, some 30 miles (45 km) away, and the legalization of gambling here in 1931. The influx of construction workers with money to burn, and the electricity and water provided by the dam, paved the way for the casino-based growth that took place in the 1940s and 1950s.

Since the 1990s, numbers of ever more extravagant resorts have been built in the city, including the impressive Bellagio, Venetian, and Aladdin, and this expansion shows no signs of slowing. For those who can tear themselves away from the city, the surrounding country has much to offer. Lake Mead and the stunning rock formations of the Valley of Fire State Park provide a range of outdoor pleasures from horseback riding to watersports.

Today, Las Vegas is the fastest growing city in the US, with more than 1,000 people moving in each week. Tourism and gaming remain the city's most successful industries – it has 18 of the 20 largest hotels in the world – but it is also known for its wedding chapels and top-quality entertainment.

Decorative stained-glass ceiling of the Tropicana Hotel's elegant casino

◁ **One of the city's oldest neon signs, "Vegas Vic" located on Fremont Street, downtown Las Vegas**

Exploring Las Vegas

L AS VEGAS HAS two centers. The wonderland of the Strip, and the older Downtown area, where the city began in 1905 (see pp96–7). The Strip is really Las Vegas Boulevard (Hwy 604), a 3.5-mile- (6-km-) long street that runs northeast through the city. The Downtown area crosses the Strip around Fremont Street (see p118). Strictly speaking, the part of the Strip that lies south of the Sahara Hotel is in Clark County, while the city proper is centered around Downtown Vegas. Ringed by mountains, canyons, and desert, the Las Vegas area also has a wealth of natural beauty in a variety of parks, some of it just a short drive from the Strip (see pp120–21).

The dazzling sight of the Las Vegas Strip, illuminated at night by myriad shimmering neon lights

GETTING AROUND

The Strip is a long road, and driving is recommended as the best way to get around. Major hotels have free parking lots, as well as valet service. The number 301 bus runs along the Strip past Downtown, and a trolley bus service operates between Hacienda Avenue in the south Strip and the Sahara Hotel in the north. Both buses stop at all the major hotels on the Strip. Taxis are also an option and are best hailed at hotels.

KEY

▢	The Strip see pp102–105
✈	International airport
🚊	Train station
🚌	Bus station
ℹ	Visitor information
▬	Interstate
▬	Major highway
▬	Highway

0 meters   500

0 yards   500

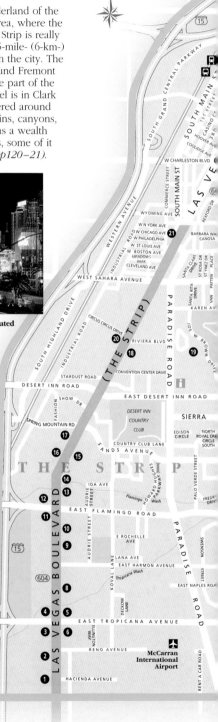

Roman-themed fantasy at the famous Caesars Palace

SEE ALSO

- *Where to stay* pp236–8

- *Where to eat* pp254–6

SIGHTS AT A GLANCE

Hotels and Casinos

Aladdin **9**
Bellagio **11**
Caesars Palace **12**
Circus Circus **20**
Excalibur **3**
Flamingo Hilton **13**
Las Vegas Hilton **19**
Luxor Las Vegas **2**
Mandalay Bay **1**
MGM Grand **5**
Mirage **16**
New York New York **4**
Paris **10**
Riviera **18**
Stratosphere **21**
Treasure Island **17**
Tropicana **6**
Venetian **15**

Historic Towns and Cities

Boulder City/Hoover
Dam **26**

Streets and Malls

Fremont Street
Experience **22**
Showcase Mall **8**

Museums and Galleries

Imperial Palace
Auto Collection **14**
Las Vegas Natural History
Museum **24**
Lied Discovery Children's
Museum **23**
Old Las Vegas Mormon
Fort **25**
Liberace Museum **7**

Areas of Natural Beauty

Lake Mead National
Recreation Area **27**
Mount Charleston **29**
Red Rock Canyon National
Conservation Area **30**
Valley of Fire State Park **28**

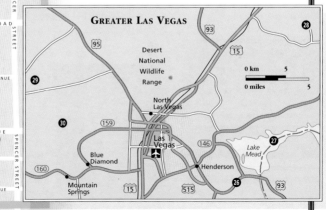

A View of The Strip I

THE HEART OF Las Vegas lies along Las Vegas Boulevard, a sparkling vista of neon known simply as "the Strip." This southern stretch of the Strip is home to a cluster of vast, lavishly-themed hotels, including Luxor, New York New York, and the Bellagio. Aiming to satisfy all a visitor's needs in one location, with restaurants, shops, and casinos, these hotels are best-appreciated at night when the lights come to life. It is in the evening that these new megaresorts become a fantasyland of such riotous design and architecture as the illuminated sphinx that fronts the Luxor hotel's striking pyramid. The exotically themed Aladdin is evidence of the city's ability to reinvent itself quickly – it took only two years to build.

View of the Strip's southern section

New York New York
A replica of the Statue of Liberty forms part of the façade of this hotel, which is composed of a host of Manhattan landmarks such as the Empire State Building ❹

Luxor
Tutenkhamun's gold sarcophagus is one of many re-created artifacts in the hotel's King Tut Museum ❷

The Boardwalk Casino
is a Holiday Inn hotel, and features a roller-coaster facing the Strip.

Mandalay Bay's
interior, with its palm trees and bamboo, re-creates a 19th century tropical paradise.

Excalibur's towers are a kitsch fantasy of medieval England.

Showcase Mall is a striking building, with its giant neon Coca-cola bottle. A huge games arcade makes the mall popular with families.

Tropicana
This casino was rebuilt in the late 1970s, with a stunning Art Nouveau-style stained-glass ceiling and glass lamps ❻

MGM Grand Hotel
This famous statue of Leo, symbol of the Hollywood film studio, MGM, rises 45 ft (15 m) above the corner of Tropicana Avenue ❺

Caesars Palace

Reproduction Roman statuary adorns the grounds of Caesars Palace. One of the Strip's oldest and most glamorous hotels, Caesars was built in 1966. Inside, the lavish Forum Shops mall features moving statues **12**

Lobby of the Bellagio

Lighting the ceiling of the hotel's elegant lobby, this colorful glass installation was designed by famous glass artist Dale Chihuly **11**

Paris resort's half-scale replica of Parisian landmark, the Eiffel Tower, dominates the Strip.

Imperial Palace

A pagoda fronts this Asian-themed hotel, famous for its classic car collection that is open to visitors **14**

W. DUNES RD

THE STRIP

FLAMINGO ROAD

| 0 meters | 300 |
| 0 yards | 300 |

Aladdin Hotel

Opened in 1963, Aladdin's reputation as one of the glitziest Strip hotels was sealed when Elvis married Priscilla here in 1967. The old building was imploded in 1998, and a new Arabian Nights-themed resort opened in 2000 **9**

Flamingo Hilton

The flaming pink and orange neon flower of the Flamingo hotel's façade is a famous Strip icon. Redesigned in the 1970s and 80s, the original 1946 building was the beloved project of gangster Bugsy Seigel (see p97) **13**

A View of The Strip II

THE FIRST CASINO resort to open on Las Vegas' Strip in 1941 was the El Rancho Vegas Hotel-Casino, which was located on the northern section of the Strip, on the corner of Sahara Avenue. A building boom followed in the 1950s, resulting in a swathe of resorts. The Sands, Desert Inn, Sahara, and Stardust hotels began the process that has transformed the Strip into a high-rise adult theme park. Many of these north Strip resorts remain, but they are now unrecognizable from their earlier incarnations – thanks to million-dollar rebuilding programs.

View of the Venetian and north Strip

Today, resorts such as the Venetian and the Mirage have established the Strip's reputation for upscale quality and almost nothing remains of the spit-and-sawdust atmosphere the city once had.

Treasure Island
Treasure Island's skull and crossbones sign lures passers by to the battling pirate ship show, held each evening on the hotel's Strip-side lagoon ⑱

The Mirage is both stylish and tacky – its beautiful, Strip-facing gardens feature an "erupting" volcano.

Dive is a family-friendly restaurant that features part of a submarine jutting onto the Strip.

The Fashion Show Mall is an upscale shoppers' paradise, with a range of stores.

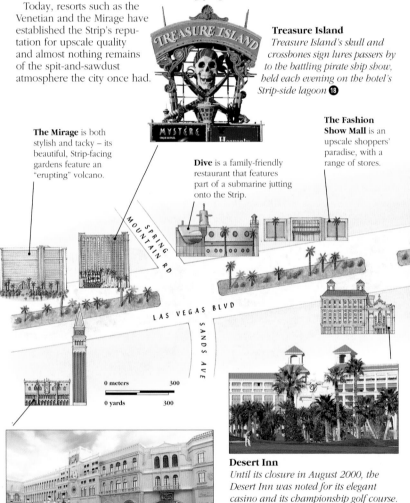

SPRING MOUNTAIN RD

LAS VEGAS BLVD

SANDS AVE

0 meters   300
0 yards   300

Desert Inn
Until its closure in August 2000, the Desert Inn was noted for its elegant casino and its championship golf course.

Venetian
One of the world's most luxurious hotels, this has mock canals flowing through its shopping area ⑮

Stardust
This famous sign, with its twinkling neon colors, is a noted Strip landmark. Originally made in 1968, today's hotel sign was altered in 1991.

Stratosphere Tower
An observation deck at the top of this 1,149-ft (350-m) tower offers fine views of the city and the ring of mountains that rise from the desert **21**

Circus Circus
Lucky the clown beckons visitors to this resort, which offers circus acts and traditional carnival games on the mezzanine floor above the casino **20**

La Concha Motel
is a rare remnant of stylish old Vegas. It was built in 1961.

The Candlelight Wedding Chapel
is located next to the Algiers Hotel. It is possible to get married here at any time of the day or night.

Algiers Hotel
Built in 1953, this is the oldest intact hotel left on the Strip. Despite extensive redecoration, the Algiers retains the low-rise motel-style of Vegas' original resorts, with its pink and blue exterior and elegant neon (see p236).

LAS VEGAS NEON
This seemingly jewel-encrusted sign from the Riviera hotel is just one of the Strip's famous neon images. The neon sign remains the dominant icon of Las Vegas, despite the fact that many of the new themed megaresorts here have opted for a more understated look. Neon is a gas discovered by British chemist Sir William Ramsey in 1898. But it was a French inventor, Georges Claude, who, in 1910, found that an electric current passed through a glass tube of neon emitted a powerful, shimmering light. In the 1940s and 50s the craft of neon sign making was elevated to the status of an art in Vegas.

The neon-lit façade of the Mandalay Bay hotel on the Las Vegas Strip

Mandalay Bay ❶

3950 Las Vegas Blvd. ☎ *(702) 632-7777; (877) 632-700.* ♿ ✉
◷ *24 hours (see p238).*
ⓦ *www.mandalaybay.com*

THE MANDALAY BAY resort aims to re-create the tropics of the late 19th century. Located at the south end of the Strip, it opened in 1999 and has 3,300 rooms. Tropical plants and white stucco architectural features such as arches and decorative cornices evoke a colonial atmosphere. Even the vast 110,000-sq-ft (10,200-sq-m) casino manages to suggest elegant 1890s Singapore. One highlight is the 10-acre (4-ha) lagoon-style swimming pool with its sandy beach and wave machine, plus a water ride around the pool. More restrained than other Strip resorts, the Mandalay Bay includes 15 restaurants, two nightclubs, and a theater which often hosts Broadway musicals. It is also the only resort on the Strip to feature a non-gaming hotel, the Four Seasons, located on the Mandalay's top four floors.

Luxor ❷

3900 Las Vegas Blvd. ☎ *(702) 262-4000; (800) 288-1000.* ◷ *24 hours (see p237).* ♿ ✉ ⓦ *www.luxor.com*

THE LUXOR'S FAMOUS 30-story bronze pyramid opened in 1993 and quickly became a Las Vegas icon. Despite the fact that the resort is modeled on the Eygptian city of Luxor, which has no pyramid, there is impressive attention to detail in the range of Ancient Egyptian architectural features. Painted temple pillars adorn the casino, and a reproduction Cleopatra's Needle graces the entrance. Visitors enter the pyramid through the legs of a giant sphinx to find themselves inside the casino where the ranks of ringing slot machines are surrounded by walls decorated with copies of paintings and hieroglyphs from the real Luxor's Karnak temple.

Although today's Luxor has removed some of the more kitsch elements of its original decor, such as a ride down the "Nile" in Cleopatra's barge, its animatronic talking camels can still be found near the walkway to the Excalibur hotel, close to the shops of the Giza Galleria. As a tribute to Egypt's ancient religions, a beam of light is projected from the pyramid's apex nightly – so powerful that it can be seen from planes cruising above Los Angeles 250 miles (400 km) away.

Among the hotel's many attractions, a free ride in the guest elevators (named "inclinators") ranks high – they travel along the inclines of the 350-ft (110-m) pyramid at an angle of 39 degrees. Also for those unafraid of heights, the **Luxor Imax™ Theater**, with its raked seats, offers 3-D films projected onto a seven-story-high screen. The experience takes viewers on a breathtaking journey in a range of environments from the Cretaceous period and its dinosaurs to the Grand Canyon. **King Tut's Tomb and Museum** is a meticulously researched reproduction of Tutankhamun's tomb as it was when archaeologists Howard Carter and

Impressive Egyptian-style lobby of the Luxor hotel

Lord Carnarvon discovered it in 1922. Traditional materials, including historically accurate dyes and linens, were used to re-create the burial chamber, and its stunning carved sarcophagus is coated in real gold.

Luxor Imax™ Theater
Luxor. ⬤ *10am–11pm Sun–Thu;*
10am–11:30pm Fri & Sat. 🎦 &

King Tut's Tomb and Museum ⬤ *9am–11pm Sun–Thu;*
9am–11:30pm Fri & Sat. 🎦 &

Excalibur's towers are designed to create a medieval fantasy castle

Excalibur ❸

3850 Las Vegas Blvd. 📞 *(702) 597-7777; (800) 937-7777.* ⬤ *24 hours*
(see p237). &
🌐 *www.excalibur-casino.com*

ONE OF THE STRIP'S larger hotels (it has more than 4,000 rooms), the Excalibur is a family friendly theme park resort with a casino attached. The medieval world of King Arthur and his knights is obvious at first sight of the castle like exterior with its white towers, turrets, moat, and drawbridge. Suits of armor line the entrance, which leads into the heavily themed casino where even the one-armed bandits have such signposts as "Medieval Slot Fantasy."

The second floor houses the Medieval Village, where quaint alleyways are lined with shops and restaurants, such as the Italian Lance-a-Lotta Pasta and Sir Galahad's Prime Rib. The Nitro Grill is a classic steakhouse with a difference – diners can experience live

World Championship Wrestling bouts from ringside tables. Costumed entertainers wander about amid the tables of dining families, and free juggling, musical, and magic acts are performed on the Jester's Stage every 45 minutes. On the floor below, a variety of simulator rides take visitors on a heart-stopping roller coaster ride or into a virtual sci-fi battle designed and directed by *Star Wars* director, George Lucas.

New York New York ❹

3790 Las Vegas Blvd.
📞 *(702) 740-6969; (800) 693-6763.*
⬤ *24 hours (see p237).* &
🌐 *www.nynyhotelcasino.com*

THIS HOTEL'S re-creation of the Manhattan skyline dominates the Tropicana Avenue corner of the Strip – no mean feat in a street of such impressive façades. Considered to be one of Las Vegas' most appealing sights, New York New York is fronted by a 150-ft (46-m) replica of the Statue of Liberty, behind which are 12 of Manhattan's most famous landmark buildings, including the Empire State, the Chrysler, and Seagram's. Every interior detail of the hotel is designed to reflect a part of New York City, from the 1930s-style wood-paneled lobby to the

Central Park casino, made to a scale of 1:3, complete with footbridges, cast-iron streetlamps, and trees with fall foliage. This fabulous casino is entered from the Strip via a replica of Brooklyn Bridge, which is one-fifth the size of the original. Roaring around the whole complex is the Manhattan Express, a roller coaster that twists and dives at speeds of 65 mph (105 kmph), and passes through the casino itself. Set among Greenwich Village brownstones is a wide range of cafés, restaurants, and bars offering a choice of live music from swing and jazz to Motown and rock.

Roller coaster at New York New York speeding through the air

MGM Grand ❺

3799 Las Vegas Blvd. [C] *(702) 891-1111; (800) 929-1111.* ○ *24 hours* (see p237). [&] [☞]
[W] *www.mgmgrand.com*

T HE EMERALD-GREEN MGM Grand building is fronted by the famous Leo, a 45-ft- (15-m-) tall bronze lion used as the symbol of the MGM Hollywood film studio. The original MGM hotel was built in the 1970s, farther down the strip on the site of the present Bally's hotel, and was named for the 1930s film, Grand Hotel, starring Greta Garbo. In 1980 the worst hotel fire in Las Vegas history destroyed the building and killed 84 people. Although the Grand did reopen on this site, it was not until 1993 that the MGM Grand of today opened, on the corner of the Strip and Tropicana Avenue. It covered a mammoth 114 acres (46 ha) and was themed on the movie The Wizard of Oz. A 1999 refurbishment expanded this theme to include all MGM movies. Over $500 million have been spent on the resort, which prides itself as Vegas' "City of Entertainment."

MGM Grand figurine

The largest hotel in the US with more than 5,000 rooms, the Grand boasts an array of entertainment and restaurants, and a 171,500-ft-sq (16,000-sq-m) casino. Its re-creation of New York's famous club,

Seen from across the Strip at night, the Tropicana hotel building

Studio 54, is one of the Strip's most popular nightspots. Another favorite, the **MGM Grand Lion Habitat**, offers the chance to see these magnificent animals at close quarters. In summer, the **Grand Adventures Theme Park** features rides, cafés, shops, and its stomach-churning roller coaster, the Sky Screamer. The Grand Garden Arena is a 17,000-seat venue famous for big-name concerts, major sports events, and world championship boxing. The smaller Grand Theater hosts the $45 million musical EFX (see p127).

🐾 MGM Grand Lion Habitat
MGM Grand. ○ *11am–11pm daily.* [&]
🎢 Grand Adventures Theme Park
MGM Grand. ○ *Opening hours and prices are seasonal.* [🎫] [&]

Tropicana Resort and Casino ❻

3801 Las Vegas Blvd. [C] *(702) 739-2222; (800) 634-4000.* ○ *24 hours* (see p238). [&]
[W] *www.tropicana.com*

O NE OF THE few 1950s boom hotels still on the Strip, the Tropicana was built in 1957. Las Vegas' famous illusionist act, Siegfried & Roy *(see p127)*, first appeared here, at its Folies Bergères in 1973. In 1995 the resort was restyled, and it now has lush tropical gardens and a fine Caribbean village façade. A 5-acre (2-ha) water park is one of the hotel's most delightful attractions, featuring three outdoor pools, a heated indoor pool, and five spas. Waterfalls and exotic flowers and foliage provide a habitat for flamingoes, black swans, and Brazilian parrots. The pool offers unusual casino action with swim-up blackjack tables which have a waterproof surface and money dryers.

A small museum within the resort is devoted to gambling history. At the **Casino Legends Hall of Fame** exhibits include a range of memorabilia and tributes to the founding fathers of Las Vegas such as Benny Binion *(see p118)*. There are also items from across Nevada, including antique slot machines and the largest collection of poker chips in the world.

🏛 Casino Legends Hall of Fame
Tropicana. *10am–6pm daily.* [🎫] [&]

Visitors viewing lions through the glass-walled tunnel at the MGM Grand

Liberace Museum ⑦

1775 E. Tropicana Ave. ☎ (702) 798-5595. ◷ 10am–5pm Mon–Sat; 1–5pm Sun. 🎥 ♿

T**HE SERENE** Spanish-style façade of the Liberace Museum is a vivid contrast to its glittering contents. Founded in 1979, the museum celebrates the life and work of one of Las Vegas's best-loved performers, Liberace (1919–87). The cars, pianos, and famously bejeweled costumes of this flamboyant personality are exhibited in three sections. The main area houses 18 of Liberace's 39 pianos, and the cars include a rare Rolls Royce covered with mirror tiles and etched galloping horses in which Liberace, dressed to match, would arrive at his Las Vegas show. Lavishly rhinestoned costumes and stage jewelry are also on show. The costumes worn at his final 1986 performance took six seamstresses, wearing protective sunglasses against the glare of the stones, several months to make. The world's largest

Liberace in his King Neptune costume

Austrian rhinestone, weighing over 50 lbs (23 kg), is also displayed here, near to Liberace's personal memorabilia, which includes several precious jewel-encrusted tiny music boxes.

Showcase Mall ⑧

3785 Las Vegas Blvd. ☎ (702) 597-3122. ◷ varies for each attraction. ♿

T**HIS NEON-CLAD** building features a 100-ft- (33-m-) high neon Coca-cola bottle. The Mall is an excellent place to take children but also offers enough to satisfy adults who are badly in need of a break from casinos. There are two main attractions – **GameWorks** (the brainchild of movie mogul Steven Spielberg), and M&M's World. While the latter is hardly more than a promotional exhibit for the company's products, it does offer fun elements and plentiful chocolate samples on the M&M's tour. GameWorks, on the other hand, offers its visitors hands-on entertainment with Indy-car simulator rides, virtual gun battles, and a daunting 75-ft (26-m) climbing wall. There is

also an Internet lounge and a choice of reasonably priced cafés and restaurants.

🎮 GameWorks

Showcase Mall. ☎ (702) 895-7626. ◷ 10am–1am Mon–Thu; 10am–2am Fri & Sat. 🎥 for climbing wall. ♿

Aladdin ⑨

3667 Las Vegas Blvd S. ☎ (702) 736-7114. ◷ 24 hours (see p237). ♿
W www.aladdincasino.com

O**NE OF LAS VEGAS'** historic hotels, the Aladdin, opened in 1963 as the Strip's first non-gaming resort, but the concept was ahead of its time and the hotel folded. Re-opened in the mid-1960s, in 1967 it hosted one of Vegas' most glamorous events, the wedding of Elvis and Priscilla Presley.
Today, the Aladdin has been completely rebuilt on the 1,001 Arabian Nights theme. It includes Desert Passage, a lavishly designed shopping, dining, and entertainment complex that re-creates the souks of North Africa. Its store-lined alleyways wind around a 7,000-seat performing arts theater. Aladdin is unusual in that it has built the first private membership club casino in addition to its public casino. "The London Club" is modeled on the exclusive European-style casinos seen in James Bond movies.

The neon lights and giant Coca-cola bottle of Showcase Mall

Paris ⑩

3645 Las Vegas Blvd. 📞 *(702) 739-411; (888) BONJOUR.* ⏱ *24 hours* (see p238). ♿ ☑
🌐 *www.parislv.com*

Located next to Bally's Hotel *(see p237)* on the Strip, Paris is a $760 million resort that looks like a Hollywood film set of the real French capital. The façade is composed of replicas of such Paris landmark buildings as the Louvre, the Hôtel de Ville, and the Arc de Triomphe. A 50-story, half-scale Eiffel Tower dominates the complex, and visitors can ride an elevator to the observation deck at the top or dine in its gourmet restaurant 100 ft (33 m) above the Strip. The casino contains architectural details that meticulously re-create Parisian streetlife, including cast-iron street lamps, and everything is set beneath a fabulous painted sky. Cobblestone streets wind along the edge of the casino and are filled with shops selling an array of expensive French goods including wine, cheese, and chocolate. The resort also boasts five lounges, a spa, two wedding chapels, and eight restaurants including the brasserie-style Mon Ami

Half-size model of the Eiffel Tower in the Paris hotel complex

de Gabi *(see p255).* This restaurant has tables outside overlooking the Strip, where diners can enjoy fine French cuisine in true Paris style.

Cocktail waitress

Bellagio ⑪

3600 Las Vegas Blvd. 📞 *(702) 693-7111; (888) 987-6667.*
⏱ *24 hours* (see p238). ♿ ☑
🌐 *www.bellagiolasvegas.com*

This $1.6 billion luxury resort opened in 1998 on the site of a previous hotel called the Dunes. Its design is based on the northern Italian town of Bellagio, with ocher-and terracotta-colored Mediterranean buildings set back from the Strip behind an 8-acre (3-ha) lake modeled on Italy's Lake Como. One of the

hotel's many attractions is the sublime fountain display on the lake that springs into action at regular intervals through the day and evening. Crowds gather to watch the free show – a choreographed water dance set to music, accompanied by visual effects including a rolling mist and, at night, stunning light effects.

No expense has been spared on the Bellagio's interior either; beautiful carpets and marble floors line the parade of upscale shops that include some of the most stylish names in Italian design, such as Armani and Prada. Delicate Carrara marble mosaics adorn all the entrance hall floors, and the main lobby ceiling is hung with sculpted glass flowers of every color. Even the casino manages to be light and airy; powerful air-conditioning helps banish the smoky atmosphere.

Perhaps the most surprising aspect of the Bellagio is its **Gallery of Fine Art**, a $300-million collection of major works of art that can hold its own against some of Europe's best galleries. The collection spans 20th-century art history from Impressionism to Pop Art and includes fine paintings by Manet, Picasso, and Jackson Pollock.

🏛 The Bellagio Gallery of Fine Art
Bellagio. 📞 *(702) 693-7722.*
⏱ *8am–11pm daily; children admitted 8–10:30am.* 🎟 ♿ 🎧

The Bellagio's famous dancing fountains shooting high into the air

Caesars Palace, seen from its entrance on the Strip at night

Caesars Palace ⓬

3570 Las Vegas Blvd.
📞 *(702) 731-7110; (800) 634-6661.*
🕐 *24 hours (see p237).* ♿
🅆 *www.caesars.com*

ROMAN STATUES, Greek
columns, and cocktail
waitresses in togas could all
be found at Caesars Palace
when it opened in 1966. The
decor and waitresses remain
part of the ambience here, but
in a less kitsch, more upscale
way since more than $600
million was spent refurbishing
the resort during the 1990s.

This classic Vegas casino was
the first themed hotel on the
Strip and quickly established
a reputation for attracting top
artists, from Andy Williams in
the 1960s to the singer Celine
Dion and the magician David
Copperfield in the 1990s. Over
the last four decades Caesars
has also hosted international
sports events, including
championship tennis, featuring
stars such as John McEnroe
and André Agassi, and boxing,
with such names as world
champions Muhammad Ali
and Mike Tyson.

Today, the hotel houses
three casinos, four lounges,
a new health spa, and the 4.5-
acre (1.8-ha) Garden of the
Gods – a pleasant landscaped
area with three swimming
pools. Caesars' elegant façade
is fronted by fountains and
cypress trees. The casinos
have all been refurbished
and, with their high ceilings
and light decor, have an
elegant, upbeat atmosphere.
The charming gaming expert

Barney Vinson gives free
weekday lessons in most
games, including craps and
blackjack *(see pp128–31)*.

The entrance to the chic
and highly exclusive Forum
Shops *(see p125)*
features a *trompe
l'oeil* sky ceiling and
a triumphal arch
topped by an
imposing statue of
a charioteer driving
four golden horses.
This is also the place
to find the thrilling
Imax™ 3-D ride,
Race for Atlantis, a virtual
reality race to save the
ancient city of Atlantis from
the bad guys. Visitors wear
3-D glasses and experience
a high-speed chariot race on
the motion simulator.

Race for Atlantis

Caesars Palace, Forum entrance.
🕐 *10am–11pm Sun–Thu;
10am–midnight Fri & Sat.* ♿

Flamingo Hilton ⓭

3555 Las Vegas Blvd. S. 📞 *(702) 733-
3111; (800) 832-2111.* 🕐 *24 hours
(see p237).* ♿ 🅆 *www.hilton.com*

THE BRILIANT pink and
orange neon flower of
the Flamingo hotel's façade
is, to many, the archetypal Las
Vegas icon. However, nothing
remains of the original 1946
casino: the last vestiges of this
building, including mobster
Bugsy Siegel's private suite,
were bulldozed in 1976
(see p97). One of the few
remaining signs of this notorious gangster's involvement in
the hotel is Bugsy's Deli, a
New York-style restaurant
with displays of 1940s and
1950s black-and-white photographs. In the 1990s a $130-
million renovation created
one of the most elegant
pool areas in Vegas.
Set among 15 acres
(6 ha) of landscaped
gardens, two
Olympic-sized pools
are veiled by tropical
plants and palm trees,
with islands that
provide a home to
African penguins and
pink flamingoes. There is a
kids' pool, two Jacuzzis, and
a water slide that leads to
three additional pools. The
hotel's pretty wedding chapel
is also set in the pool area.
Both guests and visitors may
use the renowned tennis club,
which has four floodlit night
courts, a practice court, and
a tennis shop. Professional
instructors are also available.

**Bagel-shaped sign
for Bugsy's Deli**

Exotic plants and lush palms surround the pool at the Flamingo Hilton

The Statue of Liberty dominates New York New York's Manhattan skyline façade ▷

Imperial Palace Auto Collection ⑭

3535 Las Vegas Blvd. S. 📞 *(702) 731-3311.* 🕐 *9:30am–11:30pm daily.* 🚫 &

Located on the fifth floor of the Imperial Palace Hotel's parking lot, this multi-million-dollar collection of classic cars from around the world will impress even the most autophobic of visitors. Ralph Engelstad, owner of the Imperial Palace Hotel, began his collection with a 1929 Ford Model A Roadster in 1979. Two years later, the museum was opened with enough space for 200 cars.

As well as vintage Fords, the exhibition includes such classics as Mercedes, Chevys, Cadillacs, and a range of military vehicles and fire trucks. Some of the most glamorous cars in the world can be found in this collection. These include limos from the 1920s and 1930s, such as the Duesenberg roadsters owned by film stars Clark Gable and Mae West. More recent, but no less stylish, are the Cadillacs and Chevrolets of the 1950s and 1960s with their elongated tail fins, leather seats, and chrome accessories. These include the 1963 pale blue Cadillac that once belonged to Elvis Presley, and Marilyn Monroe's pretty pink Lincoln Capri convertible. Today, many of the cars are for sale, with the gorgeous Duesenbergs sporting steep price tags of more than one million dollars.

Elvis' blue Cadillac on show at the Imperial Palace Auto collection

Venetian ⑮

3355 Las Vegas Blvd. S. 📞 *(702) 733-5000; (888) 283-6423.* 🕐 *24 hours (see p238).* & 📋 🌐 *www.venetian.com*

This astounding piece of architecture re-creates the city of Venice and currently contains more than 3,000 suites. Another 3,000 are planned, which will make the Venetian one of the largest hotels in the world. One of the new breed of luxury Vegas megaresorts, the Venetian has been built on the site of the legendary Sands Hotel. The Sands was the home of the "Rat Pack" *(see p97),* and a famous swim-up craps table, which was demolished in 1996. Facing the Strip, facsimiles of the Doge's Palace, the Campanile, and the Ca d'Oro overlook the blue waters of the Grand Canal – complete with a gondola park beneath a Rialto Bridge. Craftsmen have made sure that every detail is authentic, even the concrete has been aged to look like 400-year-old stone.

The colonnaded cloister of the Doge's Palace offers visitors one of the best views of the Strip. In front of the palace it is possible to rent a gondola to gently travel into the building along a winding canal to the Grand Canal Shoppes. The Venetian fantasy continues here with high-quality stores and restaurants set among cobblestone walkways and bridges beneath a blue painted sky that resembles a Renaissance painting. Acres of lavish marble flooring, statues, and replicas of famous Venetian paintings are found throughout this elegant complex. The stunning front lobby has a dome decorated with scenes from Venetian master paintings while the entrance to the Grand Canal Shoppes boasts a copy of Veronese's 1538 painting, *The Apotheosis of Venice.*

Entertainer at the Venetian

Mirage ⑯

3400 Las Vegas Blvd. S. 📞 *(702) 791-7446; (800) 627-6667.* 🕐 *24 hours (see p238).* & 📋 🌐 *www.themirage.com*

The Mirage hotel-casino opened in the fall of 1989 at the staggering cost of $620 million. At the time, it was the largest hotel in the US with 3,044 rooms. This new megaresort aimed to cater not only to gamblers but also to vacationers and conventioneers.

The stylish Venetian Hotel, complete with reproduction Campanile

Dramatic pirate battle on the lagoon at Treasure Island

Perhaps more than any other hotel, the Mirage revolutionized the Strip, setting out to draw visitors with attractions other than just the casino – a kind of fantasyland for adults.

The Mirage occupies an entire block along Las Vegas Boulevard between Caesars Palace and Treasure Island, and offers a range of attractions to its own guests and Vegas visitors alike. Its traffic-stopping façade introduces the complex's South Sea island theme with tropical gardens, waterfalls, and a lagoon. But the star of the show is a volcano that erupts, spewing fire and smoke every 15 minutes each evening.

Inside, an atrium filled with exotic plants, (some real, some fake) is kept suitably steamy by computerized misters. Behind the main desk a 20,000-gallon (90,000-liter) aquarium is filled with brightly colored fish and small sharks. As well as gaming, visitors can shop in designer stores, eat in one of 18 restaurants and bars, or see the famed illusionists Siegfried & Roy in an on-site theater built especially for them. Siegfried & Roy are also known for their conservation work with threatened white tigers and lions, and these amazing creatures can be seen at close quarters in a delightful zoo in the hotel's lush, landscaped gardens. Next to the zoo is a spacious dolphin pool, where dolphins can be observed at play several times daily.

Treasure Island 🕑

3300 Las Vegas Blvd.S. 🄲 *(702) 894-7111; (800) 944-7444.* 🕐 *24 hours (see p238).* 🄳 🅆 *www.treasureisland.com*

LOCATED NEXT TO its sister resort, the Mirage, Treasure Island is best-known for the pirate battle that takes place several times nightly on its lagoon on the Strip. This spectacular free show involves a full-scale battle between a pirate ship and a British frigate. Set against the background of an 18th-century Caribbean village, flying stuntmen and canon fire let rip until the pirates are victorious and the defeated frigate sinks beneath the waves. The wooden walkway that surrounds this extravaganza is thronged with visitors jostling for a better view, but a ringside seat can be gained at the Battle Bar inside the hotel. In windy conditions the show may be canceled.

Treasure Island is themed on Robert Louis Stevenson's novel of the same name. More family-friendly than many newer resorts, the hotel is also host to the stunning contemporary circus, *Mystère* by Cirque du Soleil, performed in a specially customized showroom *(see p127).*

The exotic rainforest atrium in the Mirage

Sparkling neon stars light up the Riviera façade at night

Riviera ⓱

2901 Las Vegas Blvd. ☎ (702) 734-5110; (800) 634-6753. ◯ 24 hours (see p237). ♿
Ⓦ www.theriviera.com

ONE OF THE group of Las Vegas hotels that were built on the Strip during the post-World War II building boom, the Riviera opened in 1955. Its nine-story tower made the hotel the city's first high-rise. Some of the key characters of Las Vegas' past have featured in the hotel's history. Liberace was the first headliner here, appearing with legendary Hollywood actress, Joan Crawford, who was the official hostess on opening night. Liberace was paid a record-breaking $50,000 a week. Over the next ten years the Riviera consolidated its reputation for offering glamorous entertainment, attracting such stars as Orson Welles, Ginger Rogers, and Marlene Dietrich.

Today, the Riviera occupies 1,000 ft (300 m) of the north Strip, and boasts 2,075 rooms. Several million dollars have been spent on refurbishing

Bronze sculpture of showgirls at the Riviera

the resort in recent years. While its glamor is somewhat faded the Riviera retains an "old Vegas" atmosphere, symbolized by its large, brash casino. This is one of the less expensive big Strip hotels, but still offers a good range of facilities, including an Olympic-sized pool, tennis courts, and a health spa. There are several restaurants, cafés, bars, and stores, as well as four shows. *Splash* features Mermaids, special effects, and water, and is performed in the 1,000-seater Versailles Theater.

Las Vegas Hilton ⓳

3000 Paradise Road. ☎ (702) 732-5111; (800) 732-7117. ◯ 24 hours. ♿ Ⓦ www.hilton.com/hotels

ELVIS PRESLEY is the star most associated with this hotel (which opened as The International in 1969), appearing here for a record 837 performances, all of which were sold out. Today, big-name singers such as Johnny Mathis and Chaka Khan perform here, but visitors can still pay tribute to the memory of the King at his lifesize statue just off the lobby. The hotel's proximity to the Las Vegas Convention Center makes it popular with businesspeople, but luxurious surroundings, a plush casino, and the famous **Star Trek: The Experience** attraction all draw other visitors to the resort.

The Spacequest Casino opened alongside Star Trek: The Experience, and is designed as a 24th-century space station where large windows look out onto the stars, Earth, and orbiting space shuttles. The Experience itself has been set up in partnership with Paramount Parks and offers a self-guided tour of costumes, special effects, and clips from both the TV series and movies. Visitors are then "beamed aboard" the transporter room of the USS *Enterprise* from where they are whisked off to fight the Klingons on a simulated ride of battle-filled adventure aboard a shuttle craft. Alternatively, the Deep Space Nine Promenade, from the

Visitors tour Star Trek: The Experience at the Las Vegas Hilton

Seen from the south, the brightly lit Circus Circus façade features Lucky the clown

spin-off television series first shown in the 1990s, offers themed cafés and shops such as Quark's Bar and Restaurant and Moogie's Trading Post.

Star Trek: The Experience
Las Vegas Hilton. ◯ 11am–11pm daily. ♿ 📷 Visitors must be 42 in (107 cm) tall to ride the Experience.

Circus Circus ②⓪

2880 Las Vegas Blvd. ☎ (702) 734-0410; (800) 634-3450.
◯ 24 hours (see p236). ♿
W www.circuscircus-lasvegas.com

LOCATED AT THE north end of the Strip, Circus Circus opened in 1968 and is a themed resort offering family entertainment. The hotel has a choice of reasonably priced restaurants and buffets, including a delicious steak house.

This vast property covers over 68 acres (27.5 ha) and has the largest indoor theme park in the country. The huge **Adventuredome** is housed inside a pink dome, with a re-created Southwest landscape of sandstone cliffs, caves, and a waterfall, and is maintained at a temperature of 72°F (21°C) year round. The range of rides here includes the terrifying double loop, double corkscrew roller coaster, a water flume ride that races down a mountain, and the Fun House Express – an Imax™ simulator ride.

The three casinos here cover

an incredible 100,000 sq ft (9,500 sq m). Above the main casino is the Big Top with its circular walkway of traditional games where the children are the winners – they can often be seen here carrying lots of stuffed toys. This is also the place to find the seating for the live circus acts that perform half-hourly from 11am to midnight. World-class acrobats can be seen flying high above the heads of the gamblers filling the slot machines below.

The Adventuredome
Circus Circus. ☎ (702) 794-3939.
◯ 9am–9pm daily. 📷 ♿

Stratosphere ②①

2000 Las Vegas Blvd. ☎ (702) 380-7777; (800) 99-TOWER.
◯ 24 hours. ♿ W www.stratlv.com

SOMEWHAT ISOLATED at the north end of the Strip, away from the main attractions, this resort hotel boasts the 1,149-ft- (350-m-) high Stratosphere Tower – a Vegas landmark and the tallest building west of the Mississippi River. The summit has indoor and outdoor observation decks, which offer unparalleled views of the city and the surrounding desert and mountains, and a popular revolving restaurant (see p255). The tower elevators take just

Neon sign rising above the Stratosphere

30 seconds to whisk visitors to the top, where two thrilling rides are located. **The High Roller** roller coaster twists and turns around the tower, and the **Big Shot** shoots visitors 160 ft (49 m) up in the air. At ground level the 100,000 sq ft (9,500 sq m) casino includes a poker room and a keno lounge. The Stratosphere also offers two shows, several restaurants, and a range of stores.

The High Roller and the Big Shot
Stratosphere. ◯ 10am–1am Sun–Thu; 10am–2am, Fri, Sat, & holidays. 📷 ♿ for observation deck only.

The Stratosphere Tower, landmark of Las Vegas' north Strip

Evening light show at the Fremont Street Experience

Fremont Street Experience ㉒

Light shows: hourly 6pm–midnight daily. 🚹
Ⓦ *www.vegasexperience.com*

K NOWN AS "Glitter Gulch,"
Fremont Street was in
the heart of Las Vegas when
it was incorporated in 1905.
This is where the first casinos
were located, complete with
stylish neon signs, and
famous illuminated icons
such as Vegas Vic and Vickie
lit up the night sky. However,
during the 1980s and 1990s,
Fremont Street suffered in
competition with more lavish
attractions on the Strip and
became a run-down city
center avoided by tourists.
In 1994 the city's ambitious
$70-million project to revita-
lize the area was initiated.

A vast steel canopy now
covers the street, from which
a spectacular sound-
and-light show is
projected every night.
There are five different
shows each evening;
*Odyssey – Illuminating
Journey; Swing Cat
Blues; The Heartbeat of
a Planet; Las Vegas
Legends;* and *Country &
Western Nights.* Around
35 computers operate
over two million lights
for each seven-minute
performance. The street
is now pedestrianized
and visitors can easily
stroll from casino
to casino, stopping to
snack and shop at a
variety of stalls along

the way. Although some of the
famous 1950s and 1960s neon
signs gave way to the new
show, many of the dazzling
neon façades belonging to
some of the city's oldest and
best-loved
casinos remain.
In contrast to
the Strip, the
buildings are
closer together
here, making
casino-hopping
an easy option.

For many years
the landmark casino in Vegas
was **Binion's Horseshoe**.
Benny Binion is one of the
city's legendary characters,
who is said to have arrived in
town in 1946 wearing a ten-
gallon hat and carrying a suit-
case filled with $2 million in
cash. The casino retains an
old-style Vegas atmosphere
with flocked wallpaper and
gold fittings (it was the first
casino to install carpet), and it

attracts many locals with its
low-stake games. It is still
possible to play two-dollar
blackjack and nickel slot
machines here. Today, Binion's
is famous for the annual World
Series of Poker competition,
in which players from all over
the world play for three
weeks, the winner scooping
the final pot of $1.5 million.

Other historic Las Vegas
casinos along Fremont Street
include **Jackie Gaughan's
Plaza**, built in 1971 on the
site of the original Union
Pacific Railroad depot, with
its atmospheric 1970s style.
The friendly **El Cortez**, with
its Mexican styling, faces
Fremont Street from Las Vegas
Boulevard, and is one of the
few casinos to retain architectural features from its
original 1950s
building. The
Four Queens,
named for the
owner's four
daughters, was
built in 1966 and
has one of the
best arrays of
lights on Fremont
Street. Inside, gilt mirrors and
chandeliers evoke early 19th-
century New Orleans, and the
casino claims to have the largest slot machine in the world.
At 9-ft (3-m) high and 20-ft
(6-m) wide, it takes six players
at a time. Fully renovated in
1976, the **Golden Nugget** is
bright and clean. The epony-
mous golden nugget is the
world's largest, weighing an
incredible 61 lbs 11 oz (27 kg).

**Golden Nugget neon sign
at the Fremont Experience**

Binion's Horseshoe
128 E. Fremont St. *(see p236).*
🎦 *(702) 382-1600.* FAX *(702)
382-5750.* ⏱ *24 hours.*
Jackie Gaughan's Plaza
1 Main St. *(see p236).*
🎦 *(702) 386-2110.* FAX *(702)
382-8281.* ⏱ *24 hours.* 🚹
El Cortez
600 E. Fremont St. *(see p236).*
🎦 *(702) 385-5200.* FAX *(702)
385-1554.* ⏱ *24 hours.* 🚹
Four Queens
202 E. Fremont St. *(see p236).*
🎦 *(702) 385-4011.* FAX *(702)
387-5123.* ⏱ *24 hours.* 🚹
Golden Nugget
129 E. Fremont St. *(see p236).*
🎦 *(702) 385-7111.* FAX *(702)
387-5123.* ⏱ *24 hours.* 🚹

**Façade of Binion's Horseshoe, one of
Fremont Street's most traditional casinos**

The modernist façade of the Lied Discovery Children's Museum

Lied Discovery Children's Museum **㉓**

833 Las Vegas Blvd. 【 (702) 382-3445. ◯ 10am–5pm Tue–Sun. ● Mon (except school holidays), Thanksgiving, Dec 25, Jan 1. ◪ ♿ ⓦ www.ldcm.org

A CONICAL, CONCRETE teepee forms part of this striking building, which also houses a branch of the Las Vegas City Library. Opened in 1990, this excellent museum is devoted to interactive exhibits that are fun for both adults and children. The first floor focuses on the arts and is the venue for workshops including mask-making and designing musical instruments. Children can stand inside a gigantic bubble, freeze their shadows on a wall, and hear simple phrases translated into different languages, including Navajo. The second floor features the in-house radio station and has a working television studio, which encourages children to explore how the medium works. Changing exhibitions cover a range of subjects from world cultures to art and wildlife. The gift shop here is excellent.

The Las Vegas Natural History Museum **㉔**

900 Las Vegas Blvd. 【 (702) 384-3466. ◯ 9am–4pm daily. ● Thanksgiving, Dec 25, Jan 1. ◪ ♿

A POPULAR CHOICE with the families who need a break from the Strip resorts, this museum has an appealing range of exhibits. Dioramas re-create the African savannah and display a variety of wildlife from leopards and cheetahs to several African antelope species such as nyalas, bush boks, and duikers. The Wild Nevada Room features the flora and fauna of the Mojave desert. Animatronic dinosaurs include a 35-ft- (10.5-m-) long *Tyrannosaurus rex*, while the marine exhibit has live sharks and eels. In the hands-on discovery room visitors can dig for fossils and operate a robotic baby dinosaur.

Old Las Vegas Mormon Fort **㉕**

908 Las Vegas Blvd. 【 (702) 486-3511. ◯ 8:30am–4:30pm daily. ● public holidays.

L OCATED JUST OPPOSITE the children's museum on Las Vegas Blvd., the small soft-pink adobe building that is the only remains of the Mormon Fort is a tranquil spot. The oldest building in Las Vegas, the fort dates back to 1855, when the first group of Mormon settlers arrived in the area. They constructed an adobe fort arranged around a 150-ft- (45-m-) long *placita* (small rectangular plaza) with 14-ft- (4-m-) high walls, but abandoned it three years later. The fort became part of a ranch in the 1880s and was run by Las Vegas pioneer Helen Stewart *(see p96)*. The City of Las Vegas bought the site in 1971, and restoration work has been ongoing since then.

Today, visitors enter a reconstruction of the original adobe house with its simply furnished interior much as it would have been under Mormon occupation. The building also contains an exhibition that describes the Mormon missions and their impact on Las Vegas.

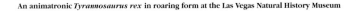

An animatronic *Tyrannosaurus rex* in roaring form at the Las Vegas Natural History Museum

Neat lawns and houses in the Boulder City suburbs

Boulder City and Hoover Dam ㉖

Road map A3. 🏔 12,500. ✈ 🚌
ℹ Hoover Dam Visitor Center, Hoover Dam, Boulder City. 📞 (702) 294-3523. 🕮 ♿

JUST EIGHT MILES (13 km) west of the colossal Hoover Dam, Boulder City was built as a model community to house dam construction workers. With its neat yards and suburban streets, it is one of Nevada's most attractive and well-ordered towns. Its Christian founders banned casinos, and there are none here today. Several of its original 1930s buildings remain, including the restored 1933 Boulder Dam Hotel, which houses the **Hoover Dam Museum**.

The Hoover Dam was built between 1931 and 1935 across the Colorado River's Black Canyon, 30 miles (48 km) east of Las Vegas. Hailed as an engineering victory, the dam gave this desert region a reliable water supply and provided

inexpensive electricity. Today, the dam supplies water and electricity to the three states of Nevada, Arizona, and California, and has created Lake Mead – a popular tourist center. Visitors to the dam have the choice of two types of guided tour, both of which begin at the visitor center. The first is a half-hour tour, which includes a video presentation on the history; the second is an hour-long hard-hat trip into the depths of the dam to see its turbines. There are superb views of the dam and the surrounding badlands (areas of sparse vegetation and intricate rock formations) from the top of the visitor center.

🏛 **Hoover Dam Museum**
444 Hotel Plaza, Boulder City.
📞 (702) 294-3515. 🕒 8:30am–
4:30pm daily. 🕮 ♿

Lake Mead National Recreation Area ㉗

Road map A3. 📞 (702) 293-8906; Alan Bible Visitor Center (702) 293-8907. 🚌 Las Vegas. 🕒 8:30am–4:30pm daily. ● Thanksgiving, Dec 25, Jan 1. 🕮 ♿ limited. ⛺

AFTER THE completion of the Hoover Dam, the waters of the Colorado River filled the deep canyons that once towered above the river to create a huge reservoir. This lake, with its 700 miles (1,130 km) of shoreline, is the centerpiece of Lake Mead National Recreation Area, a 1.5-million-acre (600,000-ha) tract of land. The focus is on water sports, especially sailing, waterskiing, and fishing. Striped bass and rainbow trout are popular catches. There are also several campgrounds and marinas dotted around the reservoir.

Power boating on Lake Mead

Valley of Fire State Park ㉘

Road map A3. 📞 (702) 397-2088. 🚌 Las Vegas. 🕮 ♿ partial. ⛺

THIS SPECTACULARLY scenic state park has a remote, desert location some 60 miles (97 km) northeast of Las Vegas. Its name derives from the red sandstone formations that began as huge, shifting sand dunes about 150 million

Extraordinary rock formations in the Valley of Fire State Park

years ago. There are two well-maintained trails across this wilderness, including the Petroglyph Canyon Trail, an easy half-mile (0.8-km) loop, which takes in several fine prehistoric Ancestral Puebloan rock carvings. Here, summer temperatures often reach 112°F (30°C). The best time to visit is in spring or fall.

The nearby town of Overton lies along the Muddy River. Ancestral Puebloan people *(see pp26–7)* settled here in around 300 BC but left some 1,500 years later, perhaps because of a long drought. Archaeologists have unearthed hundreds of prehistoric artifacts in the area since the first digs began in the 1920s. Overton's **Lost City Museum of Archaeology**, just outside the town, has a large collection including pottery, beads, woven baskets, and delicate turquoise jewelry, which was a local specialty.

🏛 **Lost City Museum of Archaeology**
721 S. Moapa Valley Blvd., Overton. ☎ (702) 397-2193. ◷ 8:30am–4:30pm daily. ● public hols. 🎦 ♿

Mount Charleston ㉙

Road map A3. ☎ (702) 872-5408. ♿ Las Vegas. Ⓐ

ABOUT 45 MILES (72 km) northwest of Las Vegas, Mount Charleston rises to 11,918 ft (35,754 m) out of Toiyabe National Forest, clad with pine, mountain mahogany, fir, and aspen. Also known as the Spring Mountain Recreation Area, it offers refuge from the Las Vegas summer heat, with a variety of hiking trails and picnic areas. In the wintertime, skiing and snowboarding are popular *(see p271)*.

A range of hikes is available, including two demanding trails that snake up to the summit: the 11-mile (18-km) North Loop Trail, and the 9-mile (14-km) South Loop Trail. Easier walks on the forested slopes are also marked, including a one-hour hike up Cathedral Rock. This appealing walk starts from a pleasant

Rainbow Mountain in Red Rock Canyon National Conservation Area

mountainside picnic area at the end of Nevada State Hwy 157. This is the more southerly of the two byroads leading to Mount Charleston off Hwy 95; the other is Hwy 156, which runs to the Lee Canyon Ski Area, catering to both skiers and snowboarders.

Red Rock Canyon ㉚

Road map A3. ☎ (702) 363-1921. ♿ Las Vegas. ◷ 8am–5pm daily. ● public hols. ♿ limited. Ⓐ

FROM DOWNTOWN Las Vegas, it is a short, 10-mile (16-km) drive west to the low hills and steep gullies of the Red Rock Canyon National

Conservation Area. Here, baked by the summer sun, a gnarled escarpment rises out of the desert, its gray limestone and red sandstone the geological residue of an ancient ocean and the huge sand dunes that succeeded it. Red Rock Canyon is easily explored on an enjoyable 13-mile (21-km) scenic road that loops off Hwy 159. Beside the road are picnic spots and trailheads for a series of short hikes that cover the area's steep winding canyons. The visitor center at the start of the road has useful displays on the Canyon's flora and fauna. There are more than 15,000 bighorn sheep in the conservation area.

THE CONSTRUCTION OF THE HOOVER DAM

Hoover Dam sign

More than 1,400 miles (2,250 km) in length, the Colorado River flows through seven states on its journey from the Rocky Mountains to the Gulf of California. A treacherous, unpredictable river, it used to be a raging torrent in spring and a trickle in the heat of summer. As a source of water it was therefore unreliable and, in 1928, the seven states it served signed the Boulder Canyon Project Act to define how much water each state could siphon off. The agreement paved the way for the Hoover Dam, and its construction began in 1931. It was a mammoth task, and more than 5,000 men toiled day and night to build what was, at 726 ft (218 m), the world's tallest dam. Named after Herbert Hoover, the 31st president of the US (1929–33), and an avid supporter of the project, it contains 17 hydroelectric generating units.

View of the Hoover Dam

PRACTICAL INFORMATION

LAS VEGAS HAS BECOME one of the world's most popular playgrounds. The Strip at night, in all its blazing glory, is a sight that never seems to tire visitors. Vegas is a city that knows how to cater to its guests, and a wealth of information about hotels, casinos, dining, and entertainment is available. However, with so much to choose from it is a good idea to do some advance planning. Most visitors spend most of their time around the Strip and the Downtown area, but there are many reward-ing day trips to be had exploring other nearby sights includ-ing Grand Canyon *(see pp58–63).*

New York New York yellow stretch cab

Façade of the Las Vegas Convention Center

GENERAL INFORMATION

CHOOSING WHEN TO GO TO Vegas can be tricky if you are looking for a bargain deal. These days the city is a highly popular destination year round, but unless you have prebooked, it is generally best to avoid the major conven-tions when the hotels can be full. New Year is also an extremely busy time.

Summers are very hot here with an average July temper-ature of 105°F (40°C). Spring and fall are sunny without such intense heat, and winters can also be warm but with occasional cold winds.

The **Las Vegas Convention and Visitor's Authority (LVCVA)** sends out excellent information packs, and they also have a website, offering information on every aspect of your trip. Once in the city there are numerous free papers such as *What's On,* as well as two daily newspapers, the *Las Vegas Review Journal* and the *Las Vegas Sun,* which contain reviews of the current shows and restaurants.

Although Las Vegas is no longer the low-cost destina-tion it once was, hotel prices do vary greatly *(see pp236–8).* Generally room rates are higher on weekends than during the week. It is always worth asking for a special rate if you are staying for a few days. Booking through a travel agent, calling the toll-free numbers, or contacting one of the online reservation agencies (such as **Lodging Express** and **Las Vegas Reservations Systems**) can also result in a less expensive deal. Each major hotel has its own website with a reserva-tions facility *(see under indi-vidual hotel pp236–8).*

TIPPING

THIS IS PART OF LIFE in Las Vegas. Bellhops expect $1 per bag, bartenders $1 a drink, waiters 15 percent of the check, and cab drivers 10–15 percent of the fare. Leave a dollar a day for the chamber maids, and a tip for croupiers, if you are lucky and win.

GETTING AROUND LAS VEGAS

THE LAS VEGAS transit authority, **Citizens Area Transit (CAT),** runs the number 301 bus, which stops at all the major hotels along the Strip for a flat fare of $2. Exact change is required; dollar bills are accepted. There are also the **Las Vegas Strip Trolleys,** green, old-style buses which travel between Hacienda Avenue and the Sahara Hotel on the Strip for a flat fare of $1.50. These services can save a great deal of pounding up and down the Strip between hotels, but both can sometimes be unpredictable and slow.

If used a lot, taxis here can work out to be an expensive way of getting around. They charge $2.20 for the first mile plus $1.50 for each addi-tional mile. A cab from the airport to the south end of the Strip (a five-minute trip) costs around $11, while a trip to the north end can be as much as $20. Cabs can be hailed on the street if their top lights are on, or, more commonly, picked up at one of the hotel lines where you will be expected to tip the doorman at least a dollar.

Citizen's Area Transit logo

Las Vegas Strip trolley bus

Monorail linking the Excalibur, Luxor, and Mandalay Bay resorts

Despite the fact that the majority of your time will be spent on one street, the Strip is a very long stretch of road, and while the properties along it appear to be near, this is an optical illusion caused by their vast size. Renting a car in Las Vegas allows you to see everything without getting footsore or spending a fortune on taxis. Parking is easy in Las Vegas; all the large Strip hotels have free parking lots. All the major car rental companies are represented here and cars may be picked up and dropped off at McCarran Airport. Rates can be as low as $20 a day. (For more information about arriving in Las Vegas see *pp286–7*).

Perhaps the ultimate Las Vegas travel experience is the limousine, particularly the stretch limo. It is possible to rent a wide range of these vehicles, including stretch and superstretch versions that come fitted out with TV, cocktail bar, and even Jacuzzi, for between $40 and $80 an hour. Several companies in the city, such as

Ambassador Limo and **Las Vegas Limousines**, rent their vehicles by the hour as well as for picking up and dropping off visitors at the airport. **A.K.A. Limousine** specializes in providing accessible cars for the disabled.

SIGHTSEEING TRIPS

FOR A BREAK from the Strip's attractions, there are a variety of day trips on offer to Las Vegas' surrounding sights. These include the gigantic Hoover Dam and nearby Lake Mead with its extensive opportunities for every kind of water sport *(see p120)*. Organized trips by **Gray Line** and **Valen Transportation** include drives through the scenic Valley of Fire State Park *(see pp120–21)* and cruises aboard the **Desert Princess** on Lake Mead.

One of the most popular excursions from Vegas is to Grand Canyon, which can be visited easily on a day trip. Airplane and helicopter rides can be arranged by various companies, including **Scenic Airlines**. Gray Line also runs

DIRECTORY

USEFUL NUMBERS

A.K.A. Limousine
📞 *(702) 257-7433.*

Ambassador Limo
📞 *(888) 519-5466.*
🌐 *www.ambassadorlasvegas.com*

Citizens Area Transit
📞 *(702) CAT RIDE.*

Desert Princess
📞 *(702) 293-6180.*

Gray Line
📞 *(800) 231-2222.*

Las Vegas Convention and Visitors Authority
3150 Paradise Rd.
📞 *(800) 332-5333.*
🌐 *www.lasvegas24hours.com*

Las Vegas Helicopters
📞 *(702) 736-0013.*

Las Vegas Limousines
📞 *(888) 696-4400.*
🌐 *www.lasvegaslimo.com*

Las Vegas Reservations Systems
📞 *(800) 233-5594.*
🌐 *www.lvrs.com*

Las Vegas Strip Trolleys
📞 *(702) 382-1404.*

Lodging Express
📞 *(800) 444-ROOM (7666).*
🌐 *www.accommodations express.com*

Scenic Airlines
📞 *(702) 638-3300.*

Valen Transportation
📞 *(800) 487-2252.*

flights to Grand Canyon as well as organizing river rafting trips along the Colorado.

City tours, which take in the Stratosphere Tower and Fremont Street Experience, can also be arranged. Perhaps the most exciting city tour is by helicopter at night; **Las Vegas Helicopters** specialize in night flights some 500 ft (150 m) above the Strip, which take in all the major resorts in their amazing settings.

Most hotels have plenty of information on trips as well as providing a booking service.

Las Vegas Helicopters' tour vehicles

SHOPPING IN LAS VEGAS

In recent years Las Vegas has consolidated its reputation as a shopper's paradise. Fun and tacky souvenirs are available in small stores along the Strip, whereas jewelry and designer clothes can be found everywhere, from hotel shops to malls. Given the city's hot climate, indoor shopping malls are the norm. All the major resorts have their own covered parades of shops, and some, such as Caesars Palace Forum Shops, are as flamboyant as the hotels themselves. Several malls in Las Vegas, such as the Strip's Fashion Show Mall, house upscale department stores such as Saks Fifth Avenue and Neiman Marcus. For bargains in adult and children's clothes and shoes as well as a variety of household items, the two outlet shopping Malls, the Beltz Factory Outlet and Factory Stores of America, are located south of the Strip. Shopping centrally can be expensive, and if you need to pick up everyday items such as shampoo or a toothbrush ordinary malls used by the locals are a short drive away.

Souvenir ornament from Circus Circus

Marble floors and a glass ceiling house elegant stores at Via Bellagio

HOTEL SHOPPING

THE INDOOR MALLS in many of the new megaresorts take shopping into a new dimension. Themed styling for the large hotels means that their resort streets are designed to look like Venice, Paris, or ancient Rome.

The **Forum Shops** at Caesars Palace are decorated with columns, arches, statuary, and a *trompe l'oeil* sky, which simulates the changes from dawn to dusk through the day. The statues adorning one ornate fountain spring to life every 90 minutes and move with light and sound depicting the Atlantis myth. Among the 140 stores found here are designer clothes and shoes at Fendi, DKNY, and Salvatore Ferragamo. An enormous moving Trojan horse sits outside the top American toy store FAO Schwarz. There are specialty candy and chocolate shops, as well as a choice of restaurants including a franchise for renowned Los Angeles chef Wolfgang Puck's Spago.

The beautiful **Grand Canal Shoppes** at the Venetian are set among pretty, winding alleys. A canal, with an amazing replica of St. Mark's Square lies at the center of the mall. Alongside the usual designer apparel, such as Jimmy Choo's shoes and clothes by Joseph, there are many specialty stores selling a variety of imported Italian goods, including art at Galleria San Marco, Murano glass at Ripa De Monti, and a fine collection of Venetian costumes and masks at Il Prato.

Novelty magnets on display in a hotel store

The recently opened **Desert Passage** at Aladdin is a fantasy based on 1,001 Arabian Nights. Stores and restaurants here are arranged around the narrow lanes and squares of a North African souk (market) built into the side of a mountain, and along a re-created harborfront complete with a full-size freighter. Stores include such US designers as Tommy Bahama and Billy Martin, as well as upscale cosmetics at Aveda, and innovative new lines such as Sephora. Some of the 14 restaurants are among the country's finest, such as Lombardi's and New York's Blue Note jazz club.

Le Boulevard at the Paris hotel is a Francophile's joy, featuring authentic-style Parisian stores selling French goods including children's

Roman statues and a painted sky at Caesars Palace's Forum Shops

Visitors entering the Fashion Show Mall on Las Vegas Boulevard

clothes, cheese, wine, and chocolate. The elegant **Via Bellagio** at the Bellagio hotel offers several upscale boutiques such as Chanel, Prada, and Gucci arranged along a marble-floored walkway with plenty of natural sunlight streaming in through an ornate glass ceiling *(see p103)*.

THE MALLS

R IGHT ACROSS THE street from Treasure Island, the **Fashion Show Mall** houses seven department stores, including Neiman Marcus, Bloomingdales, Macy's, and Saks Fifth Avenue, as well as the ubiquitous Gap and Benetton. For everyday items and lower prices head off the Strip to the **Boulevard Mall**, which at 1.2 million square ft (111,500 sq m) is Nevada's largest. The vast range of shops here includes such all-American favorites as Sears and JC Penney as well as book, gift, and jewelry stores. There is also a food court.

1970s retro Elvis sunglasses

If you're searching for real bargains, there are two outlet malls heading south along the Strip past Mandalay Bay *(see p102)*. Outlet malls are proving very popular. They sell branded goods with minor faults or excess stock, often at up to 70 percent discount. The **Belz Factory Outlet Mall** has 145 stores ranging from Levi's denims to Nike goods and Waterford Crystal. This mall also has a carousel for children and a food court.

Unusual for Las Vegas, **Factory Stores of America** is an outdoor mall with 40 stores selling everything from clothes to household goods.

Façade of Ghirardelli's specialty chocolate shop on the Strip

SOUVENIRS AND SPECIALTY STORES

T HE LAS VEGAS OF old is often associated with the tacky and kitsch, and souvenirs here can be all those things. All along the Strip stores sell memorabilia; always popular are the Elvis sunglasses, some even have sideburns attached. The largest emporium, the **Bonanza Gift and Souvenir Shop** offers a wide range of gifts, from the cheapest pair of slot machine earrings to luxury sets of poker chips.

There are also a couple of gambling stores that offer a wide range of gaming merchandise from the serious to the frivolous. However, be aware that many gaming items can be pricy. **CJ Slot Sales** has both modern and antique machines, while **JP Slot Emporium** has a larger collection of bargain-price one-armed bandits.

DIRECTORY

HOTEL SHOPPING

Desert Passage
○ 10am–11pm Sun–Thu;
10am–midnight Fri–Sat.
☎ (702) 866-0710.

Forum Shops
○ 10am–11pm Sun–Thu;
10am–midnight Fri–Sat.
☎ (702) 893-4800.

Grand Canal Shoppes
○ 10am–11pm Sun–Thu;
10am–midnight Fri–Sat.
☎ (702) 414-4525.

Le Boulevard
○ 10am–11pm Sun–Thu;
10am–midnight Fri–Sat.
☎ (702) 946-7000.

Via Bellagio
○ 10am–midnight daily.
☎ (702) 693-7111.

THE MALLS

Belz Factory Outlet Mall
7400 Las Vegas Blvd. S.
○ 10am–9pm Mon–Sat; 10am–
6pm Sun. ☎ (702) 896-5599.

Boulevard Mall
3528 S. Maryland Pkwy.
○ 10am–9pm Mon–Fri; 10am–
8pm Sat; 11am–6pm Sun.
☎ (702) 732-8949.

Fashion Show Mall
3200 Las Vegas Blvd. S.
○ 10am–9pm Mon–Fri; 10am–
7pm Sat; noon–6pm Sun.
☎ (702) 369-0704.

Factory Stores of America
9155 Las Vegas Blvd. S.
○ 10am–8pm Mon–Sat; 10am–
6pm Sun. ☎ (702) 897-9090.

SPECIALTY STORES

Bonanza Gift and Souvenir Shop
2460 Las Vegas Blvd. S.
☎ (702) 384-0005.

CJ Slot Sales
2770 Las Vegas Blvd. S.
☎ (702) 893-0660.

JP Slot Emporium
3720 Tropicana Ave. W., Ste. 8.
☎ (702) 736-4747.

ENTERTAINMENT IN LAS VEGAS

L AS VEGAS MAKES a good claim to be the entertainment capital of the world. From free spectaculars such as Treasure Island's pirate battle to lavishly produced theatrical shows, there is a full range of nightlife available. Sinatra and Elvis may be gone but headliners still appear regularly in the city's showrooms, offering a rare chance to see a favorite star in a surprisingly intimate setting. Most of the major venues are

Cirque du Soleil acrobat

concentrated in the hotels along the Strip and Downtown, and range from small lounges to 1,000-seater showrooms. While visitors can still enjoy the kitsch appeal of a Vegas burlesque show with its scantily clad showgirls, high-quality productions featuring the latest in lighting and special effects are a big draw. Comedy, magic, and music from jazz to salsa are also widely available and often for free or the price of a cocktail.

INFORMATION

T HERE IS NO shortage of information on the entertainment scene in Las Vegas. A variety of free publications lists all the major productions as well as the latest big acts in town. Magazines and free newspapers such as *Showbiz Weekly, Scope, What's On,* and *Las Vegas Weekly* can usually be picked up in all the major hotels. Even Las Vegas taxis carry free guides to the city, with information on shows and attractions. The **Las Vegas Convention and Visitor's Authority** provides up-to-date showguides, and their website has current listings and reviews *(see p123).*

Showbiz Weekly magazine

BUYING TICKETS

T HE EASIEST WAY to book tickets to the major shows or visiting headliners is to call the venue/hotel directly on their toll-free number. Prices can vary, ranging from around $30 to $100 per ticket. The ticket may also include drinks, a free program, tips, and even dinner. Check in advance if there is preassigned seating, because if there isn't, you can improve your chances of getting a good seat by tipping the maitre d'.

Reservations should always be made in advance, but the length of time varies greatly according to the show's

popularity. To see the Cirque du Soleil's stunning *Mystère* at Treasure Island you can book up to 90 days in advance, while you can reserve space for most other shows up to 14 days ahead. It is also possible to get tickets on the night of the performance by lining up at the box office an hour or so before showtime. This is especially true at times when there are no major conventions in town and it is not a public holiday. Weekdays are a better bet than weekends, although most shows have one or two days off during the week. For sports events, such as world championship boxing, or the really big rock and pop concerts, frequently held at the impressive 15,225-seater MGM Grand Garden, tickets can also be purchased through **Ticketmaster** and other agency outlets.

Famous illusionists Siegfried & Roy with one of their white tigers

Discounts for children and senior citizens may be available from the box office. Free tickets may be offered to the hotel casino's big winners.

HEADLINERS

E VER SINCE THE the Strip's early days in the 1940s, Las Vegas resorts have lured some of the world's most famous performers to

Lavish production number in the musical *EFX* at MGM Grand

Relaxing with a round of golf just minutes from the Strip

entertain their gambling guests. Stars such as Frank Sinatra, Dean Martin, Liza Minelli, and Elvis Presley played regularly here, often in relatively small "headliner" showrooms. The 1,400-seat Bally's Celebrity Room has hosted a wide range of performances by some of America's most famous entertainers, from Dean Martin and Liza Minnelli to zany magicians Penn and Teller. Today, such Vegas stalwarts as singers Wayne Newton and Tom Jones can often be seen at intimate venues, including the MGM Grand's 650-seat Hollywood Theater.

Elvis show billboard at the Boardwalk Casino

LOUNGE ACTS

FROM JAZZ AT Bally's Indigo Lounge to Latin music at the Mirage's Lagoon Saloon, there is a variety of music available in the lounge bars along the Strip. The mega-resorts generally have at least two venues providing free entertainment throughout the day. Among the livliest is New York New York's The Bar at Times Square, where requests are played and a lot of boisterous audience participation takes place.

These performances are free except for the price of buying a drink. However, each venue has a minimum drink purchase charge or cover. The wonderful views from the Stratosphere Top of the World Lounge will cost you the additional price of an elevator ticket.

OUTDOOR ACTIVITIES

ONE OF THE most popular outdoor activities here is golf. Las Vegas has dozens of superbly designed golf courses, some positioned in the midst of spectacular scenery. As well as private courses there are many public ones, some just a short distance from the Strip itself. The concierge desk in your hotel will advise and book time at one of the many nearby courses. There are also excellent tennis facilities at some hotels, including Caesars Palace, the Monte Carlo, and the Riviera.

Luxurious health spas are a standard element in the big hotels providing services such as weight rooms, personal trainers, and massages.

Hiking is available at the nearby Red Rock Canyon, as is horseback riding at **Mount Charleston** (702 872-5408).

PRODUCTION SHOWS

THE FIRST production show to be staged at a Strip resort was the musical revue *Lido de Paris*, at the Stardust, which began in 1958 and ran for 33 years. This prompted other hotels to stage their own productions. Traditionally these shows have long runs – the Tropicana staged the French *Folies Bergère* in 1959, and it is still going. Often performed in built-to-order showrooms, Vegas shows usually have two performances each evening.

GAMBLING IN LAS VEGAS

Blackjack cards

DESPITE ITS GROWING fame as an all-round adult amusement park, Las Vegas remains famous for its casinos. More than 30 million visitors come to the city every year and, on average, each spends $80 gambling every day. Don't come expecting to make your fortune; with a combined annual income of $7 billion, the casinos appear to have the advantage.

The secret pleasure of gambling is the lure of the unknown – you never know what the next card will be. Casinos know this and aim to keep you playing for as long as possible. Free drinks are available for gamblers, but it is not a good idea to gamble without a clear head. Before you start, decide on an amount that you can afford to lose and be sure to stick to it.

For a first timer, the casino can seem daunting, but, with a basic understanding of the rules, most of the games are relatively simple to play *(see p130–31)*. Some hotels have gaming guides on their in-house TV channels and Las Vegas' visitor center supplies printed guides. Several large casinos give free lessons at the tables.

Row upon row of "slots" on the gaming floor of New York New York Casino *(see p107)*

GENERAL INFORMATION

ALWAYS CARRY ID if you are young-looking and tend to be carded in bars, because it is illegal to gamble under the age of 21. Children are not welcome on the casino floor, which can make it difficult for families with children in some hotels *(see pp230–45)*.

Be aware that if you are winning it is casino etiquette to tip the dealers. It can also be to your advantage to tip when you first sit down at a table, as it is always a good idea to get the dealer on your side. Dealers can prevent inexperienced gamblers from making silly mistakes and will usually explain the finer points of the games, if asked. Head for the tables where players are talking and laughing. The chances are that a row of glum faces means that you may be in for an equally dull gambling experience.

SLOT MACHINES

SLOTS OF every kind dominate Las Vegas casinos. The simple one-armed bandit, where pulling a handle spun the reels and a win resulted from a row of cherries or some other icon, has been largely superceded by computerized push-button machines offering a bewildering variety of plays.

There are basically two kinds of slots; flat-top machines and progressive machines. A flat-top machine has a range of fixed payouts depending on different arrangements of winning symbols. There will usually be a choice of stakes, from one to three coins, and if you hit a winning display you will win less for a one-coin stake than if you play the limit. On progressive slots, you give up smaller jackpots in exchange for winning a

A Mirage coinbucket

progressive jackpot. The payout on these machines increases as you play, and the rising jackpot figure is displayed above each machine. The biggest payout is currently from the Mega-bucks slots, which operate all across Nevada. A cocktail waitress at the Desert Inn won almost $35 million on a machine there in January 2000, the highest payout ever. The majority of machines take quarters, dollars, and $5, but there are a few nickel machines left in the downtown casinos. There are also high-roller slots, which take anything from $10 to $500 for a single play.

Casino loyalty card

Tips

• Usually located together, progressive machines pay out at a certain limit. It is a good idea to ask an attendant what this limit usually is, and when it was last hit. If the jackpot hits at around $10,000 and the machines are displaying $9,000, this could be a good time to start playing.
• Always play the machine limit because if you win, you will be sure to receive the maximum amount.
• Wins on both types of machine allow you to receive coins back or else they rack up credits, which you can use for subsequent bets. Monitoring your display of credits will help keep track of how much you are spending. If your original stake was 10 quarters and you win 30, using credits allows you to decide to walk away when the credit display is down to 20, leaving you 10 quarters up on the game.
• Choose to play at the busier banks of machines where players have buckets full of quarters. Rows of unoccupied machines may mean they are not paying out well.
• Join a slot club. Most casinos have clubs that offer a range of incentives to get you to play

with them; which range from cash back to discounts on hotel rooms. Members are issued with an electronic-strip plastic loyalty card that inserts into the machine; the more money a gambler spends, the greater the rewards.

BLACKJACK

THIS CARD GAME is one of the most popular games on the floor; casino blackjack tables offer minimum bet games from $2 to $500. The aim is to get as close to 21 without going over, and to beat the dealer. Cards are worth their numerical value, with all the face cards worth 10 and an ace worth 1 or 11. Generally the dealer will deal from a "shoe" (a box containing up to six decks of cards). Each player receives two cards face up, while the dealer's second card is face down. Players must not touch the cards and should use hand signals to indicate if they wish to take another card, or "hit" (scratch the table with their forefinger to receive another card) or not take a card, "stand" (wave a flat hand over their cards.) Once each player has decided to stand or hit the 21 limit, the dealer turns over his second card and plays his hand, hitting 16 or less and standing with 17 or more. This is important because it

Traditional slot machine

is an essential part of "basic strategy" blackjack. The assumption behind basic strategy is that the dealer's second card will be a ten and that the next card in the shoe will also be a ten. This is because there are more tens in the deck than any other card (there are 96 tens in six decks).

Tips

• In basic strategy if the dealer's top card is a "bad" card (from two to six), then the player should stand from 12 up and not risk taking another card. This is because the dealer has to get to 17, so it is most likely that he will go over 21 when he hits his hand.
• If the player has between 12 and 16 and the dealer's first card is seven or higher, the player should gamble on drawing an extra card, as the probability is that the dealer's other card is a ten, which beats a hand of under 17.
• If your first two cards add up to 10 or 11, then you can "double down," or bet the same amount again. If you have a $5 chip on the table then you add another, hoping to get a ten card thereby reaching a winning total of 20 or 21 and doubling your winnings. Be aware that you are only allowed one extra card if you double down.
• Another betting option is to split your hand. If you are dealt two cards of the same value, you can choose to separate them into two hands, placing a second bet by the first on the table. Do this when you have aces and eights.

A winning hand on a blackjack table at Circus Circus *(see p117)*

Craps

Craps dice

OFTEN THE MOST fun game on the floor, a sense of camaraderie develops in craps because players are betting either with or against the "shooter" (whoever has the dice) on what the next number rolled will be. The aim of the shooter's first roll, or "coming out," is to make 7 or 11 in any combination (say 3/4, 5/6) to win. A roll of 2, 3, or 12 is craps; everyone loses and the shooter rolls the dice again. If a total of 4, 5, 6, 8, 9, or 10 is rolled, this becomes the "point" number, and the shooter must roll this number again before rolling a 7 to win. Craps etiquette says that you put your money on the table rather than handing it to the dealer; wooden holders around the table will keep your chips. Always roll with one hand; the dice must hit the end of the table. All betting and laying down of chips must be completed before the next roll.

Craps table seen from above, showing the various boxes and areas for the many bets

BETS

Craps can seem confusing as there appears to be a lot going on at any one time; this is largely due to the wide variety of bets it is possible to lay. If you are a beginner the following bets are the best ones to lay.

Laying bets during a craps game at Caesars Palace

The Pass Line Bet

With this one you are basically betting that the shooter will roll a 7/11 on the first roll in order for you to win. The odds at this point are even, so if you do win you get the same amount you laid down. If a point number is rolled, the shooter has to throw the same number before he rolls another 7. Since there are more ways to roll a 7 than any point number, it pays to take the odds once the shooter has a point, which means placing an additional bet behind your pass line bet. This will pay you the true house odds if the shooter rolls his point. The odds change according to the number, so check with the dealer first.

The Don't Pass Bet

This is the opposite of a pass line bet. The aim here is for the shooter to lose by throwing a 2 or 3 on the first roll, or by rolling a losing 7, which happens before he makes his point number.

The Come Bet

This is an optional bet you can make during the game, when your money comes to the next number that rolls. For example; if the point is 6 you make a come bet, and the shooter rolls an 8. Your come bet "comes" to the 8, and now you have two numbers in play. You can also take odds on a come bet.

The Place Bet

Another way of getting additional numbers is by making a place bet. In this case, you simply pick the number you want and make a place bet on that number. The advantage of place bets is that you pick the number yourself and you can remove your bet at any time. The disadvantage is that the casino charges you from 50 cents to $1 for each $5 bet you place.

POKER

THERE ARE several different versions of poker, including video poker, played in Las Vegas casinos. It is important to know the hierarchy of poker hands to play any of these: starting with a pair as the lowest hand, and a royal flush as the highest.

CARIBBEAN STUD POKER

A TYPE OF five-card stud poker played on a table with a layout like a blackjack table, where the aim is to beat the dealer. There is a progressive jackpot where winnings increase according to a player's hand. Players win all or part of a progressive jackpot with a Royal Flush, Straight Flush, Four of a Kind, Full House, or Flush.

PAI GOW POKER

COMBINING THE ancient Chinese game of Pai Gow with American poker, this game includes a joker in the standard 52-card pack. The joker is used as an ace or to complete a straight or flush. Each player has to make the best two-card and five-card hand possible to beat the banker's two hands.

TEXAS HOLD 'EM

THIS IS THE most popular form of poker played in the poker rooms of Las Vegas casinos. It is also the game of the famous World Series of Poker held each year at Binion's Horseshoe (see p118). Players are dealt two cards and they must make their best hand from five communal cards dealt face up on the table.

ROULETTE

ROULETTE IS quite a simple game but with a great variety of bets. A ball is spun on a wheel containing numbers 1 to 36 divided equally between red and black, plus a single and a double zero, colored green. Each player's chips are a different color so they can be easily identified

A croupier setting up roulette in a private gaming room

Casino poker chips

on the table. The aim is to guess the number that will come up on the spin of the wheel. Bets are placed on the table, which has a grid marked out with the numbers and a choice of betting options. The highest payout odds are 35 to 1 for a straight bet on one number such as 10 black. You can also make a "split bet" on two numbers, which pays 17 to 1 if either number comes up. The most popular bets are the outside bets, which are those placed in the boxes outside the numbered grid. These only pay even money, but allow you to cover more numbers such as Odd or Even, Red or Black, First 18 Numbers or Second 18 Numbers. You can also make a Column Bet covering 12 numbers, which pays 2 to 1.

BACCARAT

A VARIATION OF *chemin de fer*, baccarat is played at a leisurely pace with eight decks of cards, the deal rotating from player to player. The

Two cards in each hand of baccarat

object of the game is to guess which hand will be closest to 9: the player's or the banker's. You can bet on either hand.

KENO

ONE OF THE easiest games to play, keno is a close relative of bingo. Out of the 80 numbers on a keno ticket, players may choose up to 20. A range of bets is possible and winning depends on your chosen numbers coming up. The prize depends on the amount of numbers matched.

A screen showing a keno game in progress at Circus Circus

RACE AND SPORTS BOOK

GIANT VIDEO screens adorn these areas of the casino, where you can bet on almost any sport. The race book is for betting on thoroughbred horse racing and features live coverage from racetracks across the US. The sports book covers the main sporting events taking place around the country, as well as the major tournaments staged in Las Vegas itself. Watch the progress of your team on the nearby TVs.

SOUTHERN UTAH

Southern Utah

SOUTHERN UTAH CONTAINS an abundance of stunning natural landscapes, and boasts the highest concentration of national parks in the US. The region, which lies to the north of Grand Canyon and the blue waters of Lake Powell, owes much of its dramatic beauty to the geological wonder of the Grand Staircase, a series of steep terraces of colored rock. Weather and river erosion have sculpted this feature into the fine scenery found at Bryce, Arches, Capitol Reef, Zion, and Canyonlands National Parks. Hiking, boating, and mountain-biking are popular here, with equipment rentals available in such towns as Moab and St. George.

View of the peaks of Zion National Park in spring seen from the nearby visitor center

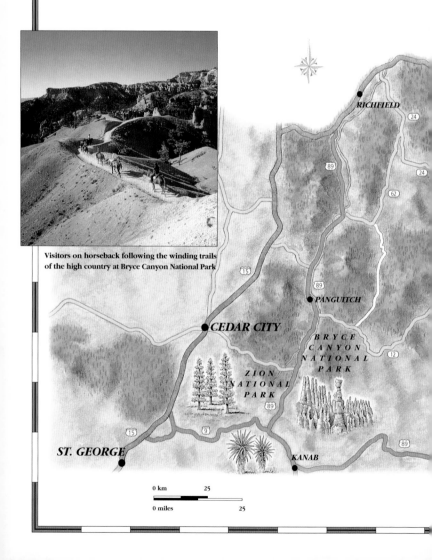

Visitors on horseback following the winding trails of the high country at Bryce Canyon National Park

RICHFIELD

24

89

24

62

15

89

PANGUITCH

CEDAR CITY

BRYCE CANYON NATIONAL PARK

12

ZION NATIONAL PARK

89

15

9

ST. GEORGE

KANAB

89

0 km   25

0 miles   25

GETTING AROUND
The best way to explore Southern Utah is by car: every road is a scenic route, and public transportation is limited. One train passes through the region, an Amtrak Super-liner, which stops at Thompson, 35 miles (58 km) north of Moab. Greyhound buses travel to some of the region's larger towns. Two Interstate Highways, I-15 and I-70, pass close to Zion and Arches National Parks respectively. Smaller paved highways include Highway 191 via Moab, and the scenic Highway 12, which skirts Grand Staircase-Escalante National Monument. A high-clearance 4WD vehicle is advisable for many of the unpaved roads.

SEE ALSO
- *Where to Stay* pp230–45
- *Where to Eat* pp246–63

KEY

▨	Interstate
▨	Major highway
▨	Highway
≈	River

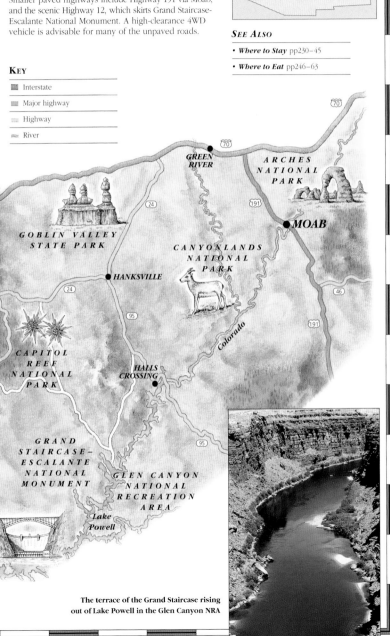

The terrace of the Grand Staircase rising
out of Lake Powell in the Glen Canyon NRA

The Mormons

THE CHURCH OF JESUS CHRIST of Latter Day Saints was founded by Joseph Smith (1805–44), a farm worker from New York State. In 1820 Smith claimed to have had visions of the Angel Moroni. The angel led him to a set of golden tablets, which he translated and later published as the *Book of Mormon*, leading to the founding of the Mormon church. This new faith grew rapidly but attracted hostility because of its political and economic beliefs, and because it practised polygamy. Seeking refuge, the Mormons moved to Illinois in 1839, where Smith was killed by an angry mob. Leadership passed to Brigham Young (1801–1877), who led church members westward. Salt Lake City was founded and Yound led his followers to establish farms across Utah's wilderness. Today, 70 percent of Utah's citizens are Mormons.

19th-century depiction of Joseph Smith's vision. The Angel Moroni is seen delivering the tablets which became the Mormon scriptures.

On the great trek westward, pilgrims rode or walked for a year, leaving Illinois in 1846 and arriving in Utah in July, 1847.

Mormon pioneers were intrepid and successful; after they had established themselves in the Salt Lake valley, church members fanned out across the west, establishing agricultural colonies in their wake. One of these colonies was in Las Vegas (see p119), where 30 Mormons, sent here by Brigham Young, built a mission and a small fort.

Brigham Young and his wives, nine of whom are seen here, illustrated Mormonism's most controversial practice, polygamy. It was outlawed in 1890 to appease the US Government and pave the way for Statehood in 1896.

THE GREAT MORMON TREK WEST

In 1847, Brigham Young led a band of Mormons west in the hope of escaping persecution and founding a safe haven in the Salt Lake valley. Young wished to find "a place on Earth that nobody wants." It was an extraordinary enterprise in which the pioneers traveled across bleak prairies and over mountains in primitive wagons, braving the fierce winter and summer weather. Those who could not afford oxen hauled all their possessions in hand carts.

Salt Lake City was painstakingly laid out in a grid system over the unpromising, and previously unsettled, landscape of Utah's Salt Lake Basin. The grid ensured wide streets, decent-sized houses, and enough land so that each family could be self-sufficient. By 1900, many farms and more than 300 towns had been founded across the West and Southwest.

BRIGHAM YOUNG

Born in Vermont in 1801 of a Protestant family, Brigham Young, carpenter, painter, and glazier, joined the Mormons in Ohio in 1832. He took charge of the great migration west from Illinois in 1846, arriving in Salt Lake City in 1847. In 1849 he established the territory of Deseret,

Brigham Young in middle-age

which encompassed present-day Utah. "Deseret" means "Honeybee" in the *Book of Mormon* and symbolizes industry. Young's vision and organizational skills helped the settlers turn the desert into fruitful farmland. During his long life, he had several disputes with the federal government, whose authority he both resisted and recognized. Despite being removed from political office in 1857, Young was head of the Mormon church until his death in 1877.

Mormon missionaries preach their faith throughout the world, placing great emphasis on their social and philosophical concerns. The church enjoys a high rate of conversion, and church membership continues to grow rapidly.

The St. George Mormon Temple *was constructed under the aegis of Brigham Young. For the eleven million Mormons worldwide, it is a potent symbol of a faith based on work, sobriety, and cooperation, with the emphasis on humanitarian service.*

SOUTHERN UTAH

WHEREVER YOU GO in southern Utah, it is hard to find a road that does not dazzle the visitor with unforgettable scenery. Winding highways lead through stunning red rock canyons, stark deserts of wind-polished rock, and cool, mountain realms of tall pines and sparkling streams. The five national parks in this region are favorite destinations, such that each is inundated with up to three million visitors a year. Despite this, even in summer there are quiet, undiscovered corners to be found across the region. The Grand Staircase–Escalante National Monument offers visitors a chance to experience this living wilderness by driving such unpaved scenic routes as the Burr Trail *(see p147)*.

The first people to live here were Paleo-Indians 12,000 years ago. Later, the Ancestral Puebloan people thrived in southeastern Utah, building cliff dwellings along the San Juan River. The Mormons arrived here in 1847, successfully establishing settlements in this harsh land.

Today, most people come to the area to enjoy the outdoors. Hiking, mountain biking, and 4-wheel driving are all popular activities, as well as riverfloat trips and whitewater adventures.

St. George and Cedar City are the biggest towns in southern Utah. A number of smaller communities, however, such as Springdale and Bluff, offer upscale stores and restaurants. Moab meanwhile offers outdoor activities by day, and entertainment by night.

SIGHTS AT A GLANCE

National and State Parks, and National Monuments
Arches National Park **1**
Bryce Canyon
  National Park **13**
Canyonlands
  National Park **3**
Capitol Reef National Park **7**
Dead Horse State Park **4**
Grand Staircase–Escalante
  National Monument **12**
Goblin Valley State Park **6**
Zion National Park **15**

Historic Towns and Cities
Boulder **8**
Cedar City **14**
Green River **5**
Kanab **16**
Moab **2**
St. George **17**

Areas of Natural Beauty
Burr Trail **9**
Hole-in-the-Rock Road **10**
Lake Powell/Glen Canyon
  National Recreation Area **11**

KEY
═══ Interstate
═══ Major highway
═══ Highway
─── Railroad

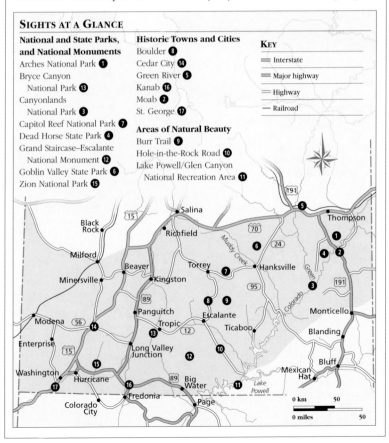

◁ **Relaxing in the rose-colored sandstone of Antelope Canyon, a narrow "slot" canyon in Glen Canyon NRA**

Arches National Park ❶

Wild flowers in the park

Aᴿᴄʜᴇꜱ ɴᴀᴛɪᴏɴᴀʟ ᴘᴀʀᴋ contains the highest number of natural stone arches found anywhere in the world. More than 80 of these natural wonders have formed over millions of years. The park "floats" on a salt bed, which once liquefied under the pressure exerted by the rock above it. About 300 million years ago, this salt layer bulged upward, cracking the sandstone above. Over time the cracks eroded, leaving long "fins" of rock. As these fins eroded, the hard overhead rock formed arches, which range today from the solid looking Turret Arch to the graceful Delicate and Landscape arches.

Devil's Garden
This area contains several of the park's finest arches, including Landscape Arch, a slender curve of sandstone more than 300 ft (91 m) long, thought to be the longest natural arch in the world.

Sunset watch at Delicate Arch
A natural amphitheater surrounds the arch, creating seating from which vistas of the La Sal Mountains are framed.

Tʜᴇ Wɪɴᴅᴏᴡꜱ Sᴇᴄᴛɪᴏɴ
In the park's Windows Section, a one-mile loop trail leads to Turret Arch, then the North and South Windows arches, situated side by side. With excellent viewing spots available, many visitors photograph North and South arches framed by the sandstone Turner Arch, as seen here.

Exᴘʟᴏʀɪɴɢ ᴛʜᴇ Pᴀʀᴋ

The park's highlights can be seen from the many viewpoints dotted along the scenic drive. The drive starts at the visitor center at the park's south end, just off Hwy 191. Several easy trails start from parking lots at the road's viewpoints. The loop at Balanced Rock is a short and easy trail suitable for children, while Delicate Arch Viewpoint Trail has disabled access. The Windows loop is suitable for families.

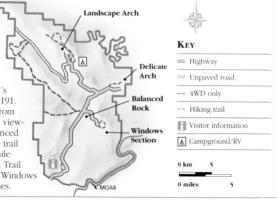

Kᴇʏ
— Highway
— Unpaved road
-- 4WD only
-- Hiking trail
ℹ Visitor information
Ⓐ Campground/RV

Landscape Arch
Delicate Arch
Balanced Rock
Windows Section
MOAB

0 km 5
0 miles 5

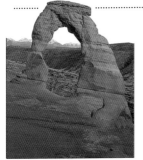

Delicate Arch
The most celebrated of all the arches here, and a state symbol, Delicate Arch appears on many Utah license plates. It is reached by a moderate 45-minute walk over sandstone.

VISITORS' CHECKLIST

Road map 2C. ℹ *Arches Visitor Center (435) 259-8161.* ⏰ *Apr–mid-Sep: 8am–6pm daily; Oct–mid-Apr: 8am–4:30pm daily.* ♿ *restrooms, campground (one site), Park Avenue Trail and Delicate Arch Viewpoint Trail only.*

Arches are formed
through a process that takes millions of years; today's arches continue to erode and will eventually collapse.

Balanced Rock
This precariously balanced boulder atop a sandstone spire is one of the park's landmarks. Good views are available from the trail as well as the scenic road route.

Western-style, timber-clad gift store on Main Street, Moab

Moab ❷

Road Map 2C. 🏠 *6500.* ℹ *Main and Center Sts. (435) 259-8825.* ⏰ *8am–8pm daily.*

A TOWN OF DRAMATIC ups and downs, Moab is currently riding its second great boom of the last 50 years. Once a quiet Mormon settlement, in 1952 a local prospector discovered the first of several major uranium deposits outside town. Overnight, Moab became one of the wealthiest communities in America. When the uranium market declined in the 1970s, the town was saved by tourism and its proximity to Arches and Canyonlands national parks.

Today, Moab is one of the top destinations for lovers of the outdoors. Mountain bikers come here to experience the famous Slick Rock Trail. They also come for the challenging ride from Moab Rim, reached by Moab Skyway, a scenic tram ride offering panoramic views of the area. There is also a vast choice of hiking and 4WD routes taking in some of this region's fabulous landscapes.

Moab is also a center for whitewater rafting on the Colorado River. **Matheson Wetlands Preserve** off Kane Creek Boulevard has 2 miles (3 km) of hiking trails along a riverside wetland that is home to birds and wildlife. The town is lively and has good facilities.

✗ Matheson Wetlands Preserve
59 East Center St. 📞 *(435) 259-4629.* ⏰ *9am–5pm daily.*

Park Avenue and the Courthouse Towers
The large, rock monoliths known as Courthouse Towers bear an uncanny resemblance to city skyscrapers. They can be seen from Park Avenue, an easy, short trail.

Canyonlands National Park ❸

Mᴵᴸᴸᴵᴏɴs ᴏꜰ ʏᴇᴀʀs ago, the Colorado and Green Rivers cut winding paths deep into rock, creating a labyrinth of rocky canyons that form the heart of this stunning wilderness. At its center, the rivers' confluence divides the park's 527 sq miles (1,365 sq km) into three districts: the Needles, the Maze, and the grassy plateau of the Island in the Sky. Established as a national park in 1964, Canyonlands is growing in popularity. Most wilderness travel, whether on foot or by vehicle, requires a permit.

VISITORS' CHECKLIST

Road map C2. ■ *Canyonlands National Park, 2282 South West Resource Blvd., Moab (435) 259-7164.* W *www.nps.gov/cany* ◯ *Visitor center: 8am–4:30pm (longer during Spring and Fall) daily.* ● *Thanksgiving, Dec 25, Jan 1.* 🈲 ♿ ☑ 🚻 Ⓐ

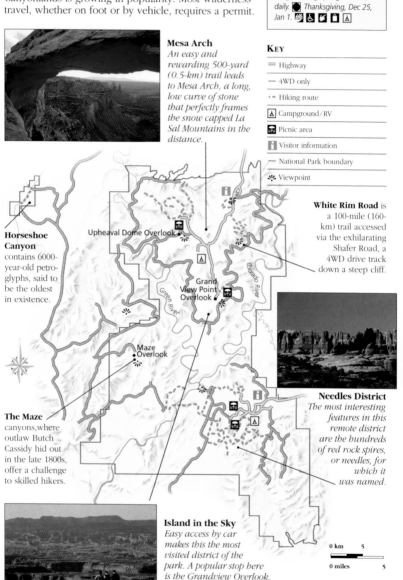

Mesa Arch
An easy and rewarding 500-yard (0.5-km) trail leads to Mesa Arch, a long, low curve of stone that perfectly frames the snow capped La Sal Mountains in the distance.

KEY

═	Highway
═	4WD only
• ▪	Hiking route
Ⓐ	Campground/RV
🈲	Picnic area
ℹ	Visitor information
—	National Park boundary
☀	Viewpoint

White Rim Road is a 100-mile (160-km) trail accessed via the exhilarating Shafer Road, a 4WD drive track down a steep cliff.

Upheaval Dome Overlook

Horseshoe Canyon contains 6000-year-old petroglyphs, said to be the oldest in existence.

Grand View Point Overlook

Maze Overlook

The Maze canyons, where outlaw Butch Cassidy hid out in the late 1800s, offer a challenge to skilled hikers.

Needles District
The most interesting features in this remote district are the hundreds of red rock spires, or needles, for which it was named.

Island in the Sky
Easy access by car makes this the most visited district of the park. A popular stop here is the Grandview Overlook, which offers panoramic views of the rocky canyons of the Green and Colorado rivers.

0 km   5
0 miles   5

The deep crevices of the canyons in the wide valley around Green River

Dead Horse Point State Park ❹

Road map C1. State Route 313 (435) 259-2614. Apr–Oct: 8am–6pm daily; Nov–Mar: 8am–5pm daily.

THE HIGH MESA of Dead Horse Point lies just outside the entry to the Island in the Sky of Canyonlands National Park. Unforgettable views of the Colorado River and the maze of deep canyons are a highpoint here. Legend has it that this park owes its name to the fact that it was once used as a natural corral for wild mustangs. A group of horses not chosen for taming were once left in this dry site, eventually dying of thirst

View of the dramatic cliffs of Dead Horse Point State Park

within sight of the Colorado River far below. The park also features several short hiking trails that follow the cliff edge, offering variations on the truly amazing view. The drama of this place has not been lost on Hollywood (see pp30–31). Famous as the spot where Thelma and Louise drove off the edge in the 1991 film of the same name, more recently these cliffs were scaled by Tom Cruise at the start of the 2000 movie Mission Impossible: 2.

Green River ❺

Road map C1. 1,000. 855 E. Main St (435) 564-3526. daily.

LOCATED IN A broad, bowl-shaped valley, the town grew around a ford of the wild Green River in the 19th and early 20th centuries. Primarily a service town, it is also a launching spot for those braving the challenging white-water that lies downstream of the Green and Colorado Rivers.

John Wesley Powell (see pp42–3) began his intrepid exploration of the Colorado River and Grand Canyon from here in 1871. Green River has the **John Wesley Powell River History Museum**, with 20,000 sq ft (1,860 sq m) of displays tracing the history of the area's exploration.

🏛 John Wesley Powell River History Museum

855 E. Main St. (435) 564-3427. Apr–Oct: 8am–8pm daily; Nov–Mar: 9am–5pm daily. public hols.

Eroded rock formations of Goblin Valley State Park

Goblin Valley State Park ❻

Road map C1. (435) 564-3633. 24 hrs daily.

THE "GOBLINS" of Goblin Valley State Park are, in fact, a group of mushroom-shaped rocks or hoodoos, intricately carved by erosion. Visitors are free to wander among these rocks, which stand up to about 10 ft (3 m) in height. Two paved, and several unpaved, trails lead down to the valley floor.

Bathed in the setting sun, the Rainbow Bridge over Lake Powell on a spring evening ▷

Capitol Reef National Park **❼**

Around 100 years ago, prospectors coming across the desert were forced to stop at the Waterpocket Fold, a vast 100-mile- (160-km-) long wall of rock that runs north–south through the desert. They likened it to an ocean reef and thought its round white domes looked like the nation's Capitol Building, hence the park's name. Covering 378 square miles (980 sq km), many people pass through the park via Fremont Canyon on Hwy 24. As famous for its long record of human habitation as it is for its beauty, Ancestral Puebloan petroglyphs and a preserved Mormon homestead can still be seen here.

VISITORS' CHECKLIST

Road map 2C. 10 miles E. of Torrey, Hwy 24. ❧ *Capitol Reef Visitor Center (435) 425-3791.*
ⓦ *www.nps.gov/care*
◯ *8am–4:30pm daily.* ◑ *Dec 25.* ♿ ♿ ♿ ⚠

Cathedral Valley

The vast rock monoliths that tower over the desert here give the valley its name. An unpaved road crosses this stunning area.

The Fremont Petroglyphs were created by the Ancestral Puebloans between 700 and 1250, and can be seen on a rock wall in the Fremont Canyon.

BICKNELL

HANKSVILLE

Capitol Gorge

Capitol Gorge can be reached from the scenic route that extends about 10 miles (16 km) into the heart of the park. Guided walking tours are available during summer, but only experienced hikers should explore the back country here.

The Gifford Farmhouse

Visitors can tour the 1908 Gifford home, which is now a cultural center dedicated to the 1880s Mormon settlement that once flourished here.

Notom-Bullfrog Road is an adventurous drive along a partly-unpaved road for 70 miles (112 km) south to Lake Powell. Cars can negotiate the road in dry weather but extra gas and water are essential.

KEY

═	Highway
═	Unmade road
▬	4WD only
🕴	Ranger station
Ⓐ	Campground/RV
🏕	Picnic
ℹ	Visitor information
☀	Viewpoint

Waterpocket Fold was formed 65 million years ago as the Earth's crust buckled upward. The multicolored ripples of rock that run the length of the park continue to be shaped by erosion.

0 km   10

0 miles   10

Boulder **8**

Road map 2C. 🚶 *755 W. Main St. Escalante (435) 826-5499.* ◯ *Apr–Oct: 7am–6pm daily; Nov–Mar: 8am–5pm Mon–Fri.*

THE TINY TOWN of Boulder nestles picturesquely among the surrounding peaks. The town is home to the Anasazi State Park, which offers restored ruins and a museum detailing the history of the Ancestral Puebloans that lived here between AD 1050 and 1200. Before Hwy 12 was built, Boulder was virtually isolated as the last town in America to receive its mail by pack mule. Today, Boulder makes a welcome rest stop along Hwy 12, which connects Hwy 89 and Capitol Reef National Park. This road boasts what may be the most spectacular and diverse array of landscapes found along any road in the country.

Between Escalante and Boulder, Hwy 12 winds through an unforgettable landscape of vividly colored, towering rock formations and twisting canyons. Visitors can stop at Calf Creek Campground to hike the short trail along Calf Creek Canyon ridge to Lower Calf Creek Falls. The falls are one of the hidden treasures of the Southwest, a 126-ft (38-m) plume that drops past lush hanging gardens into an emerald green pool. Continuing along Hwy 12, just before Boulder, the road offers white-knuckle excitement as it traverses the Hogsback, a

knife-edge ridge of rock with few guardrails and many steep drops on either side. Beyond Boulder, Hwy 12 climbs to the 9,400-ft (2,820-m) summit of Boulder Mountain.

Burr Trail **9**

Road map 2C. 🚶 *755 W. Main St. Escalante (435) 826-5499.*

THE BURR TRAIL is another partly-paved scenic road, winding through the Grand Staircase–Escalante National Monument. Heading east from Boulder, the trail crosses Capitol Reef National Park as an unpaved road before reaching Bullfrog Marina at Lake Powell *(see pp150–51.)* The first 40 miles (64 km) are paved and follow Deer Creek, rising through the winding red-rock maze of Long Canyon. At the canyon end, the view opens to reveal the pristine valleys of the Circle Cliffs and Capitol Reef National Park.

Hole-in-the-Rock Road **10**

Road map 2C. 🚶 *755 W. Main St. Escalante (435) 826-5499.*

IN 1879 A DETERMINED group of 230 Mormon settlers headed out from Panguitch, hoping to create a new settlement in southeastern Utah. Instead they were brought to a halt by the yawning 2,000-ft- (600-m-) deep abyss of Glen Canyon. Undeterred, they dynamited a

View of Lake Powell from the end of Hole-in-the-Rock Road

narrow hole through a wall of rock and constructed a primitive road down the sheer sides of the canyon. Lowering their wagons and cattle down the path by ropes they finally reached the bottom, only to repeat the whole process in reverse to ascend the far side. They finally founded the town of Bluff in 1880 *(see p172).*

Today, their original route, Hole-in-the-Rock Road, offers an impressive trip through the wild interior of the Grand Staircase–Escalante National Monument. About 18 miles (29 km) along the road, intrepid hikers can detour for Peekaboo and Spooky canyons, two slot canyons barely one foot (30 cm) wide in places. 4WD is necessary to traverse the last 6 miles (10 km) to the pioneers' "Hole in the Rock," a 50-ft (15-m) slit in the rock which offers a fine view of Lake Powell.

Hell's Backbone Bridge outside the town of Boulder, with steep mountain drops on either side

Lake Powell ⑪

See pp150–51.

Grand Staircase–
Escalante National
Monument ⑫

Road map C2. ⚑ *755 W. Main St.,
Escalante (435) 826-5499.*
◯ *Apr–Oct: 7am–6pm daily;
Nov–Mar: 8am–5pm Mon–Fri.*

Eestablished by President
Clinton in 1996, this national monument encompasses
1.9 million acres (769,000 ha)
of pristine rock canyons,
mountains, and high desert
plateaus. One of the last areas
in the US to be explored, the
Grand Staircase–Escalante
National Monument abuts
Capitol Reef National Park,
Glen Canyon National Recreation Area, and Bryce Canyon
National Park. It was named
for the four cliff faces, called
Vermilion, Grey, White, and
Pink, that rise in tiered steps
across the Colorado Plateau
(see pp18–19). Geologically
speaking, they are a recent
phenomenon, having been
raised by dramatic upheavals
just 12 million years ago.

This vast area has a special
importance, as the Bureau of
Land Management intends to
preserve its wild and largely
pristine state. No new roads,
facilities, or campgrounds will
be built in the monument,
while those roads that already
exist will not be improved.

The spectacular beauty
of the monument is
best explored on scenic
drives combined with
daylong hikes. Several
paved and dirt roads
offer access to various
parts of the park.
Highway 89 follows
the southern boundary,
in places hugging the
base of the towering
Vermilion cliffs. Just ten miles
(16 km) east of the town, a
road leads north into Johnson
Canyon, where there is a
mock Western town that has
been used for many movies
and TV shows *(see p30).*

Information on guided and
independent tours in this vast
region can be found at the
Escalante visitor center.

A few miles east of Bryce
Canyon and 9 miles (14 km)
south of Hwy 12
stands **Koda-
chrome Basin
State Park**, a
distinctive land-
scape noted for
67 free-standing
sand pipes, or
rock chimneys,
formed millions
of years ago as geyser vents.

**Vintage wagon outside
Cedar City Museum**

♣ **Kodachrome Basin
State Park**
ⓘ *(435) 679-8562; (800) 322-3770.*
◯ *Dawn–dusk daily.* 📷 ✔ 🅰

Bryce Canyon
National Park ⑬

See pp152–3.

Stage of the Globe Theatre in Cedar City

Cedar City ⑭

Road map B2. 🚶 *15,750.* ✈ 🚌
⚑ *286 N. Main St. (435) 586-5124.*

Founded in 1851 by
Mormons, this town
developed as a center for
mining and smelting iron in
the latter part of the 19th
century. Today, peaceful
Cedar City offers a choice of
hotels and restaurants within
an hour's drive
of the lovely Zion
National Park
(see pp154–5).
In town, the Iron
Mission State Park
and Museum pays
tribute to the early
Mormons' indomi-
table pioneering
spirit and features an extensive
collection of more than 300
wagons and early vehicles,
including an original Wells
Fargo overland stagecoach.
Cedar City's Shakespeare
Festival, which runs annually
from June to October, is
staged in a replica of London's
neo-Elizabethan Globe
Theatre and attracts large
audiences from the area.

Petrified ancient sand pipes rising out of the desert in the Kodachrome Basin State Park

An ATV (all-terrain vehicle) rider at the Coral Pink Sand Dunes State Park

Around 15 miles (24 km) east of the town, along Hwy 14, **Cedar Breaks National Monument** features a small but spectacular array of vibrant pink and orange limestone cliffs, topped by deep green forest. Carved by erosion out of the ancient Markagunt Plateau, sculpted columns rise in ranks of color, resembling a smaller, less-visited version of Bryce Canyon *(see pp152–3)*. In winter the monument closes, but the area remains a popular destination for cross-country skiing enthusiasts.

Cedar Breaks National Monument
(435) 586-9451. ☐ *daily. Visitor center* ☐ *May–Oct: 8am–6pm daily.*

Zion National Park ⑮

See pp154–5.

Kanab ⑯

Road map B2. 🏃 *3,900.* ⓘ *78 South 100 St. E. (520) 644-5033.* ☐ *May to Sep: 8am–6pm daily; Mar, Apr & Oct: Mon–Sat 8am–6pm; Nov–Feb: 9am–5pm Mon–Fri.*

This small town was named originally for Fort Kanab, built in 1864 but abandoned two years later because of frequent Indian attacks. Today's Kanab was established in 1874 by Mormon settlers. The town's main occupation these days is offering reasonably priced food and accommodations to vacationers traveling between Grand Canyon, Zion, and Bryce Canyon National Parks. Often referred to as the "gateway to Lake Powell," Kanab is also known as Utah's "Little Hollywood", a reference to the 200 or so movies and TV shows that have been filmed in and around the town over the past 40 years *(see pp30–31)*. Details of film sets open to the public may be obtained from the visitor center.

Environs: About 10 miles (16 km) west of Kanab and a few miles from the small town of Mount Carmel Junction, the **Coral Pink Sand Dunes State Park** is a sea of ever-shifting pink dunes that cover more than 3,000 acres (1,200 ha). This distinctive, harsh desert landscape was created when wind eroded the rich red sandstone cliffs surrounding the site, slowly depositing sand in the valley below. Interpretive signs relate the story of the dunes' geological formation. A path leads out into the dunes, allowing young and old alike to experience the thrill of sliding down the face of a huge sand dune. The park is a popular destination for riders of ATVs (all-terrain vehicles) and dune buggies.

Coral Pink Sand Dunes State Park
(435) 648-2800. ☐ *Dawn–dusk daily.*

St. George ⑰

Road map B2. 🏃 *40,000.* ✈ 🚍
ⓘ *97 E. St. George St. (435) 628-1658. Visitor center* ☐ *9am–5pm Mon–Fri; 9am–1pm Sat.*

Established in 1861 by Mormons *(see pp136–7)*, St. George has recently experienced a population boom as retirees from all over the US discover its mild climate and tranquil atmosphere. The towering gold spire that can be seen over the city belongs to Utah's first Mormon Temple, finished in 1877. A beloved project of Mormon leader and visionary Brigham Young (1801–77), it remains a key site. Only Mormons are allowed inside the temple, but the visitor center, which relates its history, is open to all. St. George's association with Brigham Young began when he decided to build a winter home here in 1871. The elegant and spacious **Brigham Young Winter Home Historic Site** is now a museum and has preserved much of its first owner's original furnishings.

Five miles (8 km) northwest of town on Hwy 18 lies Snow Canyon State Park. The park features hiking trails that lead to volcanic caves and million-year-old-lava flows. A paved bike path leads through the park and back to St. George.

Brigham Young Winter Home Historic Site
89 West St. N. *(435) 673-2517.* ☐ *Jun–Sep: 9am–8pm daily; Sep–May: 9am–6pm daily.* ● *Dec 25, Jan 1.*

Façade of Brigham Young's winter home in St. George

Lake Powell and Glen Canyon National Recreation Area ⑪

THE GLEN CANYON National Recreation Area (NRA) was established in 1972 and covers more than one million acres of dramatic desert and canyon country around the 185-mile- (298-km-) long Lake Powell. The lake was created by damming the Colorado River and its tributaries in order to supply electricity to the region's growing population. The recreation area is "Y"-shaped, following the San Juan River east almost to the town of Mexican Hat and heading northeast along the Colorado toward Canyonlands National Park (see pp142–3). Today, the lake is busy with watersports enthusiasts and touring houseboats. Glen Canyon is also one of the most popular hiking, biking, and 4WD destinations in the US.

Rainbow Bridge National Monument
Rising 290 ft (88 m) above Lake Powell, Rainbow Bridge is the largest natural arch in North America, only accessible by boat from Wahweap or Bullfrog marinas.

General View of Lake Powell
The blue waters of the man-made Lake Powell are encircled by colorful sandstone coves – once Glen Canyon's side canyons – and dramatic buttes and mesas.

Glen Canyon Dam was completed in 1963 and rises 710 ft (213 m) above the bedrock of the Colorado River.

Antelope Canyon
Bands of sandstone curve sinuously together, sometimes just a few feet apart, in this famously deep "slot" canyon.

TO GRAND CANYON

Lees Ferry was a Mormon settlement in the 19th century. Today, this outpost offers tourist facilities, including a ranger station and campground.

Wahweap Marina
*One of the best ways of
touring the area is by boat;
Wahweap Marina
offers tours and
boat hire.*

TO
CANYONLANDS
NP

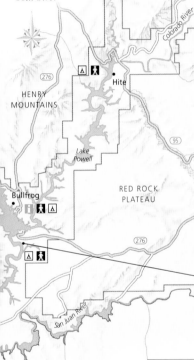

276

Hite

HENRY
MOUNTAINS

95

*Lake
Powell*

RED ROCK
PLATEAU

Bullfrog

276

San Juan River

VISITORS' CHECKLIST

Road map C2. 2m (3 km) N. of
Page on Hwy 98, off Hwy 160.
🖪 *Carl Hayden Visitor Center,
Page (520) 608-6404.*
ⓦ *www. nps.gov/glca*
☒ *to Page, Bullfrog Marina.*
◯ *Apr–Oct: 9am–6pm daily;
Nov–Mar: 8am–5pm daily.* &
visitor center only. 🖌 🖫 🍴 🕎
Ⓐ *Page and Wahweap only.*

Kayaking on Lake Powell
*On summer weekends, the lake is a
busy place as powerboats, waterskiers,
houseboat parties, jetskis, and cata-
marans explore its myriad sandstone
side canyons. The Colorado river float
trips, available below Glen Canyon
dam, are a special attraction.*

Halls Crossing has a
marina and is the starting
point for the regular ferry
service to Bullfrog Bay.

0 km   20

0 miles   20

KEY

— Highway

— Unpaved road

🏃 Ranger station

Ⓐ Campground/RV

🛈 Visitor information

☆ Viewpoint

CANYON CONTROVERSY

The completion of Glen Canyon
dam in 1963 flooded the area
described by explorer John Wesley
Powell (*see p25*) as "a curious
ensemble of wonderful features."
Controversial from the start, the
project spurred the environmen-
talist Sierra Club to campaign
against the original plans. Today,
they continue to argue for the
restoration of Glen Canyon,
believing that ancient ecosystems
are being ruined. Pro-dam advo-
cates point out the value of the
dam's ability to store water, generate power, and provide recreation.

**Lake Powell behind
vast Glen Canyon Dam**

Bryce Canyon National Park ⑬

A SERIES OF deep amphitheaters filled with flame-colored rock formations called hoodoos are the hallmark of Bryce Canyon National Park. Bryce is high in altitude, reaching elevations of 8,000–9,000 ft (2,400–2,700 m), with a scenic road traveling for 18 miles (30 km) along the rim of Paunsaugunt Plateau. The highlights here are the views of vast fields of pink, orange, and red spires; the Paiute Indians, once hunters here, described them as "red rocks standing like men in a bowl-shaped recess." The canyon's maze of pillars and channels is best appreciated on foot.

• Shakespear Point

• Mossy Cave

PINK CLIFFS

Fairyland Point

Queen's Garden Trail

Navajo Loop Trail

Sunrise Point

From this lookout it is easy to see why early settler and Mormon farmer Ebenezer Bryce, after whom the park is named, called it "a helluva place to lose a cow."

Thor's Hammer

Carved into the pink cliffs of the highest "step" of the Grand Staircase (see p148), this unusual landscape consists of eroded sandstone. Hoodoos such as Thor's Hammer are formed as rain and wind erode "fins" of harder rock that become columns, then further erode into strangely shaped hoodoos. The high altitude, ice, and wind continue the "carving" process today.

Sunset Point is one of the major lookouts in Bryce Canyon. In spite of its name it faces east, so while sunrises can be spectacular here, sunsets can be a little anticlimactic.

KEY

━━ Highway

▪▪ Hiking route

🚶 Ranger station

Ⓐ Campground/RV

Picnic area

ℹ Visitor information

☀ Viewpoint

Navajo Loop

This 1.4-mile (2-km) round-trip trail zig-zags sharply down the cliff face for 500 ft (150 m) to finish in a slow meander among slot canyons and rock stands. The climb back up the trail is particularly strenuous.

Bryce Amphitheater
This panoramic vista of snow-covered rock spires, is among the most popular views of the park. In both winter and summer the amphitheater is best seen from Inspiration Point.

VISITORS' CHECKLIST

Road map B2. Hwy 63 off Hwy 12. 🛈 *Bryce Canyon National Park, P.O. Box 170001, UT 84717–0001 (435) 834-5322.*
W *www.nps.gov/brca.*
X *Bryce Canyon Airport.*
○ *year round, daily. Visitor center* ○ *8am–4.30pm daily.*
● *Thanksgiving, Dec 25, Jan 1.*
🖾 ♿ *not on public hols.*
🖉 🍴 🛉 △

• Bryce
Point

Paria
View

PINK CLIFFS

• Swamp
Canyon
Butte

• Noon
Canyon
Butte

Natural Bridge
This graceful natural bridge is located a few yards from the park's scenic highway. It frames a picturesque view of the distant valley far below. Officially, it is a natural arch and not a bridge, as it was formed not by a river, but by the same natural forces (of wind, rain, and ice) that created the park's hoodoos.

Agua Canyon
This overlook features some of the most delicate and beautiful of the park's formations, as well as a good view of the layered pink sandstone cliffs typical of the Paunsaugunt Plateau.

Rainbow
Point

Ponderosa
Canyon

Yovimba
Point

PINK CLIFFS

0 km   2
0 miles   2

Utah Prairie Dog
Now endangered, the Utah prairie dog lives only in southern Utah: the 130 rodents that live in the park today are the largest remaining group.

Zion National Park ⑮

ZION CANYON lies at the heart of this beautiful national park and is arguably the most popular of all of Utah's natural wonders. The canyon was carved by the powerful waters of the Virgin River and then widened, sculpted, and reshaped by wind, rain, and ice. The canyon walls rise up to 2,000 ft (600 m) on both sides, and are shaped into jagged peaks and formations in shades of red and white.

Wild-flowers

The park shuttle is the only way into the canyon from April to November. Shuttles run every few minutes with numerous stops along the way. A number of short walks beginning at the stops follow marked trails to the tough 16-mile (26-km) hike through the canyon. The hike involves wading through the Virgin River.

Horseback and Mule Tours
Half- and full-day mule- and horseback tours follow several trails in the park. The Sand Bench Trail leads to a high plateau that offers fine vistas.

River Walk
At the end of Zion Canyon Scenic Drive lies the park's most popular trail. Involving no climbing, the 1.3-mile- (2-km-) paved River Walk follows the Virgin River to where the canyon walls rise to over 2,000 ft (600 m). The gentle trail offers beautiful views of the river as it winds between the canyon's red sandstone walls.

EXPLORING ZION CANYON

A guided trail takes visitors along the 6-mile (10-km) scenic road that follows the Virgin River into the ever-narrowing canyon. In summer a shuttle bus operates along the Zion Canyon and Zion-to-Mt. Carmel routes, the two major scenic drives in the park.

KEY

═ Highway

-- Hiking trail

🚹 Ranger station

Ⓐ Campground/RV

0 meters 500

0 yards 500

Weeping Rock

Emerald Pools

The Great Arch

Zion Canyon Visitor Center 🚹

South Entrance 🚹

SPRINGDALE

ZION CANYON

The lower reaches of the Virgin River meander quietly through the banks of cottonwood, oak, and willow trees that grow beneath the gradually sloping walls at the start of the canyon. The river bank is bordered with wild meadows that, in spring, sport a profusion of wild flowers. However, sudden summer rainstorms may cause floods and areas of the park near the river to be closed. Visitors are advised to check conditions first.

Hiking

Numerous guided walking and hiking tours of Zion's geology and history leave daily from the new visitor center. Popular trails are Emerald Pools Trail and Canyon Overlook Trail, which leads to the Great Arch.

VISITORS' CHECKLIST

Road map 2B. Hwy 9, near Springdale. 🛈 *Zion Canyon Visitor Center (435) 772-3256.* 🌐 *www.nps.gov/zion* ⭘ *late Mar–early Nov: 8am–8pm daily; early Nov–late Mar: 8am–5pm daily.* 🅿 🚻 *partial.* 🎟 📷 🏪 🍴 ⛺

Sculpted monoliths of rock rise above the Virgin River as it flows along the canyon.

Weeping Rock
An easy, self-guided trail leads to the rock and its hanging gardens, which are full of wildflowers in spring. This spot owes its fertility to the spring and seep-water that flows from the rock.

Luxuriant foliage along the banks of the Virgin River provides shade for the area's abundant wildlife, including birds, mule deer, and bobcats.

The Virgin River seems gentle, but the force of its current is responsible for forming the canyon.

Zion–Mt. Carmel Highway

One of the loveliest routes in the park, the Zion–Mt. Carmel highway leads upward in a set of hairpin switchbacks with splendid views back into the canyon and up to the pastel-colored sandstone of the surrounding peaks.

THE FOUR CORNERS

Exploring The Four Corners

THE FOUR CORNERS REGION is the only place in the United States where four states meet at a single point. Here, parts of Utah, Colorado, Arizona, and New Mexico make up an area of national monuments and parks, ancient ruins, and dramatic canyonlands, many set on Native American reservations. World-famous vistas include the buttes of Monument Valley, and Colorado's San Juan Skyway, where both the highway and the Durango-Silverton Narrow Gauge Railroad travel through picturesque old alpine towns.

The Keet Seel ruins at the Navajo National Monument in Arizona

One of the distinctive buttes, known as "the Mittens" in Monument Valley

GETTING AROUND

One of the least populated regions in the US, a
private car is essential for getting around the Four
Corners; a high-clearance 4WD vehicle is recommended for traveling many interesting, unpaved
regional roads. Secondary (paved) highways are
generally good, while unpaved roads are catego-
rized as follows: Good roads are suitable for all
passenger cars; high clearance roads are suitable for
2 or 4WD; 4WD roads should be tackled by only
experienced drivers in high-clearance vehicles.

THE FOUR CORNERS

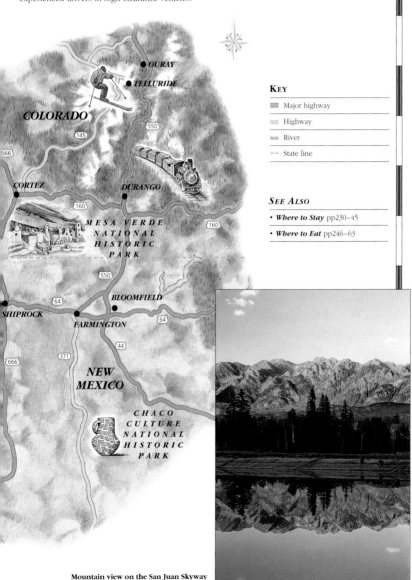

OURAY

TELLURIDE

COLORADO

145

550

666

CORTEZ

DURANGO

160

MESA VERDE
NATIONAL
HISTORIC
PARK

160

550

64

BLOOMFIELD

SHIPROCK

FARMINGTON

64

44

371

666

**NEW
MEXICO**

CHACO
CULTURE
NATIONAL
HISTORIC
PARK

KEY

▦	Major highway
▦	Highway
≈	River
--	State line

SEE ALSO

- **Where to Stay** pp230–45

- **Where to Eat** pp246–63

**Mountain view on the San Juan Skyway
between Durango and Silverton**

The Ancestral Puebloans

T HE HAUNTINGLY BEAUTIFUL and elaborate ruins left
behind by the Ancestral Puebloan people are a
key factor in the hold that this prehistoric culture has
over the public imagination. Also known as "Anasazi,"
a name coined by the Navajo meaning "Ancient
Enemy Ancestor," today they are more accurately
known as the Ancestral Puebloan people, and are
seen as the ancestors of today's Pueblo peoples.

The first Ancestral Puebloans *(see p.38)* are thought
to have settled at Mesa Verde in around AD 550, where
they lived in pithouses. By around AD 800 they had
developed masonry skills and began building housing
complexes using sandstone. From AD 1100 to 1300,
impressive levels of craftsmanship were reached in
weaving, pottery, jewelry, and tool-making.

*Ceramics, such as this bowl,
show the artistry of the Ancestral
Puebloans. Pottery is just one of
many ancient artifacts on show
in southwestern museums.*

Kivas are round pit-
like rooms dug into
the ground and roofed
with beams and earth.

*Jackson Stairway
in Chaco Canyon
is evidence of the
engineering skills
of the Ancestral
Puebloans. They
also built networks
of roads between
their communities
and extensive
irrigation systems.*

Tools *of various
types were skillfully
shaped from stone,
wood, and bone. The
Ancestral Puebloans did
not work metal, yet they
managed to produce
such beautiful artifacts
as baskets, pottery,
and jewelry.*

Bone awl

Needle

Drills

*The blue corn growing
on this Hopi Reservation
in Arizona today is a
similar plant to that
grown by Ancestral
Puebloans. They were also
skilled at utilizing the
medicinal properties of
plants, including cotton-
wood bark, which
contains a painkiller.*

The kiva *was the religious and ceremonial center of Ancestral Puebloan life. Still used by modern Pueblo Indians today, a kiva usually had no windows and the only access was through a hole in the roof. Small kivas were used by a single family unit, while large kivas were designed to accommodate the whole community.*

WHERE TO FIND ANCESTRAL PUEBLOAN RUINS

Canyon de Chelly National Monument *(see p168)*; Chaco Culture National Historical Park *(see p174)*; Mesa Verde National Park *(see page 180)*; Navajo National Monument, *(see p166)*; Hovenweep National Monument *(see p172)*.

Petroglyphs *were often used by Ancestral Puebloans as astronomical markers for the different seasons. This one was found at the Petrified Forest National Park in Arizona* (see p73).

Pueblo Bonito features many examples of the masonry skills used by the Puebloan peoples.

CHACO CANYON'S PUEBLO BONITO

At Chaco Canyon *(see pp174–5)* the largest "great house" ever built was Pueblo Bonito with more than 600 rooms and 40 kivas. One current theory is that these structures did not house populations but were, in fact, public buildings for commerce and ceremonial gatherings. The lives of the Ancestral Puebloans were short, barely 35 years, and as harsh as the environment in which they lived. Their diet was poor, and arthritis and dental problems were common. Women often showed signs of osteoporosis or brittle bones as early as their first childbirth.

THE PUEBLO PEOPLE

By AD 1300 the Ancestral Puebloans had abandoned many of their cities and migrated to areas where new centers emerged. Theories on why this occurred include a 50-year drought; the strain that a larger population placed on the desert's limited resources; and a lengthy period of social upheaval, perhaps stimulated by increasing trade with tribes as far away as central Mexico. Most archaeologists agree that the Ancestral Puebloans did not disappear but live on today in Puebloan descendants who trace their origins to Mesa Verde, Chaco, and other sacred ancestral sites.

Painstaking excavation at an Ancestral Puebloan *kiva* in Chaco Canyon

THE FOUR CORNERS

DOMINATED BY a Navajo reservation the size of Connecticut, and presenting sweeping panoramas of mesas, canyons, and vast expanses of high desert, the Four Corners is the perfect destination for those wanting to experience native culture and the real west.

Although it receives less than 10 in (25 cm) of rainfall per year, this arid land has supported life since the first Paleo-Indians arrived about 12,000 years ago. The Anasazi, today known as the Ancestral Puebloan peoples, lived here from about AD 500 until the 13th century. They are responsible for the many evocative ruins found here, including those at Mesa Verde, Chaco Canyon, and Hovenweep National Monument. Their descendants include the Hopi, whose pueblos are said to be the oldest continually occupied towns in North America. The Navajo arrived here in the 15th century and their spiritual center is Canyon de Chelly with its 1,000-ft (330-m) red rock walls.

Monument Valley's impressive landscape has been used as a backdrop for countless movies and TV shows. The region is also popular for hiking, fishing, and whitewater rafting.

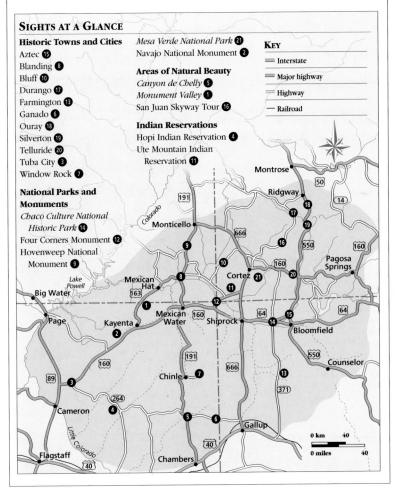

SIGHTS AT A GLANCE

Historic Towns and Cities
Aztec **15**
Blanding **8**
Bluff **10**
Durango **17**
Farmington **13**
Ganado **6**
Ouray **18**
Silverton **19**
Telluride **20**
Tuba City **3**
Window Rock **7**

National Parks and Monuments
Chaco Culture National Historic Park **14**
Four Corners Monument **12**
Hovenweep National Monument **9**
Mesa Verde National Park **21**
Navajo National Monument **2**

Areas of Natural Beauty
Canyon de Chelly **5**
Monument Valley **1**
San Juan Skyway Tour **16**

Indian Reservations
Hopi Indian Reservation **4**
Ute Mountain Indian Reservation **11**

KEY
═══ Interstate
═══ Major highway
── Highway
── Railroad

◁ **Dramatic rock formations known as "the Mittens" in the Navajo Nation's Monument Valley**

Monument Valley ●

Fᴿᴏᴍ ꜱᴄᴇɴɪᴄ ʜɪɢʜᴡᴀʏ 163, which crosses the border of Utah and Arizona, it is possible to see the famous towering sandstone buttes and mesas of Monument Valley. These ancient rocks, soaring upward from a seemingly boundless desert, have come to symbolize the American West, largely because Hollywood has used these breathtaking vistas as a backdrop for hundreds of movies, TV shows, and commercials since the 1930s *(see p30)*.

The area's visitor center sits within the boundary of Monument Valley Tribal Park, but many of the valley's spectacular rock formations and other sites are found just outside the park boundary.

Guided Tours
A row of kiosks at the visitor center offer Navajo-guided 4WD tours of the valley. The marketing tactics can be aggressive, but the tours offer an excellent way to see places in the park that are otherwise inaccessible.

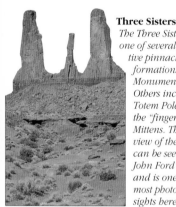

Three Sisters
The Three Sisters are one of several distinctive pinnacle rock formations at Monument Valley. Others include the Totem Pole and the "fingers" of the Mittens. The closest view of the sisters can be seen from John Ford's Point, and is one of the most photographed sights here.

Left Mitten

Art and Ruins
Petroglyphs such as this deer can be seen on Navajo-guided tours of rock art sites, which are dotted around the valley's ancient ruins.

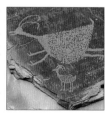

Exᴘʟᴏʀɪɴɢ Tʜᴇ Vᴀʟʟᴇʏ

The awe-inspiring beauty of Monument Valley's buttes and mesas can be viewed by travelers from Hwy 163. Visitors can also pay a fee to travel on a 17-mile (27-km) self-guided drive along a well-marked dirt road. (Fees are collected at the visitor center.) Alternatively, Navajo guides may be hired for hiking, horseback, or 4WD tours to fascinating and less-visited parts of the valley.

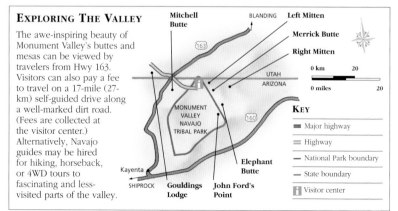

Mitchell Butte
BLANDING
Left Mitten
Merrick Butte
Right Mitten
163
0 km   20
UTAH
ARIZONA
0 miles   20
MONUMENT VALLEY NAVAJO TRIBAL PARK
160
Kᴇʏ
Kayenta
Elephant Butte
SHIPROCK Gouldings Lodge John Ford's Point

▬▬ Major highway
═══ Highway
— National Park boundary
— State boundary
🅸 Visitor center

John Ford's Point
The most popular stop along the valley drive is John Ford's Point, which is said to be the film director's favorite view of the valley. Various stands offer a range of Navajo handicrafts. A nearby native hogan *(Navajo dwelling) serves as a gift shop where Navajo weavers demonstrate their craft.*

VISITORS' CHECKLIST

Road map C2. **i** *PO Box 360289, Monument Valley. (435) 727-3353 or (435) 727-3287.* ☐ *May–Sept: 8am–7pm daily; Oct–April: 8am–5pm daily; Thanksgiving: 8am–noon.* ● *Dec 25.* 🏧 ♿ *visitor center only.* 📷 🏪 🍴 ⛺

Merrick Butte

Right Mitten

Navajo Weaver
Navajo women are usually considered to be the finest weavers in the Southwest. One rug can take months to complete and sell for thousands of dollars. Using the natural colors of the land, the weavers often add a "spirit line" to their work to prevent their spirit being "trapped" within the rug.

MONUMENT VALLEY
Monument Valley is not really a valley. The tops of the mesas mark what was once a flat plain. Millions of years ago, this plain was cracked by upheavals within the earth. The cracks widened and eroded, until all that is left today are the formations rising from the desert floor.

Gouldings Lodge
The lodge offers accommodations, a restaurant, and guided bus tours of the valley. The original trading post is now a museum of the valley's cinematic history.

Ancestral Puebloan ruins of Keet Seel at Navajo National Monument

Navajo National Monument ❷

Road map C3. [C] *(520) 672-2366.* [○] *8am–5pm daily.* [●] *Thanksgiving, Dec 25, Jan 1.* [✓] [A]

WHILE NAMED because of its location on the Navajo Reservation, this monument is actually known for its Ancestral Puebloan ruins. The most accessible ruin here is the beautifully preserved, 135-room pueblo of Betatakin, which fills a vast, curved niche in the cliffs of Tsegi Canyon. An easy one-mile (1.6-km) trail from the visitor center leads to an overlook where Betatakin is clearly visible on the far side, near the canyon floor. This is a lovely hike through piñon pines and juniper trees, and the view is captivating. From late May to early September there are daily six-hour hiking tours to Betatakin, which allow a close look at the ruins of these ancient houses.

A much more demanding 17-mile (27-km) round trip hike leads to Keet Seel, a more impressive ruin. Only a limited number of permits to

visit the ruin are issued each day. This hike requires overnight camping at a camp site with only the most basic facilities. Keet Seel was a larger and more successful community than Betatakin. Construction began on Keet Seel in about 1250, but the site is thought to have been abandoned by 1300.

These two sites are considered to mark the pinnacle of development of the area's Ancestral Puebloan people.

Tuba City ❸

Road map C3. [🏘] *17,300.* [ℹ] *Tuba City Trading Post (520) 283-5441.*

NAMED FOR TUUVI, a Hopi Indian who converted to the Mormon faith, Tuba City is best known for the 65-million-year-old dinosaur tracks found just off the main highway, 5 miles (8 km) southwest of the town. Beyond that, this is the largest community in the western section of the Navajo Reservation and is a good spot from which to explore both the Navajo National Monument and the Hopi Reservation.

Hopi Indian Reservation ❹

Road map C3. [🏘] *10,000.* [ℹ] *Highway 264, Second Mesa (520) 734-2401.* [○] *May–Sep: 8am–5pm Mon–Sat; Oct–Apr: 8am–5pm Mon–Fri & 9am–4pm Sun.*

ARIZONA'S ONLY Pueblo Indians *(see p27),* the Hopi, are believed to be direct descendants of the Ancestral Puebloan people, or Anasazi. The Hopi Reservation is surrounded by the lands of the Navajo. The landscape is harsh and barren, yet the Hopi have cultivated the land here for a thousand years. They worship, through the *kachina,* the living spirits of plants and animals, believed to arrive each year to stay with the tribe during the growing season *(see p27).* Most of the Hopi villages are located on or near one of three mesas (flat-topped elevations), named First, Second, and Third Mesa. The artisans on each of the mesas specialize in particular crafts: on First Mesa these are carved figures (representing the *kachina* spirits) and painted pottery; on Second Mesa, silver jewelry and coiled baskets are made; and on Third Mesa, craftspeople fashion wicker baskets and woven rugs.

Kachina figure

Walpi, the ancient pueblo on First Mesa, was first inhabited in the 12th century. To reach Walpi, visitors drive up to the Mesa from the Pollaca settlement to the village of Sichomovi. Nearby, the Ponsi

Historic pueblo town of Walpi on First Mesa at Hopi Indian Reservation

A range of merchandise in the general store at Hubbell Trading Post

Visitor Center is the departure point for the one-hour Walpi tours. Walpi was built to be easily defended, and straddles a dramatic knife edge of rock, extending from the tip of First Mesa. In places Walpi is less than 100 ft (33 m) wide with a drop of several hundred feet on both sides. The Walpi tour includes several stops where visitors can purchase *kachina* figurines and distinctive hand-crafted pottery, or sample the Hopi *piki* bread.

Those wishing to shop further can continue on to Second Mesa, where a range of galleries and stores offer an array of Hopi arts and crafts. The Hopi Cultural Center is home to a restaurant *(see p259)* and the only hotel *(see p241)* for miles around, as well as a museum that has an excellent collection of photographs depicting Hopi life.

On Third Mesa, Old Oraibi pueblo, thought to have been founded in the 12th century, is of note only because of claims that it is the oldest continually occupied human settlement in North America.

Walpi
(520) 737-2262. Walking tours available 9:30am–4pm daily.

Ganado and Hubbell Trading Post ❺

Road map D3. 4,500. Hubbell Trading Post, Hwy 264 (520) 755-3475.

A SMALL, BUSTLING town in the heart of the Navajo Reservation, Ganado's major attraction is the **Hubbell Trading Post National**

Historic Site. Established in the 1870s by John Lorenzo Hubbell, this is the oldest continually operating trading post in the Navajo Nation. Trading posts like this one were once the economic and social centers of the reservations. The Navajo traded sheep, wool, blankets, turquoise, and other items in exchange for tools, household goods, and food. The trading posts were also a resource during times of need. When a smallpox epidemic struck in 1886, John Lorenzo helped care for the sick, using his house as a hospital.

Navajo bracelet at Hubbell Trading Post

Today, the trading post still hums with traditional trading activities. One room is a working general store, the rafters hung with frying pans and hardware, and shelves stacked with cloth, medicines, and food. Another room is filled with beautiful hand-woven rugs, Hopi *kachina* dolls, and Navajo baskets. Another department has a long row of glass cases displaying an impressive array of silver and turquoise jewelry.

Visitors can tour Hubbell's restored home and view a significant collection of southwestern art. The visitor center features several looms where Navajo women demonstrate the art of weaving fine woolen rugs.

Hubbell Trading Post National Historic Site
A2264, near Ganado. (520) 755-3475. daily. public hols.

Window Rock ❻

Road map D3. 4,500. Highway 264 (520) 871-6413.

W INDOW ROCK is the capital of the Navajo Nation. The town is named for the natural arch found in the sandstone cliffs located about a mile north of the main strip on Hwy 12.

The **Navajo Nation Museum** located here is one of the largest Native American museums in the US. Opened in 1997, the huge hogan-shaped building houses displays that cover the history of the Ancestral Puebloans and the Navajo.

Navajo Nation Museum
Hwy 264 & Post Office Loop Rd. (520) 871-7941. 8am–5pm Mon; 8am–8pm Tue–Fri; 9am–5pm Sat.

Eroded sandstone opening of Window Rock, near Highway 12

Canyon de Chelly National Monument ❼

Flowering cactus

Few places in North America can boast a longer or more eventful history of human habitation than Canyon de Chelly. Archaeologists have found evidence of four periods of Native culture, starting with the Basketmaker people around AD 300, followed by the Great Pueblo Builders, who created the cliff dwellings in the 12th century. They were succeeded by the Hopi, who lived here seasonally for around 300 years, taking advantage of the canyon's fertile soil. In the 1700s, the Hopi left the area and moved to the mesas, returning to the canyon to farm during the summer months. Today, the canyon is the cultural and geographic heart of the Navajo Nation. Pronounced "d'Shay," de Chelly is a Spanish corruption of the Native name *Tsegi*, meaning Rock Canyon.

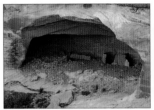

Yucca House Ruin
Perched on the mesa top, this ruin of an Ancestral Puebloan house sits in a rock hollow, precariously overhanging a sheer drop to the valley floor.

Mummy Cave Ruin
These two pueblos, separated by a central tower, were built in the 1280s by Ancestral Puebloans, who inhabited them for more than 1,000 years. An overlook provides a good view of this impressive ruin.

Stone and adobe cliff dwellings were home to the Ancestral Puebloans from the 12th to the 14th century and were built to face south toward the sun, with cooler areas within.

Navajo Fortress
This imposing rock tower was the site of a three-month siege in the early 1800s, when a group of Navajos reached the summit via pole ladders to escape the invading Spaniards. The persistence of Kit Carson (see p171) and starvation led them to surrender and they were marched to a camp in New Mexico.

Canyon Landscape
The sandstone cliffs of Canyon de Chelly reach as high as 1,000 ft (300 m), towering above the neighboring meadows and desert landscape in the distance. The canyon floor around the cliffs is fringed with cottonwood bushes, watered by the Chinle Wash.

The pale walls of the White House cliff drop 550 ft (160 m) to the canyon floor.

Hogan **Interior**
The hogan *is the center of Navajo family life. Made of horizontal logs, a smoke hole in the center provides contact with the sky, while the dirt floor gives contact with the earth. A door faces east to greet the rising sun.*

WHITE HOUSE RUINS

This group of rooms, tucked into a tiny hollow in the cliff, seem barely touched by time. The dwellings were originally situated above a larger pueblo, much of which has now disappeared. It is the only site within the canyon that can be visited without a Navajo guide, reached via a steep 2.5-mile (5-km) round-trip trail that winds to the canyon floor and offers magnificent views.

MASSACRE CAVE

The canyon's darkest hour was in 1805, when a Spanish force under Lieutenant Antonio Narbona entered the area. The Spanish wanted to subdue the Navajo, claiming they were raiding their settlements. While some Navajo fled by climbing to the canyon rim, others took refuge in a cave high in the cliffs. The Spanish fired into the cave, and Narbona boasted that he had killed 115 Navajo including 90 warriors. Navajo accounts are different, claiming that most of the warriors were absent (probably hunting) and those killed were mostly women, children, and the elderly. The only Spanish fatality came when a Spaniard attempting to climb into the cave was attacked by a Navajo woman and both plunged over the cliff, gaining the Navajo name "Two Fell Over." The Anglo name is "Massacre Cave."

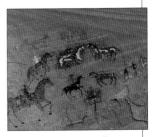

Pictograph on a canyon wall showing invading Spanish soldiers

Exploring Canyon de Chelly

Navajo ranger

CANYON DE CHELLY is startlingly different from the sparse desert landscape that spreads from its rim. Weathered red rock walls, just 30-ft- (9-m-) high at the canyon mouth, rise to more than 1,000-ft- (300-m-) high within the canyon, creating a sheltered world. Navajo *hogans (see p169)* dot the canyon floor; Navajo women tend herds of sheep and weave rugs at outdoor looms, and everywhere Ancestral Puebloan ruins add to the canyon's appeal. Navajo-led 4WD tours along the scenic North and South rims are a popular way to view the site.

Antelope House Ruin
Named for a pictograph of an antelope painted by Navajo artists in the 1830s, the oldest ruins at Antelope House date from AD 700. They can be seen from the Antelope House Overlook.

Canyon Vegetation
Within the canyon, cottonwood and oak trees line the river washes; the land itself is a fertile oasis of meadows, alfalfa and corn fields, and fruit orchards.

Map labels:
64
Chinle
7
Chinle Wash
Ledge Ruin Overlook
Standi Cc Ru
Antelope House Overlook
White House Overlook
CANYON DE CHELLY
South Rim Drive
S'idi Hou Overl

0 km   3
0 miles   3

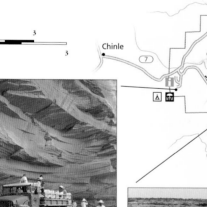

Canyon Tour
Half- and full-day tours from Thunderbird Lodge carry passengers in open flatbed or large 6WD army trucks. Of varying length and difficulty, the tours are the best way to see ruins up close.

Tsegi Overlook
This high curve along the South Rim offers good general views of the farm-studded canyon floor and surrounding landscape.

Hiking in the Canyon

Canyon de Chelly is a popular destination for hikers, but only the White House Ruins Trail may be walked without a guide. The visitor center (see p169) offers Navajo-guided hikes on trails of varying lengths.

KEY

═══	Highway
▪ ▪	Hiking route
🄰	Campground/RV
⛽	Picnic area
ℹ	Visitor information
☀	Viewpoint

TO TSAILE
WINDOW ROCK

North Rim Drive

☀ Massacre Cave Overlook

☀ Mummy Cave Overlook

Canyon del Muerto

Black Rock Canyon

Spider Rock Overlook ☀

⑦

Spider Rock

Rising more than 800 ft (245 m), Navajo legends say it was here that Spider Woman lived and gave them the skill of weaving.

KIT CARSON AND THE "LONG WALK"

In 1863, the US government sent Kit Carson under the command of General James A. Carlton to settle the problem of Navajo raids. To avoid outright slaughter Carson led his soldiers through the region, destroying villages and livestock as the Navajo fled ahead of them. In January 1864 Carson entered Canyon de Chelly, capturing the Navajo hiding there. In 1864, they were among 9,000 Navajo who were driven on the "Long Walk," a forced march of 370 miles (595 km) from Fort Defiance to Bosque Redondo in New Mexico. There, in a pitiful reservation, more than 3,000 Navajo died before the US government accepted the resettlement as a failure and allowed them to return to the Four Corners.

Fur trapper and soldier Kit Carson (1809–68)

Dramatic mesas and buttes in the Valley of the Gods near Bluff

Bluff ⑧

Road Map D2. 🏃 300. 🛈 San Juan Visitor Center, 117 S. Main St. Monticello. (800) 574-4386. Ⓐ

THE CHARMING TOWN of Bluff was settled in 1880 by the Mormons of "Hole-in-the-Rock-Road" fame *(see p147)*. Bluff's central location makes it a good base for exploring Utah's southeast corner. Float trips along the gentle San Juan River include stops at Ancestral Pueblo ruins that can be reached only by boat.

ENVIRONS: About 12 miles (20 km) north of town, a marked turn leads onto the 17-mile (27-km) dirt road through the Valley of the Gods. Like a smaller version of Monument Valley *(see pp164–65)*, this place features high rock spires, buttes, and mesas, but none of the crowds. On a quiet day visitors may have the place all to themselves and be able to imagine what the land looked like to the first settlers.

Blanding ⑨

Road Map D2. 🏃 3,800. 🛈 Edge of Cedars, State Park Museum, 660 W 400 N. (435) 678-2238. Ⓐ

A TIDY MORMON town at the base of the Abajo Mountains, Blanding is home to the Edge of Cedars State Park. The park contains modest Ancestral Puebloan ruins, including a small *kiva*, or religious chamber, which is open to visitors. The highlight is the

park museum, which has well thought-out displays on the history of these ancient people and other cultures that have inhabited the region.

Hovenweep National Monument ⑩

Road Map D2. East of Hwy 191. 📞 (970) 562-4282. ⏰ May–Sep: 8am–4pm daily; Sep–May 8am–4pm Mon–Fri. ● Thanksgiving, Dec 25, Jan 1. 🈺 ✔ Ⓐ.

ONE OF THE MOST mysterious Ancestral Puebloan sites in the Southwest, the ruins at Hovenweep lie along the rim of a shallow canyon on a remote high plateau in the southwest corner of Colorado. These well-preserved ruins, which include unique round, square, and D-shaped towers, have neither been restored nor rebuilt. Indeed, they look much as they did when W.D. Huntington, leader of a Mormon expedition, first came upon the site in 1854. The site was named later in 1874, after

an Ute word meaning "Deserted Valley." The culture here reached its peak between 1200 and 1275. Little is known of these people beyond the clues found in the pottery and tools that they left behind. Researchers have speculated on the purpose of the towers at Hovenweep and have suggested that they might have been defensive fortifications, astronomical observatories, storage silos, or the community's religious structures.

The six separate sets of ruins at Hovenweep can be visited by walking along either of the two self-guiding trails that link them.

Ute Mountain Tribal Park ⑪

Road Map D2. 🛈 Junction of Highway 160 and Highway 666. (800) 847-5485. ⏰ Apr–Oct: 8am–3:30pm daily. 🈺 ✔ obligatory.

THE RUINS of Ute Mountain Tribal Park are one of the better kept secrets of the Southwest. The Ancestral Puebloan people first arrived in this region in about AD 400.

Ancient brick tower at Hovenweep National Monument

They closely followed the Mesa Verde *(see pp180–81)* pattern of development, eventually creating numerous magnificent cliff dwellings, including the 80-room Lion House. These ruins have few visitors because of their inaccessibility. Those wishing to see them must use their own vehicles and join the dusty, half- or full-day tours led by local Ute guides.

Four Corners Monument Navajo Tribal Park ⑫

Road Map D2. *Junction of Hwys 160 and 41.* ⬛ *(520) 871-6647.* ⬜ *May–Aug: 7am–8pm; Sep–Apr: 8am–5pm.* ⬛ *Thanksgiving, Dec 25.* 🎫 ♿

THERE IS SOMETHING oddly compelling about being able to put one foot and hand in each of four states. It is fun to watch visitors try this. It is the whole premise of the Four Corners Monument – the only place in the US where four states meet at one point.

Chaco Culture National Historical Park ⑬

See pp174–75.

Farmington ⑭

Road Map D2. 🏘 *40,000.* ✈ ⬜ 🛈 *3041 E. Main St. (505) 326-7602.*

A DUSTY, HARD-WORKING ranch town, Farmington is a good base for exploring the surrounding monuments. It is also home to one of the most unusual museums in the Southwest. The **Bolack Museum of Fish and Wildlife** covers over 30,000 sq ft (2,800 sq m) and houses the largest accumulation of mounted game animals in the world collected over 70 years by wealthy oilman and rancher Tom Bolack. The interior is divided into nine themed game rooms, including African, Asian, European, and Russian. The **Farmington Museum** focuses on the local

history and geology of this area and features a popular children's gallery with several interactive exhibits.

ENVIRONS: 25 miles (40 km) west of Farmington is Shiprock, named for the spectacular 1,500-ft (457-m) rock peak that thrusts up from the valley floor about 5 miles (8 km) west of town. To the Navajo, this rock is sacred, and to early Anglo-American settlers it was a landmark visible for many miles that reminded them of a ship's prow, hence the name. Now it is only possible for sightseers to observe the peak from the roadsides of Hwys 64 or 33.

Eight miles (12 km) south, are the **Salmon Ruins**, which were once an outlying Chaco settlement. These ruins are particularly notable as they were protected from grave diggers by the Salmon family, who homesteaded here in the 1870s. As a result, a century later archaeologists recovered more than a million artifacts, many of which are on display in the excellent museum at the site. Outside the museum, trails lead to both the Salmon homestead and the ruins, the walls of which show the exceptional level of skill of these ancient stonemasons.

🏛 Bolack Museum
3901 Bloomfield Hwy. ⬛ *(435) 678-2238.* ⬜ *9am–3pm Mon–Sat, appointment only.* 🎫 ♿ 🎥 *obligatory.*

🏛 Farmington Museum
3041 E. Main St. ⬛ *(435) 678-2238.* ⬜ *9am–3pm Mon–Sat, by prior appointment only.* 🎫 ♿ 🎥

♠ Salmon Ruins
6131 Hwy 64. ⬛ *(505) 632-2013.* ⬜ *Apr–Oct: 8am–5pm Mon–Sat, noon–5pm Sun; Nov–Mar: 8am–5pm Mon–Sat, noon–5pm Sun.* 🎫 ♿ 🎥 *hourly on weekends in summer.*

Interior of the Great Kiva at Ancestral Puebloan Salmon Ruins

Aztec ⑮

Road Map D2. 🏘 *6,000.* 🛈 *110 Ash St. (505) 334-9551.*

THE SMALL TOWN of Aztec was named for its ruins, which are Ancestral Puebloan and not Aztec as early settlers believed. Preserved as a national monument, the site's 500-room pueblo was a flourishing settlement in the late 1200s. Visitors entering the large rebuilt *kiva* may imagine the complex religious rituals that once took place here.

♠ Aztec Ruins National Monument
Hwy 516. ⬛ *(505) 334-6174.* ⬜ *daily.* 🎫 ♿ 🎥

The spectacular red peak of Shiprock near Farmington

Chaco Culture National Historical Park ⑬

Arrowhead at Chaco Museum

CHACO CANYON IS one of the most impressive cultural sites in the Southwest, reflecting the sophistication of the Ancestral Puebloan civilization that existed here. With its six "great houses" (pueblos containing hundreds of rooms) and many lesser sites, the canyon was once the political, religious, and cultural center for settlements that covered much of the Four Corners. At its peak during the 11th century, Chaco was one of the most impressive pre-Columbian cities in North America. Despite its size, it is thought that Chaco's population was small because the land could not have supported a larger community. Archaeologists believe that the city was mainly used as a ceremonial gathering place, with a year-round population of less than 3,000. Probably the social elite, the inhabitants supported themselves largely by trading.

Architectural Detail
Chaco's skilled builders had only stone tools to work with to create this finely wrought stonework.

The many kivas here were probably used by visitors arriving for religious ceremonies.

PUEBLO BONITO

Pueblo Bonito is an example of a "great house." Begun around AD 850, it was built in stages over the course of 300 years. This reconstruction shows how it might have looked, with its D-shaped four-story structure that contained more than 650 rooms.

Chetro Ketl
A short trail from Pueblo Bonito leads to another great house, Chetro Ketl. Almost as large as Pueblo Bonito, at 3 sq acres (2 ha), Chetro Ketl has more than 500 rooms. The masonry used to build the later portions of this structure is among the most sophisticated found in any Ancestral Puebloan site.

Casa Rinconada
Also known as a great kiva, Casa Rinconada is the largest religious chamber at Chaco, measuring 62 ft (19 m) in diameter. It was used for spiritual gatherings.

Pueblo Alto
Pueblo Alto was built atop the mesa at the junction of several ancient Chacoan roads. Reaching the site requires a two-hour hike, but the views over the canyon are well worth it.

VISITORS' CHECKLIST

Road map 3D. 3 m (5 km) S.E. of Nageezi off Hwy 44/550.
🛈 Chaco Culture Visitor Center (505) 786-7014.
🅦 www.nps.gov/chcu.
🕐 May–Sep: 8am–6pm daily; Sep–May: 8am–5pm daily.
⬤ Public hols. 🎫 🐾 📷

This great house was four stories high.

Early Astronomers at Fajada Butte
Measurement of time was vital to the Chacoans for crop planting and the timing of ceremonies. A spiral petroglyph, carved on Fajada Butte, is designed to indicate the changing seasons through the shadows it casts on the rock.

EXPLORING CHACO

The site is accessed via a 20-mile (32-km) dirt road that is affected by flash floods in wet weather. Drivers can tour the site on the paved loop road that passes several of Chaco's highlights. There is parking near Pueblo del Arroyo. From the visitor center, a trail leads to the Una Vida great house.

KEY

═	Highway
═	Unpaved road
--	Hiking route
🅐	Campground/RV
🏞	Picnic area
🛈	Visitor information

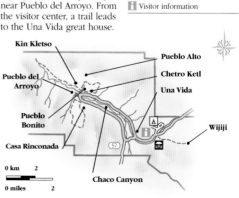

Kin Kletso
Pueblo Alto
Pueblo del Arroyo
Chetro Ketl
Una Vida
Pueblo Bonito
Wijiji
Casa Rinconada
57
Chaco Canyon

0 km 2
0 miles 2

Hundreds of rooms within Pueblo Bonito show little sign of use and are thought to have been kept for storage or for guests arriving to take part in ceremonial events.

Alta Lake surrounded by pine forests near San Juan in Southern Colorado ▷

San Juan Skyway Tour ⓰

THE SAN JUAN SKYWAY is a 236-mile (380-km) loop through some of America's finest scenery. The route travels three highways (550, 145, and 160) over the San Juan Mountains, past 19th-century mining towns and through forests and canyons. There are 14 peaks above 14,000 ft (4,200 m). Between Silverton and Ouray the road is also known as the Million Dollar Highway, having been named for the gold-rich gravel used in the road's construction or, according to another theory, because the road was expensive to build.

Tips for Drivers

Tour Route: *Highway 550 from Durango, then 145 and 160.*
Length: *236 miles (380 km).*
Stopping-off points: *Ridgeway State Park on Hwy 550 offers great views of the San Juan Mountains.*

Telluride ④
Smaller than the ski resorts of Aspen and Vail, Telluride's gentrified Western persona attracts both wealthy jet setters and serious skiers.

Ouray ③
Another very Western mining town with a history similar to Silverton's, Ouray has the added attraction of the Ouray Hot Springs.

Atlas Lake ⑤
One of many lovely alpine lakes to be found along the San Juan Skyway, Atlas Lake lies south of Telluride and just north of the high-mountain Lizard Head Pass.

Dolores ⑥
Two 12th-century Ancestral Pueblos have been preserved here as part of the Anasazi Heritage Center, together with a museum on pueblo life.

MONTROSE
Ridgway
62
Placerville
3
4
5
Ophir
Animas River
2
145
Rico
550
Dolores River
Stoner
SAN JUAN NATIONAL FOREST
6
184
Mancos River
La Plata River
160
1
FARMINGTON
0 km 10
0 miles 10

THE
FRENCH QUARTER
CAFE

Silverton ②
Silver was discovered here in 1874. Today, this classic frontier town is the scene of daily mock gunfights along Blair Street.

Durango ①
The start of the Durango and Silverton steam train trip, the town of Durango has a charming Victorian district and hot springs.

Key

- Tour route
- Other roads

Spectacular views of the Rockies from Telluride's main street

Telluride ⓱

Road map D2. 🏔 1550. ✈ 🚌
ℹ 700 W. Colorado Ave. (970) 728-4431; (800) 525-3455. ◯ daily.

ONCE A MINING town like Silverton, today Telluride is a noted ski resort, as popular with Hollywood celebrities as the equally famous Aspen in northern Colorado. Its late-Victorian center boasts upscale ski shops, boutiques, and restaurants. Yet Telluride retains its authentic charm; it is still possible to imagine the days when the notorious outlaw Butch Cassidy, who robbed his first bank in 1889, lived here.

The ski resort's exclusive Mountain Village lies across a mountain ridge easily reached by a 12-minute gondola ride. In winter, there is a variety of winter sports. In summer, there are walks and riding trails in the beautiful mountain scenery, and fishing in local lakes and rivers. The town also hosts an annual international film festival.

Ouray ⓲

Road map D2. 🏔 800. ℹ 1230 North Main St. (970) 325-4746; (800) 228-1876. ◯ daily.

THE WONDERFULLY preserved old mining town of Ouray lies 23 miles (37 km) north of Silverton on Hwy 550. Its stunning setting, amid mountain peaks, has made it a popular

base for hikers and 4WD enthusiasts. To the north of town the Ouray Hot Springs are a popular form of relaxation. To the south, a loop road leads to Box Canyon Falls Park. A short trail leads across a swinging bridge to the falls' dramatic cascade.

Silverton ⓳

Road map D2. 🏔 505. ℹ 414 Greene St. (800) 752-4494. 🅰

SILVERTON IS set among snow-covered peaks, and is one of the best preserved 19th-century mining towns in the Southwest. The entire town is registered as a National Historic Landmark, and the façades along Blair Street have altered little since the days of the 1880s silver-mining boom that gave the town its name. On Greene Street, most of the buildings date from the late 19th and early 20th centuries, including the 1902 County Jail, which houses the **San Juan County Historical Museum**, devoted to the town's mining history. Greene Street East leads 13 miles (21 km) north to the ghost town of Animas Forks – abandoned after the mines ran out of silver.

Plaque from Silverton County Jail

🏛 **San Juan County Historical Museum**
1512 Greene St. 📞 (970) 387-5838. ◯ Late May–mid-Oct: 9am–5pm daily. ● Late Oct–mid-May. ♿

Durango ⓴

Road map D2. 🏔 14,700. ✈ 🚌
ℹ 111 S. Camino del Rio (970) 247-0312; (800) 525-8855. ◯ May–Sep: 8am–6pm Mon–Sat; 10am–4pm Sun.

DURANGO IS A lovely town with shady tree-lined streets and splendid Victorian architecture. Its attractive setting, on the banks of the Animas River, draws increasing numbers of residents, making the town the largest community in this part of Colorado. It is famous as the starting point of the **Durango and Silverton Narrow Gauge Railroad**, perhaps the most scenic train ride in the US. A 1920s coal-fired steam train ferries more than 200,000 visitors each year along the Animas River valley, up steep gradients through canyons and mountain scenery, to Silverton. Passengers may choose to ride in either Victorian or open-sided "gondola" cars that offer great views. The 3.5-hour train trip makes several stops along the way, allowing hikers and anglers access to the pristine backcountry of the San Juan National Forest. A good time to make the trip is September when fall colors cover the mountainsides. This is a popular attraction, and booking ahead is recommended.

🚂 **Durango and Silverton Narrow Gauge Railroad**
479 Main Ave. 📞 (970) 247-2733; reservations (888) 872-4607. ◯ daily, year round; call for times.

Steam train on Durango and Silverton Narrow Gauge Railroad

Mesa Verde National Park ㉑

THIS HIGH, FORESTED mesa overlooking the
Montezuma Valley was home to the Ancestral
Puebloan people *(see p38)* for more than 700
years. Within canyons that cut through the mesa
are some of the best preserved and most elaborate
cliff dwellings built by these people. Mesa Verde,
meaning "Green Table," was a name given to the
area by the Spanish in the 1700s, but the ruins were
not widely known until the late 19th century. This
site provides a fascinating record of these people
from the Basketmaker period, beginning around
AD 550, to the complex society that built the
many-roomed cliff dwellings between
1000 and 1250. Displays at the Far View
Visitor Center and the Chapin Mesa
Museum provide a good introduction.

Spruce Tree House
*Tucked into a cliff niche, these
three-story structures were probably
home to as many as 100 people.*

Guided Tours
*Ranger-led tours give visitors a chance to
actually enter the ruins and get a feel for
the daily lives of these ancient people.*

CLIFF PALACE
With 150 rooms, this is the largest Ancestral
Puebloan cliff dwelling found anywhere, and is
the site that most visitors focus on. The
location and symmetry suggest that architecture
was important to the builders. Begun around
1150, it was vacated in around 1275.

HWY 160

Morefield Village

Far View
Visitor Center

Spruce
Tree
House

Wetherill
Mesa

Chapin
Mesa
Museum

Cliff Palace

Balcony House

MESA VERDE NATIONAL PARK

Most visitors start at Chapin Mesa, which has
the highest concentration of sites. A paved
scenic drive leads around the mesa and
overlooks offer excellent views.

KEY

▭	Scenic route
ℹ️	Visitor information
🚶	Ranger station
▬	Park boundary

0 km		5
0 miles		5

Balcony House
Possibly built for defense, Balcony House could not be seen from above, and access was (and still is) difficult. Visitors on tours must climb three ladders high above the canyon floor, then crawl through an access tunnel.

VISITORS' CHECKLIST

Road map D2. ▓ *PO Box 8, Mesa Verde (970) 529-4465.* ✗ *Cortez.* ◯ *Far View Visitor Center: late Apr–late Oct: 8am–5pm daily. Chapin Mesa Archaeological Museum* ◯ *daily.* 🗓 🏔 🚻 🖼 🏪 🍴

Towers were probably used as food storage areas or as lookouts for defense.

Square Tower House
This cliff site once contained 80 rooms and features a unique four-story square tower. When it was studied early in the 20th century, the tower was damaged, and the left corner had to be rebuilt from the ground up to stabilize the site.

The 23 *kivas* or religious rooms at this site are thought to indicate that there were 23 families or clans living here.

Weatherill Mesa Long House
A scenic 12-mile (17-km) drive on a winding mountain road leads to Weatherill Mesa, named for the local rancher, Richard Weatherill, who found Cliff Palace in the 1880s. Two cliff dwellings here, Step and Long houses, are open to visitors.

NEW MEXICO

Introducing New Mexico

NEW MEXICO'S SCENIC beauty, rich cultural heritage, and unique mix of Native American, Hispanic, and Anglo-American people make it a fascinating place to visit. The forested peaks of the Rocky Mountains in the north offer ski resorts in winter and cool retreats in the hot summers. Northern New Mexico is also noted for its quality of light, with stark shadows and soft colors that have attracted generations of artists to the region, especially to the creative centers of Santa Fe and Taos. Albuquerque is the state's centrally located bustling capital, and, to the south, visitors can explore ancient Native ruins at Bandelier National Monument, as well as such natural wonders as the gleaming dunes of White Sands National Monument and the cave systems of Carlsbad Caverns.

Adobe in Albuquerque's Old Town *(see pp210–11).*

KEY

▬	Interstate
▬	Major highway
▬	Highway
≈	River

SEE ALSO

- **Where to Stay** pp241–245
- **Where to Eat** pp260–263

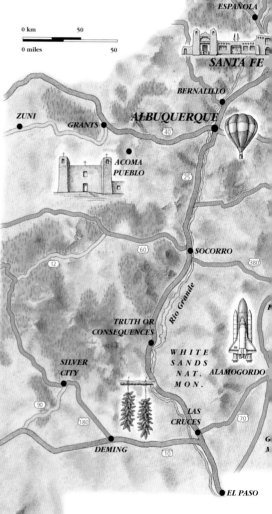

GETTING AROUND

New Mexico has two major Interstate Highways, I-25 and I-40, which cross each other in Albuquerque. Interstate 25 cuts north into Colorado and south into Mexico. Interstate 40 cuts east to west, into Texas and Arizona respectively. To the south, Interstate 10 connects the city of Las Cruces with Arizona. Albuquerque airport is New Mexico's main hub for both international and domestic flights. Greyhound buses run from Albuquerque to Santa Fe and Taos.

SANTA FE AND NORTHERN NEW MEXICO

ALBUQUERQUE AND SOUTHERN NEW MEXICO

CIMARRON

OS

KIOWA NATIONAL GRASSLANDS

SANGRE DE CRISTO MOUNTAINS

LAS VEGAS

25

39

104

40

TUCUMCARI

60

54

Pecos River

70

285

NCOLN TIONAL REST

ROSWELL

82

CARLSBAD

UPE AINS

Ancestral Puebloan cliff dwellings at Bandelier National Monument *(see p200)*

Soaptree yucca plant growing among the dunes at White Sands National Monument *(see p223)*

The Atomic Age

DURING WORLD WAR II, fears that the Germans were
developing an atomic bomb led the US to begin
its own nuclear weapons program. In 1942 Britain
and the US decided to combine their research efforts;
Los Alamos, a remote area of New Mexico, was
chosen as the location for the Manhattan Project,
which resulted in the world's first nuclear explosion
in July 1945. The clear skies, level ground, and sparse
population made it an ideal top-secret testing ground.

Fat Man and Little Boy *were
atomic bombs dropped on the
Japanese cities of Hiroshima
and Nagasaki in August 1945.
Reproductions can be seen at
the Bradbury Science Museum
in Los Alamos (see p200).*

Today, Los Alamos National Laboratory and Sandia
National Laboratory in Albuquerque are the largest
nuclear research facilities in the US, and New
Mexico's largest employers. Along with White Sands
Missile Range, they remain important centers for
military research and development. Visitors can find
out more about the region's atomic
history at museums in Los Alamos *(see
p200)* and White Sands *(see p223).*

The Nike Ajax
*missile at the
International Space
Hall of Fame in
Alamogordo (see
p224) was one of the
first guided missiles.
It was tested at the
White Sands Missile
Range in 1951.
Other rockets from
the period are on
display in the
museum grounds.*

Robert Goddard did
not live to see the age
of spaceflight. At the
time of his death in
1945, he held 214
patents in rocketry.

THE MANHATTAN PROJECT

In 1943, an innocuous former boys' school, the Los Alamos
Ranch School set high in New Mexico's remote Pajarito Plateau,
was chosen as the research site for the top secret Manhattan
Project. Work began immediately under the direction of
physicist J. Robert Oppenheimer and General Leslie R. Groves.
In just over two years they had developed the first atomic bomb,
which was detonated at the secluded Trinity Test Site (now the
White Sands Missile Range) 230 miles (370 km) south of Los
Alamos, on July 16, 1945. The decision to explode the bomb
in warfare was highly controversial, and some of the scientists
who developed the bomb signed a petition against its use. Displays
on the project can be seen at the Bradbury Science Museum.

Oppenheimer and Groves at Los Alamos, 1944

Dr. John P. Stapp testing acceleration in his Sonic Wind I rocket sled in 1954 at Holloman Air Force Base near White Sands Missile Range. His research improved aircraft seatbelt technology.

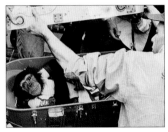

Goddard's assistants (left to right) in his workshop were N.T. Ljungquist, A.W. Kisk, and C.W. Mansur.

Ham the space chimp is helped out of his capsule after becoming the first living creature to be sent into space in 1961.

ROCKET SCIENCE

Robert Goddard (1882–1945) is often referred to as "the father of modern rocketry," developing rocket science in his workshop in Roswell, New Mexico (see p227). He launched his first liquid-fueled rocket in Massachusetts in 1926 and performed 56 flight tests in Roswell in the 1930s. By 1935 he had developed rockets that could carry cameras and record instrument readings. An altitude record was set in 1937 when a Goddard rocket reached 2 miles (3 km) above the earth.

A Goddard rocket without its casing, being studied on an "assembly frame."

The space shuttle Columbia touching down on the Northrup strip at the White Sands Missile Site on March 30, 1982. This was the first time in its three-flight history that the shuttle landed in New Mexico. Today, White Sands is a designated shuttle testing ground and landing site.

New Mexico is a major center for astronaut training and selection. Here astronaut Steven Robinson is training in a buoyancy tank to simulate life in space in preparation for his 1998 mission on the Discovery shuttle.

Hispanic Culture in New Mexico

Tᴴᴱ ʜᴇᴀʀᴛ ᴏꜰ Hispanic culture in the Southwest is found in New Mexico. Here, the Hispanic population, descendants of the original Spanish colonizers of the 16th century, outnumbers that of the Anglo-Americans. The Spanish introduced sheep and horses to the region, as well as bringing Catholicism with its saints' festivals and colorful church decorations.

Centuries of mixing with both the Southwest's native and Anglo cultures have also influenced every aspect of modern Hispanic society, from language and cooking to festivals and the arts. Contemporary New Mexican residents bear the Hispanic surnames of their ancestors, and speak English with a Spanish accent. Even English speakers use Spanish terms.

Corn *has been a staple food in the region since pre-Columbian times. It is used to make tortilla chips, which are served with guacamole (avocado dip).*

Navajo rugs *are considered a native handicraft, but their designs also show signs of Moorish patterns brought from Spain by the colonizers who first introduced sheep into the New World.*

A Bulto *(carved wooden figure) of St. Joseph sits on the altar of the Morada Bell Tower at El Rancho de las Golondrinas (see pp198–9). It is an example of a form of Hispanic folk art, which combined religious beliefs and artistic expression.*

The well was always located in the middle of the main court-yard to be easily accessible.

Hacienda Martínez *was built south of Taos in 1804 by Don Antonio Martínez, an early mayor of the town. It is one of the few Spanish haciendas to be preserved in more or less its original form. Today it is open to visitors who can watch local artisans demonstrating a variety of folk arts.*

Decorations *made from tin originated in Mexico where this metal was a cheap substitute for silver. Shapes were cut out and painted with translucent colors.* **Cockerel**

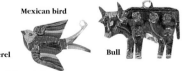

Mexican bird

Bull

Fiestas are an important element of Hispanic culture, and there are many throughout the year, particularly on saints' days (see pp32–5). Fiestas often combine both indigenous and Spanish influences. Elements of Hispanic celebrations have also been incorporated into events in other cultures; here, young girls perform traditional dances at celebrations for the Fourth of July.

Adobe beehive ovens (hornos) were introduced by the Spanish for baking bread. They were originally of Moorish design.

SPANISH INFLUENCE

The restored El Rancho de las Golondrinas *(see pp198–9)* is a living museum showing the way of life – centered on the hacienda – pioneered in the Southwest by the Spanish colonists. In a hacienda, a large number of rooms (approximately 20) would be set around one or two courtyards, reflecting the extended family style of living favored by the Spanish settlers. The Spanish Colonial style is also seen in the layout of many towns, including central Santa Fe *(see pp192–5).*

Chile ristras are garlands of dried red chiles sold as souvenirs in New Mexico. Chiles were a Native American food, unknown in Europe before Columbus landed in the Americas in 1492. However, they were adopted wholeheartedly by the Spanish.

Luminarias fill the square outside San Felipe de Neri church in Albuquerque's Old Town. These Mexican lanterns (also called farolitos) consist of a candle set in sand in a paper bag, and are displayed during religious festivals.

SANTA FE AND NORTHERN NEW MEXICO

THE BEAUTY OF the landscape and the wealth of cultural attractions make northern New Mexico one of the most popular destinations in the Southwest. Visitors drive through the forests of the San Juan Mountains and the peaks of the Sangre de Cristo Range, part of the southern Rocky Mountains, then through picturesque villages to meet the Rio Grande valley. It was this fertile landscape that probably attracted Ancestral Puebloan people in the 1100s. Their ancestors still live today in pueblo villages, and are famous for producing distinctive crafts and pottery. Taos Pueblo is the largest

of the pueblos, its fame due both to its adobe architecture and its ceremonial dances performed on feast days. Southward lies the beautiful city of Santa Fe. Founded by Spanish colonists in 1610, Santa Fe is now one of the most visited cities in the United States, renowned for its art galleries and adobe buildings. Today, tourism dominates this historic trading center, with its appealing mix of Hispanic, Native, and Anglo-American cultures

Many specialty vacations and outdoor activities are available in the area, including archaeological tours, skiing, and whitewater rafting.

SIGHTS AT A GLANCE

Historic Towns and Cities
Jemez Springs ❸
Las Vegas ❻
Los Alamos ❷
Santa Fe ❶
Taos ⓫

Historic Villages and Pueblos
Abiquiu ❾
Chama ❿
Chimayo ❽
Rancho de Taos ⓬
Taos Pueblo ⓭

Parks and National Monuments
Bandelier National Monument ❹
Pecos National Historical Park ❺

Areas of Natural Beauty
Enchanted Circle Tour ⓯
Northern Pueblo Tour ❼

Ski Areas
Taos Ski Valley ⓮

KEY

✈ International airport
═ Interstate
▬ Major highway
═ Highway
─ Railroad

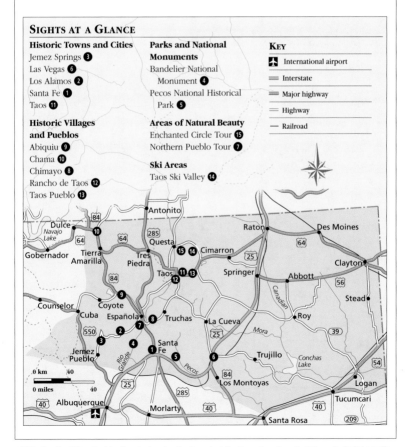

◁ The façade of Taos Pueblo church showing its characteristic stepped roofs and whitewashed adobe walls

Street-by-Street: Santa Fe Plaza ❶

THE OLDEST STATE CAPITAL in North America, Santa Fe
was founded by the Spanish conquistador Don Pedro
de Peralta, who established a colony here in 1610 *(see
p39)*. This colony was abandoned in 1680 following the
Pueblo Revolt, but settlers recaptured it in 1692 *(see p40)*.
When Mexico gained independence in 1821, Santa Fe
was opened up to the wider world and traders and settlers from the US arrived via the Santa Fe Trail *(see p25)*.

    The central plaza has been the heart of Santa Fe since
its founding, and there is no better place to begin
exploring the city. Today, it houses a Native American
market under the portal of the Palace of the Governors,
and the square is lined with shops, cafés, and galleries.

★ **Museum of Fine Arts**
*Built of adobe in 1917, this
museum focuses on the
paintings and sculpture
of Southwestern artists.*

The Plaza
*The obelisk at the center of this main square
commemorates Santa Fe's war veterans.
The Plaza is dominated by the Palace
of the Governors and lined
with old colonial buildings.*

SHERIDAN

LINCOLN

AVENUE

PALACE

BURRO ALLEY

W. SAN FRANCISCO STREET

DON GASPAR

GALISTEO STREET

WATER STREET

0 meters   100
0 yards   100

KEY

– – – – – Suggested route

STAR SIGHTS

★ **Palace of the
Governors**

★ **Museum of Fine Arts**

**Original
Trading Post**
*This historic trading
post sells Hispanic art,
antiques, and Native
American crafts.*

★ **Palace of the Governors**
This single-story adobe building dates back to the early 17th century. Now part of the Museum of New Mexico, the palace houses displays on the city's history.

Institute of American Indian Arts Museum

CATHEDRAL PLACE

E. SAN FRANCISCO STREET

SHELBY STREET

PLAZA

E. WATER STREET

La Fonda Hotel

Loretto Chapel
Built in Gothic style by French architects in the 1870s, the Loretto Chapel was modeled on Ste. Chappelle in Paris. The building and elegant spiral staircase inside were commissioned for the Sisters of Loretto.

Saint Francis Cathedral
This colorful, carved wooden statue of the Virgin stands in a chapel belonging to the original 17th-century church on which the cathedral was built in 1869.

Exploring Central Santa Fe

SANTA FE'S RICH HISTORY and beautiful architecture have made it one of the most popular destinations in the US. Sitting 7,000 ft (2,100 m) up on a high plateau, surrounded by the splendor of the Sangre de Cristo mountains, it basks in clear light and sunshine. The blending of three distinct cultures – Hispanic, Native American, and Anglo – contribute to the city's vibrancy. Santa Fe is an artists' town. About one in six residents work in the arts, and their legacy is everywhere, from the dozens of private galleries along Canyon Road to the fine collections at the Museum of New Mexico. Still, Santa Fe has a relaxed atmosphere, and a setting that offers plenty of opportunities for such outdoor activities as hiking or skiing.

Virgin at Palace of the Governors

Exploring Santa Fe

Many of the main attractions in Santa Fe are within easy walking distance of the Plaza *(see p192)*. This is also the city's main shopping district for arts, crafts, and souvenirs, and many popular cafés and restaurants line the nearby streets. Santa Fe is home to the Museum of New Mexico's four museums. Visitors are advised to buy the four-day pass that covers all of them.

🔒 Santuario de Guadalupe

100 S. Guadalupe St. 📞 *(505) 988-2027.* ⬜ *daily.*
This 1795 adobe church is dedicated to the Virgin of Guadalupe, the patron saint of both the Mexican and Pueblo peoples. Santuario de Guadalupe marked the end of the old Camino Real (Royal Road), the main trade route from Mexico. A painted altarpiece of the Virgin, dating from 1783, graces the peaceful interior, which is also used as a setting for classical concerts.

🏛 Georgia O'Keeffe Museum

217 Johnson St. 📞 *(505) 995-0785.* ⬜ *10am–5pm Sat–Tue, 10am–8pm Fri; summer: 12 noon–8pm Wed.* ⬤ *public hols.* 🎫 *free after 5pm.* ♿
Opened in 1997, this museum is dedicated to New Mexico's most famous resident artist, Georgia O'Keeffe (1887–1986; *see p203*). It is the only place in the world with a substantial collection of her works under one roof. Some of her best-loved paintings are on display here, including *Jimson*

Jimson Weed **(1932), painting at the Georgia O'Keeffe Museum**

Weed (1932), *Purple Hills II*, and *Ghost Ranch, New Mexico* (1934). Her sculpture and less well-known works, including drawings and paintings of New York, can also be seen here.

🏛 Museum of Fine Arts

107 W. Palace Ave. 📞 *(505) 476-5072.* ⬜ *10am–5pm Tue–Sun, 10am–8pm Fri.* ⬤ *Mon, public hols.* 🎫 ♿
Built to showcase New Mexico's growing art scene and completed in 1917, this building is one of the earliest

examples of modern Pueblo Revival-style architecture *(see p23)*. The design owes much to the nearby Pueblo mission churches. Exhibition spaces have square beams, hand-carved and painted decoration, and other traditional interior features. The museum's permanent collection comprises more than 7,000 pieces of Southwestern art dating from the 19th century onward.

🚩 Palace of the Governors

105 E. Palace Ave. 📞 *(505) 476-5100.* ⬜ *10am–5am Tue–Sun.* ⬤ *Mon, public hols.* 🎫 ♿
The Palace of the Governors dominates the north side of the Plaza and is the oldest public building in continuous use in America. Built in 1610, it was the seat of regional government for 300 years until 1909, when it became part of the Museum of New Mexico.

Exhibits trace the history and culture of New Mexico from 1540 to 1912. Items such as a hand-crafted rawhide violin illustrate the self-reliance and ingenuity that was needed to make a home on the isolated frontier.

🏛 Institute of American Indian Arts

108 Cathedral Pl. 📞 *(505) 988-6211.* ⬜ *daily.* ⬤ *public hols.* 🎫 ♿
Housed in a striking pink Pueblo Revival-style building, this engaging museum contains the National Collection of Contemporary Indian Art. Traditional arts such as pottery, textiles, and beadwork are displayed alongside modern paintings and mixed-media works by leading Native American artists. There is also an attractive sculpture garden.

Sculpture in the courtyard of the Museum of Fine Arts

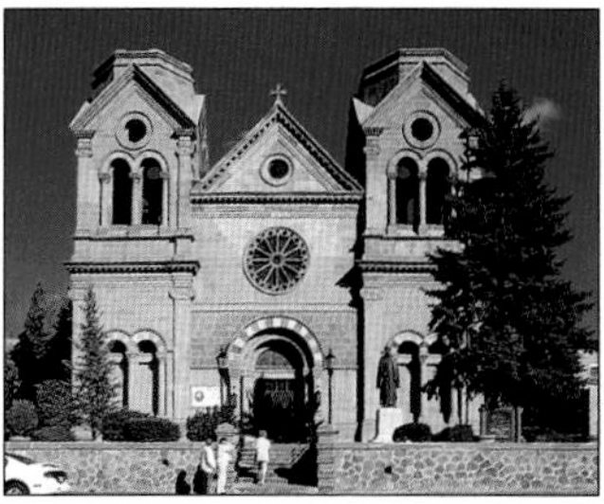

The decorative façade of St. Francis Cathedral

✝ St. Francis Cathedral

131 Cathedral Pl. ☎ *(505) 982-5619.* 🕐 *daily.* ♿

The Cathedral's French Romanesque-style façade is an anomaly in the heart of this adobe city, yet its honey-colored stone, glowing in the afternoon light, makes it one of its lovliest landmarks. It was built in 1869 under Santa Fe's first Archbishop, Jean Baptiste Lamy. The building replaced most of an earlier adobe church called *La Parroquia,* except for the side chapel of Our Lady of the Rosary. This houses the oldest statue of the Virgin Mary in North America, known as *La Conquistadora.* Carved in Mexico in 1625, the figure was brought to Santa Fe where it gained mythical status as settlers fleeing the Pueblo Revolt in 1680 *(see p40)* claimed to have been saved by the Virgin's protection.

✝ Loretto Chapel

207 Old Santa Fe Trail. ☎ *(505) 982-0092.* 🕐 *daily.* 🎟 ♿

The Loretto Chapel is famous for its miraculous staircase, a dramatically curved spiral that winds upward for 21 ft (6 m) with 33 steps that make two complete 360 degree turns. The spiral has no nails or center support and its perfect craftsmanship is all that keeps it aloft. When the chapel was originally built it lacked access to the choirloft. A mysterious carpenter appeared, built the spiral, and vanished without seeking payment. The railing was added in 1887 to calm the nuns' fear of heights.

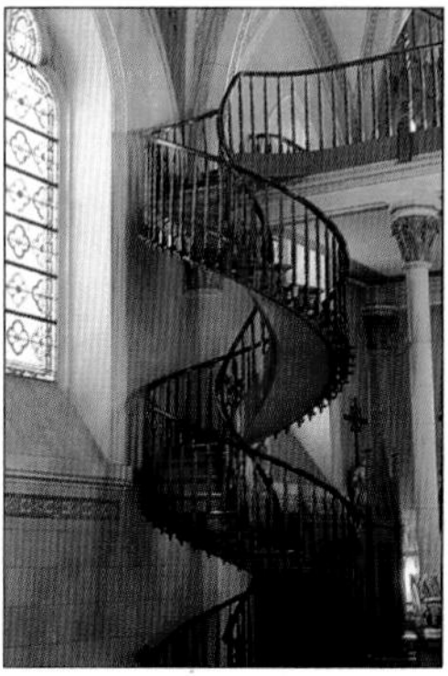

The elegant curves of the spiral staircase at the Loretto Chapel

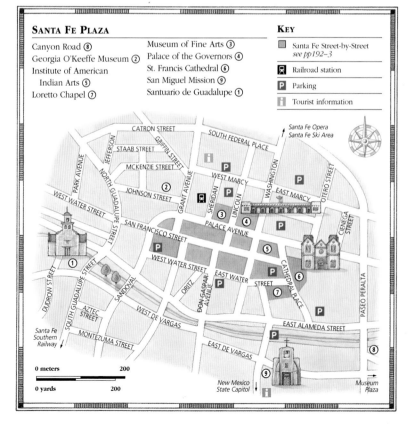

Santa Fe Plaza

- Canyon Road (8)
- Georgia O'Keeffe Museum (2)
- Institute of American Indian Arts (5)
- Loretto Chapel (7)
- Museum of Fine Arts (3)
- Palace of the Governors (4)
- St. Francis Cathedral (6)
- San Miguel Mission (9)
- Santuario de Guadalupe (1)

Key

- Santa Fe Street-by-Street *see pp192–3*
- Railroad station
- [P] Parking
- Tourist information

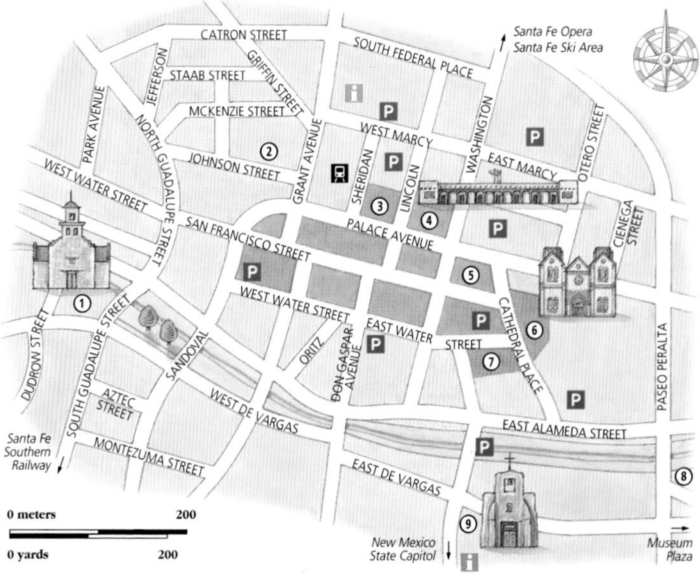

Museum of International Folk Art

Mexican jaguar mask

THIS CHARMING MUSEUM houses a stunning collection of folk art from all over the world, including toys, miniature theaters, dolls, and paintings, as well as religious and traditional art. The eastern gallery holds the fine Girard Collection, the largest collection of cross-cultural works in existence. Thousands of objects from more than 100 countries are displayed, including icons and paintings. The highlights are ceramic figures arranged in attractive scenes, ranging from a Polish Christmas to a Mexican baptism The Hispanic Heritage Wing contains Spanish colonial decorative art, such as rare hide paintings, while the Neutrogena Wing offers textiles from Africa, Asia, and South America.

★ Girard Collection Figures
Created in 1960 in Oaxaca, Mexico, this baptism scene is made up of over 50 painted earthenware villagers.

Neutrogena Collection
Specializing in rugs, textiles, blankets, and costumes, this gallery spans world culture to reveal a depth of craft and detail in each piece, as shown in this 19th-century dyed Japanese bridal sleeping cover.

La Casa Colonial is a lifesize, interactive re-creation of an early 19th-century home from Santa Fe Town Plaza.

Hispanic Heritage Wing
This hand-carved New-Mexican icon, from 1830–50, represents Mary, Our Lady of Sorrows. It is typical of the Spanish colonial and Hispanic folk art found in this wing.

The Bartlett Library in the Bartlett Wing is a research facility housing articles, photographs, and audio-visual material on world cultures.

Entrance

Library

STAR SIGHTS

★ Girard Collection

VISITORS' CHECKLIST

706 Camino Lejo. ((505) 476-
1200. ◯ 10am–5pm Tue–Sun.
● public hols. ▨ ♿ ✉ ▯

★ **Girard Collection Toy**
*This Bangladeshi toy is a
1960s addition to the more
than 100,000 artifacts
collected by US designer
Alexander Girard from
1930 to 1978.*

🚌 Canyon Road

Originally an Indian track
between the Rio Grande and
Pecos pueblos, Canyon Road
was later used by burros
(donkeys) hauling fire-
wood down from the
mountains. This
upscale road is today
lined with more than
100 private art galleries,
restaurants, and shops,
with their premises in
historic adobe houses,
such as El Zagun at
No. 545. Most of the
artworks here are for
sale, and many have
fairly high price tags.
Canyon Road runs parallel to
the river and the former
Acequia Madre, or "mother
ditch," the city's first irrigation
channel, which today is lined
with adobe buildings.

⛪ San Miguel Mission

401 Old Santa Fe Trail. ((505) 983-
3974. ◯ daily. ▨ ♿

The chapel of San Miguel is
thought to have been built
around 1610, making it one of
the oldest churches in the US.
The original dirt floor and
adobe steps are still visible at
the front of the altar. It was
built by Tlaxcala Indians, who
traveled from Mexico with the
early Spanish settlers.

This simple church contains
a number of attractive features.
The great roof beams were
restored in 1692, having been
burned 12 years earlier in the
Pueblo Revolt. A carved wood-
en *reredos* (altarpiece) frames
the centrally placed statue
of the patron saint, San Miguel,
while the side walls boast
paintings of religious scenes
on deerskin and buffalo hide.

🏛 Museum Plaza

Alongside the Museum of
International Folk Art, two
other important museums are
found in Museum Plaza.
**The Museum of Indian
Arts and Culture** is
dedicated to traditional
Native American arts
and culture. Its main
exhibit, *Here, Now &
Always*, tells the story of
the Southwest's oldest
communities in the words
of native Pueblo, Navajo,
and Apache people.

**Ancient male
figurine**

There are also exhibits
of Pueblo pottery, pet-
roglyphs, and rock art.
Established in 1937 by
wealthy philanthropist Mary
Cabot Wheelwright of Boston,
**The Wheelwright Museum
of the American Indian** is
built to resemble a Navajo
hogan (see p169). For many
years Navajo sandpaintings
were displayed here, but
these have been returned to
the Navajo Nation. Today the
museum's focus is on its
changing exhibitions of
contemporary work by Native
American artists. In the
basement, the excellent Case
Trading Post re-creates the
first trading posts established
on the Navajo reservation and
sells a fine range of traditional
handmade crafts and jewelry.

🏛 Museum of Indian Arts
and Culture

710 Camino Lejo. ((505) 476-
1250. ◯ 10am–6pm Tue–Sun.
▨ ♿

🏛 The Wheelwright
Museum of the American
Indian

704 Camino Lejo. ((505) 982-
4636. ◯ daily. ● public hols. ♿

Detail of the carved wooden *reredos* at San Miguel Mission

KEY

| ▢ Girard Collection |
| ▢ Neutrogena Collection |
| ▢ Hispanic Heritage Wing |
| ▢ Bartlett Wing |
| ▢ Changing gallery |
| ▢ Non exhibition space |

El Rancho de las Golondrinas

ESTABLISHED IN THE early 1700s, El Rancho de las Golondrinas (Ranch of the Swallows), is a historic stopping place on the Camino Real, the old royal road trading route that ran from Mexico City to Santa Fe. Home to the Baca family for 200 years, the 200-acre (89-ha) ranch was used by settlers and explorers to rest up and water their animals before heading on to the city. Located in a fertile valley just south of Santa Fe, this living history museum, with its restored buildings and historic features, re-creates life on a typical 18th-century Spanish rural hacienda. Authentic historic crops such as squash and corn are grown here, and burros and horses are used to work the fertile land.

Villager Weaving
On weekends, costumed workers demonstrate the hacienda's skills, including weaving.

Sapello Mill and Sierra Village

Lookout Post

★ La Placita
This small central court-yard contains the hornos, or beehive-shaped ovens that were used to bake bread and cookies.

★ Baca House Kitchen
The kitchen, like the rest of the Baca house, dates from the early 1800s. It features a bell-shaped oven and a built-in wall cabinet (alacena) to keep food cool.

★ Chapel
This pretty painted wooden reredos (screen) graces the chapel. Part of the original ranch, a chapel was essential for devout Catholic settlers.

VISITORS' CHECKLIST

334 Los Pinos Rd, 15 miles (24 km) south of Santa Fe off I-25. *(505) 471-2261.* Jun–Sep: 10am–4pm Wed–Sun for self-guided tours; Apr, May, Oct: guided tours only. Call ahead for reservations.

Sapello Mill
This 1870s water mill was moved here from a New Mexican village in 1972. Its millstones still grind wheat into flour on festival days.

Truchas Mill

The Entertainment Platform plays host to musicians and dancers who perform shows of traditional colonial music during festivals and special events.

Pino House (office)

STAR SIGHTS

★ La Placita

★ Chapel

★ Baca House Kitchen

Santa Fe Opera
5 miles N. of Santa Fe on Hwy 84/285. *(505) 986-5900; (800) 280-4654.* mid-Jun–Sep 1.
Located just north of Santa Fe near the pueblo villages of Tesuque and Pojoaque, the city's impressive outdoor auditorium is the setting for one of the finest summer opera companies in the world. It is renowned for innovative productions, which attract international stars. A state-of-the-art electronic system allows the audience to read translations of the libretti on the seats in front of them. Backstage tours are available in July and August. Visitors are advised to come prepared for Santa Fe's changeable weather with warm clothing, umbrellas, rugs, and waterproof gear.

Santa Fe Ski Area
Hwy 475. *(505) 982-4429.* Nov–Apr: 9am–4pm daily, weather permitting.
Just a 30-minute drive from central Santa Fe, the ski area sits in a 12,000-ft- (4,000-m-) high basin of the Sangre de Cristo mountains. The resort has 43 trails to suit skiers of every ability, from beginners to experts, and snowboarding runs are also open. A lodge, equipment rentals, ski and child care are available, as are a variety of ski packages. During the summer, chairlift rides up to cooler temperatures are popular, and offer splendid views of the Rio Grande. Bear in mind that during the winter, the slopes are open only in safe conditions; always call in advance to make sure that your preferred runs are open.

The façade of the New Mexico State Capitol with Puebloan sun motif

New Mexico State Capitol
Old Santa Fe Trail & Paseo de Peralta. *(505) 986-4589.* May–early Sep: 8am–5pm Mon–Sat; mid-Sep–Apr: 7am–7pm Mon–Fri.
Built to resemble the sun symbol of the Zia Pueblo people, the circular State Capitol houses works by New Mexican artists from the Capitol Art Collection. Paintings, photographs, sculptures, furniture, and weavings are displayed on four levels. A highlight is the mixed-media sculpture *The Buffalo* (1992), by Holly Hughes, which includes the use of paintbrushes and film for the animal's hair and mane.

Buffalo sculpture at State Capitol

Santa Fe Southern Railway
410 S. Guadalupe St. *(505) 989-8600; (888) 989-8600.*
Located in the railyard near the corner of Guadalupe Street and Montezuma Avenue, this working freight train offers rides in vintage passenger cars through spectacular desert scenery to the little village of Lamy. The stop for lunch at Lamy is included in the ticket price. The round trip takes between three and four-and-a-half hours. Train schedules change seasonally, so call ahead for times. Sunset trips and holiday specials also run.

The engine car of the Santa Fe freight train

Northern Pueblos Tour [7]

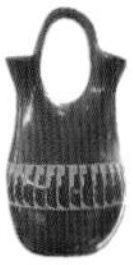

Redware pottery

THE FERTILE VALLEY OF the Rio Grande between Santa Fe and Taos is home to eight pueblos of the 19 Native American pueblos in New Mexico. Although geographically close, each pueblo has its own government and traditions, and many offer attractions to visitors. Nambe gives stunning views of the surrounding mountains, mesas, and high desert. San Idelfonso is famous for its fine pottery, while other villages produce handcrafted jewelry or rugs.

Tips for Drivers

Starting point: *Tesuque Pueblo, north of Santa Fe on Hwy 84.*
Length: *45 miles (70 km). Local roads leading to pueblos are often dirt tracks, so allow extra time.*
Note: *The pueblos welcome visitors, but remember to obey their laws and observe pueblo etiquette* *(see p278–9).* ℹ *Indian Pueblo Cultural Center (505) 843-7270.*

Santa Clara Pueblo [5]
This small pueblo is known for its artisans and their work. As in many pueblos, it contains a number of craft shops and small studios, often run by the Native artisans themselves.

Puye Cliff Dwellings [6]
Now deserted, this site contains over 700 rooms, complete with stone carvings, that were home to Native peoples until 1500.

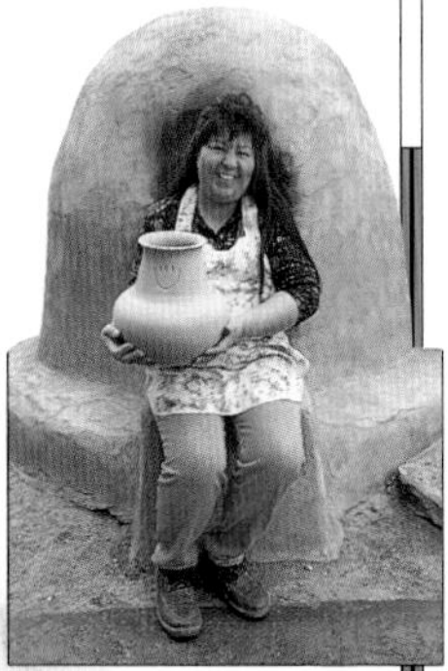

San Juan Pueblo [7]
Declared the first capital of New Mexico in 1598, this village is now a center for the visual arts and has an arts cooperative.

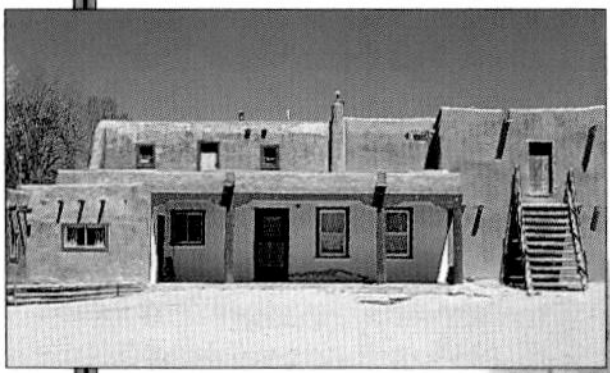

San Ildefonso Pueblo [4]
Occupied since 1300, this pueblo is best known for its etched black pottery, the proceeds of which saved its people from the Depression of the 1930s.

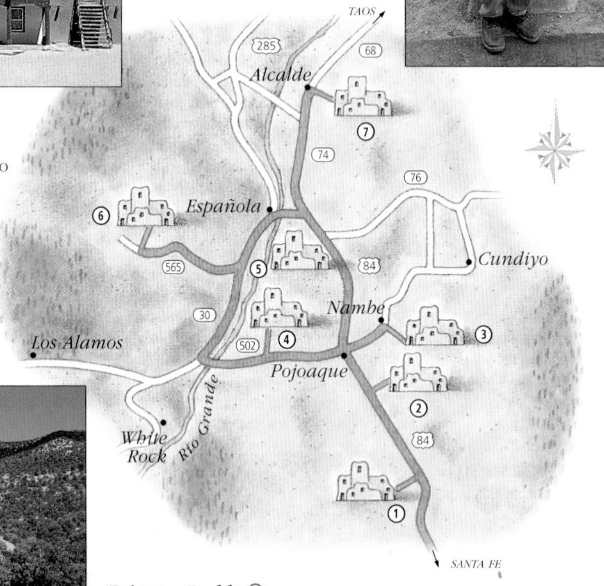

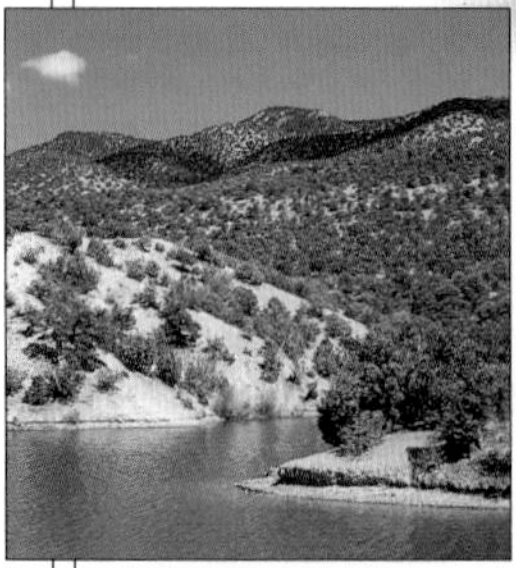

Nambe Pueblo [3]
Set in a beautiful fertile valley, this village is bordered by a lakeside hiking trail with waterfall views and a buffalo ranch.

Pojoaque Pueblo [2]
The new Peoh Cultural Center and Museum here is an excellent introduction to the pueblo way of life in these small communities.

Tesuque Pueblo [1]
The Tewa people here have concentrated on farming and pottery-making for centuries.

0 km 10
0 miles 10

Key

Tour route
Other roads

The stone façade of Chimayo Church in the Santa Fe valley

Chimayo ❽

Road map E3. 🏠 *2,800.* ℹ️ *Big Rock Shopping Center, Española (505) 753-2831.* ▲

Tʜɪs village lies 25 miles (40 km) north of Santa Fe in the Rio Grande valley. Chimayo was settled by Spanish colonists in the 1700s on the site of an Indian pueblo famous for having a healing natural spring. The site of the spring is now occupied by the Santuario de Chimayo, built by a local landowner in 1813–16 after he experienced a vision telling him to dig the foundations in earth blessed with healing powers. While digging here he found a cross that once belonged to two martyred priests, and the church became a place of healing pilgrimage. The chapel contains a beautiful *reredos* surrounding the crucifix and a tiny side-room with a pit of "the holy dirt," which visitors are allowed to take away.

Chimayo is also known for its woven blankets and rugs, which have been produced by the Ortega family for generations. Their workshop is just off the junction with Hwy 76, while farther along, Cordova and Truchas villages are also known for their fine craftwork.

Abiquiu ❾

Road map E3. 🏠 *500.* ℹ️ *Hwy 84 (505) 685-4312.*

Tʜɪs smɑll ɑdobe village with its sunlit dusty streets was the home of the Southwest's most famous artist, Georgia O'Keeffe, from 1946 until her death in 1986. Her village home and studio can be toured only by reservation and bookings need to be made in advance on (505) 685-4539. The country around Abiquiu, with its red rocks, mesas, and corrugated slopes, is now known as O'Keeffe Country because it inspired so many of her abstract landscape paintings

A few miles north of town, the fascinating **Piedra Lumbre/Rocks of Fire Visitor Center** focuses on local geology and natural history. The museum is located at the Ghost Ranch, a retreat established and now run by Presbyterians.

🏛 **Piedra Lumbre/Rocks of Fire Visitor Center**
Hwy 84, Abiquiu. 🅲 *(505) 685-4312. Reopens to visitors in summer 2001.*

Chama ❿

Road map E2. 🏠 *1,000.* ℹ️ *Chamber of Commerce, 499 Main St., (505) 756-2235.*

Fᴏᴜɴᴅᴇᴅ ᴅᴜʀɪɴɢ the 1880s silver-mining boom, the main attraction in today's Chama is the **Cumbres and Toltec Scenic Railroad**. This narrow-gauge steam train makes a spectacular 64-mile (102-km) daily trip over the Cumbres Pass and through the Toltec Gorge into Colorado, with views of the San Juan and Sangre de Cristo mountains.

🚂 **Cumbres and Toltec Scenic Railroad**
Hwy 17 🅲 *(505) 756-2151.* 🕐 *10:30am daily, mid-May to mid-Oct.* 📷 ♿

GEORGIA O'KEEFFE

One of the 20th century's foremost artists, Georgia O'Keeffe (1887–1986) has managed to achieve both critical and popular acclaim for her paintings, which, either as studies of single blooms or sun-washed landscapes of the Southwest, are universally loved. Wisconsin-born and raised, she studied art in Chicago and New York but fell in love with the light of New Mexico when her friend and patron, Mabel Dodge Luhan, invited her to her home in the area. O'Keeffe bought an old adobe in Abiquiu and there created the abstract paintings that brought the beauty of New Mexico to national attention.

Artist Georgia O'Keeffe

Dramatic red rock landscape near Abiquiu

Taos ⓫

Gun in the Kit Carson Museum

THE SMALL CITY of Taos is set between the dramatic peaks of the Sangre de Cristo Mountains and the Rio Grande River. Like Santa Fe, it is an important center for the arts but is more bohemian and relaxed in style. Its plaza and the surrounding streets are lined with craft shops, cafés, and galleries, many housed in original adobe buildings.

Taos Indians have lived in the area for around 1,000 years. With the arrival of the Spanish missionaries in 1598, a few settlers followed, but it was not until Don Diego de Vargas resettled the area, after the Pueblo Revolt in 1680, that the town's present foundations were laid *(see p40)*. In 1898, artists Ernest Blumenschein and Bert Phillips stopped in Taos to repair a broken wagon wheel, and never left. In 1915 they established the Taos Society of Artists, which still supports local artists today.

Exploring Taos

There are three parts to Taos: the central historic district, Taos Pueblo to the north, and Rancho de Taos to the south *(see p206)*. Paseo del Pueblo Norte, the main street, leads north then curves west, becoming Hwy 64. It leads to Taos Ski Valley, the Millicent Rogers Museum, and Rio Grande Gorge Bridge.

Furniture displayed in the Blumenschein Museum

🏛 Harwood Foundation Museum

238 Ledoux St. 【 *(505) 758-9826.* ⭘ *10am–5pm Tue–Sat; noon–5pm Sun.* ⬤ *Mon & public hols.* 🖼 ♿

New Mexico's second-oldest museum occupies a 19th-century adobe compound run by the University of New Mexico. It provides a tranquil setting for paintings, sculpture, prints, drawings, and photography. Work by members of the original Taos Society of Artists is displayed alongside that of contemporary local artists. A collection of Hispanic works is also featured, including 19th-century *retablos*.

🏛 Blumenschein Home and Museum

222 Ledoux St. 【 *(505) 758-0505.* ⭘ *9am–5pm daily (call for winter hours).* 🖼 ♿ *partial.*

Ernest Blumenschein (1874–1960), along with Bert Phillips and Joseph Henry Sharp, was instrumental in founding the Taos Society of Artists in 1915. The Society promoted their own work and that of other Taos artists, establishing the town's reputation as an artistic center. The Museum is located in Blumenschein's former home, sections of which date from the 1790s. Paintings by Blumenschein and his family, as well as representative works produced by the Taos Society of Artists, hang in rooms decorated with Spanish Colonial furniture and European antiques.

♜ Taos Plaza

Taos Plaza, built by the Spanish and fortified after the Pueblo Revolt of 1680, has

Shops and cafés line the narrow streets around Taos Plaza

been remodeled several times but remains the centerpoint of the town. Its shady trees and benches make it a relaxing spot to sit and people-watch. The copper-topped bandstand was a gift from Mabel Dodge Luhan, New Mexico's leading arts patron in the 1920s. A flag has flown continuously from the flagpole since the Civil War, when Kit Carson and a band of citizens raised the Union Flag to protect Taos from Confederate supporters.

🏛 Kit Carson Home and Museum

113 Kit Carson Rd. 【 *(505) 758-0505.* ⭘ *Jun–Oct: 8am–6pm daily; Nov–May: 9am–5pm daily.* 🖼 ♿ *partial.*

At the age of 17, Christopher "Kit" Carson (1809–68) ran away to join a wagon train and became one of the most famous names in the West. He led a remarkable life, working as a cook and interpreter, a fur-trapping mountain man, a scout for mapping expeditions, an Indian agent, and a military officer *(see p171)*. He purchased this house in Taos in 1843 for his 14-year-old bride, Josefa Jaramillo, and lived here for the rest of his life. Carson's remarkable story, and the unpredictable nature of frontier life, are the focus of the museum exhibits, which feature antique firearms, trapping equipment, photographs, and furniture.

Cover of a Kit Carson book

🏛 Fechin Institute

227 Paseo del Pueblo Norte. 【 *(505) 758-1710.* ⭘ *May–Oct: 10am–5pm Wed–Sun; Nov–Apr: 10am–2pm Wed–Sun.* ⬤ *Mon & Tue.* 🖼 ♿

Born in Russia in 1881, Nicolai Fechin learned woodcarving from his father. He became a talented artist producing paintings, drawings, and sculpture. Fechin moved to Taos with his family in 1927 and set about restoring his adobe home with Russian-influenced woodwork including handcrafted doors,

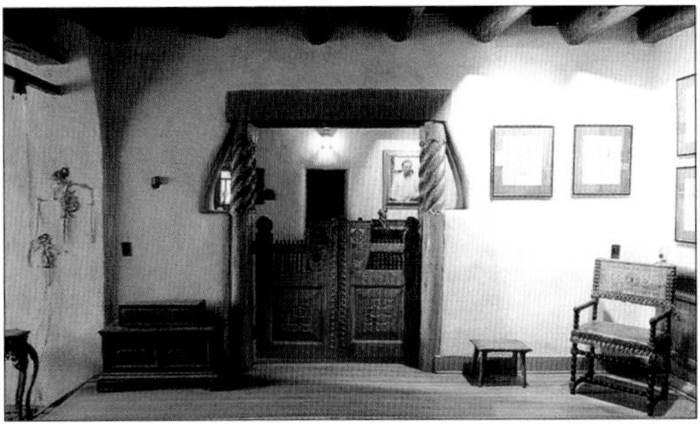

Handcrafted, wooden swing doors in the Fechin Institute

windows, and furniture. Today his house is a museum, and examples of his work are displayed in this unique building, as are exhibits by other artists.

🏛 Millicent Rogers Museum

Millicent Rogers Museum Rd.
☎ *(505) 758-2462.* ○ *Apr–Oct: 10am–5pm daily.* ● *Nov–Mar: Mon; public hols.* 💲 ♿

Beautiful heiress and arts patron, Millicent Rogers (1902–53) moved to Taos in 1947. Fascinated by the area, she created one of the country's best museums of Southwestern arts and design. Native silver and turquoise jewelry and Navajo weavings form the core of the exhibits. Also featured is the pottery of the famous Puebloan artist Maria Martinez (1887–1980), with its distinctive black-on-black style.

🏛 Governor Bent House and Museum

117a Bent St. ☎ *(505) 758-2376.* ○ *10am–5pm daily.* 💲

Charles Bent became the first Anglo-American governor of New Mexico in 1846. In 1847 he was killed by Hispanic and Indian residents protesting against American rule. The hole hacked in the adobe by his family as they tried to flee can still be seen. Today, exhibits include guns, native artifacts, and animal skins.

Visitors' Checklist

Road map E3. 👥 6,000. 🚌 *Greyhound, Taos Bus Center, Hwy 68.* [i] *1139 Paseo del Pueblo Sur (505) 758-3873; (800) 732-8267.* 🎪 🎭 *Taos Film Festival (Apr); Summer Music Festival (Jun–Aug).*

🌉 Rio Grande Gorge Bridge

☎ *(505) 758-9593.* ○ *8:30am–4:30pm daily.* ● *some festivals and tribal events.* 💲 ♿

The dramatic Rio Grande Gorge Bridge, built in 1965, is the second-highest suspension bridge in the country. At 650 ft (195 m) above the Rio Grande, its dizzying heights offer awesome views of the gorge and the surrounding stark, sweeping plateau.

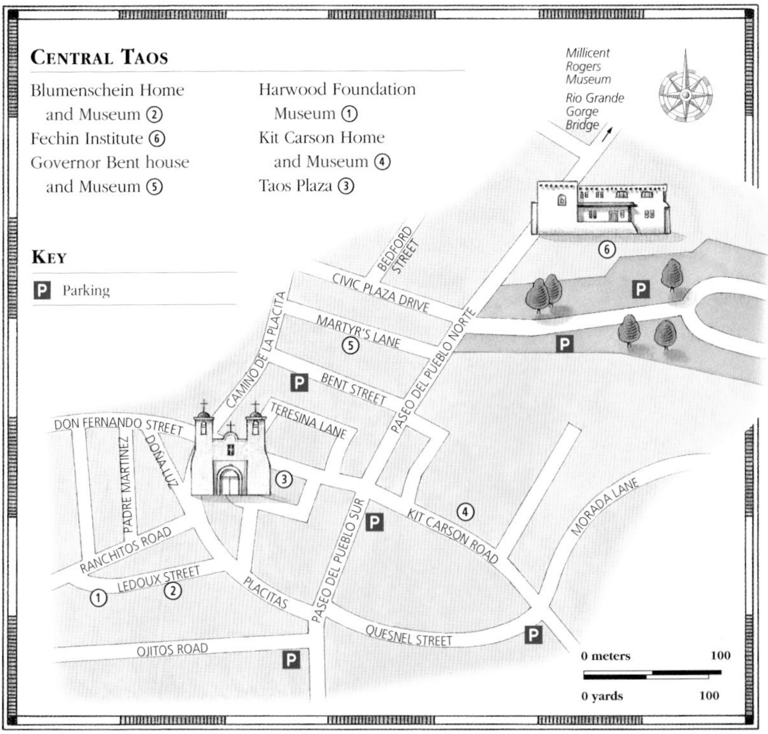
CENTRAL TAOS
Blumenschein Home and Museum ②
Fechin Institute ⑥
Governor Bent house and Museum ⑤
Harwood Foundation Museum ①
Kit Carson Home and Museum ④
Taos Plaza ③
KEY
[P] Parking
Millicent Rogers Museum
Rio Grande Gorge Bridge
BEDFORD STREET
CIVIC PLAZA DRIVE
MARTYR'S LANE
CAMINO DE LA PLACITA
BENT STREET
PASEO DEL PUEBLO NORTE
TERESINA LANE
DON FERNANDO STREET
PADRE MARTINEZ
DOÑA LUZ
KIT CARSON ROAD
MORADA LANE
RANCHITOS ROAD
LEDOUX STREET
PLACITAS
PASEO DEL PUEBLO SUR
QUESNEL STREET
OJITOS ROAD
0 meters 100
0 yards 100

Restored early-19th-century kitchen at the Hacienda Martínez

Rancho de Taos ⑫

Road map E3. 🚹 *Taos Visitor Center, 1139 Paseo de Pueblo Sur, Taos (505) 758-3873.*

Located 3 miles (5 km) southwest of central Taos, this separate community is centered on a peaceful plaza. Rancho de Taos is also home to the striking adobe church of **San Francisco de Asis**, which was built between 1710 and 1755. The church is one of the best examples of mission architecture in the Southwest and provided inspiration for many artists. It was often painted by Georgia O'Keeffe *(see p203)*.

The **Hacienda Martínez** is a Spanish Colonial house built in 1804 and one of the few still in existence *(see p188)*. Its adobe walls are 2-ft (60-cm) thick and have heavy *zaguan* (entry) gates. Inside, 21 starkly furnished rooms surround two courtyards. The first owner, Antonio Severino Martinez, prospered through trade with Mexico and later became mayor of Taos. The merchandise he sold is displayed here.

🚹 **San Francisco de Asis**
Hwy 68, Rancho de Taos.
📞 *(505) 758-2754.* ⏰ *9am–4pm Mon–Sat.* ● *Sun; Jun 1–15.* ♿
🏛 **Hacienda Martínez**
Ranchitos Road, Rancho de Taos.
📞 *(505) 758-0505.* ⏰ *Apr–Oct: 9am–5pm daily; Nov–Mar: 10am–4pm daily.* ● *public holidays.* 📷

Taos Pueblo ⑬

Road map E3. Hwy 150. 🚹 *Taos Pueblo Tourism Office, P.O. Box 1846, Taos (505) 758-9593.* 📷 📹 📷

Taos pueblo is one of the oldest communities in the US, having been occupied continuously for around 1,000 years. Two multistory adobe communal houses, with their curved edges, sit on opposite sides of the open central "square". Known as North House and South House, they are the largest pueblo buildings in the country and are thought to date from the early 1700s. More than 150 people live year-round at the pueblo, as their ancestors did, with no electricity, and water supplied only from a stream. Sights include the 1850 St. Jerome Chapel, the ruins of the earlier 1619 San Geronimo Church, and the central plaza, with its corn and chile drying-racks and adobe ovens or *hornos*. Several ground-floor dwellings are now craft shops. Guided tours are available but there is a fee of $10 for photography; permission must be granted prior to photographing a resident. No cameras are permitted during ceremonial dances, although several festivals are open to visitors throughout the year.

Downhill view of one of the celebrated ski slopes at Taos

Taos Ski Valley ⑭

Road map E2. 🚹 *(800) 992-7669; (505) 776-2291.* ♿ *village only.*

A century ago, Taos Ski Valley was a bustling mining camp. In 1955, Swiss-born skier Ernie Blake began developing a world-class ski resort on the northern slopes and snow bowls of Wheeler Peak, the 13,161-ft (3,950-m) summit that is the highest in New Mexico. Located 15 miles (24 km) north of Taos, it has 12 lifts and 72 runs for all abilities, but it is particularly known for its challenging expert terrain. The ski season itself generally runs from Thanksgiving to early April depending on the weather. The valley also makes a spectacular summer retreat popular with those seeking relief from the summer heat. Some 100 residents live in the village year-round.

Adobe buildings at the Taos pueblo, inhabited to this day by villagers

Enchanted Circle Tour [15]

THE SCENERY AROUND Taos rises from high desert plateau with its sagebrush and yucca plants to the forested Sangre de Cristo Mountains. The Enchanted Circle tour follows a National Forest Scenic Byway through some of the area's most breathtaking landscapes. Circumnavigating the highest point in New Mexico, Wheeler Peak (13,161 ft/ 3,950 m), it continues through the ruggedly beautiful Carson National Forest. Lakes and hiking trails lie off the tour, which passes through small towns and the home of English novelist D.H. Lawrence.

Tips for Drivers

Length: *84 miles (134 km.)*
Starting point: *North of Taos on Hwy 522, continuing east and south on Hwys 38 & 64.*
Getting around: *While the main roads offer smooth and rapid driving, bear in mind that many sights are located on dirt tracks and minor roads.*

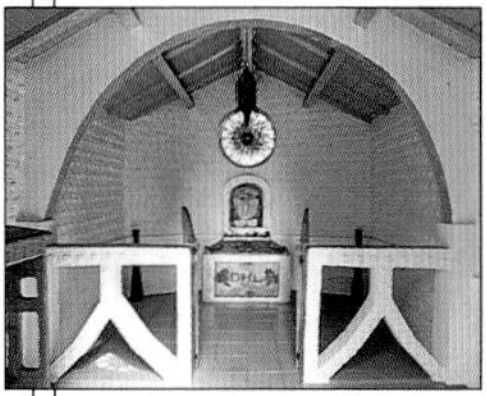

D.H. Lawrence Memorial [1]
Known for his innovative, erotic work, the writer's ashes were laid to rest near the farmhouse where he lived in the 1920s.

Questa [2]
This hamlet is the gateway to Carson National Forest, with rivers, mountains, and lakes set against a rocky backdrop.

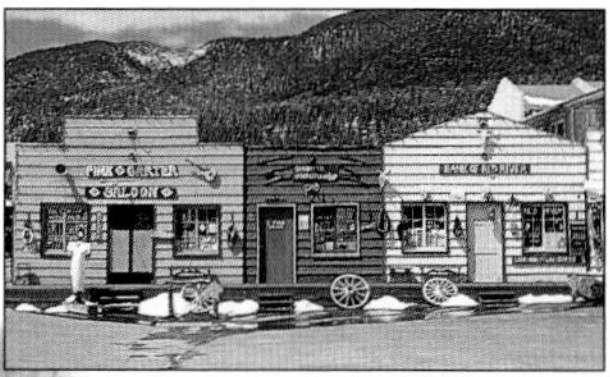

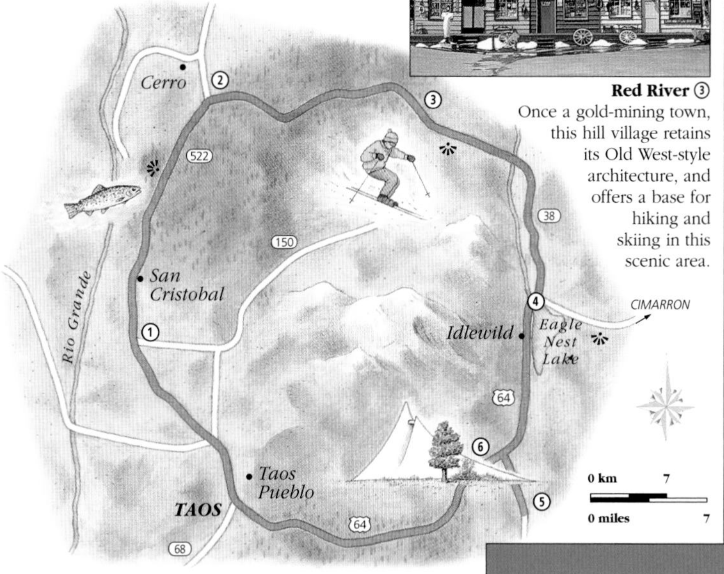
Cerro
522
150
38
San Cristobal
Rio Grande
CIMARRON
Idlewild
Eagle Nest Lake
64
Taos Pueblo
TAOS
68
0 km 7
0 miles 7

Red River [3]
Once a gold-mining town, this hill village retains its Old West-style architecture, and offers a base for hiking and skiing in this scenic area.

DAV Vietnam Veterans Memorial [6]
Located in the National Park, this dramatic modern chapel honors all the US troops who lost their lives in Vietnam.

Angel Fire [5]
Winter sports are foremost here, with sleigh rides, snowmobiling, and horseback trips through the snowy landscape available at this growing resort.

Eagle Nest [4]
Growing in popularity as a base for sports trips, this small town is conveniently located and offers ski and boat rental for the nearby mountains and lakes.

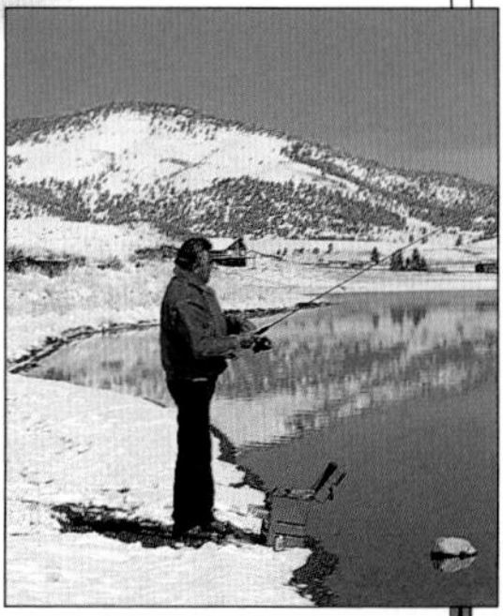

Key

- Tour route
- Other roads
- Viewpoint

ALBUQUERQUE AND SOUTHERN NEW MEXICO

SOUTHERN NEW MEXICO is home to natural wonders such as the Carlsbad Caverns, as well as modern cities thriving on hi-tech research industries. Albuquerque is the state's largest city, with an Old Town plaza and fine museums. West of here is Acoma Pueblo, the oldest continually inhabited settlement in thje country. The southern third of the state is dominated by the Chihuahua Desert, which is one of the driest in the region. Despite this, the area was cultivated by Hohokam farmers for centuries. The Gila Cliff Dwellings are the last remnants of the Mogollon people. By the 17th century Apaches occupied much of the region, whose reputation as a "Wild West" outpost stems from the 19th-century exploits of characters such as Billy the Kid.

SIGHTS AT A GLANCE

Historic Towns and Cities
Alamogordo ⑱
Albuquerque ❶
Bernalillo ❸
Carlsbad ㉓
Cloudcroft ⑲
Deming ⑫
El Paso ⑯
Grants ❻
Las Cruces ⑭
Lincoln ㉑
Mesilla ⑮
Roswell ㉔
Ruidoso ⑳
Socorro ❽

Silver City ⑪
Truth or Consequences ❾

Areas of Natural Beauty
Acoma Pueblo ❺
Sandia Peak Tramway ❷
The Turquoise Trail ❹

National Parks and Monuments
Carlsbad Caverns National Park ㉒
El Morro National Monument ❼

Fort Selden State Monument ⑬
Gila Cliff Dwellings National Monument ⑩
White Sands National Monument ⑰

KEY
✈ International airport
▬ Interstate
▬ Major highway
═ Highway
— Railroad

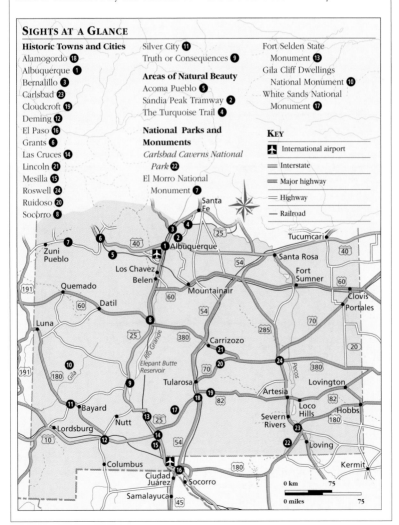

◁ **Flowering cacti cover the walls of a pueblo ruin at Coronado State Monument in Bernalillo**

Albuquerque Old Town Street-by-Street ❶

Chile pepper store sign

Occupied by native peoples from 1100 to 1300 AD, Albuquerque grew up from a small colonial group of pioneers who first settled by the Rio Grande in the wake of late 16th-century Spanish explorers of the region. In 1706, a band of 18 families won formal approval for their town from the Spanish crown by naming the city after the Spanish Duke of Alburquerque, (the first "r" in the name was later dropped).

Today's Old Town still boasts many original adobe buildings dating from the 1790s. The city's first civic structure, the imposing San Felipe de Neri church was completed in 1793. Despite many renovations, the church retains its original adobe walls. The adjacent plaza forms the heart of the Old Town and is a pleasant open space where both locals and visitors relax on benches, surrounded by the lovely adobe buildings that house craft shops, restaurants, and museums.

Agape Pueblo Pottery
This store features a selection of pueblo pottery such as this hand-crafted pot from Santa Clara Pueblo.

Church Street Café
Said to occupy the oldest house in the city, this café serves excellent New Mexican cuisine and is famous for its spicy chili.

Christmas shop

San Felipe de Neri church

ROMERO NW

CHURCH ST NW

NORTH PLAZA

SOUTH PLA

RIO GRANDE BOULEVARD NW

★ Old Town Plaza
The plaza was the center of Albuquerque for over 200 years. Today, this charming square makes a pleasant rest stop for visitors strolling around the nearby streets lined with museums and colorful stores.

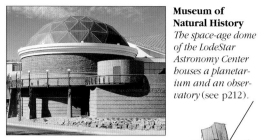

Museum of Natural History

The space-age dome of the LodeStar Astronomy Center houses a planetarium and an observatory (see p212).

VISITORS' CHECKLIST

Road map 3E. 🖼 580,000.
✈ *Albuquerque International Sunport, 5 miles (8 km) S. of Downtown.* 🚉 *Amtrak, 214 1st St. SW.* 🚌 *Greyhound, 300 Second St. SW.* ℹ *Albuquerque Convention and Visitors Bureau, 20 First Plaza, Galeria level, (505) 842-9918; (800) 284-2282.*
🎫 *American Indian Week (Apr); New Mexico Arts and Crafts Fair (late Jun); New Mexico State Fair (Sep); Kodak™ Albuquerque International Balloon Fiesta (Oct).*

MOUNTAIN ROAD NW

19TH STREET

| 0 meters | 50 |
| 0 yards | 50 |

KEY

‒ ‒ ‒ ‒ ‒ Suggested route

SAN FELIPE NW

★ Albuquerque Museum of Art and History

This full-scale model of a conquistador on horseback illustrates the kind of Spanish Colonial art and artifacts that dominate this museum's excellent displays. There is also a delightful outdoor sculpture gallery.

Rattlesnake Museum

This Eastern diamondback rattlesnake (right) is one of many species of rattler kept here. There are also displays on the snake's role in medicine, history, and Native American culture.

STAR SIGHTS

★ **Albuquerque Museum of Art and History**

★ **Old Town Plaza**

Exploring Albuquerque

Aᴌʙᴜǫᴜᴇʀǫᴜᴇ ɪs New Mexico's largest city. It has grown to fill the valley that stretches westwards from the foothills of the Manzano and Sandia Mountains and across the banks of the Rio Grande. The coming of the railroad during the 1880s brought increasing numbers of settlers and great prosperity. The city center shifted 2 miles (3 km) east from the Old Town Plaza to what is now Albuquerque's Downtown area. Today, the city has a contemporary buzz with many of its shops, museums, and high-tech industries concentrated in and around Downtown. At the eastern end of this area lies the University of New Mexico with its collection of museums and galleries.

Modern sculpture

San Felipe de Neri Church lies at the north end of Old Town Plaza

Exploring Albuquerque

The best way to see the city is by car. The major sights here are all located near highway exits, which are surprisingly close to areas of historic and architectural interest such as the Old Town. Two Interstate highways cross the center of Albuquerque, Highway 25 travels north to south across Downtown, while Highway 40 cuts west to east running just north of Downtown and close by the university campus.

✕ Albuquerque BioPark

2601 Central Ave. NW. **(** (505) 764-6200. ◯ 9am–5pm Tue–Sun. ● Thanksgiving, Dec 25. ◉ ♿
The park encompasses the Albuquerque Aquarium and the Rio Grande Botanic Garden. The Rio Grande Zoological Park is located nearby. The botanic garden occupies ten acres (4 ha) of woodland along the Rio Grande and has a variety of different gardens.

The aquarium focuses on the marine life of the Rio Grande *(see p200)* and features a fascinating walkthrough eel cave containing moray eels. There is also an impressive 285,000-gallon (627,000-liter), floor-to-ceiling shark tank.

⛫ Turquoise Museum

2107 Central Ave. NW.
((505) 247-8650. ◯ 9:30am–6pm Mon–Sat. ● Thanksgiving, Dec 25. ◉ ♿
The fascinating displays in this museum focus on consumer education, helping visitors to judge the quality of turquoise gemstones. The entrance is a replica mine tunnel that leads to the "vault," which contains an unsurpassed collection of rare and varied turquoise specimens from around the world.

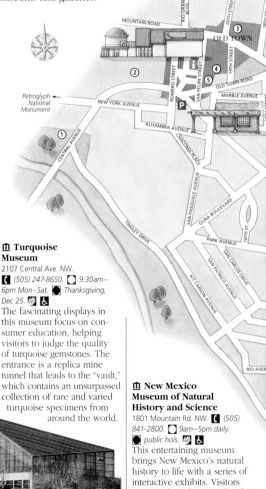

⛫ New Mexico Museum of Natural History and Science

1801 Mountain Rd. NW. **(** (505) 841-2800. ◯ 9am–5pm daily. ● public hols. ◉ ♿
This entertaining museum brings New Mexico's natural history to life with a series of interactive exhibits. Visitors can stand inside a simulated live volcano or explore an ice cave. The "Evolator" is a ride through 38 million years of the region's evolution using

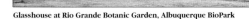

Glasshouse at Rio Grande Botanic Garden, Albuquerque BioPark

the latest video technology. Replica dinosaurs, a state-of-the-art planetarium, and a large-screen film theater are all highly popular with children.

🏛 Albuquerque Museum of Art and History

2000 Mountain Rd. NW. 📞 *(505) 242-4600.* 🕐 *9am–5pm Tue–Sun.* ⬤ *public hols.* ♿

This excellent museum depicts four centuries of history in the middle of Rio Grande Valley. A collection of well-chosen artifacts is expertly arranged for maximum impact. Exhibits focus on the Spanish Colonial period *(see p39)* and include a reconstructed 18th-century house and chapel. From April to November, walking tours of the Old Town leave from the museum.

🏛 American International Rattlesnake Museum

202 San Felipe Ave. N. 📞 *(505) 242-6569.* 🕐 *daily.* ⬤ *public hols.* 🈯 ♿

More than a mere repository for creepy-crawlies, this animal conservation museum explains the life-cycles and ecological importance of some of Earth's most misunderstood creatures. It contains the world's largest collection of live rattlesnakes, including natives of North, Central, and South America.

The snakes are displayed in glass tanks that simulate their natural habitat as closely as possible, and are accompanied by explanatory notices suitable for both adults and children. The museum also features other much-maligned venomous animals, including a Gila monster lizard, tarantulas, and scorpions.

Colorful tiles decorate the Art Deco-style façade of the KiMo Theater

🎭 KiMo Theater

423 Central Ave. NW. 📞 *(505) 848-1370.* 🕐 *call for program.* 🈯 ♿

Built in 1927, the KiMo Theater was one of many entertainment venues constructed in the city during the 1920s and 1930s. One of Albuquerque's most distinctive buildings, the theater's design was inspired by that of the nearby Native American pueblos, and created a fusion of Pueblo Revival and Art Deco styles. Today, the KiMo Theater is a community arts center staging music, dance, and drama.

🦁 Rio Grande Zoological Park

903, 10th St. SW. 📞 *(505) 764-6200.* 🕐 *9am–5pm Tue–Sun.* ⬤ *Thanksgiving, Dec 25.* 🈯 ♿

The Rio Grande Zoo forms part of the Albuquerque Bio-Park. The zoo is noted for its imaginative layout with enclosures designed to simulate the animals' natural habitats, including the African savanna. Among the most popular species here are lowland gorillas and white Bengal tigers.

🏛 Explora! Science Center and Children's Museum

800 Rio Grande Blvd. NW. 📞 *(505) 842-1537.* 🕐 *Tue–Sun.* ⬤ *public hols.* 🈯 ♿

Explora's kids-oriented science center is enjoyable for adults and children alike. Interactive exhibits allow you to direct your own laser show, fly a model plane, or race balls through liquid-filled tubes. In the Children's Museum, youngsters can look through kaleidoscopes, practice weaving, or capture their shadows.

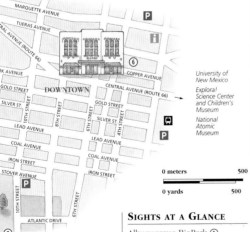

0 meters 500
0 yards 500

SIGHTS AT A GLANCE

KEY

🚌	Bus station
🅿	Parking
ℹ	Visitor information
▦	Albuquerque Old Town Street-by-Street *see pp210–11*

Indian Pueblo Cultural Center

THIS IMPRESSIVE cultural center is run by the 19 Indian Pueblos that lie along the Rio Grande around Albuquerque and Santa Fe. The complex history and varied culture of the Puebloan peoples is traced here through their oral history and is presented from their viewpoint.

The building is designed to resemble the layout of a pueblo dwelling, and is set around a large central courtyard. The center also contains a restaurant serving Pueblo Indian cooking, and an excellent group of gift shops offering high-quality pottery, jewelry, and other crafts from each pueblo.

Two female Puebloan dancers in front of a mural in the central courtyard

Puebloan Central Courtyard
Red adobe walls decorated with murals and hung with chiles emulate the layout of a Pueblo dwelling. Each weekend exuberant dance performances are held here.

KEY

- ☐ Museum (featuring Puebloan history)
- ☐ Arts and Crafts Exhibition
- ☐ Mini-theater
- ☐ Pueblo Kitchen Restaurant
- ☐ Theater
- ☐ Gift shops
- ☐ Non-exhibition space

Main entrance

Arts and Crafts Exhibition
A flower and leaf motif, colored with bold strokes of black and orange on yellow, are typical of the kind of pottery found in some villages today.

STAR FEATURE

★ **Museum**

Courtyard Mural
*Painted by Jemez Pueblo
artist Jose Rey Toledo
in 1979, this mural
shows the turtle
rain dance.*

**Museum
entrance**

★ Museum
*This wooden baby carrier
from Taos Pueblo is one of
many artifacts, from ancient
to modern, that highlight
Puebloan cultural life.*

Minutemen rockets outside the National Atomic Museum

⛫ University of New Mexico

ℹ 1700 Las Lomas Rd. NE. ((505) 277-1989.

The campus of New Mexico's largest university is known for its Pueblo Revival style architecture *(see p23)* and its museums. The **University Art Museum** contains the largest fine arts collection in the state, including Old Master paintings, sculpture, and other works from the 17th to the 20th centuries.

The **Maxwell Museum of Anthropology** is considered one of the finest of its kind in the US. It emphasizes the culture of the Southwest, with an important collection of art and artifacts, including prehistoric pottery and a reconstructed cave dwelling. It also features exhibits from South America, Asia, Africa, and Australia.

Horse at Museum of Anthropology

⛫ University Art Museum

((505) 277-4001. ☐ 9am–4pm Tue–Fri, 1–4pm Sun. ● Mon, Sat. &

⛫ Maxwell Museum of Anthropology

((505) 277-4405. ☐ 9am–4pm Tue–Fri, 10am–4pm Sat. ● Mon, Sun. &

⛫ National Atomic Museum

South Wyoming Blvd. ((505) 284-3243. ☐ daily. ● public hols. &

This singular museum is devoted to the history of nuclear weapons and atomic energy *(see pp186–7)*. The central focus here remains the story of the bomb, and artifacts range from Einstein's letter to President Roosevelt suggesting the possibility of an atom bomb to the casings of bombs themselves. Particularly sobering are replicas of Little Boy and Fat Man, the atomic bombs dropped on Hiroshima and Nagasaki in 1945.

⌂ Petroglyph National Monument

ℹ 4735 Unser Blvd. NW. ((505) 899-0205. ☐ daily. ● public hols. & limited.

This site lies on the western outskirts of Albuquerque. The area was established in 1990 to preserve nearly 20,000 images carved into rock along the 17-mile (27-km) West Mesa escarpment. The earliest petroglyphs date back to 1,000 BC, but the most prolific period is thought to be between 1300 and 1680. The pictures from this time range from human figures such as musicians and dancers to animals, including snakes, birds, and insects. Spirals and other geometric symbols are common, as are hands, feet, and animal tracks. Though the meaning of many petroglyphs has been lost over time, others have great cultural significance to today's Puebloan population.

Hundreds of petroglyphs are accessible along Boca Negra Canyon, 2 miles (3 km) north of the park visitor center, where three self-guided trails, lasting from 5 to 35 minutes, wind past them. The petroglyphs should never be touched, as they are easily damaged.

Sandia Peak tram rising over pine forest and mountains near Albuquerque

Sandia Peak Tramway ❷

10 Tramway Loop N.E. ☏ (505) 856-7325. ◯ May–early Sep: 9am–10pm daily; late Sep–Apr: 9am–8pm Thu–Tue, 5pm–8pm Wed. 🖼 &

THE SANDIA PEAK Tramway is a breathtaking ride from the foothills at the north-eastern edge of Albuquerque to Sandia Peak at 10,378 ft (3,113 m). The tram was constructed in the mid-1960s, and transports tourists from the outskirts of the city to the summit's viewing platform. The ride lasts 15 minutes and passes over stunning land-scapes, moving from low desert to ponderosa pine forests and rugged mountains at the top. The summit offers outstanding panoramic views of Albuquerque and the surrounding countryside.

Bernalillo ❸

🏠 6,000 🛈 PO Box 638 (505) 867-3311. 🅰

THE FARMING community of Bernalillo was settled by Spanish colonists in 1698. Here, against a striking back-drop on the banks of the Rio Grande, is the **Coronado State Monument**, which encompas-ses the partially restored ruins of the Kuaua pueblo. Spanish explorer Francisco Vasquez de Coronado is believed to have been here in 1540 on a quest to find Cibola, the fabled seven cities of gold (see p39).

Nearby Sandia Pueblo is home to around 300 people. Their festival on San Antonio's Day in June features tribal dancing (see p33).

ENVIRONS: Around 16 miles (26 km) northwest of Bernalillo, Zia Pueblo is famous for its redware pottery. Visitors are welcome to purchase the pottery and watercolors produced in this small community.

⋔ Coronado State Monument
State Highway 44, 1 mile west of I-25. ☏ (505) 867-5351. ◯ 8:30am–5pm daily. ● public holidays. 🖼 &

The Turquoise Trail ❹

🛈 PO Box 1335, Cedar Crest (505) 281-5233.

THE SCENIC Highway 14, known as the Turquoise Trail, runs for 52 miles (84 km) between Albuquerque and Santa Fe. Passing through the spectacular countryside of the Sandia Mountains and Cibola National Forest, it takes in the old mining towns of Golden, Madrid, and Cerillos.

Golden is the first stop in a northward direction. It is a small ghost town with ruined buildings, and an atmospheric adobe mission church, which dates back to 1830.

Madrid was a busy coal-mining town in the early 20th century. Its ramshackle houses

The interior of the Trading Post store at Cerillos

are now full of artists and New Age entrepreneurs, and there are more than 20 galleries, craft, and antique shops. **The Old Coal Mine Museum** in town displays a variety of old locomotives, vintage vehicles, buildings, and mining gear, and organizes the staging of Victorian melodramas in the nearby Engine House Theater.

Tiny Cerrillos has a 2,000-year history of mining turquoise, gold, copper, and coal. Today, its sleepy streets attract browsing tourists who particularly enjoy the fine **Casa Grande Trading Post** with its turquoise mining museum, rock and gift shop, and petting zoo.

🏛 **Old Coal Mine Museum**
2846 Hwy 14, Madrid. ((505) 438-3780. ⏰ 9:30am–5:30pm daily. ● public holidays. 🎫 ♿
🎪 **Casa Grande Trading Post**
Cerrillos. ((505) 438-3008. ♿

An old mining cottage in Madrid, midway on the Turquoise Trail

Acoma Pueblo ❺

Rte 23, off I-40. ⏰ Year-round. ● Some pueblo festivals. 🎫 ♿ 🎥 obligatory. 🏢 Acoma Tourist Center (505) 469-1052. ⏰ Apr–Oct: 8am–7pm daily; Nov–Mar: 8am–4:30pm daily.

T HE INCREDIBLE beauty of Acoma Pueblo's setting on the top of a 357-ft- (107-m-) high mesa, has earned it the sobriquet "Sky City." Looking out over a stunning panorama of distant mountains, mesas, and plains, its high position afforded the Puebloan people natural defense against enemies and helped delay submission to Spanish rule. Acoma is one of the oldest continuously

Centuries-old houses at the Acoma Pueblo on a high plateau

inhabited towns in the US, occupied since before the 12th century (see p39). Today, just 30 people live on the 70-acre (40-ha) mesa top year round; 6,000 others from local towns return to their ancestral home for festivals and celebrations.

As well as original pueblo buildings, the village features the 1629 mission church, San Esteben del Rey. There are also seven ceremonial *kivas* (see p161), their wooden ladders jutting out against the sky. Acoma can be visited only on a guided tour, where expert guides explain its rich history.

Grants ❻

🏃 8,600. 🏢 100 N. Iron Avenue. (800) 748-2142. ⛺

B ETWEEN THE 1950s and the 1980s, Grants was famous as a center for uranium mining. Yellow rocks of the mineral were found by Navajo farmer Paddy Martinez on top of Haystack Mountain, 10 miles (16 km) from town in 1951. The industry has now declined but visitors can relive its heyday at the **New Mexico Mining Museum** – tours go underground to see a re-created mine.

Today, Grants is well-placed along Hwy 40/ Route 66 for exploring sights in the area, such as the unusual volcanic badlands of El Malpais National Monument.

🏛 **New Mexico Mining Museum**
100 Iron Street. ((505) 287-4802. ⏰ May–Sep: 9am–5pm Mon–Sat, 9am–3pm Sun; Oct–Apr: 9am–4pm Mon–Sat. ● public holidays. 🎫 ♿

El Morro National Monument ❼

((505) 783-4226. ⏰ Visitor center: Oct–Apr: 9am–5pm, May–Sep: 9am–7pm; Hiking Trail: Oct–Apr: 9am–4pm; May–Sep: 7:30am–7pm. ● Dec 25, Jan 1. 🎫 ♿ 🎥 ⛺

R ISING DRAMATICALLY from the surrounding plain, El Morro is a long sandstone cliff that slopes gently upward to a high bluff, where it suddenly drops off. Its centerpiece is the 200-ft- (60-m-) tall Inscription Rock, which is covered with more than 300 petroglyphs and pictographs from early pueblo people, as well as some 2,000 inscriptions left by Spanish and Anglo travelers. For centuries, people were drawn to this remote spot by a pool of fresh water, formed by runoff and snowmelt, beneath the bluff. Here they carved their initials into the rock.

Among the signatures is that of the Spanish colonizer Don Juan de Oñate (see p39), who, in 1605, wrote "pasó por aquí," meaning "passed by here," a phrase repeated by many subsequent travelers. An easy half-mile (1-km) trail leads past the pool and the inscriptions at the base of the rock.

Handcrafted pot from Zuni

ENVIRONS: The people of the Zuni Pueblo, 32 miles (50 km) west of El Morro, are descendants of the early mesa dwellers of the region. Today, Zuni artists are known for their fine pottery and shell mosaic jewelry. Outstanding murals depicting Zuni history can be seen in the pueblo's 17th-century mission church.

Façade of San Miguel Mission in Socorro

Socorro 8

Road map E4. 🚶 *10,000.* ℹ️ *101 Plaza (505) 835-0424.*

SOCORRO, MEANING "aid" in Spanish, was named by explorer Juan de Oñate in 1598 when his party received help from the people of the Pilabo Pueblo, which once stood here. The area was re-settled in the early 1800s, and it was during the silver boom of the 1880s that many of the town's delightful Victorian buildings were constructed, including those surrounding the plaza. Just north of here is the 1821 San Miguel Mission, featuring massive adobe walls, supported by curved arches.

ENVIRONS: The **Bosque del Apache National Wildlife Refuge**, a renowned bird-watching area, lies 20 miles (32 km) south of Socorro. It attracts thousands of migrating snow geese, and sandhill and whooping cranes in winter.

🦤 Bosque del Apache National Wildlife Refuge
Hwy 1. 🞂 *(505) 835-1828.*
🞇 *daily.* ⬤ *Dec 25.* ♿

Truth or Consequences 9

Road map E4. 🚶 *7,000.*
ℹ️ *201 S. Foch St. (505) 894-3536; (800) 831-9487.* 🅰️

KNOWN BY LOCALS as "T-or-C," this town changed its name from Hot Springs to Truth or Consequences for the 10th anniversary of the game show of the same name, held here in 1950. The original hot springs still exist in the form of bath houses dotted around the town. For centuries the thermal springs had drawn Native Americans to the area, notably the famous Geronimo *(see p42).* The **Geronimo Springs Museum** has displays on local history, including a life-sized statue of the Apache chief. Outside, visitors can test the waters in a channel of the bubbling springs. The town center has an old-fashioned charm enhanced by such places as Joe's Barber Shop, the Hot Springs Bakery, and a handful of rustic gift shops.

Truth or Consequences is a popular summer resort as it is close to both the **Elephant Butte Lake** and the Caballo Lake State Parks. These are famous for a wide range of outdoor activities, including such water sports as fishing, boating, and windsurfing.

🏛 Geronimo Springs Museum
211 Main St. 🞂 *(505) 894-6600.*
🞇 *9am–5pm Mon–Sat.*
⬤ *Sun; public hols.* 🈂️ ♿
🦤 Elephant Butte Lake State Park
Off I-25. 🞂 *(505) 744-5421.*
🞇 *24 hours.* 🈂️ ♿ 🅰️

Gila Cliff Dwellings National Monument 10

Road map D4. 🞂 *(505) 536-9461.*
🞇 *late May–early Sep: 8am–6pm daily; mid-Sep–mid-May: 9am–4pm daily.* ⬤ *Dec 25, Jan 1.* 🈂️ ♿ 🅰️

THE GILA (pronounced hee-la) Cliff Dwellings are one of the most remote archae-ological sites in the Southwest, situated among the piñon, juniper, and ponderosa ever-greens of the Gila National Forest. The dwellings occupy five natural caves in the side of a sandstone bluff high above the Gila River.

Hunter-gatherers and farmers called the Tularosa Mogollon established their 40-room village here in the late 13th century. The Mimbres Mogollon people, famous for

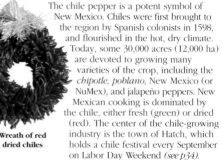

CHILE PEPPERS

The chile pepper is a potent symbol of New Mexico. Chiles were first brought to the region by Spanish colonists in 1598, and flourished in the hot, dry climate. Today, some 30,000 acres (12,000 ha) are devoted to growing many varieties of the crop, including the *chipotle, poblano,* New Mexico (or NuMex), and jalapeño peppers. New Mexican cooking is dominated by the chile, either fresh (green) or dried (red). The center of the chile-growing industry is the town of Hatch, which holds a chile festival every September on Labor Day Weekend *(see p34).*

Wreath of red dried chiles

The chile has a reputation as a cure for a range of health problems. In the 18th century, it was used to relieve the toothache. Today, capsaicin, the chemical that gives chile its heat, is added to ointments for muscle and joint pain. The chile's high vitamin C content (a large green chile contains as much as an orange), is believed to help prevent colds and flu.

One of the entrances to the Gila Cliff Dwellings, situated high above the Gila River

their abstract black-and-white pottery designs, also lived in this area *(see p38)*. The ruins are accessed by a one-mile (1.6-km) roundtrip hike from the footbridge crossing the Gila River's West Fork. Allow two hours to navigate the 40-mile (64-km) road to the site from Silver City as it winds and climbs through the mountains and canyons of the forest.

Silver City ⑪

Road map D5. 🏃 *12,000.* 🚌
i *Chamber of Commerce, 201 N. Hudson St. (800) 548-9378.* Ⓐ

As ITS NAME suggests, Silver City was a mining town. Located in the foothills of the Pinos Altos Mountains, the town's ornate Victorian architecture dates from its boom period between 1870 and the 1890s. In 1895, a flood washed away Silver City's main street, and in its place today is Big Ditch Park, an *arroyo* (or waterway) running 50-ft- (15-m-) deep through the town. This area was the site of the cabin where Billy the Kid *(see p225)* spent much of his youth.

Framed by a backdrop of mountains and forest, Silver City has three defined historic districts – Chihuahua Hill, Gospel Hill, and the old business district – all containing buildings that evoke the town's Wild West boom-town past.

The **Silver City Museum** is found in the beautiful 1881 H.B. Ailman House, and contains frontier-era memorabilia, while the **Western New Mexico University Museum** holds the Southwest's largest collection of Mimbres pottery.

Silver City is a good base for exploring the surrounding region. The nearby forest is home to elk, deer, and bear, and there are several hiking trails and picnic areas.

🏛 Silver City Museum
312 W. Broadway St. **(** *(505) 538-5921.* ⭘ *9am–4:30pm Tue–Fri; 10am–4pm Sat & Sun.* ● *public hols.* ♿
🏛 Western New Mexico University Museum
10th & W. Sts. **(** *(505) 538-6386.* ⭘ *9am–4:30pm Mon–Fri; 10am–4pm Sat & Sun.* ● *public hols.* 🖼 *donation.* ♿

Deming ⑫

Road map D5. 🏃 *14,500.* 🚗 🚌
i *800 E. Pine St. (505) 546-2674; (800) 848-4955.* Ⓐ

THE TOWN of Deming lies 60 miles (96 km) west of Las Cruces. The Deming Luna Mimbres Museum contains excellent pieces of Mimbres pottery, frontier artifacts, and a fine gem and mineral display. Rockhounding (amateur rock and mineral collecting) is a popular pastime in the nearby **Rockhound State Park** where jasper, agate, opal, crystal, and other minerals can be found. The town is also known for its Great American Duck Race, run every August *(see p33)*.

🏕 Rockhound State Park
Highway 11. **(** *(505) 546-6182.* ⭘ *7:30am–5pm daily.* 🖼 ♿

The H.B. Ailman House, which is home to the Silver City Museum

Glimmering white dunes of gypsum granules at White Sands National Monument ▷

Remains of the 1865 Fort Selden in Mesilla Valley

Fort Selden State Monument ⑬

Road map E5. ((505) 526-8911. ◯ 8:30am–5pm daily. 🖼 ♿

BUILT IN 1865, this adobe fort was established to protect settlers and railroad construction crews in the Mesilla Valley from attacks by Apaches and outlaws. Its buildings, now in ruins, once housed four companies of the 125th Infantry, a black infantry unit known as the Buffalo Soldiers. Douglas MacArthur, who was to command Allied troops in the Pacific during World War II, lived here for two years as a boy in the 1880s when his father was post commander. The fort was abandoned in 1891 when defense of the region was no longer necessary. Today, rangers dressed in period uniforms demonstrate the life of the 19th-century soldier. A small museum contains memorabilia.

Sentinel statue at Fort Selden

Las Cruces ⑭

Road map E5. 👥 78,000. ℹ 211 N. Water St. (800) 343-7827.

SPREADING OUT at the foot of the rugged Organ Mountains, *Las Cruces*, or The Crosses, was named for the graves of early settlers ambushed here by the Apache in 1787 and again in 1830. It has always been a crossroads – of

frontier trails, of the railroads, and now two Interstate Highways (10 and 25). Today, it is New Mexico's second largest city and a busy center for manufacturing, farming, and high-tech industries, as well as being the home of New Mexico State University.

While the town is best used as a base for exploring the region, there are a number of interesting museums here. They include the **Branigan Cultural Center**, which features fine displays of historic photographs alongside the work of local artists. The center also arranges tours of the nearby Bicentennial Log Cabin, a late 19th-century pioneer house of hand-hewn timber furnished with attractive antiques and artifacts from the same period.

🏛 **Branigan Cultural Center**
Downtown Mall, Lucero and Main Sts. ((505) 541-2155. ◯ 10am–4:30pm Mon–Fri; 10:30am–1pm Sat. ● Sun, public hols. ♿

Mesilla ⑮

Road map E5. 👥 2,000. ℹ 211 N. Water St. (800) 343-7827.

THIS WELL-PRESERVED historic town was established in 1850 by a group of residents who preferred to remain in Mexican territory, when most of New Mexico came under

American rule. However, with the Gadsden purchase of 1854 (*see p41*), Mesilla became part of the United States.

Today, Mesilla exudes the atmosphere of a late-19th-century frontier town, especially around the historic plaza with its adobe architecture. It was here, in Mesilla's former courthouse, that Billy the Kid (*see p225*) was sentenced to hang in 1881. **The Gadsden Museum** contains exhibits on local history and cultures.

🏛 **Gadsden Museum**
Hwy 28/Barker Rd. ((505) 526-6293. ◯ 9–11am & 1–5pm daily. ● public hols. 🖼 ♿

Billy the Kid gift shop in the 19th-century town of Mesilla

El Paso ⑯

Road map E5. 👥 630,000. ✈ 🚊 🚌 ℹ 1 Civic Center Plaza (915) 534-0653; (800) 351-6024.

LARGE AND SPRAWLING, El Paso, Texas, is a key entry point to New Mexico and the Southwest. Facing El Paso on the other side of the Rio Grande is its Mexican sister town of Ciudad Juárez. They share the border, which was established in 1963 after disputes concerning the Rio Grande had been resolved. From the city, Interstate I-10 travels north to Las Cruces and west across southern Arizona. The Amtrak train *Sunset Limited* stops at El Paso (*see p288*) three times a week.

The Spanish named their early settlement here *El Paso del Norte* (Northern Pass) in the late 16th century. It was a

The 1692 Socorro Mission on El Paso's Mission Trail

stopping place on the famous King's Highway *(Camino Real, see p25)*, which linked Mexico to Spain's northern territories. The city's history as a major hub is reflected today in its typically Southwestern mix of Native American, Hispanic, and European cultures.

El Paso has a series of outstanding mission churches, including the Ysleta and the Socorro, both dating from 1692, while the lovely Chapel San Elizario was built in 1789. **Mission Socorro** combines Native and Spanish styles, with *vigas* (wooden ceiling beams) often carved and painted with Native American designs.

El Paso's western heritage is further reflected in its links with the famous outlaw Billy the Kid *(see p225)*, who visited the town in 1876 when he got his partner, Melquiades

Segura, out of jail. Today, El Paso is a center for Western wear, with many stores selling cowboy boots and hats.

Mission Socorro
(915) 534-0677. ○ daily; call one week ahead. obligatory

White Sands National Monument ⑰

Road map E4. (505) 679-2599. ○ daily. ● Dec 25.

THE GLISTENING dunes of the White Sands National Monument rise up from the Tularosa Basin at the northern end of the Chihuahuan Desert. It is the world's largest gypsum dune field, covering around 300 sq miles (800 sq km).

Gypsum is a water soluble mineral, rarely found as sand. But here, with no drainage outlet to the sea, the sediment washed by the rain into the basin becomes trapped. As the rain evaporates, dry lakes form and strong winds blow the gypsum up into the vast fields of rippling dunes.

Visitors can explore White Sands by car on the Dunes Drive, an 8-mile (13-km) road. Four clearly marked trails lead from points along the way, including the wheelchair-accessible Interdune Boardwalk. Year-round ranger-led walks introduce visitors to the dunes' flora and fauna. Only plants that grow quickly enough not to be buried by sand survive, such as the hardy soaptree yucca. Most of the animals here are nocturnal, and include foxes, coyotes, and porcupines.

The park is surrounded by a military testing site, the White Sands Missile Range. For safety, the park and the road leading to it (Hwy 70) may close for up to two hours when testing is underway. The **White Sands Missile Range Museum** displays many of the missiles tested here, as well as the V-2 rockets used in World War II.

White Sands Missile Range Museum
US 70, 25 m (40 km) E. of Las Cruces. (505) 678-2250. ○ 8am–4:30pm Mon–Fri. ● Sat & Sun, public hols.

Soaptree yucca plants growing at White Sands National Monument

Colorful shops along Ruidoso's attractive main street

Alamogordo ⑱

Road map E4. ♔ 30,000. ✈
ℹ️ 1301 White Sands Blvd. (505)
437-6120; (800) 826-0294.

Alamogordo was established
as a railroad town in 1898
by two New York entrepreneurs, Charles and John Eddy.
Its wide streets are lined with
cottonwood trees, which reflect
its origins and are at the root of
its name – Alamogordo
means "fat cottonwood" in
Spanish. Located at the foot of
the Sacramento Mountains, the
town was a sleepy backwater
until World War II, when
construction of the nearby
Holloman Air Force Base
sparked its development as a
major defense research center.

The town is only 13 miles
(21 km) from White Sands
National Monument *(see
p223)* and offers many
opportunities for such
outdoor activities as
hiking, biking, and golf,
particularly in the Lincoln
National Forest on
Alamogordo's eastern
border. In town, the
**International Space
Hall of Fame**, is a
fascinating museum
housed in a golden-
glass, cube-shaped
building. Opened in
1976, the museum
focuses on the history
of the space race, with
exhibits detailing living
conditions inside a
space station, a full-
size replica of
Sputnik, the first
space satellite, and
a simulated walk on

**Launch vehicle at the
Space Hall of Fame**

Mars. Another simulator offers
the chance to land the space
shuttle with directions from
mission control. The Space Hall
also includes the IMAX™
Dome, a large screen theater.

🏛 **International Space
Hall of Fame**
Indian Wells Rd at Scenic Dr. 【 (505)
437-2840; (800) 545-4021. ⏱ 9am–
5pm daily. 🅿️ ♿

Cloudcroft ⑲

Road map E4. ♔ 750.
ℹ️ Cloudcroft Chamber of Commerce,
Hwy 82 (505) 682-2733. Ⓐ

The picturesque mountain
town of Cloudcroft was
established in 1898 as a center
for the lumber trade. Perched
at 8,650 ft (2,600 m) in the
Sacramento Mountains,
the village soon became a
favorite vacation spot for
those escaping the summer
heat of the valley below.
Cloudcroft remains a
popular resort, with its
summer population
more than doubling the
number of year-round
residents. Burro Avenue,
running parallel to the
main highway, looks
much as it did at the turn
of the 20th century with
its rustic timber build-
ings, many of which
house quaint gift shops.
Surrounded by the
Lincoln National Forest,
the town offers many
outdoor sports, such
as hiking, mountain
biking, hunting, fish-
ing, skiing, and golf.

Ruidoso ⑳

Road map E4. ♔ 7,000. ℹ️ 720
Sudderth Dr. (505) 257-7395. Ⓐ

Nestled high in the
Sacramento Mountains,
surrounded by cool pine
forest, Ruidoso is one of
New Mexico's fastest growing
resorts. Mecham Drive is the
long main street lined with
shops, art galleries, cafés, and
restaurants. Here, specialty
shops sell everything from
candles to cowboy boots.

Outdoor activities are the
area's major attraction, with
hiking, horseback riding, and
fishing. There are several golf
courses including the **Links
at Sierra Blanca**, a top-rated
18-hole course. Northwest of
the town is **Ski Apache**.
Owned and operated by the
Mescalero Apache Tribe, it is
famous for its warm-weather
powder snow. The town is
best known for horse racing.
Quarter horse (fast over a quarter of a mile) and thoroughbred racing at **Ruidoso
Downs Racetrack**. The track
hosts the All-American Futurity,
held every Labor Day (the
first Monday in September).
The world's richest quarter
horse race, it has prize money
in excess of $2 million. The
Ruidoso Downs Race Horse
Hall of Fame is located in the
**Hubbard Museum of the
American West**. This
museum contains Western
memorabilia, the heart of
which is a collection of more
than 10,000 pieces assembled
by a wealthy New Jersey
horsewoman, Anne Stradling
(1913–92). Formerly known

BILLY THE KID

When he died, Billy the Kid was one of the Old West's most notorious outlaws. Born Henry McCarty in 1859, it is believed he changed his name to William Bonney in 1877, when he killed his first victim in Arizona.

Billy fled to Lincoln, where he was hired by John Tunstall and Alexander McSween, who had set up a store competing with one run by Lawrence Murphy and James Dolan. In February 1878, when Dolan's men murdered Tunstall, Billy helped to form the Regulators, who set out to get justice. The Lincoln County War followed, culminating in a violent battle in July. Billy escaped, but was captured by Sheriff Pat Garrett two years later and returned to Lincoln to be hung. Once again, however, he escaped. Billy was eventually shot, by Garrett, at Fort Sumner on July 14, 1881. In spite of his violent life, Billy was a local hero. His story and deeds are memorialized in the little town of Lincoln.

Wild West outlaw, Billy the Kid

One of the historic buildings along Lincoln's main street

Lincoln ㉑

Road map E4. 🏠 *100*. 🛈 *Lincoln County Heritage Trust, Main Street.* *(505) 653-4025.* ⏰ *8:30am–5pm daily.* 🖼 ♿

THE PEACEFULNESS of this small town, surrounded by the beautiful countryside of the Capitan Mountains, belies its violent past. It was the center of the 1878 Lincoln County War, a battle between rival ranchers and merchants involving the legendary Billy the Kid. In those days, Lincoln County covered one-quarter of the state, and Lincoln itself was the county seat.

Lincoln is now a state monument, with 11 buildings kept as they were in the late 1800s. At the Lincoln County Courthouse you can see where Billy the Kid was held, and the bullet hole in the wall from his escape. Tunstall Store has its shelves stocked with original 19th-century merchandise. The Lincoln County Historical Center has displays featuring the Apache people, the early Hispanic settlers, and the Buffalo Soldiers all-black regiment from Fort Selden, as well as the Lincoln County War.

as the Museum of the Horse, its artifacts range from fine art to horse-drawn carriages. Outside is the fabulous *Free Spirits at Noisy Water* (1995), a monument of seven larger-than-life-sized horses by local artist Dave McGary (b.1958). Every October, the town celebrates life in the Old West with the Lincoln County Cowboy Symposium, which features country music and dancing, celebrity roping, and a chuck wagon cook-off.

Set on a high mesa a few miles north at Alto is the **Spencer Theater for the Performing Arts**, a state-of-the-art venue for theater, music, and dance. Built by Albuquerque architect Antoine Predock in 1997, this white sandstone building is set against a spectacular mountain backdrop.

⛳ Links at Sierra Blanca
105 Sierra Dr. 📞 *(505) 258-5330.*
🎿 Ski Apache
📞 *(505) 336-4356.*
Ruidoso Downs Racetrack
Hwy 70. 📞 *(505) 378-4431.*
⏰ *May–early Sep.* 🖼 ♿
🏛 Hubbard Museum of the American West
841 Hwy 70. 📞 *(505) 378-4142*
⏰ *May–early Sep: 9am–5:30pm daily; early Sep–Apr: 10am–5pm daily.*
⏺ *Thanksgiving, Dec 25.* 🖼 🎥 ♿
🎭 Spencer Theater for the Performing Arts
Airport Highway 200. 📞 *(505) 336-4800; (888) 818-7872.* 🖼 ♿

The bronze monument, *Free Spirits at Noisy Water* (1995), at the Hubbard Museum of the American West

Carlsbad Caverns National Park ㉒

Located in the remote southeastern corner of New Mexico, Carlsbad Caverns National Park protects one of the world's largest cave systems. Geological forces carved out this complex of chambers, and their decorations began to be formed around 500,000 years ago when dripping water deposited drops of the crystalized mineral calcite. Native pictographs near the Natural Entrance indicate that they had been visited by Native peoples, but it was cowboy Jim White who brought them to national attention, after exploring them in 1901. The caverns were made a national park in 1930, and a United Nations World Heritage Site in 1995, one of 20 in the US.

Underground Lunchroom
A paved section of the cavern is home to a popular underground diner, a kitsch souvenir store, and restrooms.

Natural
Entrance

Visitor
Information
Center

King's Palace Tour
This tour takes in the deepest cave open to the public, 830 ft (250 m) below ground.

The Boneyard is a complex maze of dissolved limestone rock.

Queens
Chamber and
Papoose Room

Doll's Theater
This small cave is named for its size. The Doll's Theater resembles a fairy grotto, filled with fine, luminous soda-straw formations.

The Big Room
A self-guided tour takes in the 14-acre (5.6-ha) Big Room and passes features such as the Bottomless Pit.

Rock
of Ages

Bottomless Pit

VISITORS' CHECKLIST

Road map F5. 3225 National Parks Hwy, Carlsbad. **⬛** (505) 785-2232; (800) 967-2283 (for tour reservations). **✖** to Carlsbad. **⬛** to White's City. **○** May–Aug: 8:30am–5pm daily; Sep–mid-May: 8:30am–3:30pm (Natural Entrance) call for last entry times. **●** Dec 25. **🔲** **♿** partial. **▨**

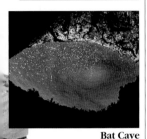

Bat Cave
Most summer evenings at dusk clouds of free-tailed bats emerge from the bat cave to cross the desert in search of food.

Doll's Theater

Painted Grotto

0 meters ————— 100
0 yards ————— 100

TOURS

━━ Big Room route

━━ Natural Entrance route

━━ King's Palace tour
(Ranger guided only)

Butterfly and lobelia flowers, Living Desert State Park

Carlsbad **㉓**

Road map F5. **🏠** 25,000. **🛈** 302 S. Canal St. (505) 887-6516; (800) 221-1224. **△**

THE TOWN OF Carlsbad is located 20 miles (32 km) northeast of Carlsbad Caverns, making it a good option for visitors to the caves. There are plenty of hotels as well as opportunities for outdoor activities. (White's City also offers accommodations; see p245.) The Pecos River winds through town, there are three lakes, and fishing, boating, and water-skiing are popular pastimes. At the northern edge of town, the Living Desert State Park has exhibits focusing on the ecology of the Chihuahuan Desert (see p20).

Roswell **㉔**

Road map F4. **🏠** 50,000. **🛈** 426 N. Main St. (505) 624-0889.

ONCE A SMALL ranching town, Roswell is now a byword for aliens and UFOs, due to the Roswell Incident. The **International UFO Museum and Research Center** is devoted to the serious investigation of visitors from outer space and features an extensive collection of newspaper clippings, photographs, and maps of the crash site. A 70-minute film contains over 400 interviews with people connected to the crash.

Roswell's **Museum and Art Center** is one of the finest small museums in the Southwest, with a collection of 2,000 artifacts on the history of the American West. The fascinating Robert H. Goddard Collection details 11 years of experiments by this famous rocket scientist (see p187). His workshops have been rebuilt at the museum.

Roswell's Alien Zone symbol

🏛 International UFO Museum and Research Center
114 N. Main St. **⬛** (505) 625-9495. **○** daily. **♿**

🏛 Roswell Museum and Art Center
100 W. 11th St. **⬛** (505) 624-6744. **○** 9am–5pm Mon–Sat; 1–5pm Sun and public hols. **♿**

THE ROSWELL INCIDENT

Near midnight on July 4, 1947 an unidentified airborne object crash-landed during a storm in the Capitan Mountains, 75 miles (120 km) northwest of town. Jim Ragsdale was camping nearby and claims to have seen a flash and a craft, 20 ft (6 m) in diameter, hurtling through the trees and the bodies of four "little people," with skin like snakeskin. However, Ragsdale did not tell his story until 1995.

The US Airforce issued a statement that a flying saucer had been recovered, and the story spread around the world. By July 9, however, they said it was just a weather balloon. Witnesses were allegedly sworn to secrecy, fuelling rumors of a cover-up and alien conspiracy theories to this day.

Officers examine "alien" material

TRAVELERS' NEEDS

WHERE TO STAY

THE SOUTHWEST has a long history of hospitality that is reflected in the wide variety of accommodations on offer to the visitor. Whether luxurious five-star resorts or simple rustic lodges suit your budget, there is a wealth of options. You can choose modern hotels, historic or cozy bed and breakfasts, convenient motels, or fully equipped apartments. For those seeking Western-style adventure, there are dude ranches, many of which are luxurious lodgings with horseback

Weatherford Hotel sign in Flagstaff

riding. Across the range, all are likely to offer private bathrooms and clean, comfortable rooms. Las Vegas hotels are noted for their themes and size and have widely varying prices, depending on occupation and whether you wish to stay mid-week or on weekends. Across the rest of the region prices also tend to vary according to the season. The listings provided on pages 232–45 recommend more than 200 places in all price ranges, each representing the best of their kind.

Traditional adobe architecture of the Hotel Santa Fe façade

HOTEL CLASSIFICATIONS

THE TOURIST industry throughout the Southwest is recognized for its quality lodgings. A guideline to travelers is the diamond rating system of the **American** and **Canadian Automobile Associations** (AAA and CAA). Every accommodation, from the one-diamond motel to the five-diamond resort hotel, is rated for service, cleanliness, and the facilities offered. AAA members also benefit from discounts when they book in advance.

TAXES

ACCOMMODATIONS tax varies across the region as it is charged by both state and city or county governments. Expect to pay between 10 and 14 percent of the room price in tax. Prices given for hotels in this book include taxes.

LUXURY HOTELS

IN THE SOUTHWEST, hotels come in every shape and size, including historic show-places, such as Grand Canyon's El Tovar (see p233), originally built to impress East Coast investors and prove that the Southwest was an exciting tourist destination. Today, some of the most lavish hotels in the US are located in the region, from the extravagant, themed mega-resorts of Las Vegas (see pp236–8) to the Wigwam Resort in Phoenix (see p235) with its three championship 18-hole golf courses, tennis dining, and gourmet dining. The area around Phoenix and southern Arizona is famous for both its luxury health and golf resorts. Small, independently owned

"boutique" hotels offer luxurious facilities combined with an intimate atmosphere and attentive service.

There are also many hotels aimed specifically at corporate travelers, offering weekly rates and computer and fax outlets in the rooms, although these services are now available in a range of hotels.

CHAIN HOTELS AND MOTELS

FOR THE MOST PART, you can count on efficient service, moderate prices, and comfortable (if bland) surroundings at a chain hotel. The most popular chains include **Holiday Inn**, **Comfort Inn**, **Best Western**, **Ramada Inns**, **Econolodge**, and **Super 8**. Particularly good value are suite hotels, such as **Country Inn and Suites** and **Embassy Suites**, which offer living rooms and kitchenettes for little more than the cost of a basic hotel room. Chain hotels also offer central reservation systems that can help you find a room at peak times.

A hotel in the Best Western chain

Motels provide rooms that are usually accessible from the parking area. They are often the only option in remote areas, and can vary from nostalgic Route 66 places (see pp50–51) to such bargain lodgings as Motel 6.

Jeanette's Bed and Breakfast in Flagstaff *(see p232)*

HISTORIC INNS AND BED AND BREAKFASTS

THERE ARE hundreds of excellent inns and bed and breakfasts located across the Southwest. Generally speaking, inns are larger, with more spacious public areas and a dining room. Bed and breakfast establishments tend to be noted for their more homey atmosphere. Both inns and B&Bs may be found in restored or reconstructed historic buildings, and many are located in charming Victorian houses in historic towns. These lodgings pride themselves on providing a warm welcome and friendly service. Visual delights often include antiques, art, and gardens. There are Bed and Breakfast and Inn associations in each state that can help you select and make bookings.

WESTERN HOTELS AND DUDE RANCHES

IF YOU'VE EVER wanted to indulge your "Old West" fantasies there are plenty of historic hotels in which to do so. Between 1880 and 1920, Western towns gained prestige through the quality and grandeur of their hotels, and many built during this time boast extravagantly ornate decor. Today, many of these places have been carefully restored and offer great settings for a vacation. Durango's Strater Hotel, for example, with its antique-furnished rooms, is both a historic hotel and a museum *(see p241)*.

Dude ranches offer visitors the chance to experience western life. They first appeared in the 1920s – the name "dude" is a colloquialism meaning "a city-dweller unfamiliar with life on the range." Choices range from relaxing vacations that include leisurely horseback rides to working ranches where you participate in such activities as cattle roundups. Meals, accommodations, and horses are usually included in the price. Arizona and Colorado have **Dude Ranch Associations** to help you find the perfect western vacation.

Barbecue on the Lazy K Dude Ranch near Tucson, Arizona

CAMPGROUNDS AND RV PARKS

CAMPGROUNDS FOR both tents and RVs (recreational vehicles) are found all over the Southwest and are especially popular in the national parks. The **National Forest Service** provides information on forest campgrounds, which range from extremely basic to those with running water and limited RV hookups.

DIRECTORY

CHAIN HOTELS

Holiday Inn
(*(800) 465-4329.*

Comfort Inn
(*(800) 221-2222.*

Best Western
(*(800) 528-1234.*

Ramada Inns
(*(800) 272-6232.*

Econolodge
(*(800) 424-4777.*

Super 8
(*(800) 800-8000.*

Country Inn and Suites
(*(800) 456-4000.*

Embassy Suites
(*(800) 362-2799.*

HISTORIC INNS AND BED AND BREAKFASTS

Bed and Breakfasts of New Mexico
Box 2805, Santa Fe, NM 87505.
(*(505) 982-3332.*

New Mexico Bed and Breakfast Association
Box 2805 Santa Fe NM 87504.
(*(505) 766-5380;*
(800) 661-6649.

Arizona Association of Bed and Breakfast Inns
Box 7186, Phoenix AZ 85011.
(*(800) 284-2589.*

DUDE RANCHES

Arizona Dude Ranch Association
P.O. Box 603, Cortaro AZ 85652.
(*(800) 444-DUDE.*

Colorado Dude and Guest Ranch Association
P.O. Box 2120, Granby, CO 80446.
(*(970) 887-3128.*

CAMPGROUNDS AND RV PARKS

National Forest Service
Southwest Regional Office,
517 Gold Ave., SW, Albuquerque, NM 87102.
(*(505) 842-3292.*
Intermountain Regional Office,
2501 Wall Ave., Ogden, UT 84401.
(*(801) 524-5030.*

Choosing a Hotel

THE HOTELS in this guide have been selelcted for their good value, excellent facilities, or location. This chart lists the hotels by region in the same order as the rest of the guide. The color codes of each region are shown on the thumb tabs. Entries are alphabetical within price category. Prices given are in-season rates but always enquire about special discounts as rates can vary from week to week and between weekdays and weekends. For restaurant listings, see pages 250–63.

Grand Canyon and Northern Arizon

Hotel	Price	Number of Rooms	Restaurant	Children's Facilities	Garden/Terrace	Swimming Pool
Boulder City: *El Rancho Boulder Motel* 725 Nevada Hwy., NV 89005. ☎ *(702) 293-1085.* With its 1940s architecture, the El Rancho Boulder Motel has clean rooms and is within walking distance of the town center. ❄ [TV] ♿ [P] 💳	$	39				■
Camp Verde: *Camp Verde Comfort Inn* 340 N. Industrial Dr., AZ 86322. ☎ *(520) 567-9000.* [FAX] *(520) 567-1828.* [W] *www.comfortinn.com* A straightforward but well-kept chain motel, near several of the state's most interesting sights. ❄ [TV] ♿ [P] 💳	$$	85				
Cottonwood: *Best Western Cottonwood Inn* 993 S. Main St., AZ 86326. ☎ *(520) 634-5575.* [FAX] *(520) 634-5576.* [W] *www.cottonwoodinn-az.com* The Best Western group has built a pleasant, spacious hotel here with comfortable rooms. ❄ [TV] ♿ [P] 🏋 💳	$$	77	●	■		■
Flagstaff: *Hotel Weatherford* 23 North Leroux St., AZ 86001. ☎ *(520) 779-1919.* [FAX] *(520) 773-8951.* The 1890s Weatherford is one of Flagstaff's most distinctive hotels. Its better rooms are decorated in antique style. ❄ [TV] [P] 💳	$	30	●			
Flagstaff: *Hilton Garden Inn* 350 W. Forest Meadows St., AZ 86001. ☎ *(520) 226-8888.* [FAX] *(520) 556-9059.* This modish, medium-sized establishment provides everything from an ironing board to a microwave in each of the rooms. ❄ [TV] ♿ [P] 🏋 💳	$$	90	●		●	■
Flagstaff: *Hotel Monte Vista* 100 San Francisco St., AZ 86001. ☎ *(520) 779-6971.* [FAX] *(520) 779-2904.* Many of the rooms in this characterful 1920s hotel are named after famous guests who stayed here, such as Bob Hope. ❄ [TV] [P] 💳	$$	46	●	■		
Flagstaff: *Little America Hotel* 2515 E. Butler Ave., AZ 86004. ☎ *(520) 779-7900.* [FAX] *(520) 779-7983.* [W] *www.littleamerica.com* This comfotable resort complex is set among pine trees, to the east of downtown Flagstaff. ❄ [TV] [24] ♿ [P] 🏋 💳	$$	247	●	■	●	■
Flagstaff: *Jeanette's Bed & Breakfast* 3380 E. Lockett Rd., AZ 86001. ☎ *(520) 226-1488.* This appealing B&B in a Victorian-style house has antique-filled rooms. A gourmet breakfast is included in the room price. ❄ ♿ Partial [P] 💳	$$	4				
Flagstaff: *Radisson Woodlands Hotel Flagstaff* 1175 West Route 66., AZ 86001. ☎ *(520) 773-8888.* [FAX] *(520) 773-0597.* One of the best chain hotels in town, this well-equipped establishment has excellent health and fitness facilities. ❄ [24] [TV] ♿ [P] 🏋 💳	$$$	183	●	■	●	■
Grand Canyon: *Phantom Ranch* Grand Canyon, AZ 86023. ☎ *(303) 297-2757.* [FAX] *(303) 297-3175.* Nestling among the cottonwoods down in the canyon, Phantom Ranch offers a central lodge and a string of timber cabins in a stunning setting. 💳	$	40	●		●	
Grand Canyon: *Bright Angel Lodge* Grand Canyon South Rim, AZ 86023. ☎ *(303) 297-2757.* [FAX] *(303) 297-3175.* Popular with hikers, Bright Angel offers both frugal rooms in the main lodge, which dates from the 1930s, and appealing log cabins. ❄ [P] 💳	$$	89	●		●	
Grand Canyon Village: *Yavapai Lodge* Grand Canyon South Rim, AZ 86023. ☎ *(303) 297-2757.* [FAX] *(303) 297-3175.* Set among the pine and juniper woods beside the visitor center, this lodge provides motel-style rooms. ⊘ Nov–Mar. ❄ [TV] ♿ [P] 💳	$$	358	●	■	●	

Price categories for a standard double room per night, inclusive of service charges, and any additional taxes:
$ under US$50
$$ US$50–$100
$$$ US$100–$150
$$$$ US$150–$200
$$$$$ US$200 plus.

RESTAURANT
Hotel restaurant or dining room usually open to non-residents unless otherwise stated.
CHILDREN WELCOME
Cribs and a baby-sitting service available. Some hotel restaurants have children's portions and high chairs.
GARDEN/TERRACE
Hotels with a garden, courtyard, or terrace.
SWIMMING POOL
Hotel with an indoor or outdoor swimming pool.

	Number of Rooms	Restaurant	Children's Facilities	Garden/Terrace	Swimming Pool
GRAND CANYON VILLAGE: *Maswik Lodge* $$$ Grand Canyon South Rim, AZ 86023. ☎ *(303) 297-2757.* [FAX] *(303) 297-3175.* Popular with families, this lodge is located at the west end of the village a short walk from the South Rim. 🛏 [TV] ♿ [P] 💳	278	●	■	●	
GRAND CANYON VILLAGE: *El Tovar Hotel* $$$$ Grand Canyon South Rim, AZ 86023. ☎ *(303) 297-2757.* [FAX] *(303) 297-3175.* Opened in 1905, this distinguished Edwardian hotel offers the most sumptuous accommodation in Grand Canyon National Park. Some rooms have panoramic views of the canyon. 🛏 [24] [TV] ♿ [P] 💳	78	●	■	●	
GRAND CANYON VILLAGE: *Thunderbird and Kachina Lodges* $$$ Grand Canyon South Rim, AZ 86023. ☎ *(303) 297-2757.* [FAX] *(303) 297-3175.* These two modern lodges offer deluxe accommodation and are situated a stone's throw from the South Rim of the canyon. 🛏 [TV] ♿ [P] 💳	110			●	
GRAND CANYON (NORTH RIM): *Grand Canyon Lodge* $ Bright Angel Point, Grand Canyon. AZ 86023. ☎ *(303) 297-2757.* [FAX] *(303) 297-3175.* The only hotel accommodation on the North Rim of the canyon, this lodge has cabins and a few modern motel rooms. Advance reservations are essential. ● Oct–May. 🛏 [TV] ♿ [P] 💳	35	●			
JEROME: *Ghost City Inn* $ 541 N. Main St., AZ 86331. ☎ *(520) 634-4678.* Occupying a handsome Victorian villa, this well-maintained inn has tastefully decorated bedrooms and fabulous views down the valley. [TV] [P] 💳	6			●	
KINGMAN: *Best Western A Wayfarer's Inn* $$ 2815 E. Andy Devine Ave., AZ 86401. ☎ *(520) 753-6271.* [FAX] *(520) 753-9608.* This well-kept hotel is up to the chain's usual high standards, with a pool and indoor spa. Buffet breakfast is included. 🛏 [TV] ♿ Partial. [P] 🍸 💳	100				■
LAKE HAVASU CITY: *Ramada Inn* $ 271 S. Lake Havasu Ave., AZ 86403. ☎ *(520) 855-1111.* [FAX] *(520) 855-6228.* Recently revamped, this stylish hotel offers spacious elegant rooms and is a short walk from London Bridge. 🛏 [TV] ♿ [P] 🍸 💳	170	●	■		■
LAKE HAVASU CITY: *Nautical Inn Resort & Conference Center* $$$ 1000 McCulloch Blvd., AZ 86403. ☎ *(520) 855-2141.* [FAX] *(520) 855-8460.* [W] *www.nauticalinn.com* This resort spreads along the shore of Lake Havasu and appeals to both family vacationers and conference organizers. Watersports facilities are available. 🛏 [TV] ♿ [P] 💳	120	●	■	●	■
SEDONA: *Star Motel* $ 295 Jordan Rd., AZ 86336. ☎ *(520) 282-3641.* Conveniently located in the center of Sedona, this unassuming motel offers some of the most reasonably priced rooms in town. 🛏 [TV] [P] 💳	11				
SEDONA: *Cozy Cactus B&B* $$ 80 Canyon Circle Dr., AZ 86351 ☎ *(520) 284-0082.* [FAX] *(520) 284-4210* Excellent lodgings are available at this upscale, ranch house B&B, which occupies a scenic setting on the southern outskirts of Sedona. 🛏 [P] 💳	5			●	
SEDONA: *Enchantment Resort* $$$$$ 525 Boynton Canyon Rd., AZ 86336. ☎ *(520) 282-2900.* [FAX] *(520) 282-9249.* [W] *www.enchantmentresort.com* Hidden away in beautiful Boynton Canyon, this ritzy complex of adobe-style houses with a full range of leisure facilities is one of the district's premier resorts. 🛏 [24] [TV] ♿ [P] 🍸 💳	222	●	■	●	■
WILLIAMS: *Fray Marcos Hotel* $$ 235 North Grand Canyon Blvd., AZ 86046. ☎ *(520) 635-4010.* [FAX] *(520) 635-2180.* [W] *www.thetrain.com* This elegant hotel, next to the terminus of the Grand Canyon Railway, has a stately wood-beamed hall. 🛏 [TV] ♿ [P] 💳	196	●		●	

For key to symbols see back flap

234 TRAVELERS' NEEDS

Price categories for a standard double room per night, inclusive of service charge, and any additional taxes:
⑤ under US$50
⑤⑤ US$50–$100
⑤⑤⑤ US$100–$150
⑤⑤⑤⑤ US$150–$200
⑤⑤⑤⑤⑤ US$200 plus.

RESTAURANT
Hotel restaurant or dining room usually open to non-residents unless otherwise stated.
CHILDREN WELCOME
Cribs and a baby-sitting service available. Some hotel restaurants have children's portions and high chairs.
GARDEN/TERRACE
Hotels with a garden, courtyard, or terrace.
SWIMMING POOL
Hotel with an indoor or outdoor swimming pool.

	NUMBER OF ROOMS	RESTAURANT	CHILDREN'S FACILITIES	GARDEN/TERRACE	SWIMMING POOL
WILLIAMS: *Mountainside Inn* ⑤ 642 E. Route 66, AZ 86046. ((520) 635-4431. FAX (520) 635-2292 Tucked away among pine trees, the Mountainside Inn offers tidy rooms, and is a convenient base for Grand Canyon. ▦ TV & P ⊞ ⊠	96	●	■		■
PHOENIX AND SOUTHERN ARIZONA					
APACHE JUNCTION: *Holiday Inn Express Apache Junction* ⑤⑤ 1101 West Apache Junction, AZ 85220. ((480) 982-9200. FAX (480) 671-6183. Convenient for the Apache Trail, this small and intimate hotel has views of the Superstition Mountains and a lavish breakfast. ▦ TV & P ⊠	40		■	●	■
BISBEE: *Shady Dell* ⑤ 1 Douglas Rd, AZ 85603. ((520) 432-3567. Unique accommodation in vintage 1950s aluminum trailers, set in a 1927 trailer park. Original decor includes black-and-white TVs. P	8	●		●	
BISBEE: **COPPER QUEEN HOTEL** ⑤⑤ 11 Howell Ave., AZ 85603. ((800) 247-5829. FAX (520) 432-4298. Atmospheric, late 19th-century hotel with rooms decorated in period style. A book in the lobby listing sightings of resident ghosts! ▦ TV & P ⊠	47	●		●	■
DOUGLAS: *The Gadsden Hotel* ⑤⑤ 1046 G Ave., AZ 85607. ((520) 364-4481. FAX (520) 364-4005. W www.theriver.com/gadsdenhotel Opened in 1907, this historic hotel has sumptuously decorated rooms and public areas. ▦ TV & P ⊠	160	●			
DRAGOON: *Triangle T Guest Ranch* ⑤⑤ I-10 exit 318, AZ 85609 (& FAX (520) 586-7533. Historic ranch in Texas Canyon close to Kartchner Caverns, Tombstone, and the outstanding Amerind Foundation *(see p93)*. Comfortable cabins with old-fashioned furnishings. ▦ & P ⊠	8	●			■
GREEN VALLEY: *Best Western Green Valley* ⑤⑤ 111 S. La Cañada, AZ 85614 ((800) 344-1441. FAX (520) 625-0215. Just 20 minutes south of Tucson, this is a great base for exploring San Xavier mission, Tubac, and Madera Canyon. Heated pool and spa. ▦ TV & P ⊠	108	●		●	■
PHOENIX: *Hotel San Carlos* ⑤⑤ 202 N. Central Ave., AZ 85004. ((602) 253-4121. FAX (602) 253-6688. Located at the heart of downtown Phoenix, this designated historic hotel, built in the 1920s, has rooms decorated in tasteful style. ▦ TV P ⊠	133	●			■
PHOENIX: *Los Olivos Hotel & Suites* ⑤ 202 E. McDowell Rd., AZ 85004. ((602) 528-9100. FAX (602) 258-7259. An inexpensive option, Los Olivos is a straightforward, downtown hotel within easy walking distance of the Heard Museum. ▦ TV & P ⊠	48	●			■
PHOENIX: *Quality Hotel & Resort* ⑤⑤ 3600 N. 2nd Ave., AZ 850133. ((602) 248-0222. FAX (602) 248-0466. W www.getawayresort.com One of the more luxurious premises in this reliable chain, with extensive facilities including a well-equipped gym, four pools, and a spa, offering a range of treatments. ▦ TV & P ⊞ ⊠	280	●	■	●	■
PHOENIX: *Ramada Inn Downtown* ⑤⑤ 401 North 1st St., AZ 85004. ((602) 258-3411. FAX (602) 258-3171. Situated in the downtown core near the convention center, the rooms here are stylish, brisk, and business-like. ▦ TV & P ⊠	162	●		●	■
PHOENIX: *Arizona Biltmore Resort & Spa* ⑤⑤⑤ 2400 E. Missouri Ave., AZ 85016. ((602) 955-6600. FAX (602) 381-7600. Designed by Frank Lloyd Wright *(see p23)*, this 1930's hotel complex excellent facilities set among landscaped grounds. ▦ 24 TV & P ⊞ ⊠	732	●	■	●	■

PHOENIX: *Best Western Executive Park Hotel* $$$ 1100 N. Central Ave., AZ 85004. (602) 252-2100. FAX (602) 252-2731. W www.bestwestern.com In the heart of the downtown business area, this chic hotel provides a complimentary airport shuttle.	107	●			■
PHOENIX: *Pointe Hilton South Mountain Resort* $$$ 7777 S. Pointe Parkway, AZ 85044. (602) 438-9000. FAX (602) 870-8181. Set among the hills south of Phoenix, this resort offers every amenity, including a golf course and four restaurants.	638	●	■	●	■
PHOENIX: *Ritz-Carlton Hotel* $$$$ 2401 E. Camelback Rd., AZ 85016. (602) 468-0700. FAX (602) 468-0793. W www.ritzcarlton.com This appealing hotel occupies a modern tower with Neo-classical flourishes. Large, comfortable rooms.	281	●			■
PHOENIX: *The Wigwam Resort* $$$$$ 300 E. Wigwam Blvd., Litchfield Pk., AZ 85251. (623) 935-3811. FAX (623) 935-3737. W www.wigwamresort.com To the west of the city, this luxurious resort boasts three 18-hole golf courses, two pools, and a choice of fabulous restaurants. Rooms are stylish, spacious, and comfortable.	331	●	■	●	■
SCOTTSDALE: *Scottsdale Princess* $$$ 7575 E. Princess Dr., AZ 85255. (480) 585-4848. FAX (480) 585-0086. A first-rate resort-hotel in a handsome setting with a full range of amenities, and several award-winning restaurants.	650	●	■	●	■
SCOTTSDALE: $$$$$ *Hyatt Regency Scottsdale Hotel at Gainey Ranch* 7500 E.Doubletree Ranch Rd., AZ 85258. (480) 991-3388. FAX (480) 483-5550. Outstanding contemporary architecture is a highlight here. Rooms are tasteful, and the gardens lush and enticing.	493	●	■	●	■
SCOTTSDALE: *The Phoenician* $$$$$ 6000 E.Camelback Rd., AZ 85251. (480) 941-8200. FAX (480) 947-4311. One of the region's most extravagant resort complexes, set among superb gardens with a stunning golf course, tennis courts, restaurants, and no less than nine swimming pools.	654	●	■	●	■
TOMBSTONE: *Best Western Lookout Lodge* $ Hwy. 80 W., AZ 85638. (520) 457-2223. FAX (520) 457-3870. W www.bestwestern.com Large rooms look out over the desert and the mountains. Complimentary Continental breakfast.	40				■
TOMBSTONE: *Silver Nugget Bed & Breakfast* $ 520 E. Allen St., AZ 85638. (520) 457-9223. FAX (520) 457-3471. W www.silvernugget@tombstone1880.com This friendly B&B overlooks Allen Street, and has a different Western theme in each of the rooms.	4				
TUCSON: *Casa Alegre Bed & Breakfast Inn* $$ 316 E. Speedway Blvd., AZ 85705. (520) 628-1800. FAX (520) 792-1880. A hot tub, pool, and peaceful gardens provide pampering at this charming Arts and Crafts-style bungalow built in 1915.	6			●	■
TUCSON: *El Presidio Bed & Breakfast Inn* $$ 297 N. Main Ave., AZ 85701. (800) 349-6151. FAX (520) 623-3860. Restored Victorian adobe mansion set around a pretty courtyard. Rooms are decorated with antiques. Delicious breakfasts included.	4			●	
TUCSON: *Windmill Inn at St. Philip's Plaza* $$ 4250 N. Campbell Ave., AZ 85718. (800) 547-4747. FAX (520) 577-0045. W www.windmillinns.com Conveniently located in an upscale shopping plaza, this hotel is great value. It features pleasant two-room suites, complimentary breakfast, and a newspaper delivered to your door.	122		■		■
TUCSON: *Arizona Inn* $$$ 2200 E. Elm St., AZ 85719. (800) 933-1093. FAX (520) 881-5830. W www.arizonainn.com This pink stucco resort hotel, opened in 1930, features spacious rooms set in lush grounds.	86	●		●	■
TUCSON: *Lodge on the Desert* $$$ 306 N. Alvernon Way, AZ 85711. (800) 456-5634. FAX (520) 327-5834. A tranquil hideaway close to the university featuring adobe-style buildings with charming rooms set amid pretty desert gardens.	35	●		●	■

For key to symbols see back flap

Price categories for a standard double room per night, inclusive of service charges and any additional taxes: $\textcircled{S}$ under US$50; $\textcircled{S}\textcircled{S}$ US$50–$100; $\textcircled{S}\textcircled{S}\textcircled{S}$ US$100–$150; $\textcircled{S}\textcircled{S}\textcircled{S}\textcircled{S}$ US$150–$200; $\textcircled{S}\textcircled{S}\textcircled{S}\textcircled{S}\textcircled{S}$ US$200 plus.	**RESTAURANT** Hotel restaurant or dining room usually open to non-residents unless otherwise stated. **CHILDREN WELCOME** Cribs and a baby-sitting service available. Some hotel restaurants have children's portions and high chairs. **GARDEN/TERRACE** Hotels with a garden, courtyard, or terrace. **SWIMMING POOL** Hotel with an indoor or outdoor swimming pool.	NUMBER OF ROOMS	RESTAURANT	CHILDREN'S FACILITIES	GARDEN/TERRACE	SWIMMING POOL
TUCSON: *Hacienda del Sol Guest Ranch Resort* $\textcircled{S}\textcircled{S}\textcircled{S}\textcircled{S}$ 5601 N. Hacienda del Sol Rd., AZ 85718. **(** (800) 728-6514. FAX (520) 299-5554. W *www.haciendadelsol.com* Overlooking desert landscape, this luxury retreat in the hills above town has been popular since the 1940s when stars such as Katherine Hepburn used to visit. 🔲 TV & P 🔲		30	●		●	■
TUCSON: *Lazy K Bar Guest Ranch* $\textcircled{S}\textcircled{S}\textcircled{S}\textcircled{S}\textcircled{S}$ 8401 N. Scenic Dr., AZ 85743. **(** (800) 321-7018. FAX (520) 744-7628. W *www.lazykbar.com* An authentic ranch offering trail rides through the desert and square dances as part of the package. 🔲 & P 🔲		23	●	■	●	■
LAS VEGAS						
DOWNTOWN: *Binion's Horseshoe* $\textcircled{S}$ 128 E. Fremont St., NV 89109. **(** (702) 382-1600 FAX (702) 384-1574. Known for hosting the world series poker championship, all rooms have been remodeled in shades of pink *(see p118)*. 🔲 24 TV & P 🔲		366	●			■
DOWNTOWN: *El Cortez* $\textcircled{S}$ 600 E. Fremont St., NV 89101. **(** (702) 382-9938. FAX (702) 474-3626. This low-rise adobe brick building, dating from 1941, has pleasant rooms, although some have showers only *(see p118)*. 🔲 24 TV & P 🔲		300	●			
DOWNTOWN: *Fitzgeralds Casino Holiday Inn* $\textcircled{S}\textcircled{S}$ 301 E. Fremont St., NV 89109. **(** (800) 274-5825. FAX (702) 388-2181. The rooms here have recently been redecorated to a high standard, many with great views across the city to the mountains beyond. 🔲 TV & P 🔲		638	●			
DOWNTOWN: *Four Queens* $\textcircled{S}\textcircled{S}$ 202 E. Fremont St., NV 89109. **(** (800) 634-6045. FAX (702) 887-5160. With its impressive glittering façade, the Four Queens retains the glamorous atmosphere of old Las Vegas. Many rooms offer views of the Fremont Street Experience *(see p118)*. 🔲 24 TV & P 🔲		690	●			
DOWNTOWN: *Golden Nugget* $\textcircled{S}\textcircled{S}$ 129 E. Fremont St., NV 89101. **(** (800) 634-3454. FAX (702) 386-8362. The most luxurious hotel in the Downtown area *(see p118)*. All the rooms have large marble bathrooms. 🔲 24 TV & P 🔲 🔲		1805	●			■
DOWNTOWN: *Jackie Gaughan's Plaza* $\textcircled{S}\textcircled{S}$ 1 Main St., NV 89101. **(** (800) 634-6575. FAX (702) 386-2378. This comfortable hotel has rooms in its North Tower that overlook the Fremont Street Experience *(see p118)*. 🔲 TV & P 🔲 🔲		1037	●	■		■
THE STRIP: *Sahara* $\textcircled{S}$ 2535 Las Vegas Blvd. S., NV 89109. **(** (888) 696-2121. FAX (702) 791-2027. This friendly hotel is conveniently located for attractions at the north end of the Strip, including the Stratosphere Tower *(see p117)*. 🔲 TV & P 🔲 🔲		1720	●			■
THE STRIP: *Stratosphere* $\textcircled{S}$ 2000 Las Vegas Blvd. S., NV 89104. **(** (702) 380-7777. FAX (702) 383-5334. W *www.grandcasinos.com* Panoramic views of the city offset this hotel's distant location at the north end of the Strip *(see p117)*. 🔲 24 TV & P 🔲		1500	●			
THE STRIP: *Algiers Hotel* $\textcircled{S}\textcircled{S}$ 2845 Las Vegas Blvd. S., NV 89109. **(** (800) 732-3361. FAX (702) 792-2112. One of the best bargains on the Strip, this 1950s hotel is also one of the oldest. Spacious, clean rooms but no casino. 🔲 24 TV & P 🔲		105	●			■
THE STRIP: *Barbary Coast* $\textcircled{S}\textcircled{S}$ 3595 Las Vegas Blvd. S., NV 89109. **(** (800) 634-6755. FAX (702) 894-9954. W *www.barbarycoastcasino.com* This intimate hotel has beautifully decorated rooms and a choice of restaurants. 🔲 24 TV & P 🔲		200	●			

THE STRIP: *Circus Circus* $$ 3744
2880 Las Vegas Blvd. S., NV 89109. 📞 (800) 634-3450. FAX (702) 734-2268.
🌐 www.circuscircus.com A vast property with a range of rooms and child-friendly attractions, including a theme park (see p117). 🛏 24 TV ⚂ P ✇

THE STRIP: *Excalibur* $$ 4032
3850 Las Vegas Blvd. S., NV 89109. 📞 (702) 597-7777. FAX (702) 597-7009.
🌐 www.excalibur-casino.com In keeping with its kitsch medieval theme, rooms feature fake stone walls, and wall sconces (see p107). 🛏 24 TV ⚂ P ✇

THE STRIP: *Imperial Palace* $$ 2700 L N N
3535 Las Vegas Blvd. S., NV 89109. 📞 (800) 634-6441. FAX (702) 735-8328.
🌐 www.imperialpalace.com One of the few hotels to feature balconies overlooking the Strip. Extremely good value. 🛏 24 TV ⚂ P 🍴 ✇

THE STRIP: *Luxor* $$ 4467
3900 Las Vegas Blvd. S., NV 89119. 📞 (800) 288-1000. FAX (702) 262-4404.
🌐 www.luxor.com This opulent Egyptian-themed hotel features a huge atrium and a reconstruction of Tutankhamun's tomb. Rooms are decorated in tastefully muted tones (see p106). 🛏 24 TV ⚂ P 🍴 ✇

THE STRIP: *MGM Grand* $$ 5034
3799 Las Vegas Blvd. S. Nevada 89109. 📞 (800) 929-1111. FAX (702) 891-1030.
🌐 www.mgmgrand.com Despite being one of the largest hotels in the world the Grand maintains a relaxed, friendly atmosphere and boasts a particularly luxurious spa (see p108). 🛏 24 TV ⚂ P 🍴 ✇

THE STRIP: *Monte Carlo* $$ 3002
3770 Las Vegas Blvd. S., NV 89109. 📞 (800) 311-8999. FAX (702) 730-7250.
🌐 www.monte-carlo.com An elegant European theme is reflected in the large rooms, each with a marble bathroom. 🛏 24 TV ⚂ P 🍴 ✇

THE STRIP: *New York New York* $$ 2024
3790 Las Vegas Blvd. S., NV 89109. 📞 (800) 693-6763. FAX (702) 740-6920.
🌐 www.nynyhotelcasino.com Rooms here are decorated in authentic Art Deco style, with lots of inlaid wood (see p107). 🛏 24 TV ⚂ P 🍴 ✇

THE STRIP: *Riviera* $$ 2075
2901 Las Vegas Blvd. S., NV 89109. 📞 (800) 634-6753. FAX (702) 794-9541.
One of the Strip's oldest hotels, the Riviera was opened in 1955 by Liberace (see p109). Comfortable rooms (see p116). 🛏 24 TV ⚂ P 🍴 ✇

THE STRIP: *Stardust* $$ 1700
2535 Las Vegas Blvd. S., NV 89109. 📞 (888) 696-2121. FAX (702) 791-2027.
A Vegas icon since it opened in 1958, guests can stay in the hotel's towers or the Motor Inn, which has motel-style rooms with parking bays outside each one. 🛏 24 TV ⚂ P 🍴 ✇

THE STRIP: *Aladdin* $$$ 2657
3667 Las Vegas Blvd S., NV 89109. 📞 (877) 333-9474. FAX (702) 785-5558.
🌐 www.aladdincasino.com Spacious rooms themed in an Arabian Nights-style are offered at this hotel, which also has the vast Desert Passage shopping and entertainment complex (see p109). 🛏 24 TV ⚂ P 🍴 ✇

THE STRIP: *Bally's* $$$ 2814
3645 Las Vegas Blvd. S., NV 89109. 📞 (800) 634-3434. FAX (702) 794-2413.
🌐 www.ballyslv.com Friendly, with an olympic-size swimming pool and large, luxurious rooms, many with good views of the Strip. 🛏 24 TV ⚂ P 🍴 ✇

THE STRIP: *Caesars Palace* $$$ 2454
3570 Las Vegas Blvd.S., NV 89109. 📞 (800) 634-6001. FAX (702) 731-6636
🌐 www.caesars.com This Vegas institution is famous for its luxurious rooms and suites, all with marble bathrooms. TVs in the rooms offer gaming lessons on the in-house channel (see p111). 🛏 24 TV ⚂ P 🍴 ✇

THE STRIP: *Flamingo Hilton* $$$ 3999
3555 Las Vegas Blvd. S., NV 89109. 📞 (702) 733-3111. FAX (702) 733-3353.
🌐 www.hilton.com This tropical-themed hotel is renowned for having one of the best pool areas in Vegas (see p111). 🛏 24 TV ⚂ P 🍴 ✇

THE STRIP: *Harrah's* $$$ 2700
3475 Las Vegas Blvd., NV 89109. 📞 (800) 427-7247. FAX (702) 369-5008.
🌐 www.harrahs.lv.com Friendly hotel with comfortable rooms. It is also possible to play keno through the room's TV set. 🛏 24 TV ⚂ P 🍴 ✇

For key to symbols see back flap

Price categories for a standard double room per night, inclusive of service charges and any additional taxes:

$ under US$50
$$ US$50–$100
$$$ US$100–$150
$$$$ US$150–$200
$$$$$ US$200 plus.

RESTAURANT
Hotel restaurant or dining room usually open to non-residents unless otherwise stated.

CHILDREN WELCOME
Cribs and a baby-sitting service available. Some hotel restaurants have children's portions and high chairs.

GARDEN/TERRACE
Hotels with a garden, courtyard, or terrace.

SWIMMING POOL
Hotel with an indoor or outdoor swimming pool.

	NUMBER OF ROOMS	RESTAURANT	CHILDREN'S FACILITIES	GARDEN/TERRACE	SWIMMING POOL
THE STRIP: *Mandalay Bay* $$$ 3950 Las Vegas Blvd. S., NV 89119. **(** (877) 632-7000. **FAX** (702) 632-7228. **W** www.mandalaybay.com Ornate yet elegant rooms provide a host of amenities including two phone lines with computer jacks. The popular pool area has a "beach" and a gently-flowing "river" where guests may enjoy a leisurely swim (see p106).	3646	●			■
THE STRIP: *Paris* $$$ 3655 Las Vegas Blvd. S., Nevada 89109. **(** (888) 266-5687. **FAX** (702) 546-4405. **W** www.paris-lv.com The charming rooms here are modeled on 18th-century Paris. Bathrooms are luxurious, and every amenity from in-room voice mail to cable TV is available (see p110).	2916	●		●	■
THE STRIP: *Tropicana* $$$ 3801 Las Vegas Blvd. S., NV 89109. **(** (800) 634-4000. **FAX** (702) 739-2492. **W** www.tropicana.lv.com Noted for the lush gardens and waterfalls around its delightful pool area, the Tropicana is a popular Vegas institution. Guests can soak in one of three outdoor Jacuzzis (see p108).	1874	●		●	■
THE STRIP: *Treasure Island* $$$$ 3300 Las Vegas Blvd. S., NV 89109. **(** (888) 696-2121. **FAX** (702) 894-7446. **W** www.treasureislandlasvegas.com Despite a lack of children's facilities, this hotel is a popular choice with families, because of its Pirate theme and nightly battle attraction (see p115).	2885	●			■
THE STRIP: *Venetian* $$$$ 3355 Las Vegas Blvd. S., NV 89109. **(** (888) 283-6423. **FAX** (702) 414-4884. **W** www.venetian.com All rooms are luxury suites with a minibar, two TVs, fax, and three telephone lines, all set among the palatial splendor of the hotel's gloriously executed Venice theme (see p114).	3036	●		●	■
THE STRIP: *Bellagio* $$$$$ 3600 Las Vegas Blvd. S., NV 89109. **(** (888) 987-6667. **FAX** (702) 693-8546. **W** www.bellagiolasvegas.com One of the most sophisticated resorts in Las Vegas, the Bellagio's rooms are decorated to a high standard with imported carrara marble bathrooms and silk furnishings. The hotel re-creates an authentic Italian atmosphere (see p110).	3000	●			■
THE STRIP: *Mirage* $$$$$ 3400 Las Vegas Blvd. S., NV 89109. **(** (702) 791-7111. **FAX** (702) 791-7446. **W** www.themirage.com Conveniently located in the center of the Strip, the Mirage is famous for its tropical atrium, pretty pool area, and Siegfried and Roy's white tigers (see p127). All the rooms are spacious and have stylish, elegant decor (see p114–5).	3000	●		●	■
SOUTHERN UTAH					
BOULDER: *Boulder Mountain Lodge* $$ 20 N. Hwy. 12, UT 84717. **(** (800) 556-3446. **FAX** (435) 335-7461. An attractive Western style lodge located along the scenic Highway 12, the hotel is surrounded by fabulous red rock canyons. It also houses one of the best restaurants in Southern Utah (see p256).	20	●			
BRYCE CANYON: *Bryce Canyon Lodge* $$$ Bryce Canyon National Park, UT 84717. **(** (435) 834-5361. **FAX** (303) 297-3175. This Western classic boasts elegant period decor, romantic cabins with fireplaces, and suites and rooms with a tasteful Southwestern motif. Located 100 yds (30 m) from the canyon rim. Reserve early.	115	●		●	
BRYCE CANYON: *Best Western Ruby's Inn* $$$ Bryce Canyon National Park, UT 84764. **(** (800) 528-1234. **FAX** (435) 834-5265. This busy modern inn, located just outside the park, offers two restaurants, a gas station, and a host of other services, tours, and activities.	368	●			■

CEDAR CITY: *Holiday Inn Cedar City* $$ 100
1575 W. 200 North, UT 84720. ☎ *(800) 432-8828.* FAX *(435) 586-1010.*
A good-quality formula Holiday Inn that is new enough to make
it one of Cedar City's best hotels. 🛏 📺 P 🖉

CEDAR BREAKS NATIONAL MONUMENT: *Cedar Breaks Lodge* $$$ 47
223 Hunter Ridge Rd., UT 84719. ☎ *(888) 282-3327.* FAX *(435) 677-2211.*
This is Brian Head Ski Resort's premier lodging. Large rooms with
superb views are standard. Reasonable summer rates. 🛏 📺 P 🖉

ESCALANTE: *Prospector Inn* $ 50
380 W. Main St., UT 84726. ☎ *(435) 826-4653.* FAX *(435) 826-4285.*
This is one of Escalante's nicer family hotels. The spacious rooms
are comfortable, and all have two beds. 🛏 📺 P 🖉

KANAB: *Parry Lodge* $$$ 89
89 E. Center St., UT 84741. ☎ *(800) 748-4104.* FAX *(435) 644-2605.*
This picturesque hotel has clean and pleasant rooms. Movie stars
John Wayne and Charleton Heston once stayed here. 🛏 📺 P 🖉

KANAB: *Shilo Inn* $$$ 118
296 W.100 North, UT 84741. ☎ *(800) 222-2244.* FAX *(435) 644-5333.*
A new hotel featuring mini-suites equipped with refrigerators and micro-
waves. A Continental breakfast is included in the room rate. 🛏 📺 P 🖉

MOAB: *Hotel Off-Center* $ 8
96 E. Center St., UT 84532. ☎ *(435) 259-4244.* FAX *(435) 259-3366.*
This quirky budget place is a hit with younger travelers. Rooms are themed;
one is done up like a miner's shack. Bathrooms down the hall. 📺 P 🖉

MOAB: *The Landmark Hotel* $$ 36
168 N. Main St., UT 84532. ☎ *(800) 441-6147.* FAX *(435) 259-5556.*
A downtown Colonial brick building with spacious rooms. Particularly good
value for large families. Continental breakfast included. 🛏 ☰ 📺 P 🖉

MOAB: *Pack Creek Ranch* $$$ 13
La Sal Mountain Loop Rd., UT 84532. ☎ *(435) 259-5505.* FAX *(435) 259-8879.*
This working western ranch at the foot of the La Sal Mountains offers
hiking trails and stunning scenery. Guests stay in log cabins. 🛏 P 🖉

MOAB: *Redstone Inn* $$ 52
535 S. Main, UT 84532. ☎ *(800) 772-1972.* FAX *(435) 259-2717.*
A pleasant motel in the heart of town offers rooms with kitchenettes. For
travelers with pets, there are 16 pets-welcome rooms. 🛏 📺 P 🖉

MOAB: *Sunflower Hill Bed and Breakast Inn* $$$ 11
185 N. 300 East, UT 84532. ☎ *(800) 662-2786.* FAX *(435) 259-3065.*
A charming Victorian house and cottage surrounded by pretty gardens.
Rooms are stylishly furnished, and breakfast is excellent. 🛏 📺 P 🖉

MOAB: *The Gonzo Inn* $$$ 43
100 W. 200 South, UT 84532. ☎ *(800) 791-4044.* FAX *(435) 259-6992.*
Elegant and eclectic, this very trendy establishment features a warm
Southwestern motif furnished with kitsch 1950s furniture. 🛏 📺 P 🖉

PAGE: *Best Western Inn and Suites* $$$ 99
207 N. Lake Powell Blvd., AZ 86040. ☎ *(800) 637-9183.* FAX *(520) 645-9552.*
This modern suite hotel has a nice pool and is conveniently
close to Lake Powell. Lots of room for the price. 🛏 📺 P 🖉

PAGE: *Courtyard by Marriott* $$$ 153
600 Clubhouse Dr., AZ 86040. ☎ *(800) 851-3855.* FAX *(520) 645-5004.*
This beautiful, upscale hotel features great views of Glen Canyon
and the mountains. Room service, spa, and pool. 🛏 📺 P 🖉

PANGUITCH: *Best Western New Western* $ 55
180 E. Center St., UT 84759. ☎ *(800) 528-1234.* FAX *(435) 676-8876.*
A clean, modern, and tasteful Best Western. Pleasant and moderately
priced and just 30 minutes from Bryce Canyon. 🛏 📺 P 🖉

SPRINGDALE: *Zion Park Inn* $$ 120
1215 Zion Park Blvd., UT 84767. ☎ *(800) 934-7275.* FAX *(435) 772-2499.*
This modern resort is decorated with understated elegance and is set
amid landscaped grounds just outside the park. 🛏 📺 P 🖉

Price categories for a standard double room per night, inclusive service charges and any additional taxes: $ under US$50; $$ US$50–$100; $$$ US$100–$150; $$$$ US$150–$200; $$$$$ US$200 plus.	RESTAURANT Hotel restaurant or dining room usually open to non-residents unless otherwise stated. CHILDREN WELCOME Cribs and a baby-sitting service available. Some hotel restaurants have children's portions and high chairs. GARDEN/TERRACE Hotels with a garden, courtyard, or terrace. SWIMMING POOL Hotel with an indoor or outdoor swimming pool.	NUMBER OF ROOMS	RESTAURANT	CHILDREN'S FACILITIES	GARDEN/TERRACE	SWIMMING POOL
ST. GEORGE: *Ranch Inn* $ 1040 S. Main St., UT 84770. ((800) 332-0400. FAX (435) 656-3983. Clean, modern suites with kitchenettes and a modest price make this a good place for a longer stay. 🔲 TV P 🌿		52			●	▧
ST GEORGE: *Bluffs Inn & Suites* $ 1140 S. Bluff St., UT 84770. ((800) 832-5833. FAX (435) 673-8705. Good value and pleasant family-style motel with large comfortable rooms and a pleasing pastel decor. 🔲 TV P 🌿		61	●			▧
ST. GEORGE: *Seven Wives Inn* $$ 217 N. 100 West,. UT 84770. ((800) 600-3737. FAX (435) 628-4538. This elegant inn comprises two large Victorian houses decorated with antiques. Most of the rooms have fireplaces and balconies, and huge gourmet breakfasts are included. 🔲 TV P 🌿		13			●	▧
TORREY: *Wonderland Inn* $$$ 875 E. Hwy 24, UT 84775. ((800) 458-0216. FAX (435) 425-3212. A bright and cheerful property with pleasant rooms conveniently located close to Capitol Reef National Park. 🔲 TV P 🌿		50	●		●	▧
WAHWEAP: *Wahweap Lodge* $$$ Lakeshore Dr., UT 86040. ((800) 528-6154. FAX (520) 645-1031. This elegant modern lodge, offers views of Lake Powell from some rooms. It also has a restaurant, marina, and boat rentals. 🔲 TV P 🌿		375	●			▧
ZION NATIONAL PARK: *Zion Lodge* $$ Nr. Springdale, UT 84767. ((435) 772-3213. FAX (435) 772-2001. Spacious lodge, located in Zion National Park, offering comfortable rooms and cabins surrounded by natural beauty. 🔲 P 🌿		121	●		●	

THE FOUR CORNERS

AZTEC: *Step Back Inn* $$ 103 W. Aztec Blvd., NM 87410. ((505) 334-1200. FAX (505) 334-9858. Aztec's newest hotel is clean, comfortable, and close to the amenities of the downtown area. 🔲 TV P 🌿		39				
BLUFF: *Recapture Lodge* $ Hwy 191, UT 84512. ((435) 672-2281. FAX (435) 672-2284. This comfortable country lodge hosts regular speakers on the area's geology and archaeology, and offers adventure tours. 🔲 TV P 🌿		28				▧
BLUFF: *Valley of the Gods Bed and Breakfast* $$ Valley of the Gods Rd., UT 84531. ((970) 749-1164. W www.valleyofthegods.cjb.net As "away from it all" as you can get, this pleasant house is the only building in the Valley of the Gods. 🔲 P 🌿		4				
CAMERON: *Cameron Trading Post* $ Rte 89, AZ 86020. ((800) 338-7385. FAX (520) 679-2350. This working trading post also has a cool, delightful garden and fine Native art gallery. The rooms, built in 1916, are comfortable. 🔲 TV 🌿		66	●		●	
CHINLE: *Holiday Inn* $$ Garcia Trading Post, Canyon de Chelly, AZ 86503. ((520) 674-5000. FAX (520) 674-8264. A large hotel complex built around the historic Garcia Trading Post, which houses the hotel's Garcia Restaurant *(see p258)*. Tours of Canyon de Chelly can be arranged from here. 🔲 🍽 TV ♿ P 🌿		108	●		●	▧
CHINLE: *Thunderbird Lodge* $$$ Canyon De Chelly, AZ 86503. ((800) 679-2473. FAX (520) 674-5844. Part of the excellent complex at the mouth of Canyon de Chelly. Rooms are tastefully decorated in Southwestern style. 🔲 🍽 TV ♿ P 🌿		72	●			

CORTEZ: *Kelly Place* $$ 10

14663 Rd. G, CO 81321 **☎** *(800) 745-4885.* **FAX** *(970) 565-3540.*
A few miles from town, this quiet country retreat is set among contrasting
landscapes of fruit orchards and red rock canyons, and offers group
workshops on local Native culture and archaeology. 🔲 **P** 🔳

DURANGO: *Jarvis Suite Hotel* $$$ 22

125 W. 10th St., CO 81301. **☎** *(800) 824-1024.* **FAX** *(970) 259-6190.*
Each of the clean and very pleasant suites in this excellent value hotel
offer a well-equipped kitchen and a living room with sofa bed. 🔲 **TV** **P** 🔳

DURANGO: *Strater Hotel* $$$ 93

699 Main Ave., CO 81301. **☎** *(800) 247-4431.* **FAX** *(970) 259-2208.*
Built in 1887, this Durango landmark building is one of the great luxury
hotels of the Old West. Comfortable rooms are furnished with period
antiques, as well as having delightful bathrooms. 🔲 **TV** **P** 🔳

DURANGO: *Tall Timber Resort* $$$$$ 10

1 Silverton Star, CO 81301 **☎** *(970) 259-4813.*
A deluxe Western resort hidden in the Animas Valley, it is accessible by
the Silverton & Durango steam train or complimentary helicopter only.
Private, spacious cottages and gourmet dining of the highest caliber. 🔲 🔳

FARMINGTON: *Best Western Inn at Farmington* $ 192

700 Scott Ave., NM 87401. **☎** *(800) 528-1234.* **FAX** *(505) 327-1565.*
This good-value and dependable chain hotel has a pool, which is
very inviting in summer. 🔲 **TV** **P** 🔳

MESA VERDE NATIONAL PARK: *Far View Motor Lodge* $$ 150

Mancos, CO 81328. **☎** *(800) 449-2288.* **FAX** *(970) 533-7831.*
Away from the hustle and bustle of the park, this is a modern hotel that
offers superb views across the mesa and Montezuma Valley. 🔲 **P** 🔳

MONUMENT VALLEY: *Gouldings Lodge* $$$ 62

Off Hwy 163, UT 84536. **☎** *(800) 874-0902.* **FAX** *(435) 727-3344.*
This famous inn has hosted movie stars and directors from almost every
movie made here *(see p164–5).* Each room has a balcony with a superb
view of Monument Valley. There is also a museum, which features the
cabin John Wayne used in an early movie 🔲 **TV** **P** 🔳

TELLURIDE: *New Sheridan Hotel* $$$ 26

231 W. Colorado Ave., CO 81435. **☎** *(800) 200-1891.* **FAX** *(970) 728-5024.*
Built in 1895, this atmospheric and luxurious hotel is in Telluride's
historic district. Although busy during the skiing season, attractive off-
peak rates and rooftop hot tubs are available. 🔲 **TV** 🔳

TELLURIDE: *The Victoria Inn* $$$ 31

401 W. Pacific Ave., CO 81435. **☎** *(800) 611-9893.* **FAX** *(970) 728-3233.*
A clean modern hotel within walking distance of Telluride's historic district,
this is one of the town's most reasonably priced inns. The hotel also
boasts a pleasant garden area. 🔲 **TV** **P** 🔳

TELLURIDE: *The Peaks at Telluride* $$$$$ 174

136 Country Club Dr., CO 81435. **☎** *(800) 789-2220.* **FAX** *(970) 728-3291.*
Located in Mountain Village, a gondola ride above Telluride, this luxury
hotel has fabulous views of the surrounding mountain peaks. Advance
reservations are recommended. 🔲 **TV** **&** **P** 🔳

SECOND MESA, HOPI RESERVATION: *Hopi Cultural Center Hotel* $ 33

Rte. 264, AZ 86043. **☎** *(520) 734-2401.* **FAX** *(520) 734-6651.*
This recently renovated hotel with an adobe look outside and pleasant
pastel interior is the best accommodation for miles around. 🔲 **TV** **P** 🔳

WINDOW ROCK: *Navajo Nation Inn* $ 56

48 W. Rte 264, AZ 86515. **☎** *(800) 662-6189.* **FAX** *(520) 871-5466.*
This attractive, comfortable hotel is one of the reservation's showpieces.
Rooms are immaculately clean with bathrooms. 🔲 **TV** **P** 🔳

SANTA FE AND NORTHERN NEW MEXIC

ABIQUIU: *Abiquiu Inn* $ 19

Highway 84, NM 87510. **☎** *(800) 447-5621.* **FAX** *(447) 447-5621 ext 2*
This roadside inn with pleasant modern rooms and amenities is the only
place to stay in Abiquiu. It also has a good restaurant. 🔲 **TV** **P** 🔳

For key to symbols see back flap

Price categories for a standard double room per night, inclusive of service charges and any additional taxes:
$ under US$50
$$ US$50–$100
$$$ US$100–$150
$$$$ US$150–$200
$$$$$ US$200 plus.

RESTAURANT
Hotel restaurant or dining room usually open to non-residents unless otherwise stated.

CHILDREN WELCOME
Cribs and a baby-sitting service available. Some hotel restaurants have children's portions and high chairs.

GARDEN/TERRACE
Hotels with a garden, courtyard, or terrace.

SWIMMING POOL
Hotel with an indoor or outdoor swimming pool.

	Price	Number of Rooms	Restaurant	Children's Facilities	Garden/Terrace	Swimming Pool
CHAMA: *The Gandy Dancer Bed & Breakfast* 299 Maple Ave., NM 87520. ((505) 756-2191. FAX (505) 756-9110. Located one block from the Cumbres and Toltec Scenic Railroad, this delightful B&B is set in a purple Victorian mansion. 🖥 TV P 🗐	$$	7			●	
CHIMAYO: *Casa Escondida* County Rd. 100, House 64, NM 87522. ((800) 643-7201. FAX (505) 351-2575. Charming B&B set in an adobe hacienda. Attractive rooms, furnished with Arts and Crafts-style antiques. Delicious breakfasts. 🖥 TV P 🗐	$$	8			●	
CHIMAYO: *Hacienda Rancho de Chimayo* County Rd. 98, NM 87522. ((505) 351-2222. FAX (505) 351-2222. All the rooms here have antique beds and are furnished with hand-woven Chimayo rugs and draperies. 🖥 TV 🗐 P 🗐	$$	7	●		●	
CIMARRON: *Cimarron House Bed & Breakfast* 600 18th St., NM 87714. ((505) 376-2616. This pleasant B&B overlooks the Cimarron River. Comfortable rooms have king-size beds, fireplaces, and cedar paneling. 🖥 TV P 🗐	$	6				◼
CIMARRON: *St. James Hotel* Rte 1, Box 2, NM 87714. ((800) 748-2694. FAX (505) 376-2623. This landmark hotel dating from 1880 has been restored with period furniture. Jesse James and Buffalo Bill once stayed here. 🖥 TV 🗐 P 🗐	$	24	●			
TAOS: *Holiday Inn Don Fernando de Taos* 1005 Paseo del Pueblo Sur, NM 87571. ((800) 759-2736. FAX (505) 758-0055. Hand-carved furniture and adobe walls add a regional touch to this hotel, which has a tennis court, heated pool, and hot tub. 🖥 24 TV 🗐 P 🗐	$$	124	●	◼		◼
TAOS: *American Artists Gallery House Bed & Breakfast* 132 Frontier Lane, NM 87571. ((800) 532-2041. FAX (505) 758-0497. Simply, but beautifully decorated in Southwestern style with whitewashed walls and carved furniture. Delicious gourmet breakfasts. 🖥 TV 🗐 P 🗐	$$$	10			●	
TAOS: *Fechin Inn* 227 Paseo del Pueblo Norte, NM 87571. ((800) 811-2933. FAX (505) 751-7338. W www.fechin-inn.com/rc This elegant inn next to the Fechin House Museum was designed by the artist Nicolai Fechin and features hand-carved woodwork, paintings, and prints by the artist. 🖥 TV 🗐 P 🍴 🗐	$$$	85			●	
TAOS: *Taos Inn* 125 Paseo del Pueblo Norte, NM 87571. ((888) 461-8267. FAX (505) 758-5776. W www.taosinn.com This historic inn just north of the plaza has rooms in adobe buildings dating from the 1800s, which are decorated with Mexican tiles, locally made furniture, and hand-woven bedspreads. 🖥 TV 🗐 P 🗐	$$$$	36	●		●	◼
TAOS: *Casa de las Chimeneas* 405 Cordoba Road, NM 87571. ((877) 758-4777. FAX (505) 758-3976. A romantic B&B set in beautiful gardens near the town center. Fabulous breakfasts and complimentary evening buffet. 🖥 TV 🗐 P 🍴 🗐	$$$$	8			●	
TAOS SKI VALLEY: *Hotel Edelweiss* PO Box 83, NM 87525. ((800) I LUV SKI. FAX (505) 776-2533. W www.taosnet.com/edelweiss This year-round alpine lodge has many luxuries, from the outdoor hot tubs and in-room massage to the down comforters on all the beds. 🖥 TV P 🗐	$$$	8	●	◼		
TESUQUE: *The Bishop's Lodge* Bishop's Lodge Rd., NM 87501. ((800) 732-2240. FAX (505) 989-8739. W www.bishopslodge.com A luxurious, upscale resort with well-appointed rooms and a wide range of activities available, including horseback riding, tennis, and hiking. 🖥 TV 🗐 P 🍴 🗐	$$$$$	111	●	◼	●	

SANTA FE: *Camas de Santa Fe* $$ **15**
323 Palace Ave., NM 87501. ((800) 632-2627. W www.camasdesantafe.com
Intimate B&B a short walk from the plaza. Most rooms feature hardwood
floors with simple, stylish furnishings. 🚗 TV & P 🍽

SANTA FE: *El Rey Inn* $$ **86**
1862 Cerrillos Rd., NM 87505. ((800) 521-1349. FAX (505) 989-9249.
W www.elreyinnsantafe.com One of the lower-priced hotels on
Cerrillos Road, this pleasant hotel has rooms decorated in Southwestern style
set among lush gardens. Breakfast included in room rate. 🚗 TV & P 🍽

SANTA FE: *Dancing Ground of the Sun* $$$ **20**
711 Paseo de Peralta, NM 87501. ((800) 745-9910. FAX (505) 986-8082.
Charming 1930s bungalows in the heart of town feature rooms decorated
with handcrafted furniture. Continental breakfast included. 🚗 TV & P 🍽

SANTA FE: *Grant Corner Inn* $$$ **11**
122 Grant Ave., NM 87501. ((800) 964-9003. FAX (505) 983-1526.
W www.grantcornerinn.com This 1905 Colonial manor creates a wonderful
country ambience in the heart of downtown. 🚗 TV & P 🍽

SANTA FE: *Inn of the Turquoise Bear* $$$ **10**   L
342 E. Buena Vista St., NM 87501. ((800) 396-4104. FAX (505) 988-4225.
W www.turquoisebear.com B&B in an adobe villa set in acres of gardens, rock
terraces, and tall pines. Great rooms and delicious breakfast. 🚗 TV & P 🍽

SANTA FE: *Hotel St. Francis* $$$$ **83**
210 Don Gaspar Ave., NM 87501. ((800) 529-5700. FAX (505) 989-7690.
W www.hotelstfrancis.com Built in 1920, this elegant hotel has attractive rooms
and serves traditional afternoon tea in the spacious lobby. 🚗 TV & P 🍽

SANTA FE: *Hotel Santa Fe* $$$$ **128**
1501 Paseo de Peralta, NM 87501. ((800) 210-6441. FAX (505) 984-2211.
W www.hotelsantafe.com Charming Native American-owned hotel with
spacious rooms and contemporary decor. Fine Native American cuisine
is served in the hotel's Corn dance Cafe (see p260). 🚗 TV & P 🍽 🍽

SANTA FE: *Inn on the Alameda* $$$$ **68**
303 East Alameda, NM 87501. ((800) 289-2122. FAX (505) 986-8825.
W www.inn-alameda.com This beautiful Pueblo-style hotel prides itself on
attention to detail. Rooms and suites are elegantly decorated in soothing
earth tones, and the buffet breakfast is fabulous. 🚗 TV & P 🍽 🍽

SANTA FE: *Territorial Inn* $$$$ **20**
215 Washington St., NM 87501. ((800) 745-9910. FAX (505) 986-9212.
Romantic Victorian B&B close the Plaza, famous for its "brandy turn-
downs" in the evening. Generous breakfast included. 🚗 TV & P 🍽

SANTA FE: *Inn of the Anasazi* $$$$$ **59**
113 Washington Ave., NM 87501. ((800) 688-8100. FAX (505) 988-3277.
W innoftheanasazi.com Luxurious rooms with four-poster beds. Elegant
restaurant serving Southwestern cuisine (see p261). 🚗 TV & P 🍽

SANTA FE: *La Fonda Hotel* $$$$$ **167**
100 E. San Francisco, NM 87501. ((800) 497-8165. FAX (505) 982-6367.
W www.lafondasantafe.com A Santa Fe landmark, this handsome 1920s
hotel stands on the site of an original 1610 adobe. 🚗 TV & P 🍽

SANTA FE: *La Posada de Santa Fe* $$$$$ **159**
330 E. Palace, NM 87501. ((800) 727-5276. FAX (505) 982-6850.
W www.laposadadesantafe.com Romantic adobe cottages set amid fragrant
gardens. Rooms are individually decorated. 🚗 TV & P 🍽

ALBUQUERQUE AND SOUTHERN NEW MEXICO

ALAMORGORDO: *White Sands Inn* $ **93**
1020 S. White Sands Blvd., NM 88310. ((505) 434-4200. FAX (505) 437-8872.
Comfortable, good-value motorlodge with large rooms and suites, near
to attractions and restaurants. Deluxe breakfast included. 🚗 TV & P 🍽

ALBUQUERQUE: *Wyndham Garden Hotel* $ **151**
6000 Pan American Freeway NE, NM 87109. ((800) 996-3426. FAX (505) 798-4305.
This welcoming hotel has simple Southwestern decorations and an
atrium lobby and bright, comfortable rooms. 🚗 TV & P 🍽 〰

For key to symbols see back flap

Price categories for a standard double room per night, inclusive service charges and any additional taxes:					
$ under US$50					
$$ US$50–$100					
$$$ US$100–$150					
$$$$ US$150–$200					
$$$$$ US$200 plus.					

RESTAURANT
Hotel restaurant or dining room usually open to non-residents unless otherwise stated.

CHILDREN WELCOME
Cribs and a baby-sitting service available. Some hotel restaurants have children's portions and high chairs.

GARDEN/TERRACE
Hotels with a garden, courtyard, or terrace.

SWIMMING POOL
Hotel with an indoor or outdoor swimming pool.

		NUMBER OF ROOMS	RESTAURANT	CHILDREN'S FACILITIES	GARDEN/TERRACE	SWIMMING POOL
ALBUQUERQUE: *W. J. Marsh House Victorian B&B* $$ 301 Edith SE., NM 87102. ((505) 247-1001. FAX (505) 842-5213. W www.marshhouse.com Rooms here are decorated with Victoriana, and a gourmet breakfast is served on antique china and crystal. 🚗 P 🗷						
ALBUQUERQUE: *Holiday Inn Mountain View* $$ 2020 Menaul Blvd., NM 87107. ((505) 884-5732. FAX (505) 881-4806. Attractive hotel with spacious rooms, conveniently located near the junction of I-25 and I-40. Views of the nearby mountains. 🚗 TV 🔥 P 🍴 🗷		360	●			■
ALBUQUERQUE: *La Posada de Albuquerque* $$ 125 2nd Street NW., NM 87102. ((800) 777-5732. FAX (505) 242-1945. Built in 1939, this boutique-style hotel features a two-story atrium lobby with Spanish tile floors and carved beams and woodwork. 🚗 TV 🔥 P 🗷		113	●			
ALBUQUERQUE: *Albuquerque Doubletree Hotel* $$$ 201 Marquette Ave., NW., NM 87102. ((888) 223-4113. FAX (505) 247-7025. W www.doubletreehotels.com Very comfortable, friendly, well-appointed hotel in the heart of downtown. 🚗 TV 🔥 P 🍴 🗷		295	●			■
ALBUQUERQUE: *Albuquerque Hilton* $$$ 1901 University Blvd., NE., NM 87102. ((800) 274-6835. FAX (505) 880-1196. Resort-like facility in the heart of downtown, with attractive courtyard gardens, and outdoor and indoor pools. 🚗 TV 🔥 P 🍴 🗷		263	●		●	■
ALBUQUERQUE: *Bottger-Koch Mansion B&B* $$$ 110 San Felipe NW., NM 87104. ((800) 758-3639. FAX (505) 243-4378. W www.bottger.com Victorian luxury is on offer at this family-run B&B, set in this delightful historic mansion. Rooms have four-poster beds, and there is a courtyard garden. 🚗 TV P 🗷		8			●	
ALBUQUERQUE: *Hacienda Antigua* $$$ 6708 Tierra Dr., NW., NM 87107. ((800) 201-2986. FAX (505) 345-3855. W www.haciendantigua.com This grand old adobe home has rooms decorated with colorful quilts, polished antiques, and fresh flowers. 🚗 P 🗷		6			●	
ALBUQUERQUE: *Sheraton Albuquerque Uptown* $$$ 2600 Louisiana NE., NM 87110. ((800) 252-7772. FAX (505) 881-3736. W www.sheratonuptown.com Great value at this beautiful hotel, near two major shopping malls, with quick access to Old Town and the airport. Rooms are large, comfortable, and tastefully appointed. 🚗 TV 🔥 P 🍴 🗷		296	●			■
ALBUQUERQUE: *Casas de Sueños* $$$$ 310 Rio Grande Blvd., SW., NM 84104. ((800) 242-8987. FAX (505) 842-8493. Near the Old Town Plaza, this "House of Dreams" was an artists' colony in the 1930s. Charming cottages surround a lovely courtyard. 🚗 TV 🔥 P 🗷		22	●		●	
CARLSBAD: *Holiday Inn Carlsbad* $$ 601 S. Canal St., NM 88220. ((505) 885-8500. FAX (505) 887-5999. Attractive, reliable chain property with many amenities, such as heated pool, whirlpool, sauna, playground, and cable TV. 🚗 TV 🔥 P 🍴 🗷		100	●	■	●	■
CEDAR CREST: *Elaine's Bed & Breakfast* $$ 72 Snowline Estates, NM 87008. ((800) 821-3092. FAX (505) 281-1384. W www.elainesbnb.com This three-story, timber-built home is located in the evergreen Sandia Peaks. Very comfortable rooms are furnished with antiques, and have alpine views. 🚗 🔥 P 🗷		5			●	
CLOUDCROFT: *The Lodge* $$$ 1 Corono Place, NM 88317. ((800) 395-6343. FAX (505) 682-2715. W www.thelodge-nm.com This historic mountain railroad resort, built in 1911, offers superb service amid Victorian ambience. An excellent restaurant, Rebecca's *(see p263)* and golf course are also available. 🚗 TV 🔥 P 🍴 🗷		61	●	■	●	■

GILA: *Casitas de Gila Guesthouses* $$ 310 Hooker Loop, NM 88038. ☎ *(505) 535-4455.* [FAX] *(505) 535-4456.* [W] *www.casitasdegila.com* These cozy adobe guesthouses with rustic Mexican furniture are set in grounds at the edge of Gila National Forest. ❄ ♿ [P] 💳	5			●	
GRANTS: *Travelodge* $ 1608 E. Santa Fe Ave., NM 87020. ☎ *(505) 287-7800.* [FAX] *(505) 287-7800, ext 401.* Well-appointed, spacious rooms decorated with New Mexican art. Indoor heated pool and complimentary breakfast. ❄ [TV] ♿ [P] 💳	60				■
JEMEZ SPRINGS: *The Dancing Bear* $$ 314 San Diego Dr., NM 87025. ☎ *(800) 422-3271.* [FAX] *(505) 829-3395.* Nestled beneath a red rock mesa, comfortable rooms have views of the mountains and look out on the Jemez River. ❄ [TV] [P] 💳	4				
LAGUNA: *Apache Canyon Ranch B&B* $$$$ 4 Canyon Dr., NM 87026. ☎ *(800) 808-8310.* [FAX] *(505) 836-2922.* [W] *www.apachecanyon.com* This high-desert ranch inn is set in the sweeping landscape east of Grants. Beautiful rooms. ❄ [TV] ♿ [P] 💳	4			●	
LAS CRUCES: *Hilltop Hacienda B&B* $ 2600 Westmoreland, NM 88012. ☎ *(505) 382-3556.* [FAX] *(505) 382-3556.* Fantastic views of the mountains and desert valley from this hilltop B&B. Comfortable, pleasant rooms with fireplaces. Pets allowed. ❄ [TV] ♿ [P] 💳	3				
LAS CRUCES: *T.R.H. Smith Mansion B&B* $$ 909 North Alameda Blvd., NM 88005. ☎ *(800) 526-1914.* [FAX] *(505) 524-8227.* [W] *www.smithmansion.com* Characterful 1914 home with bedrooms representing different areas of the world: the Americas room has a fireplace and loveseat. Full German breakfast is included. [P]	4				
LINCOLN: *Ellis Store & Co. Country Inn* $$ Hwy 380, NM 88338. ☎ *(800) 653-6460.* [FAX] *(505) 653-4610.* Old West charm and gracious hospitality are offered in this 1850s adobe home. Rooms feature handmade quilts and fireplace or woodburning stove. Delicious breakfast included. ♿ [P] 💳	10	●		●	
ROSWELL: *Roswell Inn* $ 1815 N. Main St., NM 88201. ☎ *(505) 623-4920.* [FAX] *(505) 622-3831.* Set in spacious grounds with a landscaped courtyard, this pleasant place has large rooms with contemporary decor. ❄ [TV] ♿ [P] 💳	121	●		●	■
ROSWELL: *Best Western Sally Port Inn* $$ 2000 N. Main St., NM 88201. ☎ *(505) 622-6430.* [FAX] *(505) 623-7631.* The top hotel in Roswell, with heated pool, whirlpool, saunas, tennis court, and video game room. ❄ [TV] ♿ [P] 🏋 💳	124	●			■
RUIDOSO: *Dan Dee Cabins* $$ 310 Main Rd., NM 88345. ☎ *(505) 257-2165.* [W] *www.ruidoso.com* Surrounded by acres of forest but just minutes from town, these charming mountain cottages feature rustic decor. Ideal for families. ❄ [TV] ♿ [P] 💳	13				
RUIDOSO: *Inn of the Mountain Gods* $$$ Carrizo Canyon Rd., NM 88340. ☎ *(505) 257-5141.* [FAX] *(505) 257-6173.* Upscale resort set among pine forests on the Mescalero Apache reservation, offering fishing, canoeing, horseback riding, tennis, and golf. The Dan Li Ka restaurant *(see p263)* is one of the area's best. ❄ [TV] ♿ [P] 💳	230	●	■	●	■
SILVER CITY: *Bear Mountain Guest Ranch* $$ 2251 Bear Mountain Rd., NM 88061. ☎ *(800) 880-2538.* Built in the 1920s, this large ranch house is set on 160 acres (64 ha), just north of town. Local outdoor activities include bird-watching, hiking, and mountain biking. The rooms are lovely and meals are included. ❄ ♿ [P] 💳	14	●			
SILVER CITY: *Carter House Bed and Breakfast Inn/AYH Hostel* $$ 101 N. Cooper St., NM 88061. ☎ *(505) 388-5485.* [FAX] *(505) 524-0123* This 1906 oak-trimmed house has a youth hostel with dormitory beds on the ground floor, and five private B&B rooms above. ❄ [P] 💳	5				
WHITE'S CITY: *Best Western Cavern Inn & Guadalupe Inn* $ 17 Carlsbad Caverns Hwy., NM 88268. ☎ *(505) 785-2291.* [FAX] *(505) 785-2283.* These two hotels are part of White's City, the small resort that is the nearest accommodation to Carlsbad Caverns. Rooms are large, comfortable, and well appointed with amenities such as HBO. Good value. ❄ [TV] ♿ [P] 💳	107	●	■	●	■

WHERE TO EAT

Pub sign in Flagstaff

As well as offering a top-class regional cuisine, which is rapidly gaining international recognition, the Southwest offers a diverse range of eating experiences, especially in its larger cities. Santa Fe, Phoenix, Albuquerque, Tucson, and Las Vegas rival any city in the country for the quality of ingredients and variety of cuisine available, with ambiences ranging from rustic to romantic. Southwestern cuisine is increasingly served in casual but stylish cafés. Mexican food is often best at local restaurants in New Mexico, Arizona, and Colorado, while Utah favors American fare. Restaurants with a cowboy or Mexican theme are usually inexpensive and can be entertaining. Hotel restaurants often serve the best food in small towns.

The restaurants listed on pages 250–63 have been chosen for their quality, variety, and good value. Some typical dishes available in the Southwest are shown on pages 248–9.

Acclaimed regional restaurant, Coyote Café, in Santa Fe

EATING HOURS

As found elsewhere in the US, breakfast is often a banquet: restaurants have extensive breakfast menus to choose from while hotels often have large buffets. Bacon, eggs, hash brown potatoes, pancakes, waffles, cereals, toast, and muffins appear on most menus. Sunday brunch is a feast to be lingered over, with seafood, meat, and poultry dishes served as well. Breakfast times range from 6 or 6:30am to 10:30 or 11am, though "all-day breakfasts" are popular at many cafés. Brunch is frequently served until 2pm.

Lunch is generally served from around 11:30am until 2:30 or 3pm. Many of the pricier restaurants offer scaled-down versions of their evening menu, which can be good value. Evening meals are served from 5:30 or 6pm, and the last seating is seldom later than 9pm. In small towns, many restaurants are closed in the evening. At the other extreme, Las Vegas' 24-hour culture offers a variety of meals at any time of the day or night.

PRICES AND TIPPING

Eating out in the Southwest is very reasonable, and even the most expensive restaurants offer good value. Light meals in cafés and diners usually cost between $5–$10, while chain restaurants serve complete dinners such as chicken or steak with potatoes and vegetables or salad for under $10. Mexican restaurants generally offer huge combination plates for $8–$12. At finer restaurants and upscale cafés, dinner entrées range from $15–$30, and a three-course meal, excluding wine, can still be found for under $50. In Las Vegas, the casino buffets serve myriad dishes, such as roasts, salads, pasta, and fish, to a high standard at reasonable prices (usually all-you-can-eat for under $15).

The standard tip is 15 percent of the cost of the meal, before tax. Tipping should be based on service, and if it is outstanding, leave up to 20 percent. Bartenders expect to be tipped accordingly for each round of drinks.

Sales tax will not be shown on menu prices, but apply to each item of food and drink. Although they vary from state to state and from city to city, these usually add around 5–7 percent to the cost of a meal.

TYPES OF FOOD AND RESTAURANTS

Dining establishments in the Southwest come in a wide variety of shapes and sizes from small and friendly diners offering hearty burgers and snacks to gourmet restaurants serving the latest Southwestern and fusion cuisine, to the lavish dining rooms in some of the area's top resorts, particularly in Phoenix and Las Vegas.

Starting at the lower end of the scale, fast food is a way of life throughout the country, and a string of outlets such as McDonald's, Burger King, Wendy's, and Arby's are found along the main strips of most towns in the region. They serve the usual inexpensive variations on burgers, fries, and soft drinks. Chains such as Applebee's and Denny's offer more variety, with soups, salads, sandwiches, meals, and desserts. These are generally good value, but the quality varies from one establishment to the next. Pizza chains are also ubiquitous in the region.

Mid-range restaurants can include a range of ethnic cuisine, such as Italian, Greek, Chinese, Japanese, and Indian food. Many good restaurants of this type can be found at shopping malls.

Mexican restaurants proliferate in the region, especially in New Mexico and southern Arizona, and vary from roadside stands and snack bars to upscale restaurants where the food is complemented by the architecture. These are often set in adobe buildings with lush interior courtyards that provide a romantic ambience.

"Southwestern" cuisine is a fusion of Native American, Hispanic, and international influences, and is increasingly showcased in the region's finest restaurants. These often feature a renowned resident chef (such as Mark Miller in Santa Fe's Coyote Café, *see p261*). Las Vegas is also home to some of the most elegant restaurants in the country. In the 1990s, several of the city's best hotels recruited celebrity chefs. Now, every hotel has at least one upscale restaurant with a world-class menu and the involvement of such influential names as

Hollywood's Wolfgang Puck of Spago's fame, who owns several restaurants along the Strip including Spago at Caesars Palace *(see p255)*.

Traditional American diner, Lindy's, in Albuquerque

COFFEE HOUSES AND CAFÉS

COFFEE HOUSES are popular throughout Southwest resorts and major cities. Along with specialty coffees, they generally serve pastries, bagels, desserts, and delicatessen fare. Cafés range from simple establishments serving sandwiches to trendy eateries offering Southwestern cuisine.

VEGETARIAN

SOUTHWESTERN AND American cuisine is largely meat based. Vegetarians may not find much variety outside the larger cities and resorts. However, salad bars are big

everywhere, from fine restaurants to fast-food chains. Salads can be a meal in themselves; they usually come with meat and seafood, but vegetarian orders are often accommodated. Many fast food chains also now serve salads, soups, or baked potatoes to cater to the more health conscious customer.

ALCOHOL

BEER, PARTICULARLY the *cervezas* imported from Mexico, is the most popular drink in the region, although Las Vegas is renowned for its cocktails. Visitors need to be 21 to buy alcohol. Be sure to carry I.D. as it is often requested before you are served. Utah's licensing laws, influenced by the Mormon community, are stricter, with liquor stores open for shorter hours and never on a Sunday. Alcohol is forbidden on all native reservations.

DISABLED FACILITIES

ESTABLISHMENTS ARE required to provide wheelchair access and a ground-level restroom by law, but check with older places in advance.

CHILDREN

WHILE LAS VEGAS is not primarily a family resort, the Southwest is generally child-friendly. Restaurants often serve children's portions and will provide a high chair.

DRESS CODES

DINING IS CASUAL throughout the Southwest. Even in upscale restaurants, there is seldom a need for a jacket and tie. In the land of cowboys, jeans are acceptable almost everywhere. In Las Vegas, however, dress smartly for the classier restaurants.

SMOKING

ALMOST ALL restaurants have smoking and non-smoking areas, although many ban smoking entirely throughout the establishment, including the bar area.

Southwestern decor at the Two Micks Cantina Grill in Tucson

An Introduction to Southwestern Food

SOUTHWESTERN FOOD reflects the region's strong Hispanic and Native cultures. Mexican food and its more refined cousin, Southwestern cuisine, enjoy a following around the globe. One of the pleasures of a visit to the region is discovering that a great variety of dishes are available; made with the freshest ingredients, and cooked with expertise. Those with tender tastebuds need not fear the chile pepper, which is at the heart of the cuisine. Chiles can pack a powerful bite, but milder varieties add flavor without heat. Most menus in restaurants frequented by tourists provide an explanation of the dishes, and staff are happy to offer advice. The region's other great staple is beef, and there is no shortage of good steaks and burgers in most areas. Santa Fe is possibly the culinary capital of the Southwest, with a range of restaurants in all price categories *(see pp260–61)*.

Red and green chiles

A tortilla and bean stall at Tumacacori, southern Arizona

NEW MEXICAN FOOD

THE MAIN ingredients of Southwestern cuisine are similar to those found in Mexican cooking, including corn, beans, cheese, tomatoes and, of course, chile. But there the similarity ends, for the combination and method of Southwestern cooking is different to that of Mexico.

New Mexican cuisine has its roots in the Pueblo culture, whose foods and cooking methods were adapted by early settlers. Today, a great variety of dishes can be found across the region. The distinctive taste of many local dishes may come from such ingredients as home-grown chiles or nuts from the piñon pine, which are considered a delicacy, as well as from the use of precious family recipes. More unusual regional ingredients include *nopales*, the fruit of the prickly pear cactus, the *chayote* (similar to zucchini), or the *tomatillos*, a walnut-sized green berry.

Mexican food and its Anglo version, Tex-Mex, are found all over the Southwest, but the fundamental distinction of New Mexican regional food lies in its chile sauces. In New Mexico these are made wholly of fresh or ground chile and form the basis for many dishes. In Mexican food the sauces are often tomato-based with chile added as a

spice. New Mexican sauces use puréed green or red chile diluted with water; garlic, salt, and sometimes herbs are added for seasoning and flour for thickening. Meat may be added in some sauces.

RED OR GREEN?

YOU WILL OFTEN hear this question when ordering Southwestern cuisine. They're talking about chile, of course, which is more of a staple than a specialty in much of the region. Many dishes can

A selection of dried chiles

be served with either green or red chile on top. Contrary to popular myth, one is not necessarily hotter than the other. The heat depends on the variety of chile, how many seeds it contains, and on the soil conditions that year. Restaurants used by locals generally serve a hotter chile than those catering to tourists. If you're unsure, many restaurants will let you have a little dish of each on the side – this is known as "Christmas" *(see p218)*. There are more than a hundred types of chile available, including NuMex, *poblano*, *mulato*, jalapeño, and *chipotle*. Very hot varieties include cayenne and habanero.

WHAT TO DRINK

A margarita, a tequila cocktail served in a salt-rimmed glass, is the classic drink with Mexican food, as are Mexican beers such as Corona, Tecate, and San Miguel. (Beer is also known to cool burning chile mouths.) California wines feature on most wine lists, but consider trying some of the little-known local wines. There are small regional wineries in southern Arizona and New Mexico. Sonoita Vineyards, near Elgin, Arizona, has received national recognition for its Pinot Noir and Cabernet wines. New Mexico's winemaking tradition stretches back to the first Spanish missionaries. Among its 19 wineries, the Gruet winery is known for its excellent sparkling wines. The Tucson and New Mexico tourist offices can provide details on various tours and tastings.

Corona Extra

Mexican beer

A margarita cocktail

CLASSIC SOUTHWESTERN DISHES

Tortillas are flat pancakes made of wheat or corn. They are the basis of many Southwestern dishes, since they can be stuffed or rolled, served soft or crispy (fried), and are the perfect partner for such classic ingredients as beef, chicken, or bean and cheese filling and topped with chile or salsa. Variations on the tortilla include the burrito, or the larger burro, a soft floury pancake, which becomes a crispy chimichanga when deep-fried. Flautas, also fried, are similar, but the burrito is rolled rather than folded around its ingredients. Enchiladas are rolled corn tortillas, filled with cheese, beef, or chicken, and usually topped with a red chile sauce and melted cheese. Small, fried tortillas or tacos are a popular snack food. They are folded in half and filled with ground beef, beans, onions, tomatoes, lettuce, and grated cheese.

Salsa is found on almost every table in the region. This cold spicy sauce of tomatoes, onions, chiles, herbs, and spices is served with many dishes. Guacamole is another topping or dip, made from avocados, lime or lemon juice, chile, cilantro (coriander), and spices.

Classic grilled T-bone steak with accompaniments

Steak sauce — T-bone steak
Baked potato — Corn on the cob

The chile relleno is perhaps the region's signature chile dish. A whole green chile is stuffed with cheese, dipped in a light egg batter, and deep fried. It is sometimes stuffed with rice or meat. Chiles are frequently eaten at breakfast, especially huevos rancheros – fried eggs on a soft tortilla, served with chile, melted cheese, and refried beans.

Popular desserts include *sopaipilla*, a light pastry that puffs up when fried and is served with honey to drizzle over the top, and *flan*, a firm, creamy, caramel custard.

MEAT, POULTRY, AND FISH

Southwestern cooking also features some great meat and poultry dishes. *Carne asada* means roasted, or sometimes grilled meat, while *carne seca* is beef that has been dried in the sun before cooking. *Carnitas* is beef or pork slow-roasted in green chile and spices, then served shredded with flour tortillas.

The Southwest is a ranching region, so sirloins, T-bones, and other cuts of steak are in plentiful supply. Both fish and seafood are popular, and the quality is high since fresh fish is flown in from California.

NATIVE AMERICAN SPECIALTIES

There are few specifically Native American restaurants. Indian fry bread – a flat, fried dough served with honey or other toppings – is often sold at food stands outside tourist attractions or at events. Navajo tacos are made with a base of fry bread rather than tortilla. Hopi piki bread is made from ground corn and boiling water and cooked in a thin layer over a hot surface.

At festivals special foods may be offered to visitors such as fried rabbit meat, or Three Sisters Stew made with corn, beans, and squash.

Enchiladas

Huevos rancheros

Tacos with guacamole

Chile relleno

COOKING SCHOOLS

If you wish to learn to cook Southwestern meals, two cooking schools offer a variety of courses. These are the Santa Fe School of Cooking, 116 W. San Francisco Street, Santa Fe, tel: (505) 983-4511, and Jane Butel's Southwestern Cooking School, c/o La Posada de Albuquerque, 125 2nd Street NW, Albuquerque, tel: (505) 243-2622 or (800) 472-8229.

Choosing a Restaurant

THE RESTAURANTS in this guide have been selected across a wide range of price categories for their exceptional food, good value, or interesting location. Entries are listed by region, in alphabetical order within price category. The thumb tabs on the pages use the same color-coding as the corresponding regional chapters in the main section of this guide.

	OUTDOOR EATING	VEGETARIAN SPECIALTIES	BAR AREA	FIXED-PRICE MENU	CHILDREN'S FACILITIES
GRAND CANYON AND NORTHERN ARIZONA					
FLAGSTAFF: *Downtown Diner* $ 7 E. Aspen Ave., AZ 86001. **(** (520) 774-3492. An atmospheric spot, popular with the locals, the Downtown Diner serves inexpensive, filling American meals from early each morning. 🗐		●			
FLAGSTAFF: *San Felipe's Cantina* $ 103 N. Leroux, AZ 86001. **(** (520) 779-6000. A popular and lively spot, offering an excellent range of authentic Mexican dishes at reasonable prices. The enchiladas are especially tasty. 🗐🗐		●	■		■
FLAGSTAFF: *Black Bart's* $$ 2760 E. Butler Ave., AZ 86001. **(** (520) 779-3142. Enjoy great steaks and burgers in this appealing converted barn. Waiting staff sing Western favorites on a wooden stage . 🗐🗐					■
FLAGSTAFF: *Charly's Pub & Grill* $$ 23 N. Leroux, AZ 86001. **(** (520) 779-1919. This fast-moving restaurant is a popular spot, serving an enticing range of burgers and sandwiches, as well as Mexican specialties. 🗐🗐		●	■		
FLAGSTAFF: *Pasto* $$ 19 E. Aspen, AZ 86001. **(** (520) 779-1937. A busy, downtown restaurant, offering excellent Italian cuisine with bargain daily specials. Vegetarian and wheat-free dishes are also served. 🗐🗐	■	●	■		
FLAGSTAFF: *Cottage Place Restaurant* $$$ 126 W. Cottage Ave., AZ 86001. **(** (520) 774-8431. One of Flagstaff's best restaurants, an imaginative menu includes vegetarian dishes as well as a good selection of seafood and meats. 🗐🗐🗐		●			
GRAND CANYON: *Bright Angel Restaurant* $ Bright Angel Lodge, AZ 86023. **(** (520) 638-2631. This bustling café-restaurant serves light meals and salad, as well as full meals. Reservations are not accepted, so you may have to line up. 🗐🗐		●			■
GRAND CANYON: *Grand Canyon Lodge* $$ Bright Angel Point, AZ 86023. **(** (520) 638-2611. Though remote, this lodge (*see p233*) manages to sustain a good restaurant, where American dishes are the order of the day. 🗐 *Partial.* 🗐		●	■		
GRAND CANYON: *Phantom Ranch* $$ Grand Canyon, AZ 86023. **(** (303) 297-2757. Situated on the canyon floor and accessible only by hiking or mule trail, Phantom Ranch (*see p232*) has a canteen providing meals by advance reservation only. The house specialty is the "Hiker's Stew". 🗐🎵🗐	■	●			
GRAND CANYON VILLAGE: *Maswik Cafeteria* $ Grand Canyon South Rim, AZ 86023. **(** (303) 297-2757. Maswik Lodge (*see p233*) offers this inexpensive, self-service café, with Mexican food as its specialty. There is also a cocktail lounge. 🗐🗐		●	■		■
GRAND CANYON VILLAGE: *El Tovar Hotel* $$$ Grand Canyon South Rim, AZ 86023. **(** (303) 297-2757. El Tovar (*see p233*) has a large dining room overlooking the South Rim of Grand Canyon. The menu is wide-ranging and portions are large. Reservations for dinner are pretty much essential. 🗐🗐		●	■		
JEROME: *English Kitchen* $ 119 Jerome Ave., AZ 86331. **(** (520) 634-2132. This café serves standard but well-prepared snacks and meals in premises that served as an opium den in Jerome's wild past. 🗐	■	●			

	OUTDOOR EATING	VEGETARIAN SPECIALTIES	BAR AREA	FIXED-PRICE MENU	CHILDREN'S FACILITIES

Price categories for a three-course meal for one, including half a bottle of wine (where available) and service:
$Ⓢ$ under US$25
$ⓈⓈ$ US$25–$35
$ⓈⓈⓈ$ US$35–$50
$ⓈⓈⓈⓈ$ US$50–$70
$ⓈⓈⓈⓈⓈ$ over US$70

OUTDOOR EATING
Some tables on a patio or terrace.
VEGETARIAN SPECIALTIES
One menu always includes a selection of vegetarian dishes.
BAR AREA
There is a bar area or cocktail bar within the restaurant, available for drinks and/or bar snacks.
FIXED-PRICE MENU
A fixed-price menu available at a good rate, for lunch, dinner or both, usually with three courses.
CHILDREN'S FACILITIES
Small portions and/or high chairs available on request.

		OUTDOOR EATING	VEGETARIAN SPECIALTIES	BAR AREA	FIXED-PRICE MENU	CHILDREN'S FACILITIES
JEROME: *Flatiron Café* 416 N. Main St., AZ 86331. (*(520) 634-2733.* Great salads are a specialty of this amiable café in the center of Jerome. Also try the tasty scrambled eggs at breakfast. ● D. 🔊🌿	$Ⓢ$		●			▣
KINGMAN: *Mr Díz Route 66 Diner* 105 E. Andy Devine, AZ 86401. (*(520) 718-0066.* Painted pink and peppermint green, there is no missing this cheerful diner, which is crammed with Route 66 memorabilia. 🔊🌿	$Ⓢ$					▣
LAKE HAVASU CITY: *London Bridge Brewery* 422 English Village, AZ 86403. (*(520) 855-8782.* This microbrewery in the London Arms pub is a popular spot. Breakfasts, lunches, and dinners are served along with specialty beers. 🔊🎵🌿	$Ⓢ$	▣	●	▣		
LAKE HAVASU CITY: *Miguel's Mexican Restaurant* 1550 Palo Verde Blvd., AZ 86403. (*(520) 453-1550.* This busy restaurant features the very best of Mexican cuisine, an exemplary range of authentic and spicy dishes at very affordable prices. 🔊🌿	$Ⓢ$		●	▣		▣
SEDONA: *Black Cow Café,* 229 N. Highway 89A, AZ 86336. (*(520) 203-9868.* Bright and breezy, this café makes an excellent pit stop, serving filling sandwiches, cakes, and pastries. The homemade ice cream is irresistible. 🔊🌿	$Ⓢ$		●			
SEDONA: *Dahl & Diluca Ristorante Italiano* 2321 W. Hwy 89A, AZ 86336. (*(520) 282-5219.* A cozy place offering dishes inspired by Tuscan cuisine. Its claim that guests can "dine in Italy without leaving Sedona" is entirely justifiable. 🔊🌿	$ⓈⓈ$		●	▣		
SEDONA: *El Rincon* Tlaquepaque Mall, 336 Hwy. 179, AZ 86336. (*(520) 282-4648.* This well-established restaurant specializes in tasty Mexican and Navajo-influenced dishes. The margaritas are superb. ● *Mon; Feb.* 🔊🍷🎵🌿	$ⓈⓈ$	▣	●	▣		
SEDONA: *Oaxaca Restaurante & Cantina* 231 N. Highway 89A, AZ 86336. (*(520) 282-4179.* A lively and appealing café-restaurant serving Southwestern and Mexican dishes. Open for breakfast, lunch, and dinner. 🔊🌿	$ⓈⓈ$	▣	●	▣		
SEDONA: *Takashi Japanese Restaurant* 465 Jordan Rd., AZ 86336. (*(520) 282-2334.* Traditional Japanese cuisine to eat in or take out is available at this friendly restaurant. Dishes include tempura, teppan, teriyaki, and sushi. 🔊🌿	$ⓈⓈ$	▣	●	▣		
SEDONA: *Shugrue's Hillside Grill* Hillside Courtyard, 671 Hwy 179, AZ 86336. (*(520) 282-5300.* Arguably the best steaks in town can be enjoyed at this brisk, modern restaurant. The service is excellent; both efficient and courteous. 🔊🌿	$ⓈⓈⓈ$		●	▣		
WILLIAMS: *Miss Kitty's Steakhouse* Mountainside Inn, 642 E. Route 66, AZ 86046. (*(520) 635-9161.* A local tradition, Miss Kitty's offers tasty steaks, ribs, and more at good prices. There is live music and dancing most nights of the week. 🔊🎵🌿	$Ⓢ$			▣		▣
WILLIAMS: *Twisters Soda Fountain* 401 E. Route 66, AZ 86046. (*(520) 635-0266.* One of the few of the town's old diners that has survived, Twisters is furnished with colorful retro American memorabilia. 🔊🌿	$Ⓢ$					▣
WILLIAMS: *Rod's Steak House* 301 E. Route 66, AZ 86046. (*(520) 635-2671.* Established in 1946, this traditional steak house has long been a Route 66 landmark. The steaks are well prepared and service is first-rate. 🌿	$ⓈⓈ$			▣		▣

Price categories for a three-course meal for one, including half a bottle of wine (where available) and service:

$ under US$25
$$ US$25–$35
$$$ US$35–$50
$$$$ US$50–$70
$$$$$ over US$70

OUTDOOR EATING
Some tables on a patio or terrace.

VEGETARIAN SPECIALTIES
One menu always includes a selection of vegetarian dishes.

BAR AREA
There is a bar area or cocktail bar within the restaurant, available for drinks and/or bar snacks.

FIXED-PRICE MENU
A fixed-price menu available at a good rate, for lunch, dinner or both, usually with three courses.

CHILDREN'S FACILITIES
Small portions and/or high chairs available on request.

		OUTDOOR EATING	VEGETARIAN SPECIALTIES	BAR AREA	FIXED-PRICE MENU	CHILDREN'S FACILITIES

PHOENIX AND SOUTHERN ARIZONA

		OUTDOOR EATING	VEGETARIAN SPECIALTIES	BAR AREA	FIXED-PRICE MENU	CHILDREN'S FACILITIES
APACHE JUNCTION: *Mining Camp Restaurant & Trading Post* 6100 E. Mining Camp St., AZ 85217. **(** (480) 982-3181. This well-established restaurant, in a modern version of a miners' canteen, offers tasty traditional American dishes at affordable prices. 🍽 ● *Jul–Sep.*	$				●	■
BISBEE: *Copper City Brewing Co.* 2 Copper Queen Plaza, AZ 85603. **(** (520) 432-7787. This bright, cheerful, family-run restaurant serves burgers, sandwiches, and steaks. The microbrewery on site churns out interesting brews such as Sweet Bordello Brown, homemade root beer, and ginger ale. 🦽 🍽	$		●	■		
GLOBE: *La Luz del Dia* 304 N. Broad St., AZ 85001. **(** (520) 425-8400. For something distinctive, try this Mexican bakery and coffee shop. A good place to fill up before exploring this attractive town and its surroundings.	$		●			
NOGALES: *La Roca Restaurant* Calle Elias 91, AZ 85628. **(** (888) 527-0220. This spacious restaurant is built into a rocky outcrop. The interior has Spanish colonial decor and folk art. The margaritas are superb. 🦽 🍽	$$			■		
PHOENIX: *Ed Debevic's* 2102 E. Highland Ave., AZ 85016. **(** (602) 956-2760. Good food and fun are the hallmarks of this lively diner, which features many 1950s accoutrements, including a mini-jukebox on most tables. 🍽	$					
PHOENIX: *Ironwood Café* Heard Museum, 2301 N. Central Ave., AZ 85004. **(** (602) 252-8848. A stylish café, with an emphasis on traditional dishes at reasonable prices. The Sonoran corn stew, at just $7, is highly recommended. 🦽 🍽	$	■	●			■
PHOENIX: *Aunt Chilada's at Squaw Peak* Dreamy Draw Dr., AZ 85020. **(** (602) 944-1286. Mexican food is the specialty of this popular restaurant, which occupies an imaginatively modernized, 19th-century general store. 🦽 🎵 🍽	$$	■	●	■		
PHOENIX: *Avanti Restaurant* 2728 E. Thomas Rd., AZ 85016. **(** (602) 956-0900. With justification, the Avanti bills itself as a Valley tradition – it has been serving up first-rate Italian cuisine for nearly 30 years. 🦽 🍷 🍽	$$$		●			
PHOENIX: *Arizona Kitchen* Wigwam Resort, 300 Wigwam Blvd., Litchfield Pk., AZ 85340. **(** (623) 935-3811. Diners can watch the innovative native Southwestern cuisine being prepared in this charming open-plan restaurant at the exclusive Wigwam. 🦽 🍽	$$$$		●	■		
PHOENIX: *Compass Restaurant* Hyatt Regency, 122 N. 2nd St., AZ 85004. **(** (602) 440-3166. Phoenix's only revolving restaurant has fabulous views across the city. The food is first-rate too, featuring regional American dishes. 🦽 🍷 🍽	$$$$		●	■		
PHOENIX: *Vincent's on Camelback* 3930 E. Camelback Rd., AZ 85251. **(** (602) 224-0225. This classy restaurant offers an imaginative menu that blends French and Southwestern cuisine. Advance reservations are recommended. 🦽 🍷 🍽	$$$$$		●	■		
SCOTTSDALE: *Ristorante Sandolo* Hyatt Regency, 7500 E. Doubletree Ranch Rd., AZ 85258. **(** (480) 991-3388. This stylish café-restaurant serves the freshest of pasta dishes. The singing servers offer a serenade that precedes – if you book it – a gondola ride on the canal behind the hotel. 🦽 🍷 🎵 🍽	$$$	■	●	■		

SCOTTSDALE: *Ruth's Chris Steakhouse* ⓢⓢⓢ
7001 N. Scottsdale Rd., AZ 85253. **(** *(480) 991-5988.*
One of the best steakhouses in town, noted for its corn-fed and aged
US prime beef. Chicken and seafood dishes are also available. 🔥 🗑

SCOTTSDALE: *The Squash Blossom* ⓢⓢⓢ
Hyatt Regency, 7500 E. Doubletree Ranch Rd., AZ 85258 **(** *(480) 991-3388.*
The emphasis of this excellent café is on Southwest cuisine with
such delicacies as fajitas and a delicious taco salad. 🔥 🗑

SCOTTSDALE: *La Hacienda* ⓢⓢⓢⓢⓢ
Scottsdale Princess, 7575 E. Princess Dr., AZ 85255. **(** *(480) 585-4848.*
This top-flight restaurant features a superb range of authentic Mexican
dishes and is ideal for a leisurely and luxurious night out. Strolling
Hispanic musicians serenade guests while they eat. 🔥 🍷 🎵 🗑

SCOTTSDALE: *Mary Elaine's* ⓢⓢⓢⓢⓢ
The Phoenician, 6000 E. Camelback Rd., AZ 85251. **(** *(480) 941-8200.*
One of the city's smartest restaurants, Mary Elaine's focuses on
contemporary French cuisine with an Italian twist. The location offers a
plush setting and fine views over the valley. Men need jackets. 🔥 🍷 🗑

TEMPE: *Rustler's Rooste* ⓢⓢⓢ
Pointe South Mountain Resort, 7777 S. Pointe Pkwy., AZ 85044. **(** *(602)
431-6474.* Those with a hankering for Western country-style fixings can enjoy
delicious mesquite-grilled steaks and ribs. Live country music. 🔥 🎵 🗑

TUCSON: *El Charro Café* ⓢ
311 N. Court Ave., AZ 85701. **(** *(520) 622-1922.*
Tucson's oldest Mexican restaurant is critically acclaimed as serving some
of the best traditional Mexican food in the country. Try the famous *carne
seca* – beef that is sun-dried on site – a Tucson specialty. 🔥 🗑

TUCSON: *El Corral* ⓢ
2201 E. River Road, AZ 85718. **(** *(520) 299-6092.*
This inexpensive steak house is set in an old adobe hacienda with wood
beams, fireplaces, and stone floors. The specialty is prime rib. ⬤ L. 🔥 🗑

TUCSON: *Schlotzsky's Deli* ⓢ
3270 E. Valencia Blvd., AZ 85706. **(** *(520) 741-2333.*
This exceptional chain serves healthy and delicious sandwiches, salads,
and pizzas. Try the "Original" sandwich that made them famous. 🔥 🗑

TUCSON: *Café Poca Cosa* ⓢⓢ
88 E. Broadway, AZ 85701. **(** *(520) 622-6400.*
A friendly restaurant serving fine authentic Mexican cuisine, with dishes
from several regions. Vibrant Mexican-style decor. ⬤ Sun. 🔥 🗑

TUCSON: *La Cocina* ⓢⓢ
Old Town Artisans, 201 N. Court Ave., AZ 85701. **(** *(520) 622-0351.*
Dine outdoors in the lush shady courtyard, or indoors surrounded by
art shows. The dishes are works of art as well. ⬤ Mon–Wed D. 🔥 🍷 🗑

TUCSON: *The Grill* ⓢⓢⓢ
5601 N. Hacienda del Sol Rd., AZ 85718. **(** *(800) 728-6514.*
The Grill offers American regional cooking at its finest. Fresh ingredients
and inspired combinations make the menu truly memorable. 🔥 🍷 🗑

TUCSON: *Janos* ⓢⓢⓢⓢⓢ
Westin La Paloma, 3770 E. Sunrise Dr., AZ 85718. **(** *(520) 615-6100.*
One of Tucson's most elegant restaurants, Janos blends French cooking
techniques with Southwestern ingredients. The menu changes seasonally
and the extensive wine list is chosen to match. ⬤ Sun & public hols. 🔥 🍷 🗑

TOMBSTONE: *Big Nose Kate's* ⓢ
417 E. Allen St., AZ 85638 **(** *(520) 457-3107.*
This restaurant has a great old-fashioned saloon atmosphere, with an
original cowboy bar and loads of Western memorabilia. 🔥 🎵 🗑

TOMBSTONE: *O.K. Café* ⓢ
3rd & Allen Streets, AZ 85638. **(** *(520) 457-3980.*
Charbroiled buffalo, emu, and ostrich burgers are the main dishes at this
historic café, along with soups, salads, daily lunch specials, and tasty
desserts. The service is fast and friendly. ⬤ D. 🔥

For key to symbols see back flap

Price categories for a three-course meal for one, including half a bottle of wine (where available) and service:

$ under US$25
$$ US$25–$35
$$$ US$35–$50
$$$$ US$50–$70
$$$$$ over US$70

OUTDOOR EATING
Some tables on a patio or terrace.
VEGETARIAN SPECIALTIES
One menu always includes a selection of vegetarian dishes.
BAR AREA
There is a bar area or cocktail bar within the restaurant, available for drinks and/or bar snacks.
FIXED-PRICE MENU
A fixed-price menu available at a good rate, for lunch, dinner or both, usually with three courses.
CHILDREN'S FACILITIES
Small portions and/or high chairs available on request.

	OUTDOOR EATING	VEGETARIAN SPECIALTIES	BAR AREA	FIXED-PRICE MENU	CHILDREN'S FACILITIES
TUMACACORI: *Wisdom Café* $ 19316 Frontage Rd., AZ 85640. ((520) 398-2397. Serving outstanding Mexican fare based on old family recipes, this café is famous for its crispy chimichangas and fruit-filled burros. ● *Sun.* &		●			

LAS VEGAS

	OUTDOOR EATING	VEGETARIAN SPECIALTIES	BAR AREA	FIXED-PRICE MENU	CHILDREN'S FACILITIES
DOWNTOWN: *Center Stage* $ At Jackie Gaughan's Plaza, 1 Main St., NV 89101. ((702) 386-2110. Housed in a second-story glass dome this American restaurant offers great views of the Fremont Street Experience *(see p118)*. ● *L.* &					
DOWNTOWN: *California Pizza Kitchen* $$ At the Golden Nugget, 129 E. Fremont St., NV 89101. ((702) 385-7111. Features an enormous range of gourmet wood-fired pizzas, as well as a choice of pastas, salads, and delicious desserts. &		●			
DOWNTOWN: *The Steakhouse* $$ At Binion's Horseshoe, 128 E. Fremont St., NV 89101. ((702) 382-1600. Classic American steakhouse fare includes prime rib as well as seafood at reasonable prices in this venerable Las Vegas casino. ● *L.* &					
DOWNTOWN: *Second Street Grill* $$$ Fremont Hotel, 200 E. Fremont St., NV 89109. ((702) 385-3232. Distinctive Pacific Rim fusion food served in a South Sea island-themed room. Delicious fish such as ahi tuna is a specialty. ● *L Mon–Fri.* &			▪		
DOWNTOWN: *Hugo's Cellar* $$$$ At Four Queens, 202 Fremont St., NV 89101. ((702) 385-4011. Hugo's has a romantic atmosphere, due to the privacy of the dining booths, and the rose given to every female guest on arrival. ● *L.* & ♀			▪		
THE STRIP: *Bugsy's Deli* $ At the Flamingo, 3555 Las Vegas Blvd. S., NV 89109. ((702) 733-3111. One of few remaining signs of Bugsy Seigel's involvement in the hotel *(see p237)*, are the photographs of the gangster displayed on the walls. Classic New York-style deli food is served at reasonable prices. &		●			▪
THE STRIP: *Dive* $ 3200 Las Vegas Blvd. S., NV 89109. ((702) 369-3483. The front of a submarine crashing through a wall of water forms the striking exterior of this restaurant, which serves classic American food. &		●		●	▪
THE STRIP: *Harley Davidson Café* $ 3725 Las Vegas Blvd. S., NV 89109. ((702) 740-4555. A giant Harley Davidson motorbike juts out from the façade of this American restaurant. This is a popular eatery with families. &				●	▪
THE STRIP: *Penny's Liberty Café* $ 27975 Marglan Parkway and Las Vegass Blvd.N., NV 89104. ((702) 383-0101. This classic American diner, apparently untouched since the 1950s, is one of the city's best-kept secrets. It serves the most delicious burger, fries, and milkshake in Vegas and all for no more than $5. &		●		●	▪
THE STRIP: *Rik'Shaw* $ At Riviera, 2901 Las Vegas Blvd.S., NV 89109. ((720) 734-5110. Authentic Cantonese cuisine at a bargain price. Specialties include lemon chicken, abalone with black mushrooms, and pineapple duck. & ♫		●	▪		
THE STRIP: *Andre's in the Monte Carlo* $$ At Monte Carlo, 3770 Las Vegas Blvd. S., NV 89109. ((702) 798-7151. An intimate restaurant, designed to emulate a Renaissance French chateau, serving award-winning French cuisine. ● *L.* & ♀			▪		

THE STRIP: *Mon Ami Gabi* $$
At Paris, 3655 Las Vegas Blvd.S., NV 89109. (888) 266-5867.
This Parisian-style bistro serves classic French offerings such as steak frites, quiche Lorraine, and delicious salads and desserts. It is also one of the few Vegas restaurants to have a terrace onto the Strip.

THE STRIP: *Morton's of Chicago* $$
400 E. Flamingo, NV 89103. (702) 893-0703.
The friendly atmosphere of this steakhouse chain is enhanced by its decor. The walls are hung with photographs of celebrity patrons. ● L.

THE STRIP: *Noodle Kitchen* $$
At the Mirage, 3400 Las Vegas Blvd. S., NV 89109. (702) 791-7223.
Located among the tropical foliage of the Mirage's Caribe Café, this is one of the most respected Chinese restaurants in Vegas.

THE STRIP: *Smith & Wollensky* $$
3767 Las Vegas Blvd.S., NV 89109. (702) 862-4100.
Part of a small chain that originated in New York, this classic steak house offers prime rib, fresh seafood, and lunch menus in its Strip-front grill.

THE STRIP: *Tony Roma's - A Place For Ribs* $$
Stardust Resort and Casino, 3000 Las Vegas Blvd. S., NV 89109. (702) 732-6111. The favorite dishes of this popular family chain include ribs with a secret sauce, barbequed chicken, and onion-ring loaf. ● L.

THE STRIP: *Top of the World* $$
Stratosphere Tower, 2000 Las Vegas Blvd. S. NV89104 (702) 380-7711.
Panoramic views are available from this restaurant 833 ft (255 m) above the Strip. The menu is European with great meat and seafood.

THE STRIP: *Buccaneer Bay Club* $$$
At Treasure Island, 3300 Las Vegas Blvd. S., NV 89109. (702) 894-7350.
Overlooking Treasure Island's lagoon *(see p238)*, this restaurant is a good place from which to view the nightly sea battles re-enacted outside. Friendly service and sophisticated cooking make a visit here a real treat.

THE STRIP: *Mizuno's Japanese Steak House* $$$
At the Tropicana, 3801 Las Vegas Blvd. S., NV 89119. (702) 739-2713.
Dazzling displays of Japanese meat slicing are performed at tableside grills. Thin slices of steak, shrimp, and chicken are served with miso soup and freshly stir-fried vegetables. ● L.

THE STRIP: *Rosewood Grille* $$$
3339 Las Vegas Blvd.S., NV 89109. (702) 792-5965.
This is one of Las Vegas's landmark restaurants, famous for its good seafood, especially the Maine lobsters, and extensive wine list.

THE STRIP: *Spago* $$$
At Caesars Palace, 3500 Las Vegas Blvd. S., NV 89109. (702) 369-6300.
Spago's contemporary interior echoes its famous sister restaurant in Los Angeles. Fusion cooking mixes Asian and American with Italian styles in such dishes as fried salmon on soba noodles. ● L.

THE STRIP: *Trattoria del Lupo* $$$
At Mandalay Bay, 3950 Las Vegas Blvd. S., NV 89109. (702) 632-7410.
Owned by famous chef, Wolfgang Puck, who is credited with combining classic Italian cooking with contemporary California cuisine.

THE STRIP: *Emeril's New Orleans Fish House* $$$$
At MGM Grand, 3799 Las Vegas Blvd. S., NV 89109. (702) 891-7374.
One of the most popular restaurants in Las Vegas, noted for its mix of Creole and Cajun cooking. Snacks are available at the Seafood Bar.

THE STRIP: *Pinot Vegas* $$$$
At the Venetian, 3355 Las Vegas Blvd. S., NV 89109. (702) 733-5000.
Sister to the prize-winning Los Angeles restaurant of chef Joachim Splichal, noted for offering French cuisine with a California twist.

THE STRIP: *Coyote Café* $$$$$
MGM Grand, 3799 Las Vegas Blvd. S., NV 89109. (702) 891-7349.
With its Southwestern decor, this popular place offers regional fusion cooking with an exciting mix of Native American, Mexican, and Cajun flavors. Reservations required in the grill room but not the café.

For key to symbols see back flap

Price categories for a three-course meal for one, including half a bottle of wine (where available) and service:

$ under US$25
$$ US$25–$35
$$$ US$35–$50
$$$$ US$50–$70
$$$$$ over US$70

OUTDOOR EATING
Some tables on a patio or terrace.
VEGETARIAN SPECIALTIES
One menu always includes a selection of vegetarian dishes.
BAR AREA
There is a bar area or cocktail bar within the restaurant, available for drinks and/or bar snacks.
FIXED-PRICE MENU
A fixed-price menu available at a good rate, for lunch, dinner or both, usually with three courses.
CHILDREN'S FACILITIES
Small portions and/or high chairs available on request.

	Outdoor Eating	Vegetarian Specialties	Bar Area	Fixed-Price Menu	Children's Facilities
THE STRIP: Gatsby's $$$$$ At MGM Grand, 3799 Las Vegas Blvd. S., NV 89109. (702) 891-7337. This gourmet restaurant offers an eclectic mix of European and Asian cooking by noted chef Terence Fong. ● Sun & Mon D.				●	
THE STRIP: Aureole $$$$$ At Mandalay Bay, 3950 Las Vegas Blvd. S., NV 89109. (702) 632-7401. Contemporary American cuisine produced by famous New York chef, Charlie Palmer. The room features a glass tower of wine.		●			
THE STRIP: Nero's $$$$$ At Caesars Palace, 3570 Las Vegas Blvd.S., NV 89109. (702) 731-7731. The Moroccan-style decor of Nero's belies the delicious Italian food cooked using the top-quality ingredients by chef Mario Capone.		●			
THE STRIP: Picasso $$$$$ At the Bellagio, 3600 Las Vegas Blvd. S., NV 89109. (702) 693-7111. One of Vegas's premier dining experiences. Set in a coolly elegant room, the walls are adorned with several original Picasso paintings.	■		■	●	
THE STRIP: Renoir $$$$$ At the Mirage, 3400 Las Vegas Blvd. S., Nevada 89109. (702) 791-7223. The late 19th-century decor of the Renoir is enhanced by the many Impressionist paintings on the walls, including originals by Auguste Renoir himself. Fresh, seasonal ingredients are used in the dishes.	■		■	●	
OFF STRIP: Ricardo's $ 2380 E. Tropicana Ave., NV 89119 (702) 798-4515. Considered one of Vegas' best Mexican restaurants, Ricardo's offers friendly service, delicious fajitas, and award-winning margaritas.			■	●	■
OFF STRIP: Ruth's Chris Steakhouse $$ 4561 W. Flamingo Road., NV 89103. (702) 248-7011. Top quality steaks and wine list served in a traditional clubroom setting with mahogany fittings draws both visitors and locals. ● L.			■		
OFF STRIP: Piero's $$$ 355 Convention Center Dr., NV 89109. (702) 369 2305. This is an elegant Italian restaurant, popular with Vegas residents including, it is rumored, several local celebrities.			■		
OFF STRIP: Ferraro's Italian Restaurant $$$ 5900 W. Flamingo Road., NV 89103. (702) 364-5300. One of the best Italian eateries in town, Ferraro's is well-known for its osso buco, homemade gnocchi, and lamb chops.		●			
SOUTHERN UTAH					
BOULDER: Hell's Backbone Grill $$ 20 N. Hwy. 12, UT 82716. (435) 335-7464. One of the best restaurants in Southern Utah, the menu offers dazzling and creative takes on traditional Southwestern cuisine.		●			■
BRYCE CANYON NATIONAL PARK: $$ *B-Bar Wagon D Covered Wagon Company* 1089 W. Main St., UT 84764. (435) 834-5202. A family oriented theater experience starting with a wagon ride, followed by a chuckwagon dinner and country music. ● Sun; Nov–mid-May.	■				
BRYCE CANYON NATIONAL PARK: Bryce Canyon Lodge $$ Bryce Canyon National Park, UT 84717. (435) 834-5361. The best fine dining establishment in the area, serving continental cuisine in an elegant setting. Meals are traditional and well done.	■	●			■

CEDAR CITY: *Market Grill* $
273 N. 1500 W., UT 84720 ((435) 586-9325.
This unique eatery is located at the livestock yards offers up hearty fare
including rib-eye steaks and cowboy-sized breakfasts. ● *Sun.* ⚲ ✎

CEDAR CITY: *Adriana's* $$
164 S. 100 W., UT 84720. ((435) 865-1234.
A Cedar City institution, Adriana's offers high quality classic dishes such
as chicken cordon bleu and filet mignon. The restaurant's "Olde English"
ambience make this a fine dining experience. ● *Sun.* ⚲ ✎

KANAB: *Parry Lodge Restaurant* $$$
89 E. Center St., UT 84741. ((435) 644-2601.
Prime Rib, poached salmon, and other American favorites are on offer at
this restaurant, famous for feeding John Wayne and other stars. ⚲ ✎

MOAB: *Eddie McStiff's* $
57 S. Main St., UT 84532. ((435) 259-4282.
Pizza, pasta, and McStiff's own award-winning microbrewed beer are the
specialties here. The pizza is legendary, the prices modest. Another favorite
is skewered steak and chicken satay in Pacific Rim marinade. ⚲ ✎

MOAB: *Moab Diner* $
189 S. Main St., UT 84532. ((435) 259-4006.
A fun, 1950s-style diner offering full breakfasts, hearty burgers, and great
ice cream sundaes. Famous for their green chili. ✎

MOAB: *Center Café* $$$
92 E. Center St., UT 84532. ((435) 259-4295.
International cuisine featuring specialties such as grilled trout with Asian
spice rub or pan-seared lamb loin with roasted garlic flan. Specials can
include exotic but tasty dishes featuring ostrich or bison. ⚲ ♟ ✎

MOAB: *Slickrock Café* $$$
5 N. Main St., UT 84532 ((435) 259-8004.
Trendy café with clever pastas and vegetarian dishes. After a great dinner
you can buy a tee-shirt with their lizard-dog mascot on it. ⚲ ✎

MOAB: *Sunset Grill* $$$
900 N. Route 191, UT 84532 ((435) 259-7146.
Located on a hill above town, this is Moab's best fine dining establishment.
Serves a mix of high-end European and American cuisine. ⚲ ♟ ✎

PANGUITCH: *Cowboy's Smokehouse* $$
95 N. Main St., UT 84759. ((435) 676-8030.
A meat lovers treat with real mesquite cooked steaks and house-smoked
barbecued ribs. The decor and the music are solidly country. ⚲ ♫ ✎

SPRINGDALE: *Oscars Café* $
948 Zion Park Blvd., UT 84767. ((435) 772-3232.
Light and healthy sandwiches and Mexican dishes. The most popular
dishes are green chili chimichangas, mesquite-roasted chicken
enchiladas, and garlic burger on a homemade roll. ⚲

SPRINGDALE: *Bit and Spur Saloon* $$
1212 Zion Park Blvd., UT 84767. ((435) 772-3498.
An excellent, atmospheric Mexican restaurant, offering surprises like the
Bistek Asado, a chile-rubbed rib eye. ● *L; Tue & Wed Nov–Mar.* ⚲ ♫ ✎

SPRINGDALE: *Spotted Dog Café* $$
Fairmont Inn, 428 Zion Park Blvd., UT 84767. ((435) 772-3244.
Upscale steak and seafood place with local specialties such as fresh trout
and rabbit. Features a patio café that makes a good lunch spot. ⚲ ♟ ✎

ST. GEORGE: *Pancho and Lefty's* $
1050 S. Bluff St., UT 84770. ((435) 628-4772.
Good value, fun, and lively Mexican restaurant. House favorites include
the Elmedio taco and enchilada plate and fajitas. ⚲ ✎

ST. GEORGE: *Basila's Greek & Italian Café* $$$
2 W. St. George St., UT 84770 ((435) 673-7671.
Fine Greek and Italian cuisine is found in this popular local restaurant
located in the heart of St. George. Specialties include spanakopita and
kabobs (kebabs). ● *Mon & Sun.* ⚲ ♟ ✎

For key to symbols see back flap

<table>
<tr><td colspan="6">

Price categories for a three-course meal for one, including half a bottle of wine (where available) and service:

$ under US$25
$$ US$25–$35
$$$ US$35–$50
$$$$ US$50–$70
$$$$$ over US$70

OUTDOOR EATING
Some tables on a patio or terrace.
VEGETARIAN SPECIALTIES
One menu always includes a selection of vegetarian dishes.
BAR AREA
There is a bar area or cocktail bar within the restaurant, available for drinks and/or bar snacks.
FIXED-PRICE MENU
A fixed-price menu available at a good rate, for lunch, dinner or both, usually with three courses.
CHILDREN'S FACILITIES
Small portions and/or high chairs available on request.

</td></tr>
</table>

	OUTDOOR EATING	VEGETARIAN SPECIALTIES	BAR AREA	FIXED-PRICE MENU	CHILDREN'S FACILITIES
TORREY: *Capitol Reef Café* $$ 360 W. Main St., UT 84775. ☎ *(435) 425-3271.* Located near Capitol Reef National Park, this unusual find features locally-farmed smoked or grilled trout, stir fries, vegetarian entrees, and a host of imaginative dishes. Delicious homemade soups and salads. ♿ 🎵 ✉		●			■
TORREY: *Café Diablo* $$$ 599 W. Main St., UT 84775. ☎ *(435) 425-3070.* An award-winning gastronomical oasis in the culinary desert of southern Utah, serving wonderfully creative dishes with a Southwestern theme. ♿ ✉	■	●			■
WAHWEAP: *Rainbow Room* $$$ Wahweap Lodge, Lakeshore Dr., UT 86040. ☎ *(520) 645-2433.* This elegant lodge offers specials such as seared crab cakes with angel hair pasta, and has sweeping views of Lake Powell. ♿ ✉			■	●	
WAHWEAP: *Dam Bar and Grill* $$$ 644 N. Navajo Dr., AZ 86040. ☎ *(520) 645-2161.* Eclectic industrial-dam decor complements the contemporary steak and pasta dishes served here. ● *Dec & Jan: Sun; Feb & Mar: Mon.* ♿ 🍷 🎵 ✉	■	●	■	●	
ZION NATIONAL PARK: *Zion Lodge* $$ Zion National Park, UT 84767. ☎ *(435) 772-3213.* Better than average tourist fare, with a very good breakfast buffet and dinners that include steak and trout. ♿ ✉					■

THE FOUR CORNERS

	OUTDOOR EATING	VEGETARIAN SPECIALTIES	BAR AREA	FIXED-PRICE MENU	CHILDREN'S FACILITIES
BLUFF: *Cow Canyon Trading Post* $ Intersection of Hwy. 191 and Hwy. 163, UT 84512 ☎ *(435) 672-2208.* This former trading post and gas station is now a delightful small restaurant, gift shop, and gallery. The limited but innovative menu changes regularly to use the best fresh ingredients. ● *L. Tue & Wed.* ✉					
BLUFF: *Twin Rocks Café* $ Navajo Twins Dr., UT 84512. ☎ *(435) 672-2341.* Located below the twin sandstone pillars that gave the place its name, this restaurant serves sandwiches, Mexican dishes, and pastas. ♿ ✉	■	●			
BLUFF: *Cottonwood Steakouse* $$ Highway 191, UT 84512 ☎ *(435) 672-2282.* Guests have a choice of eating inside or around the outdoor barbecue pit under a giant cottonwood tree. The grilled steaks are substantial. ♿ ✉	■				
CAMERON: *Cameron Trading Post* $ Route 89, AZ 86020. ☎ *(520) 679-2231.* Hearty breakfasts and dinners feature standard but tasty versions of chicken, steak, and fish, as well as the ubiquitous Navajo taco. ♿ ✉					■
CHINLE: *Thunderbird Lodge* $ Canyon De Chelly, AZ 86503. ☎ *(520) 674-5841.* Cafeteria-style place serving large portions of classic American diner food from breakfast through dinner. Excellent value and tasty. ✉					
CHINLE: *Garcia's Restaurant* $$ Garcia Trading Post, Canyon de Chelly, AZ 86503 ☎ *(520) 674-5000.* Classic Southwestern dishes, as well as Native and Mexican specialties, are served here, including fajitas and the marinated cowboy sirloin. ♿ ✉	■	●			■
CORTEZ: *Homesteaders* $ 45 E. Main Cortez, CO 81321. ☎ *(970) 565-6253.* Barbecued pork ribs and steaks with homemade bread and pies served amid a stylish country decor of antiques and old license plates. ✉			■		

DURANGO: *Carver's Bakery and Brew Pub* $
1022 Main Ave., CO 81301 ((970) 259-2545.
A pleasant establishment that combines a bakery with a sit-down
Southwestern café and a microbrewery. 🔊 🎵 🗷

DURANGO: *Red Snapper* $$
144 E. 9th St., CO 81301. ((970) 259-3417.
A rarity in the beef-loving West, this seafood restaurant features dishes such
as Hawaiian tuna and salmon Wellington. ● *Thanksgiving, Dec 25.* 🔊 🍴 🗷

FARMINGTON: *Señor Pepper's* $
1400 W. Navajo, NM 87401. ((505) 327-0436.
A bright, friendly fiesta-style Mexican restaurant that uses fresh
ingredients. Featuring comedy shows Friday and Saturday nights. 🔊 🗷

FARMINGTON: *Clancy's Pub* $$$
2701 E. 20th St., NM 87401 ((505) 325-8176.
A friendly, oak- and-fern type bar with better than average sandwiches,
steaks, and lots of cold imported beer. ● *major hols.* 🔊 🗷

KAYENTA: *Amigo Café* $
Highway 163, AZ 86033. ((520) 697-8448.
This simple but delicious Mexican food is a welcome treat in the remote
northern Four Corners region. Efficient and cheerful service. ● *Sun.* 🗷

MONUMENT VALLEY: *Stagecoach Dining Room* $$
Goulding's Lodge, UT 84536. ((435) 727-3231.
This large, touristy restaurant serves standard American fare. The
highlight here is the stunning view of Monument Valley. 🗷

OURAY: *St. Elmo Restaurant* $
426 Main St., CO 81427. ((970) 325-0550.
This Espresso Bar is a good bet for well-prepared, light meals. Specialties
include pizza, ultra-fresh salads, omelettes, bagels, and quiche. 🗷

SECOND MESA, HOPI RESERVATION: *Hopi Cultural Center Restaurant* $$
Route 264, AZ 86043. ((520) 734-2401.
Traditional dishes like Hopi stew can be interesting, though standard
Mexican and American fare is also served. ● *Thanksgiving; Dec 25* 🔊 🗷

ST. MICHAEL'S: *Tullers Café* $
Rte. 264 St. Michael's, AZ 86511. ((520) 871-4687.
This tiny trailer is where the locals enjoy such regional specialties as
Navajo stew and Navajo tacos. Well-cooked, satisfying food. 🗷

TELLURIDE: *Maggie's Bakery and Café* $
217 E. Colorado, CO 81401. ((970) 728-3334.
The light sandwiches here are really just a prelude to diving into the
huge fluffy, homemade pastries and other baked goodies. 🗷

TELLURIDE: *South Park Café* $
300 W. Colorado Ave., CO 81435. ((970) 728-5335.
Thick pizzas with a wide range of toppings, tasty pastas, and a good
assortment of local beers makes this one of Telluride's favorite hangouts. 🗷

TELLURIDE: *Excelsior Café* $$
200 W. Colorado Ave., CO 81435. ((970) 728-4250.
An upscale eatery famous for its inventive and eclectic blend
of delicious American and nouveau-Italian dishes. 🔊 🗷

TUBA CITY: *Anasazi Grey Mountain Restaurant* $
Tuba Trading Post, Grey Mountain, AZ 86016. ((520) 679-2203.
A typical regional restaurant featuring Mexican, Native, and American
dishes with lots of frybread, hamburgers, and tacos. 🔊 🗷

TUBA CITY: *Hogan Restaurant* $
PO Box 247, AZ 8604 ((520) 283-5260.
Located next to the Quality Inn, Hogan's offers a full Mexican/American
Menu, which is a cut above the average diner fare. 🔊 🗷

WINDOW ROCK: *Navajo Nation Inn Dining Room* $
48 West Highway. 264, AZ 86515. ((520) 871-4108.
This is where the Navajo businessmen and politicians eat. Traditional
dishes are served in a room decorated with native art. ● *Sat & Sun D.* 🔊

For key to symbols see back flap

Price categories for a three-course meal for one, including half a bottle of wine (where available) and service:

$ under US$25
$$ US$25–$35
$$$ US$35–$50
$$$$ US$50–$70
$$$$$ over US$70

OUTDOOR EATING
Some tables on a patio or terrace.
VEGETARIAN SPECIALTIES
One menu always includes a selection of vegetarian dishes.
BAR AREA
There is a bar area or cocktail bar within the restaurant, available for drinks and/or bar snacks.
FIXED-PRICE MENU
A fixed-price menu available at a good rate, for lunch, dinner or both, usually with three courses.
CHILDREN'S FACILITIES
Small portions and/or high chairs available on request.

		OUTDOOR EATING	VEGETARIAN SPECIALTIES	BAR AREA	FIXED-PRICE MENU	CHILDREN'S FACILITIES

SANTA FE AND NORTHERN NEW MEXICO

		OUTDOOR EATING	VEGETARIAN SPECIALTIES	BAR AREA	FIXED-PRICE MENU	CHILDREN'S FACILITIES
CHIMAYO: *Restaurante Rancho de Chimayo* $$ County Rd. 98, NM 87522. **(** (505) 351-4444. Authentic New Mexican cuisine, prepared with locally grown produce. Relaxed dining in a hacienda-style building, with lovely views of the Chimayo valley. ● *Nov–Mar Mon.* 🛗 🎵 *Summer weekends.* 🗎			●	▪		▪
RANCHO DE TAOS: *Trading Post Café* $$ 4179 Hwy 68 (at Hwy 518), NM 87557. **(** (505) 758-5089. This 125-year-old adobe building once housed the largest general store in Taos. Today it's a relaxed and charming restaurant, featuring contemporary American cuisine with Italian influences. ● *Sun.* 🛗 🍷 🗎		▪	●	▪		
SANTA FE: *Dave's Not Here* $ 1115 Hickox St., NM 87501. **(** (505) 983-7060. This popular local eaterie features good-sized portions of New Mexican favorites, including chile rellenos and tacos, for around $5. 🛗 🗎		▪	●	▪		
SANTA FE: *Blue Corn Café and Brewery* $ 133 W. Water St., NM 87501. **(** (505) 984-1800. Friendly pub serving traditional northern New Mexican fare. A variety of microbrews are on tap in the bar, and sports events are shown on TV. 🛗 🗎		▪	●	▪		
SANTA FE: *Cowgirl Hall of Fame* $ 319 S. Guadalupe, NM 87501. **(** (505) 982-2565. Texas, Cajun, and Caribbean-style dishes served in a casual, fun, Wild-West atmosphere. A ranch breakfast is served at weekends. 🛗 🎵 🗎		▪	●	▪		
SANTA FE: *Maria's New Mexican Kitchen* $ 555 W. Cordova Rd., NM 87501. **(** (505) 983-7929. This very busy local restaurant serves authentic old Santa Fe-style cooking. Margaritas are the specialty of the house. 🛗 🎵 🗎				▪		
SANTA FE: *San Francisco Street Bar & Grill* $ 114 W. San Francisco St., NM 87501. **(** (505) 982-2044. This lively, late-night spot in Plaza Mercado is said to make the best burgers in Santa Fe. Also recommended are the grilled meats. 🛗 🗎			●	▪		
SANTA FE: *The Shed* $ 113 E. Palace Ave., NM 87501. **(** (505) 982-9030. The Shed occupies the quaint rooms of a 17th-century adobe building. Its menu features excellent New Mexican dishes. ● *Sun D.* 🛗 🗎		▪	●	▪		
SANTA FE: *Tomasita's* $ Santa Fe Station, 500 S. Guadalupe, NM 87501. **(** (505) 983-5721. Tomasita's is a favorite spot for northern New Mexican cuisine. The chili is hot, and the atmosphere busy, friendly, and fun. ● *Sun* 🛗 🗎		▪	●	▪		
SANTA FE: *Espiritu* $$ 731 Canyon Rd., NM 87501. **(** (505) 820-2226. Sophisticated dining on Italian cuisine and gourmet pizzas, served in a tranquil, garden room. Jazz vocalist Chris Calloway performs regularly. ● *Sun.* 🛗 🎵 🗎		▪	●	▪		
SANTA FE: *The Pink Adobe* $$ 406 Old Santa Fe Trail, NM 87501. **(** (505) 983-7712. Relaxed dining in a 300-year-old adobe home. Mexican dishes are served alongside beef, chicken, and seafood entrées. ● *Sat, Sun L.* 🛗 🍷 🎵 🗎			●	▪		
SANTA FE: *Corn Dance Café* $$$ 1501 Paseo de Peralta, NM 87501. **(** (505) 982-1200. This pleasant restaurant serves Native American cuisine with a contemporary twist such as fry bread filled with goat's cheese. 🛗 🎵 🗎		▪	●	▪		▪

SANTA FE: *El Farol* $$$
808 Canyon Rd., NM 87501. (505) 983-9912.
Spanish cuisine is served in small, intimate dining rooms – tapas are the
specialty at this popular local hangout.

SANTA FE: *Café Paris* $$$
31 Burro Alley, NM 87501. (505) 986-9162.
Charming small café serving excellent French cuisine with South Pacific
influences. Specialties include chicken cordon bleu and cassoulet
Bretonne. Good wines and delicious desserts. *Sat.*

SANTA FE: *Paul's* $$$
72 W. Marcy St., NM 87501. (505) 982-8738.
This intimate, imaginative restaurant serves delectable à la carte entrees, such
as baked salmon with a pecan herb crust and sorrel sauce. *Sun L.*

SANTA FE: *Prana* $$$
320 S. Guadalupe, NM 87501. (505) 983-7705.
The creative menu of this French-Asian restaurant includes such dishes
as Burmese seafood stew and pumpkin-Thai basil ravioli.

SANTA FE: *Café Pasqual's* $$$$
121 Don Gaspar Ave., NM 87501. (505) 983-9340.
Famous for its innovative New Southwestern cuisine, the menu, which
changes often, may feature such delights as grilled banana leaf-wrapped
salmon, or free-range chicken in a spicy chocolate sauce. *Limited.*

SANTA FE: *Julian's* $$$$
221 Shelby St., NM 87501. (505) 988-2355.
Italian bistro serving superb regional Italian dishes of duck, chicken,
fish, and veal. Voted the city's most romantic restaurant. *L.*

SANTA FE: *La Casa Sena* $$$$
20 Sena Plaza, 125 E. Palace Ave., NM 87501. (505) 988-9232.
Located in an 1860s home, this elegant restaurant serves innovative Southwestern cuisine, such as pan-seared molasses duck breast.

SANTA FE: *Anasazi Restaurant* $$$$$
Inn of the Anasazi Hotel, 113 Washington St., NM 87501. (505) 988-3236.
Contemporary Western cuisine, served in a large, elegant dining room
featuring woven textiles. Dinner entrées include spicy piñon-apricot
stuffed quail and cinammon-chile rubbed chop.

SANTA FE: *Coyote Café* $$$$$
132 W. Water St., NM 87501. (505) 983-1615.
Highly acclaimed Southwestern cuisine from celebrity chef Mark Miller. The
fixed-priced menu is a good way to sample a range of dishes.

SANTA FE: *Geronimo* $$$$$
724 Canyon Rd., NM 87501. (505) 982-1500.
This is a romantic adobe restaurant, with small, intimate dining rooms.
The menu is an impressive blend of New Mexican and Mediterranean
cuisine, using only the freshest seasonal ingredients *Mon L.*

TAOS: *Orlando's New Mexican Café* $
2 miles N. of the Plaza, Hwy 64, NM 87571. (505) 751-1450.
Great New Mexican dishes are served at this nice little restaurant,
decorated with tile tabletops and Southwestern knickknacks. The green
and red chile is a favorite with local patrons. *Sun.*

TAOS: *Apple Tree Restaurant* $$$
123 Bent St., NM 87571. (505) 758-1900.
Cozy adobe house near the central Plaza, serving a creative menu to
please all tastes. There is a pretty shaded patio for dining al fresco.

TAOS: *Doc Martin's* $$$$
125 Paseo del Pueblo Norte, NM 87571. (505) 758-1977.
Located in the historic Taos Inn, dating from 1600, this perennial favorite
serves fine New Mexican food in an Old-West atmosphere.

TAOS: *Lambert's of Taos* $$$$
309 Paseo del Pueblo Sur, NM 87571. (505) 758-1009.
Organic and fresh local produce is the secret of Lambert's consistently
outstanding cuisine. The ambience is casual and low-key. *L.*

For key to symbols see back flap

Price categories for a three-course meal for one, including half a bottle of wine (where available) and service:
$ under US$25
$$ US$25–$35
$$$ US$35–$50
$$$$ US$50–$70
$$$$$ over US$70

OUTDOOR EATING
Some tables on a patio or terrace.
VEGETARIAN SPECIALTIES
One menu always includes a selection of vegetarian dishes.
BAR AREA
There is a bar area or cocktail bar within the restaurant, available for drinks and/or bar snacks.
FIXED-PRICE MENU
A fixed-price menu available at a good rate, for lunch, dinner or both, usually with three courses.
CHILDREN'S FACILITIES
Small portions and/or high chairs available on request.

ALBUQUERQUE AND SOUTHERN NEW MEXICO

Restaurant	Price	Outdoor Eating	Vegetarian Specialties	Bar Area	Fixed-Price Menu	Children's Facilities
ACOMA: *Sky City Casino* I-40 at Exit 102, NM 87034. ☎ *(505) 552-6017.* This pleasant casino restaurant serves delicious food, 24 hours a day. The all-you-can-eat lunch and dinner buffets are recommended. ♿ 💳	$	■				
ALAMOGORDO: *Keg's Brewery* 817 Scenic Dr., NM 88310. ☎ *(505) 437-9564.* This fun 1950s and 1960s-style diner serves such American favorites as burgers, steaks, and seafood, with fruit pies for dessert. There is a micro-brewery on site and Western dancing in the bar on weekends. ♿ ♫ 💳	$			■		
ALAMOGORDO: *Ramona's* 2913 N. White Sands Blvd., NM 88310. ☎ *(505) 437-7616.* This popular restaurant serves fine Mexican food; chimichangas with homemade salsa are the specialty. American food is also served. ♿ 💳	$					
ALBUQUERQUE: *66 Diner* 1405 Central Ave. NE., NM 87106. ☎ *(505) 247-1421.* In this fabulous 1950s diner on old Route 66, hot dogs and burgers are served among the neon signs, comfy booths, and nostalgic tunes. ♿ 💳	$					
ALBUQUERQUE: *Black-eyed Pea* 601 Juan Tabo, NM 87123. ☎ *(505) 299-0997.* Classic home-style food such as Mom's meatloaf and chicken-fried steak are served here. The restaurant is a good place for families. ♿ 💳	$					■
ALBUQUERQUE: *Church Street Café* 2111 Church St. NW., NM 87124. ☎ *(505) 247-8522.* Situated in the Old Town just behind San Felipe de Neri church, this atmospheric restaurant is found in one of the oldest buildings in the state. Highly acclaimed for its authentic Hispanic fare. ⛔ *D.* ♿ 💳	$	■	●			■
ALBUQUERQUE: *Garduño's Restaurant & Cantina* 2100 Lousiana, NM 87111. ☎ *(505) 880-0055.* This fun, local chain has a great atmosphere with Mexican decor. Enchiladas and margaritas are the favorites here. ♿ ♫ 💳	$		●	■		■
ALBUQUERQUE: *Maria Teresa's Restaurant* 618 Rio Grande NW., NM 87104. ☎ *(505) 242 3900.* Located in a 19th-century adobe hacienda in the Old Town, this restaurant specializes in modern American and New Mexican fare. ♿ 💳	$	■	●	■		■
ALBUQUERQUE: *El Pinto* 10500 4th St. NW., NM 87114. ☎ *(505) 898-1771.* Mexican cuisine served in a maze of atmospheric rooms with Southwestern decor, or on the patio with a view of the Sandia Mountains. ♿ ♫ 💳	$$	■	●	■		■
ALBUQUERQUE: *Kanome Asian Diner* 3128 Central Ave. SE, NM 87106. ☎ *(505) 265-7773.* This delightful diner serves eclectic Asian-inspired food, including noodle dishes, wrapped foods, and chef's specialties. ⛔ *Mon, L.* ♿ 💳	$$	■	●			
ALBUQUERQUE: *La Hacienda Restaurant* 302 San Felipe NW., NM 87104. ☎ *(505) 243-3131* Atmospheric New Mexican restaurant in an old adobe building, painted with a mural of the first settlers. Fajitas and seafood are specialties. ♿ 💳	$$	■	●			■
ALBUQUERQUE: *Monte Vista Fire Station* 3201 Central Ave. NE., NM 87106. ☎ *(505) 255-2424.* Now a National Historic Site, this art-deco Pueblo Revival building was once a fire station. A local favorite, it serves creative Southwestern cuisine. ♿ 💳	$$		●	■		■

ALBUQUERQUE: *Yanni's* $$
3109 Central Ave. NE., NM 87106. ((505) 268-9250.
This top-rated local favorite serves delicious Greek dishes, along with
Mediterranean-style pizza, pasta, calzones, and vegetarian dishes.

ALBUQUERQUE: *The Artichoke Café* $$$
424 Central Ave. SE., NM 87102. ((505) 243-0200.
Relaxed but stylish downtown restaurant is decorated art and serves French-
American bistro fare. You can eat outside in good weather. ● *Sat L. Sun*

ALBUQUERQUE: *Landry's Seafood House* $$$
5001 Jefferson St. NE., NM 87110. ((505) 875-0101.
Fresh seafood and great scenery at this 1940s-style restaurant, with
beautiful views of the lake and mountains from the large deck.

ALBUQUERQUE: *High Finance Restaurant and Tavern* $$$$
40 Tramway Rd. NE., NM 87122. ((505) 243-9742.
Stunning location at the top of the Sandia Peak tramway, with fantastic
views. Fish, seafood, steaks, and slow-roasted prime rib are served.

ALBUQUERQUE: *Rio Grande Yacht Club* $$$$
2500 Yale Blvd. SE., NM 87106. ((505) 243-6111.
This restaurant with a nautical theme boasts Albuquerque's largest
seafood selection. Oyster bar Wednesdays and Fridays 5–7 pm.

CARLSBAD: *The Flume* $$
1829 S. Canal St., NM 88220. ((505) 887-2851.
This casual restaurant is one of the best in Carlsbad. It is famous for its
prime rib, but steaks, chicken, and seafood are also served.

CLOUDCROFT: *Rebecca's* $$$
The Lodge, 1 Corona Pl., NM 88317. ((505) 682-2566.
Rebecca's offers fine dining in a relaxed but elegant setting. The food is
superb – beef, seafood, and poultry with a Southwestern flare.

GRANTS: *Grants Station Restaurant* $
200 W. Santa Fe, NM 87020. ((505) 287-2334.
Fun, casual restaurant that serves good food in a great atmosphere.
Try the sizzling hot fajitas or other Mexican dishes.

LINCOLN: *Isaac's Table* $$$
Mile marker 98, Hwy. 38, NM 88338. ((800) 653-6460.
Gourmet dining in the historic Ellis Store. The six-course, fixed-price dinner
features wild game, prime beef, lamb, and seafood. ● *Sun–Tue.*

MESILLA: *Double Eagle* $$
308 Calle de Guadalupe, NM 88004. ((505) 523-6700.
Housed in a historic building on Mesilla's Plaza. Bourbon pepper steak
and chicken Mesilla, made with green chile, are favorites.

MESILLA: *La Posta de Mesilla* $$
2410 Calle de San Albino, NM 88046. ((505) 524-3524.
This adobe restaurant was built in 1857 and serves delicious steaks and
Mexican-Indian dishes, including chile rellenos and tamales. ● *Mon.*

RUIDOSO: *Café Rio* $
2547 Sudderth Dr., NM 88355. ((505) 257-7746.
Wonderful food in cheerful, relaxed surroundings, featuring interesting
dishes such as Portuguese kale soup and shrimp jambalaya.

RUIDOSO: *Cattle Baron Steak & Seafood Restaurant* $$
657 Sudderth Dr., NM 88345. ((505) 257-9355.
Prime rib and a fresh catch of the day lead the menu at this casual family
restaurant. Salad bar, chicken, steaks, and chops also served.

RUIDOSO: *Dan Li Ka* $$$
Carrizo Canyon Rd., NM 88340. ((505) 257-5141.
This fine restaurant features spectacular views of the mountains and lake.
Food ranges from steak and seafood to spicy Southwestern dishes.

SILVER CITY: *The Buckhorn Saloon & Opera House* $$
32 Main St., Pinos Altos, NM 88053. ((505) 538-9911.
Steakhouse and saloon in a beautifully restored building dating from the
1860s. Fine dining, Old West decor, and stone fireplaces. ● *L.*

For key to symbols see back flap

SHOPPING IN THE SOUTHWEST

ITH SUCH AN EXCITING range of Native American, Hispanic, and Anglo-American products, shopping in the Southwest is a cultural adventure. Native crafts, including rugs, jewelry, and pottery, top the list of things that people buy. The Southwest is also a center for the fine arts, with Santa Fe *(see pp192–9)* famous for its many galleries selling everything from Georgia O'Keeffe-inspired landscapes and the latest

Chile-shaped pot

contemporary work to kitsch bronze sculptures of cowboys or Indians. Across the region, specialty grocery stores and supermarkets stock a range of Southwestern products from hot chile sauces to blue corn tortilla chips. In the major cities there is a choice of glamorous fashion districts, usually situated in air-conditioned, landscaped malls. Las Vegas also ranks shopping among its attractions, with its themed malls *(see pp124–5)*.

SHOPPING HOURS AND PAYMENT

OST MAJOR STORES are open from 9 or 10am to between 8 and 10pm, seven days a week, although some stores may close just after midday on Sunday or Monday.

Most stores take Mastercard, VISA, and ATM cards. Other credit cards and out-of-state checks are often not accepted. A sales tax will be added to the price of 3 percent in Colorado, 4.75 percent in Utah, 5 percent in Arizona and New Mexico, and 6.5 percent in Nevada.

NATIVE ARTS AND CRAFTS

ISCOVERING THE spiritual beliefs that are bound up with all types of Native art can make shopping for these items a rewarding experience, especially when purchasing direct from native artists in

their homes. The best places to buy such pieces are generally reservation trading posts and in Pueblo or museum stores. The quality of Native crafts can vary greatly, and it is worth following a few guidelines before you buy. The term "Indian hand-made" means that the item has been made solely by Native Americans, while "Indian crafted" means that they have been involved in the production. Buying directly from the artist not only ensures authenticity but also gives money to the local Native American community.

Pot from the Cameron Trading Post

Many artists display their work at tourist stops such as those at Canyon de Chelly or on reservations. Trading posts such as the **Hubbell Trading Post** *(see p167)* on the Navajo Reservation were established specifically to sell Native

products such as rugs to the region's first tourists in the late 19th century. Other sources of authentic good-quality items include **Cameron Trading Post** near Flagstaff, which has been converted to a gallery displaying historic and modern rugs, pottery, baskets, and carvings. Hopi House at the South Rim of Grand Canyon, **Fifth Generation Trading Company** in Farmington, and **Sewell's Indian Arts** in Sedona also offer a wide choice of goods.

The Indian Pueblo Cultural Center in Albuquerque is a co-operative of 19 Pueblos and offers Pueblo Indian art at fair prices *(see p214)*. The Second Mesa Jewelry Co-operative on the Hopi reservation is a training facility that offers some of the finest Hopi silverwork *(see p166)*.

Museum shops such as the Heard's in Phoenix *(see p79)* and Flagstaff's Museum of Northern Arizona *(see p68)* sell a selection of paintings, sculpture, and *kachina* dolls.

MALLS

HE SEARING temperatures of southern Arizona and New Mexico have spawned some of the most stunning malls in the US, all of which feature air-conditioning, plant-filled atriums, and fine restaurants. The biggest concentration is in Phoenix, with the largest mall in the Southwest being

Native American rugs in the Cameron Trading Post

the city's **Metrocenter**. Large department stores such as Neiman Marcus can be found at the **Scottsdale Fashion Square**. Phoenix's **Biltmore Fashion Park** sells designer clothing and kitchenware, as well as offering some of the best dining options in town.

Themed malls are abundant in the region. **Borgata of Scottsdale** is a mall set in a 14th-century-style village with medieval courtyards. The Arizona Center in Phoenix is an oasis of restaurants and shops set among gardens, fountains, and a waterfall. The **Tucson Art District** has more than 40 fine art galleries.

Most of the major Las Vegas hotels feature designer shopping areas (*see pp106–17*).

ART GALLERIES

T HE SOUTHWEST has a vibrant artistic heritage and Santa Fe is the country's second largest art market after New York City. Its art district stretches from the downtown plaza for 2 miles (3 km) along Canyon Road (*see p197*). More than 200 galleries specialize in locally produced art. Native and Hispanic artists are also well represented, the latter producing carved *santos* and

bultos depicting saints and other religious figures. Top quality antique and reproduction Hispanic furniture and paintings can be found at markets organized by the **Spanish Colonial Arts Society**.

Typical southwestern boots and hats on sale in Phoenix

WESTERN WEAR

A MONG THE most popular souvenirs of the Southwest are hand-tooled cowboy boots, cowboy hats, and decorative leather belts. Western wear is made to high standards throughout the region. Phoenix is a famous center for cowboy clothes, but El

Paso (*see p222–3*) is also noted for its leather goods. **Aztec Hats of Phoenix** has the largest selection of cowboy hats in the Southwest, while **Saba Western Store** has been outfitting customers in western fashions since 1927. **Bacon's Boots and Saddles**, located in the historic mining town of Globe (*see p83*), is owned by craftsman Ed Bacon who has been making fine boots and saddles for more than 50 years. Parents who want to dress their children in cute western-wear might try Albuquerque's **Lil' Bit Southwest**.

FOOD

S OUTHWESTERNERS ARE proud of their cuisine and in most malls you will find grocery stores selling an array of chile sauces, salsa dips, and blue corn chips. Farmers' markets are another good source of local produce, and usually stock a range of the strings of dried chiles, known as *ristras*. Several companies have websites where you can order such gourmet regional foods as hand-made corn chips, coffee made with piñon tree nuts, and prickly pear jam.

ENTERTAINMENT
IN THE SOUTHWEST

**Museum Club
sign**

THE SOUTHWEST'S blend of cultures has made the region a thriving center for arts and entertainment. The large cities of Phoenix, Santa Fe, Tucson, and Albuquerque have vibrant artistic communities and offer opera, ballet, classical music, and major theatrical productions. The smaller resort towns of Sedona and Taos are famous for their resident painters and sculptors and regularly host noted touring productions, as well as regional theater, dance, and musical events. And almost every city and major town has a lively nightlife that includes country music, jazz, and rock, as well as dinner theater and standup comedy. Sports fans will be happy here with major league and college football, baseball, and basketball teams playing across the region.

Displaying traditional cowboy skills at one of the region's rodeos

INFORMATION

THE BEST source of events information is in the entertainment guides of local newspapers. Phoenix's *The Arizona Republic*, Tucson's *Daily Star*, the *Santa Fe New Mexican*, and *Albuquerque Journal* are the most useful. Most of these newspapers also have websites. There are several regional magazines that review events and nightlife. Most hotels offer magazines, such as *Where* and *Key*, that feature dining, attractions, and entertainment. You can book tickets for most events through **Ticketmaster** outlets, or at www.ticketmaster.com, their online booking service.

RODEOS AND
WILD WEST SHOWS

SINCE BUFFALO BILL'S first Wild West shows in the 1880s, the Southwest has been a mecca for Western-style entertainment. Traditional cowboy skills such as roping steers and breaking wild horses have been transformed into categories of rodeo contest, offering winners substantial money prizes. Rodeos owe their name to the Spanish word for round-up, harking back to the 19th century when herds of cattle crossed New Mexico on their way to California. Today's rodeo circuit is highly competitive and dangerous, attracting full-time professionals whose high pay reflects this risky career. Nevertheless, the allure is comparable with the magic of the circus. Among the largest and most popular rodeos are Tucson's Fiesta de los Vaqueros, Albuquerque's New Mexico State Fair and Rodeo, and Prescott's Frontier Days Rodeo *(see pp32–5).*

The Southwest offers plenty of opportunities for visitors to sample the atmosphere of the Wild West, either in the many ghost towns or in historic frontier towns such as **Tombstone** *(see p92),* which stages daily mock-gunfights and tours of its Victorian buildings. There are also Western towns built originally as film studios, such as **Old Tucson Studios** *(see p86).* Tours of the sets are available. **Rawhide**, north of Scottsdale, has an Old West museum, an old-fashioned ice cream parlor, a famous music venue, and Western theme attractions.

SPORTS

Baseball player

THE THREE most popular spectator sports in the Southwest, as in the rest of the country, are football, baseball, and basketball. The region's largest concentration of major teams is in the Phoenix area. There is only one major league football team in the Southwest, the **Arizona Cardinals** in Phoenix. The Arizona Diamondbacks baseball team joined the majors in 1998 and is based at the $275-million **Bank One Stadium** in Phoenix. Professional basketball is represented by the Phoenix Suns, who share the **America West Arena** with a hockey team, the

Phoenix Coyotes. While tickets may be hard to obtain for league games, it is easy to gain entrance to the many college games in any sport throughout the region. Phoenix's warm climate also attracts the Cactus League, a series of training games for seven major league baseball teams in February and March.

CLASSICAL MUSIC, BALLET, AND OPERA

I N ARIZONA, the excellent Phoenix Symphony and Arizona Opera both perform at the **Phoenix Symphony Hall** building. The city's $14-million refurbishment of the Spanish Baroque-style **Orpheum Theater** makes it a stunning addition to more than 20 major venues for arts, sports, and entertainment in and around Phoenix. Ballet Arizona and two theater companies occupy the **Herberger Theater Center**, offering a regular program of performances. With more than 20 theater companies in Phoenix, there is an impressive array of plays to choose from, as well as touring Broadway shows and big-name entertainers.

New Mexico's major cultural activities are based in Santa Fe and Albuquerque. Santa Fe has more than 200 art galleries and is also respected for its performing arts. The **Santa Fe Opera** performs both traditional and contemporary operas in its open-air arena during July and August. Santa Fe's Chamber Music Festival, held at venues throughout the city in July and August, is one of the finest in the US. The **New Mexico Symphony Orchestra** is based in

Spectacular outdoor setting of the Santa Fe Opera company

Albuquerque, best known for its classics concerts. The city's **Musical Theater Southwest** offers a range of entertainment including Broadway musicals, and its **New Mexico Jazz Workshops** stage more than 30 concerts each year.

Dancing couple at the Museum Club in Flagstaff, Arizona

NIGHTLIFE

I N ALMOST EVERY town there are restaurants, bars, and nightclubs that offer country music and dancing. Among the most famous country music venues is the Western theme town of Rawhide in Scottsdale, where well-known bands play. The **Museum Club** in Flagstaff is a venerable Route 66 *(see p51)* establishment that hosted such top country music names as Hank Williams in the 1950s and still offers a lively selection of Southwestern bands.

Major cities offer virtually every type of evening entertainment. Jazz bars and cafés are gaining in popularity, and standup comedy and rock music is available in countless venues. Clubs and arenas based in Phoenix, Tucson, Albuquerque, and Santa Fe are regular stops for big stars on US tours. However, the entertainment capital of the region, and some would say the world, is Las Vegas *(see pp126–7)*. The Las Vegas Strip on a single night hosts as much top talent as all the other cities in the Southwest do in a year: everything from Broadway shows and dazzling homegrown productions to a range of free music in the casinos.

SPECIALTY VACATIONS
AND ACTIVITIES

W ITH THOUSANDS of miles of deep rock canyons, spectacular deserts, and towering, snow-capped mountains, few places in the world offer so many opportunities for outdoor entertainment as the American Southwest. Much of the wilderness here is protected by the Federal Government in national parks, formed during the early 20th century when the region first began to attract tourists. Increasing numbers of visitors are being drawn to the region, and it is now a magnet for climbers,

Mountain bike rental sign

mountain bikers, hikers, and 4WD enthusiasts. The range of organized tours includes whitewater rafting and horseback riding, as well as cultural heritage tours of the many ancient Native American sites. Wildlife enthusiasts, particularly birdwatchers, can spot rare species on the spring and fall migration routes that cross the Southwest. The region is also a center for sports activities, especially for golfers and skiers. For information on the main events in the Southwest's sports calendar see pp266–7.

GENERAL INFORMATION

T HE MAIN centers for outdoor activities in the region are Moab *(see p141)*, Durango *(see p179)*, and Sedona *(see p71)*, with their excellent equipment shops and visitor information centers. Advance planning is advisable for activities such as whitewater rafting along the Colorado River in Grand Canyon, or mule trips into the canyon, as these are often booked up to a year ahead *(see pp58–63)*. Hikers and campers exploring the backcountry will also need permits from the National Park Service as well as detailed maps, which can be obtained from either the Bureau of Land Management, the **U.S.D.A. Forest Service**, or the **US Geological Survey**. Both state and local tourist offices can supply the latest advice on trails, permits, and weather conditions at most attractions. Anyone exploring desert or canyon country should be aware of the potential for flash floods and should check weather reports daily, especially during the summer months of July and August.

GOLF

W ITH AROUND 275 golf courses in Arizona alone, many of them top-rated, the Southwest is a golfer's paradise. This is particularly true of Southern Arizona with its year-round warm weather. The town of Scottsdale *(see pp80–1)*, is considered by some to be America's premier golf spot and is famous for such resorts as **The Boulders** and the legendary Phoenician, both top-rated championship courses. Tucson is also a well-known golfing area with such offerings as the Jack Nicklaus-designed golf resort **Westin La Paloma**. New Mexico is also known for its courses and affordable greens fees. Albuquerque's Arroyo del Oso is a challenging municipal course with immaculate fairways. Information on the various courses can be found through **Golf Arizona** and **Golf New Mexico**.

Golf course at Phoenix's top-rated Wigwam Resort *(see p235)*

HIKING

H IKING IS the single most popular outdoor activity in the Southwest. Day hikes and longer trips draw large numbers of residents and visitors who feel that this is the best way to see the region's stunning scenery. Virtually all of the national parks have excellent well-marked trails as well as fascinating ranger-led hikes that focus on the local flora, fauna, and geology. One of

Whitewater rafting trip on the Colorado River

Mountain biking along one of many red-rock trails near Moab

the most famous, and arduous, hikes in the Southwest is a rim-to-rim hike of Grand Canyon along the Bright Angel and Kaibab trails *(see pp60–3)*. It takes most hikers two to three days to complete. Longer trips into the vast wilderness of Grand Staircase-Escalante National Monument *(see p148)* and the Glen Canyon Recreation Area *(see pp150–51)* are among the highlights of wilderness exploration for hikers. Around the Four Corners region, there are many hikes that explore archaeological sites such as the Ancestral Puebloan ruins at Chaco Canyon where there is an 8-mile (13-km) trail to the pueblo houses at Chetro Ketl *(see pp174–5)*.

Hikers on the trail to Pueblo Alto at Chaco Canyon *(see pp174–5)*

ROCK CLIMBING

ITS DRY, SUNNY CLIMATE and extensive mountains, canyons, and sheer rock faces make the Southwest a popular climbing spot. Favored sites include the sheer cliffs of Zion National Park *(see pp154–5)*, the rocky landscape around Moab *(see p142)*, and Utah's Canyonlands National Park *(see p142–3)*. Moab has a good selection of equipment shops, such as the **Moab Climbing Shop**. Red Rock Canyon, 15 miles (24 km) west of Las Vegas, is another favorite area, with guided climbs offered by **Jackson Hole Mountain Guides**.

MOUNTAIN BIKING AND FOUR-WHEEL DRIVING

ALL OF THE region's national parks have trails open to mountain biking, but the centers of this activity are Moab and Durango, Colorado *(see p179)*. The state of Utah has declared itself the mountain bike capital of the world, and the Moab area is something of a pilgrimage site for mountain bikers. Named after a well-known bike trail, **Poison Spider Bicycles** sells and repairs bikes as well as housing Nichols Tours, which

leads groups through wilderness areas. Moab is famous for the Slick Rock Trail, a demanding run across more than 12 miles (19 km) of precipitous rock with stunning views. However, during the summer months the trail can become very crowded.

Around Durango, Colorado, cooler and greener conditions prevail with rides through the pine forests of the Rocky Mountains. Popular bike trails include the level, but scenic, Animas Valley Loop or the more rugged, hilly Animas Mountain Loop.

4WD at wetlands near Moab

There are also several 4WD trails, leading to remote and beautiful backcountry. Again, Moab is one of the top centers for off-road drivers, with rentals and tours available from **Farabee Adventures**. Canyonlands National Park and Canyon de Chelly are also popular. Monument Valley in Arizona *(see pp164–5)* is a prime location for 4WD tours to areas not accessible by a regular car, often led by Navajo guides from **Monument Valley Tours**. Also in Arizona, Sedona's red-rock canyons may be toured by 4WD, and **Pink Jeep Tours** is a local legend. In Scottsdale, **Walk Softly Tours** offers 4WD trips through the Sonoran Desert.

WHITEWATER RAFTING AND KAYAKING

THE GREEN, San Juan, and Colorado rivers make the Southwest one of the world's top destinations for whitewater rafting. These rivers run fast and deep, offering a thrilling ride, often through breathtaking canyons. Trips ranging from beginner to experienced are offered by most outfitters. Tour companies provide rafts, paddles, and lifejackets, and for multi-day trips that involve camping, food and tents may also be provided. Visitors are advised to check a variety of companies to make sure they get the river experience that suits them best. It is also a good idea to check their safety records and expertise.

One of the most exciting rafting trips in the Southwest is the 12–20 day trip along the Colorado River through Grand Canyon. As numbers for some trips may be limited to eight or fewer people, tours can be booked by as much as a year in advance. Many outfitters offer Grand Canyon raft trips: one of the best known is **Canyon Explorations**.

The confluence of the Green and Colorado rivers lies near Moab, Utah. Just beyond their convergence lies Cataract Canyon, one of the most famous whitewater rapids in the world. Shooting these waters should be undertaken only by experienced rafters. One of the best outfitters to take visitors through the canyon is **Sheri-Griffith Expeditions**. The company also offers raft tours of varying degrees of difficulty on the smaller rivers in the area. **Canyon Voyages** offers rafting trips ranging from peaceful river journeys to thrilling whitewater adventures. They also offer kayak workshops.

Wild River Expeditions' one-day, gentle drift through the canyons of the Four Corners' San Juan River is led by guides who are also archaeologists and geologists. There are stops at Bluff (*see p172*) and Mexican Hat, as well as at Ancestral Puebloan ruins.

Powerboating near Parker Dam in western Arizona

WATER SPORTS

THE DAMS along the Colorado River have created a chain of artificial lakes starting with Lake Powell (*see pp150–51*) and extending to Lake Mead (*see p120*) and Lake Havasu (*see p70*). A variety of water sports are available, including powerboating and jetskiing.

Set in the one million-acre (400,000-ha) Glen Canyon Recreation Area, Lake Powell is famous for its houseboat cruises. These offer visitors the chance to experience the many beaches and canyons around the lake. All visitors are shown how to operate the boats and are given an instruction manual. There is also a variety of guided tours available, including cruises to Rainbow Bridge and Antelope Canyon. Gentle raft trips between Glen Canyon Dam and Lees Ferry are offered by **Aramark Inc.**, the main tour concession for the lake. **Lake Powell Resorts and Marinas** rents out both houseboats and powerboats.

On Lake Havasu all kinds of water sports equipment, from waterskis to scuba gear, can be rented from Fun Time Boat Rentals. At Lake Mead numerous shops rent fishing boats and jetskis and offer waterskiing lessons. The **Lake Mead Visitor Center** is a useful source of information.

Boaters on all the lakes are provided with information to make water-based vacations safe and pleasurable. Children aged 12 and under must wear lifejackets, and all boats must be driven at wakeless speed within harbor or beach areas.

FISHING

LAKES MEAD, Powell, and Havasu are also noted as popular locations for fishing. The lakes are well stocked with game fish such as striped, largemouth, and smallmouth bass during the fishing season, which runs

Fishing in a lake at Cedar Breaks National Monument, Southern Utah (*see p149*)

Mountain views from the Sandia Peak Tramway near Albuquerque

from March to November. River anglers can also fish for salmon and trout. Each state has different regulations and fishing licenses, although catch and release is the rule in many areas. Information about licenses, tournaments, and tours can be obtained from marinas, outdoor equipment stores, local gas stations, and state **Fish and Game Departments**.

SKIING AND WINTER SPORTS

IN GENERAL, the ski season in Southwestern resorts runs from November to April. A range of skiing trips is available, from all-inclusive packages to day-trips from nearby towns. There are plenty of equipment rental outlets, although resort packages usually include skis, lift passes, and lessons if necessary. Other winter sports such as snowboarding, snowmobiling, and cross-country skiing are becoming increasingly popular, with runs and equipment now available in most resorts.

Utah hosts the Winter Olympics in 2002 and offers some of the best skiing in the region. The **Telluride Ski Area** is set among the 19th-century towns and mountain scenery of southwestern Colorado. The facilities and runs here, with elevations of more than 11,500 ft (3,450 m), attract many visitors during the season, including many of the country's celebrities. **Purgatory-Durango Ski Resort** is less chic and less pricey, but provides just as

much challenge with vertical drops of over 2,000 ft (600 m). New Mexico's **Taos Ski Valley** includes world-class slopes, and the Arizona Snowbowl near Flagstaff *(see p67)* is particularly popular with cross-country skiers.

HORSEBACK RIDING

HORSEBACK riding is synonymous with the Southwest, and almost every area has stables that rent horses. Some ranches offer guided trail rides as well as the chance to live and work as a cowboy. The range of trips is impressive: from hour-long rides to two-week dude ranch vacations *(see p231)*.

Ranches are dotted across the region, but the best-known are those in southern Arizona, particularly near the town of Wickenburg. The area's pleasant winter climate attracts thousands of visitors, and even large cities such as Phoenix and Tucson have riding stables and offer trails through beautiful desert scenery. Cooler summer locations such as Sedona and Pinetop Lakeside in Arizona are also popular riding centers.

Most of the national parks offer trail-riding tours, but the noted mule trip into Grand Canyon *(see p62)* needs to be booked well in advance. **Amfac Travel** offers adventurous mule rides that last two days from the South Rim, overnighting on the canyon floor at the famous Phantom Ranch *(see p232)*.

AIR TOURS

AIR TOURS are a good option for those time-restricted travelers who wish to see the more remote attractions. Canyonlands National Park is famous for its vast wildernesses: **Aerowest** offers one-hour flights over all three districts in Canyonlands, as well as over the stunning Dead Horse Point State Park *(see p143)*. **Slickrock Air Guides of Moab** offer three-hour tours that cover Canyonlands, Lake Powell, Capitol Reef National Park, and the north rim of Grand Canyon. The striking red-rock pinnacles formations of Bryce Canyon *(see pp152–3)* can be seen by both plane and helicopter on tours lasting from 17 minutes to one hour. The most popular air tours are those over Grand Canyon. Several of these are offered from Las Vegas *(see p123)*, and there are ten companies based in Tusayan at the park's southern entrance. However, increasing numbers of airborne tourists are raising the issue of noise pollution as a pressing problem throughout the canyon. Increasing numbers of visitors complain that engine noise diminishes what should be a tranquil experience of the area's beauty.

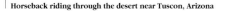

Horseback riding through the desert near Tuscon, Arizona

International Balloon Fiesta in Albuquerque, New Mexico *(see p34)*

HOT AIR BALLOONING

COOL STILL mornings, dependable sunshine, and steady breezes have made the Southwest the top hot air ballooning destination in America. Balloon trips around Albuquerque are a popular excursion, particularly in October, when the International Balloon Fiesta takes place *(see p34)*. Outfitters such as **Discover Balloons** offer a one-hour flight with champagne brunch.

You can also drift over the canyons of Sedona with **Northern Light Balloon Expeditions**, and over the Sonoran Desert with **Hot Air Expeditions**.

BIRDWATCHING

WITH MORE than 200 species of bird, including many rare breeds, bird-watching is a popular pastime in the Southwest, particularly in spring, early summer, and fall. These are peak migration seasons for warblers, fly-catchers, and shorebirds, while nesting waders and ducks may be seen in New Mexico's **Bosque del Apache Wildlife Refuge**. The refuge also boasts a winter population of more than 17,000 sandhill cranes. Several habitats across the region suit desert birds such as the roadrunner and elf owl, particularly Saguaro National Park in the Sonoran Desert. Capitol Reef *(see p146)* and Bryce Canyon *(see pp152–3)* national parks attract yellow warblers, northern orioles, and black-chinned hummingbirds.

Broad-billed hummingbird

Southern Utah and southern Arizona are noted for their hummingbird population. Tours devoted to the study of these enchanting creatures are run by **Victor Emmanuel's Nature Tours**. **The Southeastern Arizona Bird Observatory** also offers educational tours in the region.

Many species of hawk may be spotted in the Southwest, and birds of prey such as red-tailed hawks, golden eagles, and peregrine falcons are regular visitors to Bryce Canyon.

LEARNING VACATIONS

IN THE SOUTHWEST, some of the most interesting learning vacations focus on native cultures and ancient civilizations. Two organizations, **The Crow Canyon Archaeological Center** and **The Four Corners School**, offer a range of vacation courses on geography, flora and fauna, ancient ruins, and Native arts. Archaeology courses often involve working on digs with professional archaeologists; Native culture courses may study both modern and ancient Native groups, their way of life, religious practices, and arts. Most programs last between four and ten days, and visitors are housed either in college campuses or in motels. The **Smithsonian Institution** offers a popular program on past and present arts of the Hopi, Zuni, and Navajo tribes.

The distinctive cuisine of the region has led to an array of courses on Southwestern cooking. The **Santa Fe Cooking School** and the **Santa Fe Workshops** offer a variety of courses for beginners and professionals. The Workshops also offer photography and painting courses that take advantage of the unique light and landscapes of Santa Fe.

In Arizona, Sedona *(see p73)* is a mecca for those interested in New Age philosophy. The Center for the New Age is just one place offering courses in yoga, nutrition, counseling, and aromatherapy. There are also guided tours of the vortexes (points of the Earth's energy) said to be found in the area.

DIRECTORY

INFORMATION

United States Geological Survey (U.S.G.S.)
12201 Sunrise Valley Drive, Reston, VA 20192.
W www.usgs.gov
((703) 648-4748.

U.S.D.A Forest Service
517 Gold Avenue SW., Albuquerque, NM 87102.
((505) 842-3898.

GOLF

Boulders Resort
34631 N. Tom Darlington Drive, Carefree AZ 85377.
((800) 553-1717.

Golf Arizona
((480) 837-2706.

Golf New Mexico
((505) 342-1563.

Westin La Paloma
3800 East Sunrise, Tucson AZ 85718.
((520) 742-6000.

ROCK CLIMBING

Jackson Hole Mountain Guides
8201 West Charleston, Suite B, Las Vegas, NV 89117.
((702) 254-0885.

Moab Climbing Shop
550 N. Main Street, Moab UT 84532.
((435) 259-2725.

MOUNTAIN BIKING AND 4WD

Farabee Adventures, Inc.
401 N. Main St., Moab, UT 84532.
((435) 259-7494.

Goulding's Lodge Monument Valley Tours
Highway 163, Goulding, UT 84536.
((435) 727-3231.

Pink Jeep Tours
204 N. Highway 89A, PO Box 1447, Sedona AZ 86339.
((520) 282-5000; (800) 873-3662.

Poison Spider Bicycles
497 N. Main St., Moab, UT 84532.
((800) 635-1792.

Walk Softly Tours
PO Box 5510, Scottsdale, AZ 85261.
((480) 473-1148.

WHITEWATER RAFTING

Canyon Explorations
PO Box 310, Flagstaff, AZ 86002.
((520) 774-4559; (800) 654-0723.

Canyon Voyages
690 S. Main St., Moab UT.
((801) 259-6007.

Sheri-Griffith Expeditions
PO Box 1324, Moab, UT 84532.
((800) 332-2439.

WATER SPORTS

Aramark Inc.
50 S. Lake Powell Blvd., Page, AZ 86040.
((520) 645-3279.

Lake Mead Visitor Center
601 Nevada Hwy, Boulder City, NV 89005.
((702) 293-8906/8907.

Lake Powell Resorts and Marinas
PO Box 1597, Page, AZ 86040.
((520) 645-2433 or (602) 278-8888; (800) 528-6154.

FISHING

Arizona Game and Fish Department
2222 Greenway Road, Phoenix, AZ 85023.
((602) 942-3000.

Colorado Division of Wildlife
6060 Broadway, Denver, CO 80216.
((303) 291-7533.

New Mexico Department of Game and Fish
Villagra Building, Sante Fe, NM 87503.
((505) 827-7911.

Utah Division of Wildlife Resources
1596 West North Temple, Salt Lake City, UT 84116.
((801) 596-8660.

SKI RESORTS

Purgatory-Durango Mountain Resort
Route 550 Durango, CO 81301.
((970) 247-9000.

Taos Ski Valley
PO Box 90, Taos Ski Valley, NM 87525.
((505) 776-2291.

Telluride Ski Area
Route 145, Telluride, CO.
((970) 728-6070.

HORSEBACK RIDING

AmFac Tours
((303) 297-2757.

AIR TOURS

Aerowest
((435) 259-7421; (800) 842-9251.

Slickrock Airguides of Moab
((435) 259-6216.

HOT AIR BALLOONING

Discover Balloons
205C San Felipe Northwest, Albuquerque, NM 87104.
((505) 842-1111.

Hot Air Expeditions
2243 East Rose Garden Loop Suite 1, Phoenix, AZ 85024.
((480) 502-6999; (800) 831-7610.

Northern Light Balloon Expeditions
PO Box 1695, Sedona, AZ 86339.
((520) 282-2274; (800) 230-6222.

BIRDWATCHING

Bosque del Apache Wildlife Refuge
1001 Hwy 1, San Antonio, NM 87832.
((505) 835-1828.

Southeastern Arizona Bird Observatory
PO Box 5521, Bisbee, AZ 85603.
((520) 432-1388.
W www.sabo.org

Victor Emmanuel's Nature Tours
PO Box 33008, Austin, TX 78764.
((512) 328-5221; (800) 328-8368.

LEARNING VACATIONS

The Crow Canyon Archaeological Center
23390 County Road K, Cortez, CO 81321.
((970) 565-8975.

The Four Corners School
Box 1028, Monticello, UT 84535.
((435) 587-2859.

The Santa Fe Photographic Workshops
Box 9916, Santa Fe, NM 87504.
((505) 983-1400.

The Santa Fe School of Cooking
116 West San Francisco Street, Santa Fe, NM 87501.
((505) 983-4511.

The Smithsonian Institution,
1000 Jefferson Drive SW, MRC702, Washington DC 20560.
((202) 357-4700.

SURVIVAL
GUIDE

PRACTICAL INFORMATION

THE SOUTHWEST US is an area of spectacular natural beauty. Arizona, New Mexico, the Four Corners, and Southern Utah are dotted with dramatic rock formations, canyons, ancient archaeological sites, and wild desert scenery that offer visitors a choice of pleasures, including a wide variety of outdoor activities. The cities here are famous for their combination of laid-back Southern culture and sophisticated urban pursuits with excellent museums and great dining. The unique attractions of Las Vegas, Nevada *(see pp98–131)* also make for

Arizona State Parks sign

an exciting experience, popular with millions across the world. Accommodations are of international standard *(see pp230–45)*, and visitor information centers are plentiful, even in small towns.

The following pages contain useful information for all visitors planning a trip to this region. Personal Security and Health *(see pp280–81)* recommends a number of precautions, while Banking and Communications *(see pp282–3)* answers financial and media queries. There is also information on traveling around the country by both public transportation and car.

WHEN TO GO

THE SOUTHWEST has the advantage of being a year-round destination. Generally speaking the climate tends to be dictated by the varying elevations in the region. The high-lying areas of northern Arizona and New Mexico, and southern Utah have cold, snowy winters, making them popular destinations for skiing and other winter sports activities. In contrast, the lower elevations of the southern portions of the states are noted for their warm and sunny winter weather, with temperatures averaging a comfortable 70°F (21°C) in the Phoenix area, which receives thousands of winter visitors. Be aware, however, that the summer months of July and August have average temperatures of 100°F (37°C) in Phoenix, making it one of the hottest cities outside the Middle East. Spring and fall are ideal seasons to visit the southwestern United States – there are fewer visitors, and the milder temperatures make outdoor activities, especially hiking, a popular option. However, some services may be closed at these times; the North Rim of Grand Canyon in northern Arizona is open only between May and October, while the mesa tops of the ancient Pueblo site of Mesa Verde in Colorado may

be inaccessible because of snow as late as April or May. Whatever the time of year, this is a region known for having a great deal of sun, with northern areas averaging well over 200 days of sunshine each year, and the southern parts famous for having more than 300 sunny days.

Wet weather warning sign in southern Utah

ENTRY REQUIREMENTS

CITIZENS FROM Australia, New Zealand, South Africa, and the UK, and many other European countries can visit the US without the need for a visa. Instead, they are required to have a passport that is valid for at least six months after the trip they are

planning and to complete a Visa Waiver Form, usually on the incoming flight. This allows for a stay of up to 90 days. Having passed through US Immigration, visitors may then use these documents to cross the border into Mexico. Canadians do not need their passports, but when they enter the US they are required to show a photo I.D., such as a citizenship card. It is a good idea to contact the nearest United States embassy to obtain the latest information on which countries are currently participating in the visa waiver program.

Visitors from countries who do need a visa must apply to a US consulate or embassy, and may be asked for evidence of financial solvency, as well as for proof that they are intending to return to their country of origin.

Any visitor wishing to extend their stay beyond the 90-day limit should contact the nearest US Immigration and Naturalization Service (I.N.S.) well in advance of the date stamped on their visa waiver form or visa.

TOURIST INFORMATION

VISITOR INFORMATION centers in the US are noted for the quality of their information, offering everything from local maps to hotel and B&B bookings. Special tours such as guided history walks, ranger-led archaeological tours, and wildlife watching can often be arranged through these offices. In addition, all the national and state parks have their own visitor centers, which provide hiking maps, safety advice, and special licenses for wilderness hiking and camping. Some of these areas are managed by special Public Land Management Agencies, which can also be contacted for information.

Each state has a department of tourism, as do all the major towns and cities. Smaller urban centers and sights of special interest have offices that usually provide maps and guides. Information can also be obtained from the network of chambers of commerce throughout the region. If you are planning your trip in advance contact the visitor center of the state you are visiting, and they will be pleased to send you an information pack. Each department of tourism, as well as many individual sights, also have websites, which offer comprehensive information and online booking services for accommodations. Bear in mind that many of the Southwest's attractions, such as the pueblos of New Mexico and the Navajo Nation in the Four Corners, are located on reservation lands

New Mexico tourist sign

and are managed by different Native American tribal councils. For advice on etiquette, opening times, and admission charges to such sights contact the local **Bureau of Indian Affairs** or the **Navajo Tourism Department**.

Ranger on a guided tour at Keet Seel, Navajo National Monument

OPENING HOURS AND ADMISSION CHARGES

OPENING TIMES are seasonal. As a rule, most of the major sights are open later through the summer months. Museums and galleries tend to be open through the weekends and closed for one day during the week. Surprisingly, several attractions are open year-round, including many national parks and nearly everything in Las Vegas. In general those places

that do close will be shut for such major public holidays as Thanksgiving, Christmas Day, and New Year's Day *(see p35)*.

Most museums, parks, and other attractions in the region charge an admission fee. The amount can vary enormously, and many sights offer discounts for families, children, and senior citizens. Local newspapers may carry discount coupons, while student cards or an I.D. that proves you are over 65 guarantees reduced-cost entry to most major attractions in the Southwest.

TIME ZONES

THERE ARE only two time zones that affect the area covered by this book – Mountain Standard Time, which covers Arizona, New Mexico, Colorado, and Utah, and Pacific Time in Nevada. Mountain Standard Time is one hour later than Pacific Time. If it is noon in Las Vegas then it will be 1pm across the rest of the region. However, daylight-saving time runs from late spring to early fall, and the clocks are set forward by one hour, except in Arizona, which does not have daylight-saving.

To confuse matters even more, it is important to also be aware that the Navajo Nation (across Arizona and part of New Mexico) does not use daylight-saving time, but the Hopi Indian Reservation (in the middle of the Navajo Reservation), does.

Water fountains in the courtyard of the Heard Museum in Phoenix

SENIOR TRAVELERS

ALTHOUGH THE AGE when you are considered a senior in the US is 65, a multitude of discounts are also available to people over the age of 50. Reduced rates of up to 50 percent can apply to meals, accommodations, public transportation, and entrance fees, and are often better than those offered to students.

National Park Service sign

There are several organizations in the US through which discounts can be obtained. The **National Park Service** offers Golden Age Passports that reduce the cost of tours and services in the parks. **Elderhostel** arranges educational trips to various academic institutions for travelers over the age of 55. These include inexpensive accommodations on campus, lectures, and meals. For around $10 senior citizens can join the **American Association of Retired Persons** (AARP), which also offers good travel discounts.

TRAVELING WITH CHILDREN

THE SOUTHWEST offers a wide range of attractions, theme parks, and museums suitable for families traveling with young children. However, the age at which a child is eligible for discounts varies greatly from four and under, to under 18 years. Most types of accommodations state whether or not they welcome children, and in many hotels a child can share the parent's room at no extra cost. The more expensive hotels also provide babysitting services and children's clubs offering supervised activities. Restaurants in the Southwest are generally child-friendly, providing reasonably priced children's menus and high chairs (see p247). Although discounted flight tickets are available for children, these can often work out more expensive than an adult Apex fare (see p287). Reduced fares for children on public transportation tend to vary from city to city, and if you are renting a car it is possible to reserve car seats for children in advance.

TRAVELERS WITH DISABILITIES

THE US IS famous for having excellent facilities for travelers with physical disabilities. Hotels, restaurants, galleries and museums, and other public buildings are legally required to be wheelchair-accessible and to have suitably designed restrooms. Public transportation also comes under this law, and trains, buses, and taxis are designed to accommodate wheelchairs, while road crossings in busy city centers have introduced dropped curbs to enable easier access. Service animals such as guide dogs for the blind are the only animals allowed on public transportation.

Many national parks and major archaeological sights have paved walkways suitable for wheelchairs. The National Park Service offers free Golden Access passes, which grant free entry to all national parks for one year to those who are disabled or blind. The **Access-Able Travel Source** and the **Society for the Advancement of Travel for the Handicapped** are two organizations which offer a whole range of advice on traveling for the disabled, from how to rent specially adapted cars to qualifying for parking permits. They also have excellent websites.

STUDENT TRAVELERS

STUDENTS FROM outside the US need to have an identity card, such as the International Student Identity Card (ISIC), to prove their status. This entitles the holder to substantial discounts on admission prices to museums, galleries, and other popular attractions. If you are planning to stay in hostels you will need to join **Hostelling International/American Youth Hostel** (HI/AYH).

Wheelchair access

ETIQUETTE AND TIPPING

THE SOUTHWEST is noted as one of the US's most relaxed regions. Dress tends to be informal, practical, and dependent on the climate. Jeans may be worn even in upscale restaurants or the theater. In general, people are friendly and polite and, as this is a multicultural country, visitors are expected to be aware of and respect the customs of different peoples.

Some of the region's most famous sights, such as Canyon de Chelly (see pp168–71), and Monument Valley (see pp164–5), are located on reservation land. Visitors are

Youngsters enjoying the child-friendly environment of the Southwest

welcome but should be sensitive as to what may cause offense. It is illegal for alcohol to be brought onto reservations – even a bottle visible in a locked car will land you in trouble. Always ask before photographing anything, especially ceremonial dances or Native homes, and take into consideration that a photography fee may be requested. Do not go wandering off marked trails as this is forbidden. Try to dress respectfully – for example, the Hopi people request that people do not wear shorts.

Apart from Las Vegas, most of the Southwest follows the rest of the US in restricting smoking in public places. The majority of hotels are non-smoking, although a few have smoking rooms, or allow customers to smoke in bar areas. However, many restaurants have now banned smoking altogether.

Service is not included on restaurant checks, and you should leave 15 percent of the total as a tip. Hotel bell-hops expect $1–2 per bag, and chamber maids around $1 for each day of your stay.

ELECTRICITY

Throughout the US the electrical current is 110 volts and 60 Hertz. Visitors from abroad will need an adaptor plug for the two-prong sockets and a voltage converter to operate 220-volt appliances, such as hairdryers and rechargers for cell phones and laptop computers.

CONVERSION CHART

Bear in mind that one US pint (0.5 liter) is smaller than one UK pint (0.6 liter).

US Standard to Metric
1 inch = 2.54 centimeters
1 foot = 30 centimeters
1 mile = 1.6 kilometers
1 ounce = 28 grams
1 pound = 454 grams
1 US quart = 0.947 liter
1 US gallon = 3.8 liters

Metric to US Standard
1 centimeter = 0.4 inch
1 meter = 3 feet 3 inches
1 kilometer = 0.6 miles
1 gram = 0.04 ounce
1 kilogram = 2.2 pounds
1 liter = 1.1 US quarts

Relaxing in the informal surroundings of a Southwestern restaurant

DIRECTORY

STATE OFFICES

Arizona Office of Tourism
2702 N. 3rd Street,
Suite 4015, Phoenix,
AZ 85004.
(602) 230-7733;
(800) 842-8257.
W www.arizonaguide.com

Bureau of Indian Affairs
PO Box 10, Phoenix,
AZ 85001.
(602) 379-4511.

Colorado Tourism Office
1625 Broadway, Denver,
CO 80202.
(800) 265-6723.
W www.colorado.com

Navajo Tourism Department
PO Box 663, Window
Rock, AZ 86515.
(520) 871-6436.

New Mexico Department of Tourism
491 Old Santa Fe Trail,
Santa Fe, NM 87503.
(505) 827-0291;
(800) 733-6396.
W www.newmexico.org

Public Lands Information Center
W www.publiclands-usa.org

Utah Travel Council
Council Hall, Capitol Hill,
Salt Lake City, UT 84114.
(801) 538-1030.
W www.utah.com

SENIOR TRAVELERS

Elderhostel
75 Federal Street,
Boston, MA 02110.
(617) 426-7788.
W www.elderhostel.org

National Park Service
(see also under individual
sights)
Intermountain Area,
PO Box 25287,
Denver, CO 80225.

American Association of Retired Persons
3200 E. Carson Street,
Lakewood, CA 90712.
(800) 424-3410.
W www.aarp.org

DISABLED TRAVELERS

Society for the Advancement of Travel for the Handicapped (SATH)
347 Fifth Avenue,
Suite 610, New York,
NY 10016.
(212) 447-7284.
W www.sath.org

Access-Able Travel Source
PO Box 1796,
Wheat Ridge, CO 80034.
(303) 232-2979.
W www.access-able.com

STUDENT TRAVELERS

Hostelling International/ American Youth Hostel (HI/AYH)
733 15th Street NW,
Suite 840, DC 20005.
(202) 783-6161.
W www.iyhf.org.

US EMBASSIES

London
24/31 Grosvenor Square,
London W1A 1AE.
020 7499-9000.

Canada
1095 W. Pender St.,
Vancouver, BC VCE2M6.
(604) 685-4311.

Personal Security and Health

Santa Fe police badge

T HE SOUTHWEST IS a relatively safe place to visit as long as some general safety precautions are observed. In contrast to other US cities, the urban centers of the Southwest have lower crime rates, but it is wise to be cautious and to find out which parts of town are unsafe at night. When traveling across remote country roads, take a reliable local map and follow the advice of local rangers and visitor information centers. These sources also offer invaluable information on survival in the wilderness for hikers and on the normal safety procedures that should be followed by anyone engaging in any of the outdoor activities available in the region *(see pp268–73)*. It is also advisable to check the local media such as newspapers, television, and radio for current weather and safety conditions.

Pedal-pushing policeman on duty in Santa Fe, New Mexico

PERSONAL SAFETY

M OST TOURIST AREAS in the Southwest are friendly, unthreatening places. However, there is crime here and it is wise to observe a few basic rules. Never carry large amounts of cash, wear obviously expensive jewelry, or keep your wallet in your back pocket, as these are the main temptations for pickpockets. It is also a good idea to wear pocketbooks (handbags) and cameras over one shoulder with the strap across

Police car

your body. Keep your passport separate from your cash and travelers' checks. Most hotels have safety deposit boxes or safes in which you should store any valuables.

If you are driving, be sure to lock any valuables in the trunk, and to park only in well-lit parking lots. Similarly, when walking at night it is a good idea to stay where there are other people and to be aware of which areas are most likely to be unsafe.

LOST PROPERTY

I T IS UNLIKELY that small items of lost or stolen property will be retrieved, but it is necessary to report all such incidents to the police in order to make an insurance claim. Telephone the **Police Non-Emergency Line** to report the loss or theft, and they will issue you with a police report so that you can make a claim with your insurance company.

If a credit card is missing, call the credit company's toll-free number immediately. Lost or stolen travelers' checks should also be reported to the issuer. If you have kept a

record of the checks' numbers, replacing them should be a painless experience, and new ones are usually issued within 24 hours.

If you lose your passport, contact the nearest embassy or consulate. They will be able to issue a temporary replacement as visitors do not generally need a new full passport if they plan to return directly to their home country. However, if you are traveling on to another destination, you will need a full passport. It is also useful to hold photocopies of your driver's license and birth certificate, as well as notarized passport photographs if you are considering an extended visit or need additional identification.

TRAVEL INSURANCE

T HE UNITED STATES has excellent medical services, but they are very expensive. All visitors to the US are strongly advised to make sure they have comprehensive medical and dental coverage for the duration of their stay.

MEDICAL TREATMENT

F OR SERIOUS EMERGENCIES requiring assistance from the medical, police, or fire services call 911. The national organization, **Traveler's Aid Society**, may offer help in a variety of emergencies.

City hospitals with emergency rooms can be found in the Blue Pages of the telephone directory, but they are often overcrowded, particularly in larger cities. Private hospitals offer more personal treatment and are listed in the Yellow Pages of the telephone book. You may be required to provide evidence of your ability to pay before a doctor will agree to treat you, hence the importance of adequate medical insurance.

Hotels will usually call a doctor or recommend a local dentist, and nonprescription painkillers and other medicines can be obtained from drugstores, many of which are open 24 hours. Prescription drugs can be dispensed only from a pharmacy. If you

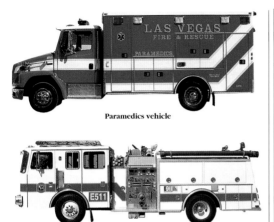

Paramedics vehicle

Fire engine

DIRECTORY

EMERGENCY SERVICES

All emergencies
911 and alert police, fire, or medical services.

Police Non-Emergency Line
Las Vegas
(702) 795-3111.
Phoenix
(480) 644-2211.
Santa Fe
(505) 827-9126.

Traveler's Aid Society
Las Vegas
(702) 798-1742.
Tucson
(520) 622-8900.

CONSULATES

The consulates closest to the Southwest are found in California.

Australian Consulate
1 Bush St., Suite 700,
San Francisco, CA 94104-4413.
(415) 362-6160.

British Consulate
11766 Wilshire Blvd., Suite 400,
Los Angeles, CA 90025.
(310) 477-3322.

Canadian Consulate
550 South Hope St., 9th Floor,
Los Angeles, CA 90071-2627.
(213) 346-2700.

New Zealand Consulate
12400 Wilshire Blvd., Suite 1150,
Los Angeles, CA 90025.
(310) 207-1605.

are already taking prescribed medication, be sure to carry extra supplies for your trip.

No specific vaccinations are required before entering the US. However, it is always a good idea to have a tetanus booster before setting out, particularly if you are planning to engage in adventurous outdoor activities.

Pharmacy sign

OUTDOOR HAZARDS

THE WEATHER in the Southwest can present visitors with a variety of dangerous situations, especially in Southern Utah's canyon country and parts of southern Arizona, where sudden summer storms can cause flash floods. Visitors may obtain the latest weather information from the ranger stations in the national parks, as well as by listening to the reports on local radio and television channels.

If you are planning a hike in wilderness territory, always tell someone where you are going and when you expect to return.

The dry heat of the region's summers can often be under-estimated by visitors, and hikers especially are advised to carry with them at least a gallon (4 liters) of drinking water per person for each day of walking. It is also extremely important for visitors to guard against the risk of forest fires, which can affect the area with devastating results.

At the higher elevations the sun can be surprisingly strong, even on cloudy days. If you are planning on hiking or engaging in other outdoor activities during the summer, an effective sunscreen and a sunhat should always be worn.

While the wilderness of the Southwest is home to certain venomous creatures such as snakes, scorpions, and the Gila monster lizard (see p21), these creatures

Park Ranger at the Petrified Forest National Park, Arizona

Fire Department badge, Sedona

generally avoid humans; it is unlikely you will be bitten if you avoid their habitats. Mostly they hide under rocks and in crevices during the heat of the day. Be careful where you step, and do not turn over rocks. Do not reach up to touch rock ledges with your hands. Insect stings and bites may hurt but are rarely fatal to adults. Always carry a snakebite kit or a first aid kit if you are going into snake or scorpion country. If bitten by a snake or scorpion, seek medical help immediately.

Banking and Currency

ASIDE FROM THE risk of gambling away all of their money in the Vegas casinos, visitors should encounter no problems with financial transactions in the Southwest. Banks and foreign currency exchanges are plentiful throughout the region, although it is wise to check out opening times. There are a great number of automated teller machines (ATMs) in towns and cities that enable visitors to make cash withdrawals 24 hours a day. Credit cards are a more common form of payment than hard currency, especially at hotels or car rental companies, although they can be used to withdraw cash at ATMs.

The most common international systems are Cirrus and Plus. Ask both your own bank and credit card company which ATM system your card can access, and how much you will be charged for transactions of differing amounts. Withdrawals from ATMs may provide a better foreign currency exchange rate than cash transactions.

WIRING MONEY

IF YOU NEED extra cash, it is possible to have money wired from your bank at home in minutes using an electronic money service. Cash can be wired to major bank branches or to any **Western Union**, **Thomas Cook**, or **American Express Moneygram** outlet.

CURRENCY

AMERICAN CURRENCY, based on the decimal system, has 100 cents to the dollar. Bills are all the same size and color, so check the number before paying. Smaller denominations are preferred in small towns and remote gas stations.

Large $500–10,000 bills are no longer printed but are still legal tender, usually found in the hands of collectors. The 25-cent piece is useful for public telephones and Las Vegas slot machines. Always carry cash for tips, public transportation, and taxis.

Automated teller machine (ATM), open 24 hours a day

BANKS AND FOREIGN CURRENCY EXCHANGES

BANK OPENING times vary throughout the Southwest, but generally they are open between 9 or 10am and 5 or 6pm. Banks in the larger centers will change foreign currency and traveler's checks, but branches in small towns may not provide this service.

TRAVELER'S CHECKS

TRAVELER'S CHECKS are safer than cash because they can be replaced if lost or stolen. Foreign currency traveler's checks may be cashed at large banks or at major hotels. Airports also have foreign currency exchanges where traveler's checks can be changed, while cities and most large towns have branches of **American Express** and **Thomas Cook**, who will also change them at a slightly higher rate than that offered at a bank. If you buy checks in US dollars they are accepted as cash in many restaurants, hotels, and stores, and you

will not be subject to a transaction fee. A passport is required as identification when using traveler's checks.

CREDIT, CHARGE, AND DEBIT CARDS

CREDIT AND CHARGE cards are practically essential when traveling in the US. The cards are accepted as a guarantee when renting a car *(see p290)*, and are used to book tickets for most forms of entertainment. The most widely used cards are VISA, American Express, MasterCard, and Diner's Club.

All credit, charge, and debit cards can be used to draw money from an ATM. These are usually found at banks, train and bus stations, airports, and convenience stores. Withdrawing cash on a debit card costs less than doing it on a credit or charge card.

American Express charge cards

Bank of Colorado building in the town of Durango

Coins

America's coins (actual size shown) come in 1-dollar, 50-, 25-, 10-, 5-, and 1-cent pieces. The new Golden Dollar, released on January 26, 2000, features the likeness of Sacagawea, an enslaved Shoshone Indian who assisted and guided the Lewis and Clark expedition across the northwest US. On the flip side is a Bald Eagle and 17 stars, indicating the 17 states at the time of this exploration.

25-cent coin (a quarter)

10-cent coin (a dime)

5-cent coin (a nickel)

1-cent coin (a penny)

$1 coin

Bank Notes

The Golden Dollar has not replaced the dollar bill which is still the more widely used form of this unit of currency. Paper bills were first issued in 1862 when coins were in short supply and the Civil War needed financing. The size of the notes, the portraits, and the back designs were decided in 1929; in the 1990s the artwork for most of the bills was re-engraved.

1-dollar bill ($1)

5-dollar bill ($5)

10-dollar bill ($10)

20-dollar bill ($20)

50-dollar bill ($50)

100-dollar bill ($100)

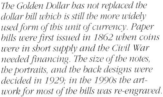

DIRECTORY

Western Union
Wiring money, US
📞 1 (800) 325-6000.

Wiring money, UK
📞 0800 833833.

American Express
Moneygram US only
📞 1 (800) 543-4080.

Check replacement
📞 1 (800) 221-7282.

Stolen credit and charge cards
📞 1 (800) 528-4800.

Thomas Cook (and MasterCard)
Check replacement and stolen credit cards
📞 1 (800) 223-9920.

Visa
Check replacement
📞 1 (800) 227-6811.

Stolen credit cards
📞 1 (800) 336-8472.

Diner's Club
Check replacement and stolen credit cards
📞 1 (800) 234-6377.

Media and Communications

US mail stamp

T HE UNITED STATES has some of the most sophisticated communications systems in the world. Telephone, mail, and Internet services are all readily available, providing fast and efficient services to destinations both local and worldwide. There is a plentiful supply of public pay phones across much of the Southwest region. They can be found in public buildings, cafés, bars, gas stations, hotels, and motels. However, bear in mind that this is a region of remote wildernesses, such as the Four Corners and southern Utah, where mailboxes or pay phones may be hard to find.

AT&T phonecards, available from local stores and vending machines

TELEPHONES

P AY PHONES ARE plentiful in the US and are easy to use with the instructions clearly marked on each phone. All numbers within a local area have seven digits.

To dial long-distance, add a one and the three-digit area code in front of the seven-digit number. The cost of a local call within the same area code is now 35 cents for three minutes. Long-distance calls are to any number outside the area code you are in and cost less when dialed direct and at

off-peak times, generally in the evenings and at weekends. Be aware that if you use your hotel telephone to make calls you may find you are charged at a much higher rate.

International numbers are preceded by 011, then the country code, followed by the city code (dropping the initial 0), and the number. International calls can be made from a pay phone, but you may need a stack of change to dial direct and will be interrupted by the operator for more money when your time runs out. It is easier

to buy a phonecard from one of the major telephone companies such as **AT&T**. These can be obtained from hotels, convenience stores, and vending machines for up to $50 dollars worth of calls. They usually operate by

USEFUL DIALING CODES

- To make a direct-dial call outside the local area code, but within the US and Canada, dial **1** before the area code. Useful area codes for the Southwest include: Utah **435**; (**801** for the Salt Lake City area); Las Vegas **702**; New Mexico **505**; Arizona **520**; (**602** or **480** for the Phoenix area); Colorado **970**.
- For international direct-dial calls, dial **011** followed by the appropriate country code. Then dial the area code, omitting the first 0, and the local number.
- To make an international call via the operator, dial **01** and then follow the same procedure as detailed above.
- For international operator assistance, dial **01**.
- For local operator assistance, dial **0**.
- For international directory inquiries, dial **00**.
- For local directory inquiries, dial **411**.
- For emergency police, fire, or ambulance services, dial **911**.
- **1-800**, **877**, and **888** indicate a toll-free number.

USING A COIN-OPERATED PHONE

1 Lift the receiver.

3 Press the number.

Coins
Make sure you have the correct coins before you dial.

5 cents

10 cents

25 cents

2 Insert the necessary coin or coins. The money drops as soon as you insert it.

4 If you wish to cancel a call before it connects, or if the call does not get through, you can retrieve the coin(s) by pressing the coin release lever.

5 If the call is answered and you talk longer than the allotted three minutes, the operator will interrupt and ask you to deposit more coins. Pay phones do not give change.

giving you a series of code numbers to punch into the phone, which accesses your account and tells you how much call time you have left before you dial. There are clear instructions on how to use them on each card. If you have any difficulty getting through, call the operator and request to be connected as a collect call (in which case the recipient will be liable for the cost of the call).

Toll-free calls have 1-800, 877, or 888 numbers, and are widely-used in the US, offering free calls to a range of businesses and services such as hotels and car rental companies. If you call a toll-free number from outside the US, you will hear a message explaining how you will actually be charged for the call, at the usual toll rate.

CELL PHONES, E-MAIL, AND FAX SERVICES

IT IS POSSIBLE to rent a cell (mobile) phone while on vacation, or to have your own cell phone tuned into local networks. Another increasingly popular method of communication for both US citizens and visitors is e-mail. These days many hotels provide modem outlets in their rooms, and there are Internet cafés in most of the cities and larger towns. Faxes can often be sent from the larger hotels, as well as from post offices and copy centers. Charges are based on the time of day of the transmission, destination, and the number of pages.

MAIL SERVICES

WITHIN THE US all mail is first class and generally takes between one and five days to arrive. The correct zip (postal) code usually ensures a swifter delivery.

International mail sent by air takes between five and ten days to arrive, but parcels that are sent at the surface parcel rate may take as long as four to six weeks. There are two special parcel services run by

the federal mail: Priority Mail promises faster delivery than normal first class mail, while the more expensive Express Mail guarantees next day delivery within the US and up to 72 hours delivery for international packages.

Several private international delivery services offer swift, next-day delivery for overseas mail, the best known being **Federal Express** and **DHL**.

US mailbox

All the major cities have a main post office as well as several local offices. In addition, there are post offices in airports, grocery stores, and drugstores. If you have the correct value of postage stamps, both letters and parcels can be mailed in any one of the many mail boxes dotted around every town. These are generally dark blue and have the collection times posted on them. It is also possible to buy postage stamps from convenience stores, vending machines, and in hotels.

NEWSPAPERS, TELEVISION, AND RADIO

THE BEST-SELLING daily papers country-wide are the *Wall Street Journal, New York Times, USA Today,* and *Los Angeles Times,* which cover the country as a whole. However, there is a wide selection of local newspapers available at even the smallest town in the region, and these are invaluable for local information. Visitor centers also often carry free papers

detailing local news, events, and weather conditions; they may also contain discount vouchers for local attractions.

Various radio stations offer local news bulletins and weather forecasts. National Public Radio is a good source of commercial-free news and entertainment, and is usually located along the FM band.

The US is famous for having a multitude of TV channels, provided by the four networks – ABC, CBS, FOX, and NBC – as well as many cable channels including magazine programs, sitcoms, cartoons, and special Spanish language channels. Most hotel and motel rooms provide at least the network channels (which all have local services), as well as PBS, the public subscription channel (with no commercials), and Cable News Network (CNN). Other popular cable channels include Home Box Office (HBO), which shows movies and entertainment shows. Most daily newspapers provide network program times, and hotel rooms are often equipped with local television schedules.

Reading the paper over coffee in a southwestern café

TRAVEL INFORMATION

PHOENIX, Salt Lake City, and Las Vegas are the main gateways for international visitors arriving in the Southwest by air. There are other major airports at Albuquerque and El Paso, Texas, which serve as entry points to the region. Visitors also arrive by car, long-distance bus or, less frequently, by Amtrak train. However, the US is a nation devoted to driving, and the automobile remains the preferred

United Airlines plane

mode of transport for those touring the Southwest. This is a country with an excellent, well-maintained network of highways, inexpensive gas, and comfortable, air-conditioned cars.

Even in the centers of the major cities here, public transportation tends to be the least-favored option. There are no urban train services and only limited bus networks, offering a minimal service on evenings and weekends.

Las Vegas's McCarran airport with close-up view of the Luxor *(see p106)*

ARRIVING BY AIR

UNLIKE MANY other American destinations, there are few nonstop flights into the Southwest from outside the US. Most visitors will have to connect via one of the country's major hubs such as Los Angeles, San Francisco, Chicago, or Dallas airports. Travelers from Pacific countries generally change at Honolulu, Hawaii. An exception to this is Las Vegas, which has more direct international flights arriving in the city each year, including a service from

London on **Virgin Atlantic** and several flights from Japan and Southeast Asia. Those carriers that fly directly to the Southwest tend to arrive at either Phoenix or Salt Lake City. The few major international airlines that do offer direct flights into the Southwest region include **British Airways**, **Air Canada**, and **Aero Mexico**.

Each state in the Southwest has a major airport as well as some smaller ones, and a range of airlines here offer

SkyWest AIRLINES

Skywest Airlines logo

connecting flights to and from cities and towns across the country *(see directory box)*. The largest airport in the region is Phoenix's Sky Harbor International, which has three terminals and receives the bulk of domestic arrivals. Phoenix is also a center for major American airlines offering both international and domestic routes, including **American Airlines**, **Continental Airlines**, **Delta Airlines**, **Frontier Airlines**, **Mesa Air**, **Northwest Airlines**, **Scenic Airlines**, **Skywest Airlines**, **Southwest Airlines**, **United Airlines**, and **American West**. From Phoenix, American West flies to Tucson, Sedona, and Yuma. Albuquerque Sunport International airport is a base for **Mesa Air**, which runs services to and from Denver, Dallas (via Roswell), Santa Fe, and other towns across New Mexico. Tucson International Airport in southern Arizona flies to Mexico City, but most travelers to and from abroad have to connect at a larger

AIRPORT	INFORMATION	DISTANCE TO CITY CENTER	TRAVEL TIME BY ROAD
Phoenix	(602) 273-3300	4 miles (6.4 km)	15 minutes
Las Vegas	(702) 261-5743	2.5 miles (4 km)	10 minutes
Albuquerque	(505) 842-4366	5 miles (8 km)	20 minutes
El Paso	(915) 772-4271	5 miles (8 km)	20 minutes
Tucson	(520) 573-8000	8 miles (12.8 km)	30 minutes

airport. Although there are immigration and customs here, there are no money changing facilities inside the airport. El Paso airport is a base for several southwestern airlines including America West, and provides links with Tucson, Phoenix, and Albuquerque among other destinations.

Mesa Airlines logo

Visitors rarely choose to travel to southern Utah by air, but there is a small airfield near Moab (*see p141*), serviced by **Aerowest**. In the Four Corners, the largest airport is the Durango-La Plata County Airport serviced by American West and United Express. The nearest airport to Mesa Verde National Park (*see pp180–81*) is the tiny Cortez-Montezuma Airport, served by United Express.

Airport official unloading bags from a tourist flight

INTERNATIONAL ARRIVALS

IF YOU ARE arriving at one of the major Southwestern airports and you are not a US citizen or resident you must present your passport and visa to the immigration officials before claiming your baggage. If you are catching a connecting flight you will have to pick up your baggage at the first point of entry and check it on to your final destination. Completed customs declaration forms are also given to immigration officials on arrival. Adult nonresidents are permitted to bring in a limited amount of duty free goods. These include 0.2 gallons (1 liter) of alcohol, 200 cigarettes, 50 cigars (but not Cuban), and up to $100 worth of gifts. Cash amounts over $10,000 should be declared, but there is no legal limit on the amount of money brought into the US.

The three major airports offer a good range of services, and several Las Vegas hotels will now check you into your room at the airport. Car rental, shuttle bus, and taxi services are plentiful and most terminals offer facilities for the disabled.

AIR FARES

THERE IS AN array of fare types and prices available for travel to and around the Southwest. If you are traveling from outside the US, research the market well in advance of your trip, as the least expensive tickets are usually booked early, especially for travel during busy seasons, which are between June and September, as well as around the Christmas and Thanksgiving holidays.

Although there are several websites offering bargains on last minute bookings, such as telme.com, or lastminute.com, direct flights to the Southwest are more likely to be booked in advance through an airline or travel agent. Agents are a good source of information on the latest bargains and ticket restrictions. They may also offer special deals to those booking rental cars, accommodations, and domestic flights in addition to their international ticket. Fly-drive deals, where the cost of the ticket includes car rental, are generally also a lower-priced option.

It is always less expensive to book an APEX (Advanced Purchase Excursion) fare, which must be bought no less than seven days in advance. However, these tickets impose such restrictions as a minimum (usually seven days) and a maximum (between three and six months) length of stay. It can also be difficult to alter dates of flights after purchase, and you should consider insuring yourself against delays or cancellations.

BAGGAGE RESTRICTIONS

INTERNATIONAL AND domestic passengers are allowed two bags each with an average weight of 70 lb (32 kg), plus one piece of hand luggage. On smaller domestic or sightseeing flights on light aircraft only one piece of hand luggage is accepted.

Traveling By Train And Bus

Greyhound Bus logo

TRAIN AND BUS travel in the Southwest can be slower than the more popular car and plane travel, but it can also be an enjoyable means of exploring the region. Long-distance buses are the least expensive way to travel here, and they also offer the widest choice of destinations. Within the major cities, public transportation is by local bus only. Although these buses tend to focus on daytime services for local commuters, they are also useful to visitors since most routes include centrally placed attractions. Booking a tour can often be the best way of seeing both major city sights and some of the more remote scenery of the Southwest, if you are not driving yourself. Taxis are also an efficient means of traveling around cities.

Amtrak booking desk for train tickets in the Southwest

TRAVELING BY TRAIN

THE SAD DECLINE of railroad travel in the US has left only a few lines, run by **Amtrak**, which cross the Southwest traveling east and west across the country. Visitors can no longer make the epic, nonstop journey from New York in the east to Los Angeles in the west, but the evocatively named *Southwest Chief* runs daily between Chicago and Los Angeles, stopping at the village of Lamy, near Santa Fe, and at Albuquerque, before heading west, via Navajo and Hopi country at Winslow and Gallup, to Flagstaff. From Flagstaff, Amtrak run a connecting bus service to Grand Canyon, and a bus from Lamy takes passengers into Santa Fe. Two other Amtrak services cross the area covered in this book. The *California Zephyr* begins in Chicago and follows a more northerly route to San Francisco, stopping at

Thompson in southern Utah, which lies 35 miles (56 km) north of Moab and the attractions of Arches and Canyonlands national parks. The *Sunset Limited* service travels from Miami through Texas and along the southern sections of New Mexico and Arizona. Southwest stops on this service include El Paso, Tucson, (which has a connecting bus service to Phoenix), and Yuma.

All three trains are Amtrak Superliners, which means they have two-tier cars offering a choice of accommodations from luxurious cabins with bathrooms to sleeping recliner chairs. The trains also possess full-length domed windows on the upper level for viewing the spectacular scenery, as well as lounge, restaurant, and snack cars.

SPECIALTY TRIPS

THERE ARE THREE railroad trips on historic rail stock that offer visitors the chance to enjoy some of the region's most delightful scenery. The **Cumbres and Toltec Scenic Railroad**, runs between Chama, New Mexico *(see p203)* and Antonito, Colorado through 64 miles (103 km) of peaks, tunnels, and gorges on a narrow gauge steam locomotive during the summer months. Colorado's **Durango & Silverton Narrow Gauge Railroad** *(see p179)* travels through the foothills of the Rockies past rugged mining country, often including abandoned machinery and wooden shacks, while the **Grand Canyon Railway** offers both diesel and steam rail trips from Williams *(see p70)* to Grand Canyon. The trip takes a little over two hours and offers packages including meals and overnight accommodations at the canyon and features Western entertainments – including a posse of bad guys staging an attack on the train. For rail enthusiasts there is also the **Santa Fe Southern**

Durango & Silverton Narrow Gauge Railroad train

Railway, which offers a 36-mile (58-km) round trip excursion on a freight train between Santa Fe and the village of Lamy. There are restored vintage cars and special sunset trips with dinner included.

Greyhound bus crossing southwestern desert landscape

LONG-DISTANCE BUSES

THE MAJOR BUS company in the US is **Greyhound**. Along with a few affiliated companies, it links all the major and many of the smaller towns and cities across the Southwest region. Greyhound buses also provide essential links with the major airports and Amtrak services. The Amtrak Thruway is a bus service connecting train stops with the major cities. For example, a bus service takes passengers from the *Southwest Chief* train at Flagstaff on to Phoenix.

Some of the most useful bus links operate out of airports. From Albuquerque airport the Greyhound affiliate, **TNM&O** (Texas, New Mexico, and Oklahoma Coaches), provides routes to Durango, Carlsbad, Farmington, and Roswell. From Phoenix's Sky Harbor airport there are 27 different daily routes throughout Arizona, as well as eight daily trips direct to Tucson.

Greyhound and a number of other companies also offer package tours, which can provide visitors with a more leisurely way of sightseeing. Everything from national parks such as Grand Canyon to archaeological attractions such as Chaco Canyon can be

Valley Metro bus in Phoenix

seen as part of a comfortable tour on luxury, air-conditioned buses, and the package includes meals and accommodations. **Greyline of Albuquerque** offer daily tours of Acoma Pueblo, Santa Fe, and Albuquerque. Check local papers or the Yellow Pages telephone directory for listings of other bus and coach companies that provide similar types of services.

TICKETS AND BOOKINGS

IN GENERAL, BOTH Amtrak and Greyhound tickets should be booked in advance. Not only does this usually mean less expensive fares but you will also be guaranteed a seat. Through Greyhound you can also get Ameripasses, which are discounted tickets valid for varying lengths of time from 7 to 60 days. Discounts are available for children under 12, students, seniors, military families, and veterans.

Reservations are essential on long-distance Amtrak Superliner services operating in the Southwest, and can be made up to 11 months in advance of the trip. Lower fares are available during off-peak times, between January and mid-May and from mid-September through mid-December.

PUBLIC TRANSPORTATION IN CITIES

WITH THE EXCEPTIONS of Santa Fe and Flagstaff, which are best explored on foot, the major cities of the Southwest, such as Phoenix and Albuquerque, cover large areas and are increasingly plagued by traffic problems. In these places you might want to consider using some form of public transportation. Albuquerque's metropolitan bus system, **Sun Tran**, covers most parts of the city, including the airport, Old Town, and University District (*see pp210–15*). Phoenix and Scottsdale (*see pp76–81*) are covered by the **Valley Metro** bus system, as well as by

(see pp210–15). (see pp76–81)

DIRECTORY

RAIL COMPANIES

Amtrak
📞 1 800 872-7245.
🖥 www.amtrak.com

Cumbres and Toltec Scenic Railroad
📞 (505) 756-2151 or (888) 286-2737.

Durango & Silverton Narrow Gauge Railroad
📞 (970) 247-2733 or 1 (888) 872-4607.
🖥 www.durangotrain.com

Grand Canyon Railway
📞 (520) 773-1976 or 1 (800) 8438-7246.

Santa Fe Southern Railway
📞 (505) 989-8600.

BUS COMPANIES

Greyhound
📞 1(800) 231-2222.
🖥 www.greyhound.com

Greyline of Albuquerque
📞 (505) 242-3880.

TNM&O
📞 (505) 243-4435.

CITY PUBLIC TRANSIT

Downtown Dash
Phoenix.
📞 (602) 253-5000.

Ollie the Trolley
Scottsdale.
📞 (480) 970-8130.

Sun Tran
Albuquerque.
📞 (505) 843-9200.

Valley Metro
Phoenix.
📞 (602) 253-5000.

Ollie the Trolley, a bus service that runs between Scottsdale's resorts and its many shopping districts. Downtown Phoenix also has the convenient **Downtown Dash**, which travels between the State Capitol, Arizona Center, and the Civic Plaza from Monday to Friday for the bargain price of only 30¢.

Traveling By Car and Four-Wheel Drive

Gas pump

WHEN THE MOVIE characters Thelma and Louise won a kind of freedom on the open roads of the Southwest, they promoted the pleasures of driving in this visually spectacular region. However, for both residents and visitors, driving is a necessary part of life in the US, particularly in the Southwest, and a car is often the only means of reaching remote country areas. Tours of such picturesque regions as central Arizona *(see p71)*, the Enchanted Circle *(see p207)* in New Mexico, or the San Juan Skyway in Colorado *(see p178)* are best made by car. This is possible because the entire region is served by a network of well-maintained roads, from multilane highways to winding, scenic routes.

mean the best deal. Check that the price includes unlimited mileage and basic liability insurance, which is a legal requirement and covers any damage to another car. There is also a rental tax of 10 percent. Collision damage waiver saves you from being charged for any visible defects on the car. Return the car with a full tank of gas, and leave plenty of time to complete any formalities.

If you are traveling in summer air conditioning is a necessity. Most rental cars have automatic transmission, although some companies offer a stick shift. Child seats or cars for disabled drivers must be arranged in advance.

Spectacular mountain scenery along the San Juan Highway

RENTING A CAR

VISITORS FROM ABROAD must have a full driver's license that has been issued for at least a year before the date of travel. International Driving Licenses are not necessary, but they can be helpful if your license is in a script other than Roman.

Although it is legal to rent a car to those over the age of 21, some rental companies charge extra to those under 25. It is also essential to have a credit card to pay the rental deposit, as few companies are willing to accept a cash deposit.

There are rental car companies all over the Southwest. Most of the major businesses, such as **Alamo**, **Avis**, and **Hertz**, and some of the budget dealers, such as **Dollar Rent-A-Car**, and **Thrifty Auto**, have outlets at airports

and in towns and cities across the region. However, if you are planning to arrive at one of the major hubs such as Las Vegas or Phoenix, the least expensive option is to arrange a fly-drive deal. If you depart from a different airport than the one you arrived at you may be charged a drop-off fee.

There is a central computerized booking system for most of the car companies, so use the toll-free number to find the best rates. Bargains can also be had by booking in advance and for travel during off season. Rates vary from state to state, and there may be deals for business travelers, frequent flyers, or members of the **American Automobile Association** (AAA or Triple A.) Currently, discounts are also offered by booking on the Internet. However, the cheapest rates do not always

Hertz car-rental logo

RULES OF THE ROAD

THE MAJOR HIGHWAYS in the US are known popularly as either Freeways or Interstates. Highway speed limits are set by each state. In the Southwest the speed limit on the major highways varies between 55 mph (90 km/h) and 75 mph (120 km/h). The Highway Patrol imposes these rules rigorously, and anyone caught speeding will be fined.

SPEED LIMIT 55
Speed limit (in mph)

REST AREA
Rest area indicated off an Interstate

NEXT 5 MILES
Wildlife warning

STOP
Stop at intersection

ONE WAY
Traffic flows in a single direction

Traffic signs
A range of different traffic signs offer warnings and instructions to drivers and should be adhered to.

Gas service station on the legendary Route 66 *(see pp50–51)*

(see pp50–51)

DIRECTORY

CAR RENTAL COMPANIES

Alamo
§ 1 (800) 354-2322.
W www.alamo.com

Avis
§ 1 (800) 331-1212.
W www.avis.com

Budget
§ 1 (800) 527-0700.
W www.budget.com

Dollar Rent-A-Car
§ 1 (800) 654-3131.
W www.dollar.com

Hertz
§ 1 (800) 654-3131.
W www.hertz.com

Thrifty Auto Rental
§ 1 (800) 847-4389.
W www.thrifty.com

USEFUL ORGANISATIONS

American Automobile Association
4100 E. Arkansas Drive,
Denver, CO 80222.
§ (303) 753-8800.
W www.aaa.com

In cities, watch for signs indicating the speed limit, as it can vary from 45 mph (75 km/h) to as little as 15 mph (35 km/h) in school zones. (Note that it is illegal to pass a stationary school bus.) Pay attention to road signs, especially in remote areas where they may issue warnings

Back Country Byway sign

about local hazards. Heavy penalties are exacted from those who drink and drive, and the alcohol limit is low.

Get information on US traffic rules from your rental company or the AAA. Some rules may seem strange to foreigners. For example, you can turn right on a red light if there is no oncoming traffic, and the first vehicle to reach a Stop sign junction has the right of way. Americans also drive on the right. The AAA provides maps and may offer help to those affiliated with foreign motoring clubs.

GAS AND SERVICE STATIONS

DESPITE THERE being a gasoline tax, gas is cheap in the US, although prices do vary, with service stations in remote areas being more expensive. It is sold by the gallon, rather than the liter as in Europe. Service stations may have a pump attendant or be self-service, in which case it is usual to pay before filling up. If you are planning

a long trip, be aware that gas stations can be less common than many visitors expect, so fill your tank before driving across remote areas.

BACKCOUNTRY DRIVING

FOR ANY TRAVEL in remote parts of the Southwest such as southern Utah's canyon country or the desert regions of Arizona and New Mexico, it is very important to check your route to see if a 4WD-vehicle is required. Although some backcountry areas now have roads able to carry conventional cars, a 4WD is essential in some wild and remote areas. Grand Staircase-Escalante National Monument *(see p148)*, for example, intends to maintain its environment by prohibiting further road building. Motoring organizations and tourist centers can provide information to assess your trip properly.

Unimproved road sign in Utah's Kodachrome Basin *(see p148)*

There are basic safety points to be observed on any trip of this kind. Plan your route and carry up-to-date maps. When traveling between remote destinations, inform the police or park wardens of your departure and expected arrival times. Check road conditions before you start, and be aware of seasonal dangers such as flash floods in Utah's canyonlands. Carry plenty of food and water, and a cell (mobile) phone as an added precaution. If you run out of gas or break down, stay with your vehicle since it offers protection from the elements. If you fail to arrive at the expected time, a search party will look for you.

Native flora and fauna must not be removed or damaged. Do not drive off-road, unless in a specially designated area and especially not on reservation land. If driving an RV, you must stop overnight in designated campgrounds.

General Index

Acknowledgments

DORLING KINDERSLEY would like to thank the following people whose contributions and assistance have made the preparation of this book possible.

MAIN CONTRIBUTORS

Donna Dailey is a writer and photographer who has traveled extensively throughout the Southwest and the Rockies. She has written guidebooks to Denver, Los Angeles, the American West, Kenya, Scotland, and Greece.

Paul Franklin is a travel writer and photographer specializing in the United States and Canada. He is the author of several guide books and magazine articles, and is based in Washington.

Michelle de Larrabeiti is a writer and editor who has traveled widely in the United States, Europe, and Asia. Based in London, she has worked on several Dorling Kindersley travel guides.

Philip Lee is a veteran travel writer and is the author of numerous articles and travel books about countries throughout the world. He has traveled widely, particularly in the United States, Canada, and Europe.

FOR DORLING KINDERSLEY

SENIOR PUBLISHING MANAGER
Louise Bostock Lang
PUBLISHING MANAGER Jane Ewart
SENIOR DESIGNER Marisa Renzullo
DIRECTOR OF PUBLISHING Gillian Allan
US EDITOR Mary Sutherland
PRODUCTION Marie Ingledew
MAP CO-ORDINATORS Casper Morris,
Dave Pugh

DESIGN AND EDITORIAL ASSISTANCE

Tessa Bindloss, Zoë Ross

ADDITIONAL PHOTOGRAPHY

Steve Gorton, Dave King, Andrew McKinney, Neil Mersh, Tim Ridley, Clive Streeter.

CARTOGRAPHY

Ben Bowles, Rob Clynes, Sam Johnston, James Macdonald (Colourmap Scanning Ltd).

FACT CHECKING

Eileen Bailey, Alan Chan, Jessica Hughes, Marshall Trimble, Barney Vinson

PROOF READER

Sam Merrell

INDEXER

Hilary Bird

SPECIAL ASSISTANCE

Many thanks for the invaluable help of the following individuals: Margaret Archuleta, Heard Museum; Myram Borders, Las Vegas CVA; Jennifer Franklin; Phoenix CVB; Louann C. Jordan, El Rancho de las Golondrinas; Ken Kraus, Utah Travel Council; Joyce Leonsanders, Albuquerque CVB; Steve Lewis, Santa Fe CVB; Jean McKnight, Tucson CVB; Rekha Parthasarathy, Arizona Office of Tourism; Pat Reck, Indian Pueblo Cultural Center; Gary Romero, New Mexico Department of Tourism; Theresa Valles Jepson, Flagstaff CVB; Charles B. Wahler, Grand Canyon National Park; and all the national park staff in the region.

PHOTOGRAPHY PERMISSIONS

Dorling Kindersley would like to thank all the cathedrals, churches, museums, hotels, restaurants, shops, galleries, national and state parks, and other sights for their assistance and kind permission to photograph at their establishments.

Placement Key - t=top; tl=top left; tlc=top left center; tc=top center; trc=top right center; tr=top right; cla=center left above; ca=center above; cra=center right above; cl=center left; c=center; cr=center right; clb=center left below; cb=center below; crb=center right below; bl=bottom left; b=bottom; bc=bottom center; bcl=bottom center left; br=bottom right; d=detail.

Works of art and images have been produced with the permission of the following copyright holders: Albuquerque Museum of Art and History Museum Purchase, 1993 General Obligation Bond Estella Loretto *Earth Mother, Offerings for a Good Life (No wa Mu Stio)*, 1994 212tl;

Capitol Art Foundation, Santa Fe, New Mexico, Capitol Art Collection Holly Hughes *Buffalo* 1992 mixed media sculpture 74" x 50" x 25" 199c; courtesy of Kit Carson Historic Museum 13t, 28c/bl, 204t/cl/cr, 206t; courtesy of the Frank Lloyd Wright Foundation 23b, 81b; Museum of Indian Arts and Cultures/Laboratory of Anthropology, Museum of New Mexico, 44857/12 Ceramic Figurine, Cochiti Pueblo ca. 1885 197tr; University of Arizona Fine Arts Oasis Barbara Grygutis *Front Row Center* 84t.

The publishers would like to thank the following individuals, companies, and picture libraries for their kind permission to reproduce their photographs:

AFP:Spaceimaging.com 11t; ARIZONA OFFICE OF TOURISM: Chris Coe 50tl; ARIZONA STATE LIBRARY: Archive+Public Records, Archive Division, Phoenix no.99–0281 36; ARIZONA STATE PARKS: K L Day 93t; ASSOCIATED PRESS: 35b, 96b, Roy Dabner 266b; Louisa Gauerke 51tl; Mickey Krakowski 33b; Julia Malakie 45c; Lennox McLendon 17b; Douglas C. Pizac 31t; Susan Sterner 33t; AURA/NOAO/ NATIONAL SCIENCE FOUNDATION: 91b.

BRIDGEMAN ART LIBRARY: Christie's London Walter Ufer (1876–1936) *The Southwest* 8–9; Private Collection/Index Frederic Remington (1861–1909) *The Conversation or Dubious Company* 1902 54b; Museum of Fine Arts Houston, Texas, USA, Hogg Brothers Collection, Gift of Miss Ima Hogg, Frederic Remington (1861–1909) *Aiding a Comrade* c.1890 54–5; University of Michigan, Museum of Art, USA Charles Ferdinand Wimar (1829–63) *The Attack on the Emigrant Train* 1856 42–3.

CIRQUE DU SOLEIL: photo Véronique Vial costumes Dominique Lemieux 126t; CORBIS: 25t, 38c, 41c, 43tl, 43b, 45t, 95, 97cbr, 136t, 203tr, 229, James L. Amos 172t; Tom Bean 2–3, 153b, 161c, 285b; Patrick Bennett 287b; Bettmann 39c/b, 41t, 42c, 42b, 43tr, 44c, 54cb, 96cl, 97t, 103bl, 136b, 171b, 187tr, 225tl, 227b; D. Boone 95–6; Jan Butchofsky-Houser 26c; W. Cody 1; Richard A. Cooke 38t; Raymond Gehman 153t;

Aaron Horowitz 219t; Liz Hymans 161t; Dewitt Jones 160t; Wolfgang Kaehler 206b, Danny Lehman 189br; Buddy Mays 279; Joe McDonald 87t; David Muench 20cr, 153cb, 160–1; Richard T Nowitz 286c; Pat O'Hara 52bl; Progressive Image/Bob Rowan 26t; Charles E Rotkin 97cla; Phil Schermeister 32b; Baldwin H Ward + Kathyrn C.Ward 186–7; Adam Woolfitt 266c.

DIANA DICKER: 27c, 160b; © Mrs. Anna Marie Houser/The Allan Houser Foundation 29t.

EFX: 126b; MARY EVANS PICTURE LIBRARY: 42t, 157.

GOULDING LODGE: 165b; GRAND CANYON CAVERNS: 50br; GRANGER COLLECTION, NEW YORK: 133; RONALD GRANT ARCHIVE: MGM 31br; Paramount Pictures 31cr; Universal Pictures 30br; courtesy GREYHOUND LINES, INC: 289t.

ROBERT HARDING PICTURE LIBRARY: Geoff Renner 134c; Nerda Westwater 33c, 189t; Adam Woolfitt 190; HEARD MUSEUM: 79b; Fred Harvey Collection 79ca; DAVE G HOUSER: 32c, 223t; Ellen Barone 34; Rankin Harvey 35t; HULTON GETTY COLLECTION: 186b.

IMAGE BANK, LONDON: Archive Photos 97b; IMPACT PHOTOS: Jacqui Spector 50bl.

JAMES AGENCY/LIBERACE MUSEUM: 109c.

KOBAL COLLECTION, LONDON: Hollywood Pictures/Cinergi 31clb; MGM Cinerama 30ca; MGM/PATHE 30cb; Paramount Pictures 55b; RKO 31cla; United Artists 30bl.

LAS VEGAS VISITORS' NEWS BUREAU: 96cra.

MGM GRAND HOTEL: 108c; MUSEUM OF CHURCH HISTORY AND ART, Salt Lake City: American Publishing Co. 137t; © by Intellectual Reserve, Inc CCA Christensen *Handcart Company* 1900 oil on canvas 136–7; MUSEUM OF INTERNATIONAL FOLK ART, A UNIT OF THE MUSEUM OF NEW MEXICO: Charles D. Carroll Bequest, Photo Blair Clark *Nuestra Señora de los Dolores/Our*

Lady of Sorrows (A.78.93–1) Arroyo Hondo Carver, New Mexico 1830–50 196b; Girard Foundation Collection, Photo Michel Monteaux *Baptism* by the Aguilar family, Octolan de Morelos, Oaxaca, Mexico C.1960 196tr, *Jaguar Mask* Mexico C.1960. 196tl, *Toy Horse* Bangladesh, Indian.C.1960. 197tl; Neutrogena Collection, Photo Pat Pollard *Yogi (Bridal Sleeping Cover)* Probably Kyushu Island, Western Japan. 19th century. 196c; courtesy of the MUSEUM OF NEW MEXICO: Fray Orci *Portrait of Don Juan Bautista de Anza* 1774 neg. no. 50828 40br(d).

NASA: 45br, 187c; NHPA: Stephen Dalton 227tl; Rich Kirchner 272b; Stephen Kraseman 21bl; David Middleton 21bcl; Rod Planck 20bl; Andy Rouse 21tl; John Shaw 12, 21cr/br, 90b; courtesy of the NATIONAL PARK SERVICE, CHACO CULTURE NATIONAL HISTORIC PARK: 161b; Dave Six 160cb, 174tl; PETER NEWARK PICTURES: 24c, 25c/b, 37c, 39t, 40t, 43c, 44t/bl, 54ca, 55t, 136c, 137c; NEW MEXICO TOURISM: 32t.

GEORGIA O'KEEFFE MUSEUM: Gift of the Burnett Foundation ©ARS, NY and DACS, London. 2001. Georgia O'Keeffe *Jimson Weed* 1932 194c;

PRIVATE COLLECTION: 9, 24t, 40c, 47, 183, 275.

BRANSON REYNOLDS: 27b, 282b; JOHN RUNNING: 26b, 27t.

SANTA FE OPERA: Robert Reck 267b; SCOTTSDALE CVB: Tom Johnson 265; SCIENCE PHOTO LIBRARY: NASA 187tl/b; STONE: Tom Bean 35c; Paul Chesley 162; Stewart Cohen 97clb; Kerrick James 112–3; Steve Lewis 51tr; Jake Rajs 96crb; Randy Wells 272t.

TELEGRAPH COLOUR LIBRARY: Colorific/David Burnett/Contact 137br; F.P.G. (C) T.Yamada 182–3; TUMACACORI NATIONAL HISTORIC PARK: Cal Peters 24b.

UNIVERSITY OF NEVADA, LAS VEGAS LIBRARY: Courtesy of Helen J. Stewart Collection 96t.

WIGWAM RESORT: 268c.

YUMA CONVENTION AND VISITORS BUREAU: ©Robert Herko 1999 90t.

Front endpaper: all special photography except ROBERT HARDING PICTURE LIBRARY: Adam Woolfitt br; STONE: Paul Chesley tr.

Jacket all special photography except: CORBIS: David Muench Front t; GETTYONE.STONE: Back b;

COUNTRY GUIDES

AUSTRALIA • CANADA • CRUISE GUIDE TO EUROPE AND THE
MEDITERRANEAN • FRANCE • GERMANY • GREAT BRITAIN
GREECE: ATHENS & THE MAINLAND • THE GREEK ISLANDS
IRELAND • ITALY • JAPAN • MEXICO • POLAND
PORTUGAL • SCOTLAND • SINGAPORE
SOUTH AFRICA • SPAIN • THAILAND
GREAT PLACES TO STAY IN EUROPE
A TASTE OF SCOTLAND

REGIONAL GUIDES

BALI & LOMBOK • BARCELONA & CATALONIA • CALIFORNIA
FLORENCE & TUSCANY • FLORIDA • HAWAII
JERUSALEM & THE HOLY LAND • LOIRE VALLEY
MILAN & THE LAKES • NAPLES WITH POMPEII & THE AMALFI
COAST • NEW ENGLAND • NEW ZEALAND
PROVENCE & THE COTE D'AZUR • SARDINIA
SEVILLE & ANDALUSIA • SICILY • VENICE & THE VENETO

CITY GUIDES

AMSTERDAM • BERLIN • BOSTON • BRUSSELS • BUDAPEST
CHICAGO • CRACOW • DELHI, AGRA & JAIPUR • DUBLIN
ISTANBUL • LISBON • LONDON • MADRID
MOSCOW • NEW YORK • PARIS • PRAGUE • ROME
SAN FRANCISCO • STOCKHOLM • ST PETERSBURG
SYDNEY • VIENNA • WARSAW • WASHINGTON, DC

NEW FOR AUTUMN 2001

EGYPT • EUROPE • A TASTE OF TUSCANY
NEW ORLEANS • SOUTHWEST USA & LAS VEGAS

FOR UPDATES TO OUR GUIDES, AND INFORMATION ON
DK TRAVEL MAPS & PHRASEBOOKS

VISIT US AT
eyewitnesstravel.dk.com

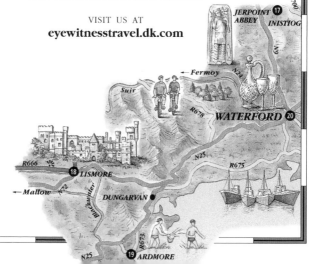

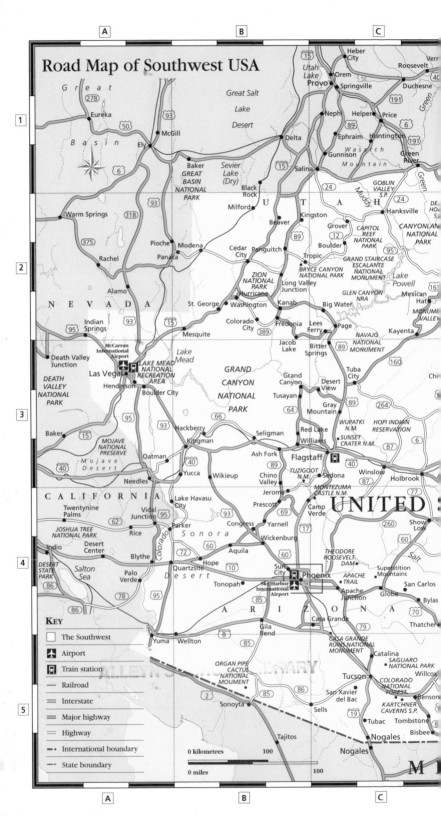